"A central cultural site for debates along America's racial divide is the issue of language. For several decades, Geneva Smitherman has been the preeminent scholar of African-American language and culture. Her impressive body of scholarly research has educated and informed an entire generation of African-Americans on the meaning of black language. Dr. Smitherman writes with power as well as grace. She provokes and challenges readers to rethink the complicated relationship between language and power within society. In the great tradition of African-American scholars such as W. E. B. Du Bois and Carter G. Woodson, Dr. Smitherman grounds her analysis in a passionate commitment to the liberation of her people. *Talkin that Talk* presents her impressive intellectual vision that examines the issue of language rights for African-Americans."

Manning Marable, *Professor of History, Director, Institute for Research in African-American Studies*

"No one in the current generation has been a more articulate voice and active presence in the struggle for the recognition of the African-American language than Geneva Smitherman. This unique collection of old and new articles captures the essence of her forceful contribution to understanding of language, education, and politics as it has developed from the 1960s into the new millennium."

Walt Wolfram, *William C. Friday Professor, English Department, North Carolina State University*

Geneva Smitherman, a native speaker of African American Language and a leading scholar, here presents her take on Ebonics and related issues.

Presented in her uniquely accessible style, the essays and interlinking commentaries guide the reader through the current Ebonics controversy which is also linked to past issues about the language, culture and education of people of African descent in the United States.

This highly readable collection draws together Smitherman's most important articles and essays, spanning a period from 1972 to the present day, and includes an autobiographical piece entitled "From Ghetto Lady to Critical Linguist".

Geneva Smitherman (aka "Dr. G") is University Distinguished Professor of English at Michigan State University. A linguist and educational activist, she has been at the forefront of the struggle for language rights for over 20 years. She has forged a writing style which combines academic discourse and African American Language that has become widely celebrated for efficacy in making the medium the message. Her previous publications include *Talkin and Testifyin* and *Black Talk*, and she is a contributor to *African American English* (1998).

For Anthony, Amber, and
the next generation

TALKIN
THAT TALK

LANGUAGE,
CULTURE, AND
EDUCATION IN
AFRICAN AMERICA

GENEVA SMITHERMAN

London and New York

First published 2000 by
Routledge
11 New Fetter Lane,
London EC4P 4EE

Simultaneously published in the USA and Canada by
Routledge
29 West 35th Street, New York, NY 10001
Routledge is an imprint of the Taylor & Francis Group

Typeset in Bembo and Gill by The Florence Group, Stoodleigh, Devon
Printed and bound in the United States of America

British Library Cataloguing in Publication Data
A catalogue record for this book is available from the British Library

Library of Congress Cataloging in Publication Data
Smitherman, Geneva
    Talkin that talk: language, culture, and education in African America /
        Geneva Smitherman.
            p.   cm.
        Includes bibliographical references (p.).
        ISBN 0–415–20864–5   ISBN 0–415–20865–3 (pbk.)
            1. African-Americans – Language.   2. African-Americans – Education –
    Language arts.   3. African-Americans – Social life and customs.
    4. Black English.   5. Americanisms.   I. Title.
    PE3102.N4S63 1999
    427′.973′08996073 – dc21   99–10323
                                                                            CIP

ISBN 0–415–20865–3 (Pbk)
ISBN 0–415–20864–5 (Hbk)

CONTENTS

Part six
THE STRUGGLE CONTINUES

ILLUSTRATIONS

ESSAYS FROM
THE ENGLISH INSTITUTE

Since 1944, the English Institute has presented
work by distinguished scholars in English and
American literature, foreign literatures and
related fields. A volume of papers selected for
the meeting is published annually.

Also available in the series from Routledge:

Comparative American Identities:
Race, Sex and Nationality in the Modern Text
Edited with an Introduction by
Hortense J. Spillers

English Inside and Out:
The Places of Literary Criticism
Edited with an Introduction by
Susan Gubar and Jonathan Kamholtz

Borders, Boundaries and Frames:
Essays on Cultural Criticism and
Cultural Theory
Edited with an Introduction by
Mae Henderson

Performativity and Performance
Edited with an Introduction by
Andrew Parker and
Eve Kosofsky Sedgwick

Human, All Too Human
Edited with an Introduction by
Diana Fuss

WHEREAS, numerous validated scholarly studies demonstrate that African American students as a part of their culture and history as African people possess and utilize a language described in various scholarly approaches as "Ebonics" (literally Black sounds) ... BE IT RESOLVED that the Board of Education officially recognizes the existence, and the cultural and historic bases of West and Niger-Congo African Language Systems, and each language as the predominantly primary language of African American students ... BE IT FURTHER RESOLVED that the Superintendent in conjunction with her staff shall immediately devise and implement the best possible academic program for imparting instruction to African American students in their primary language for the combined purposes of maintaining the legitimacy and richness of ... "Ebonics" ... and to facilitate their acquisition and mastery of English language skills ...

The Oakland, California School Board
Ebonics Resolution, December 18, 1996

Looking back at what has now been a generation in the vineyards, I bear witness to that old saying that the more things change, the more they remain the same. I thought we linguists had at least established that Black Talk was systematic and had rules, and that its speakers were normal, intelligent people who just happened to speak a language different from that of television newscasters and bank presidents. Of course I didn't have any illusions that everybody liked that different language, or its speakers, just that at least most people recognized and accepted these linguistic facts. But in December, 1996, when the Oakland, California School Board passed its resolution on Ebonics, seem like everybody and they momma start trippin – dissing the Oakland Board, calling Oakland's Black students outa they names, and even tryin to come up wit laws against Ebonics! (See my "Some Folk Don't Believe Fat Meat Is Greasy" for more on this legal campaign.) It became obvious that despite decades of research and scholarly work on Ebonics, there are still large numbers of people who do not accept the scientific facts about this language spoken by millions of Americans of African descent.

Nonetheless, I also bear witness to the power of collective action to make change. Check it out: the linguistically-biased speech tests for students going into teaching have been banished; there is a hard-working cadre of school and college teachers who are innovatively "tapping the potential" of African American and other students of Color, who were once linguistic outcasts; and the Africanization of American English is all over the public culture.

This collection brings together my most important writings on Ebonics, also known as Black Talk, African American Vernacular English, Black English, Pan African Language Systems, and Black Language. The works offered here reflect a variety of styles and focus on the interrelationship between language, education, and culture in African America. The writings present a snapshot of the struggle for language rights and my role in that struggle over the years. My insistence on writing in the Black Language Thang, particularly in the pieces written in the 1970s, added a layer of complication to my work for unhip editors. And on top of all this, there was in those "good old days" the bias against women scholars, particularly those who defy academic conventions (which is not to say that there ain't still some latent sexism around).

This book analyzes these contradictory linguistic and cultural forces and concludes on a note of optimism about the struggle for language rights for African Americans and others on the linguistic margins.

Dr. G.
November, 1998

ACKNOWLEDGEMENTS

It was scholar-poet Dr. Keith Gilyard, who planted the seed for this project. Glancing over my book shelf one day, he noticed several of my essays which he did not know existed. He told me that it was time to sum up, to get all my work out there. And so I got busy. Big ups, Bro.

Thanks to Drs. John Rickford and Arthur Spears who read the introductory Ebonics essay and gave me critical and valuable commentary. Special props, Brothers.

I thank Routledge editor Louisa Semlyen for guidance, attentiveness and most of all, for patience.

A big debt of gratitude is owed to Rachel Forbes-Jackson for help with library work, with the compilation of references for the book, and for just generally being on the case when I needed her. Thanks to Lorraine Hart for undertaking the tedious tasks involved in clearing permissions. And a special shout-out to copyeditor, Martin Barr, for diligence, thoroughness, and a keen eye.

Of course, I take responsibility for any mistakes or shortcomings herein.

Acknowledgement is due to copyright holders for their kind permission to include the following material in this book:

CHAPTERS

"From African to African American" (originally titled "What is Africa to Me?") from *American Speech* (1991), © University of Alabama Press.

"White English in Blackface or, Who Do I Be?" from *Black Scholar* (May–June 1973), pp. 32–9 © *Black Scholar*.

"Discriminatory Discourse on African American Speech" from *Discourse and Discrimination*, 1988, pp. 144–75 © Wayne State University Press.

"'A New Way of Talkin': Language, Social Change, and Political Theory" from *Sage Race Relations Abstracts* 14:1 © Sage Publications Ltd.

"Review of Noam Chomsky's *Language and Responsibility*" from *Language in Society*, 12:3 (Fall 1983), pp. 349–55 © 1983 Cambridge University Press; reprinted with the permission of Cambridge University Press.

"English teacher, why you be doing the thangs you don't do?" from *English Journal*, 61:1 (January 1972), pp. 59–65 © NCTE.

"'What Go Round Come Round': *King* in Perspective" from *Harvard Educational Review*, 51:1 (February 1981), pp. 40–56 © 1981 by the President and Fellows of Harvard College; all rights reserved.

"Ebonics, *King*, and Oakland: Some Folks Don't Believe Fat Meat is Greasy" from *Journal of English Linguistics*, © Sage Publications, Inc.

"Black English, Diverging or Converging?: The View from the National Assessment of Educational Progress" from *Language and Education Journal*, 6:1 (1992), © Multilingual Matters Ltd.

"'The Blacker the Berry, the Sweeter the Juice': African American Student Writers in the National Assessment of Educational Progress" from *The Need for Story*, ed. Ann Dyson and C. Genishi, 1994, © NCTE.

"'How I Got Ovuh': African World View and Afro-American Oral Tradition" from *Talkin and Testifyin*, 1986, pp. 73–100; first published by Houghton Mifflin, 1977 © Houghton Mifflin and Wayne State University Press.

"'If I'm Lyin, I'm Flyin': The Game of Insult in Black Language" from *Double Snaps* (1995) © William Morrow.

"Makin A Way Outa No Way: The Proverb Tradition in the Black Experience" from *Journal of Black Studies*, 17:4 (June 1987), pp. 482–508 © Sage Publications, Inc.

"Testifyin, Sermonizin, and Signifyin: Anita Hill, Clarence Thomas, and the African American Verbal Tradition" from *African American Women Speak Out on Anita Hill – Clarence Thomas*, 1995, pp. 224–42 © Wayne State University Press.

"'The Chain Remain the Same': Communicative Practices in the Hip Hop Nation" from *Journal of Black Studies*, 28:1 (September 1997), pp. 3–25 © 1997 Sage Publications, Inc.

"African Americans and 'English Only'" from *Language Problems and Language Planning*, 1992 © John Benjamins Publishing Company, Amsterdam.

"The Mis-Education of the Negro – and You Too" from *Not Only English*, ed. Harvey Daniels, 1990, © NCTE.

"Review of Heugh *et al.*, *Multilingual Education for South Africa*" from *Multilingua*, 17:2/3 (1998), pp. 321–3 © Mouton de Gruyter, A Division of Walter de Gruyter GmbH & Co. KG Publishers, Berlin.

"Soul 'N Style" from *English Journal* (February–March 1974, September 1975, February 1976), pp. 12–16 © NCTE.

"Black English: So Good It's 'Bad'" from *Essence* (September 1981), p. 154 © Geneva Smitherman.

"'Still I Rise': Education Against the Odds in Cuba" from *East Lansing Voice* (Winter 1993), © Michigan Education Association.

"CCCC and the 'Students' Right to Their Own Language'" (original unrevised version) from *English Journal* (January 1995) © NCTE.

QUOTATIONS

extract from "My Mind is Playing Tricks on Me," Geto Boys 1992, lyrics reprinted with permission © N-The Water Publishing, Inc.

extract from "Trust Nobody" by DJ Battlecat and Kam, 1995 © Famous Music Corporation, Vent Noir Music Publishing, and I-Slam Music.

extracts from "Mind Playin' Tricks" and "Do It Like a G.O." by Geto Boys, 1992 © N-The-Water Publishing, Inc.

extract from "Heritage" by Countee Cullen reprinted by permission of GRM Associates, Inc., Agents for the Estate of Ida M. Cullen, from *Color by Countee Cullen* © 1925 Harper & Brothers; copyright renewed by Ida M. Cullen.

extract from "People Everyday" by Arrested Development from *3 Years, 5 Months, 2 Days in the Life of* . . ., Chrysalis/EMI, 1990 © Vagabond/Speech Productions.

extract from "What Can I Do?" by Ice Cube, 1993, used by permission of Street Knowledge Music (ASCAP).

extract from "By the Time I Get to Arizona," by P.E. 1991, reprinted courtesy of Bring the Noiz Inc.

extract from "Shoop" by James, Denton, Roberts, Turner and Martin, reprinted courtesy of IZA Music Corporation.

extract from "Back in the Day" by Ahmad, courtesy of Wind Swept Music, Deep Technology Music and Kendal Soul Music.

ILLUSTRATIONS

Doonesbury cartoon © 1974, G.B. Trudeau. Reprinted with permission of Universal Press Syndicate.

Kudzu cartoon © Creators Syndicate, by permission of Doug Malette and Creators Syndicate.

"Bootsie" cartoons by the late Ollie Harrington © Dr Helma Harrington.

Herb and Jamal cartoon, Tribune Media Services.

"Talk American" cartoon, Tribune Media Services.

While every effort has been made to contact owners of copyright material which is reproduced in this book, we have not always been successful. In the event of a copyright query, please contact the publishers.

I WAS BORN into a sharecropping community[1] in rural Tennessee and started school at age four, quickly learning to read under the tutelage of "Miss Earline," a Black teacher with two years of college who had responded to DuBois's call to the Talented Tenth.[2] As Life would have it, Miss Earline was to be the *only* African American teacher in all my years of schooling, from "primer" (as we called it) through Graduate School. In those years, I was monolingual, speaking the Ebonics of my family, my Traditional Black Church, and my sharecropping community. Miss Earline had deep roots in our community; she understood the language of us kids, and sometimes she even spoke our language. After a few years, my family moved to the "promised land," first to Southside Chicago, then Black Bottom Detroit. It was here, "up South," as Malcolm X once called the North, that I had my first taste of linguistic pedagogy for the Great Unwashed. Teachers who didn't look like me and who didn't talk like me attacked my language and put me back one grade level. Back then, educators and others attributed "Black Dialect" to the South, although nobody ever satisfactorily accounted for the fact that Black Northerners used linguistic patterns virtually identical to those of Black Southerners.

Thus effectively silenced, I managed to avoid these linguistic attacks and to be successful in school by just keeping my mouth shut — not hard for a ghetto child in those days. I was eventually elevated to my right grade and even advanced three years. My nonverbal strategy worked until one month after my fifteenth birthday. It was at that point in my life that I became a college student and was forced to take a speech test in order to qualify for the teacher preparation program. I flunked the speech test.

At that time, many teacher-training programs had such tests, and they were linguistically and culturally biased against all varieties of US English other than that spoken by those who, as linguist Charles C. Fries had put it back in 1940, "carry on the affairs of the English-speaking people." Although the overwhelming majority of those who failed these tests were People of Color, I recall that there were a couple of whites in my group. I said to myself, "Now, what dem white folk doing up in here?" As it turned out, one of "dem white folk" was a speaker of what we now call "Appalachian English." The other was from the Bronx in New York City!

It wasn't that young people of Color and whites from working-class backgrounds could not be understood. By this stage in our lives, we had developed adequate enough code-switching skills that we were intelligible to those who "carry on the affairs of the English-speaking people." Rather, the problem was that there existed a bias against this different-sounding American English emanating from the margins. Yet our sounds were as "American as apple pie," having been created as a result of the historical processes that went into the making of America – the African Holocaust, the conquest of Native American peoples, the disenfranchisement of Latinos in the Westward Movement and American expansionism, and the exploitation of people for profits.

As descendants of those caught up in these forces, we found ourselves in a classroom with a speech therapist who wasn't sure what to do with us. Nobody was dyslexic. No one was aphasic. There was not even a stutterer among us. I mean, here was this young white girl, a teaching assistant at the university, who was just trying to get her Ph.D., and she was presented with this perplexing problem of people who didn't have any of the communication disorders she had been trained to deal with. Her solution: she taught us the test. Each of us memorized the pronunciation of the particular sounds that we needed to concentrate on. I recall two of my key areas were the post-vocalic -r sound in words like "four" and "more" (which for me were "foe" and "mow"), and the final -th sound in words like "mouth" and "south" (for me, "mouf" and "souf"). These are patterns that I now know reflect West African language influence dating from the enslavement era. But there I was living in the hood trying to mouth sounds like "more" and "sore" when all my girls was sayin "mow" and "so."

To the extent that such a story can have a happy ending, I can tell you that we all memorized and passed the speech test. I can also report that in the aftermath of the social movements that raged across "America, the beautiful" during the 1960s and 1970s, this oppressive language policy – once the requirement to enter the teaching profession in many states – no longer exists.

Ironically, that speech therapy experience rescued me from the ghetto streets (where, at the time, I was enjoying a high degree of success – details in my memoirs). It became a symbol of the social and historical forces confronting my community. It aroused the fighting spirit in me, sent me off into critical linguistics, and I eventually entered the lists of the language wars. However, for every African American student like me, who wasn't driven back to the streets, and who survived, not just to enter the System, but to come into the System and call the Question – for every Geneva Napoleon Smitherman, there are many thousands gone. Some of them was my girls that I used to kick it wit on the corner of 47th and Wabash in Chicago, one of whom was killed while out there hustlin on Chicago's Southside. Among the others who have fallen was the Brothas me and my girls sang doo-wap background for in the songs that was gon help them escape the broken-down front porches of Joseph Campau Street in Detroit.

Intellectual insight into this early experience with language oppression came from my baptism in the fire of the Black Intellectual Tradition. (There was no Critical Linguistics way back then when I was in that speech therapy class; it had yet to be named and codified.) Reading the works of the intellectually versatile W. E. B. DuBois, historian Carter G. Woodson, educator Horace Mann Bond, linguist Lorenzo Turner, psychiatrist Frantz Fanon, and – finally, a Sista! – linguist Beryl Bailey – reading the works of these Elders and then later discussing their work in study groups with other African Americans, I began to gain an understanding of language and power.

DuBois made me confront the question, "Whither the Black intellectual?" In his essay by that title, and in his turn-of-the-century book, *The Souls of Black Folk*, he argued that the Talented Tenth should commit itself to using its knowledge, research, and scholarship for the upliftment of the entire Black group. DuBois taught me that the role of the intellectual – *any* intellectual, not just the *Black* intellectual – is not just to understand the world but to change it. Because he well understood the far-reaching ramifications of the production of knowledge, DuBois taught that one should work like a scientist but write like a writer. On the language front, DuBois had proposed Mother Tongue instruction as long ago as 1933 when he laid out his pedagogical philosophy in "The Field and Function of the Negro College":

> the American Negro problem is and must be the center of the Negro university ... A French university is founded in France; it uses the French language and assumes a knowledge of French history ... In the same way,

a Negro university in the United States of America begins with Negroes. It uses that variety of the English idiom which they understand; and above all, it ... should be founded on a knowledge of the history of their people in Africa and in the United States, and their present condition.

(p. 93)

It was Carter G. Woodson who gave me an understanding of the critical significance of history. In 1926, Woodson, an avowed race man, established *Negro History Week*, which has evolved into *African American History Month*. His critique of the post-Emancipation education of Blacks in America blasted the ahistorical, Eurocentric focus of this education. It had become a blueprint for maintaining the "back door" status of Blacks. He decried the pathological consequences of this education, which was *away* from, rather than *toward* the culture of Africans in America. Reading and studying Woodson's *Mis-education of the Negro* (1933) alerted me to the origin of those linguistic patterns that had landed me in speech therapy back in the day – a therapy that was *not* designed to help me discover the wellspring of those linguistic patterns, nor, obviously to celebrate them. Rather, the therapy was a linguistic eradication program, designed around what white linguist James Sledd has called "the linguistics of white supremacy" (1969). Commenting on the matter of language in *Mis-education*, Woodson noted that

In the study of language in school pupils were made to scoff at the Negro dialect as some peculiar possession of the Negro which they should despise rather than directed to study the background of this language as a broken down African tongue – in short to understand their own linguistic history, which is certainly more important for them than the study of French Phonetics or Historical Spanish Grammar.

(p. 203)

Revolutionary psychiatrist Frantz Fanon introduced me to the psychological aspects of race and racism. His studies of the colonized personality clarified the deep wounds to the Black psyche that had been caused by colonialism and enslavement. Like DuBois, he articulated the problem of the dual dimension of the Black personality, and as a psychiatrist devoted himself to understanding the source of this duality. As a healer, he sought ways to bring a wholeness to the divided Black self that imitated things European and attributed inferiority to Black Culture. Although the "subjects" of his clinical research were mainly Africans colonized by the French, he was cognizant that his work applied to Africans elsewhere around the globe, and in fact, as he put it, to "every race that has been subjected to colonization." Fanon ascribed a fundamental significance to language. He viewed it as basic in deconstructing and healing the wounded complexity of the Black psyche. In "The Negro and Language," Fanon argued that:

> Every colonized people – in other words, every people in whose soul an inferiority complex has been created by the death and burial of its local cultural originality – finds itself face to face with the language of the civilizing nation; that is, with the culture of the mother country ... The Negro of the Antilles will be proportionately whiter ... in direct ratio to his mastery of the French language ... the fact that the newly returned Negro [i.e., from school in France] adopts a language different from that of the group into which he was born is evidence of a dislocation, a separation ... The middle class in the Antilles never speak Creole except to their servants. In school the children ... are taught to scorn the dialect ... Some families completely forbid the use of Creole ... The educated Negro adopts such a position with respect to European languages ... because he wants to emphasize the rupture that has now occurred.
>
> (1967, pp. 18ff.)

Lorenzo Dow Turner's *Africanisms in the Gullah Dialect* (1949) brought the history and the language together for me. Gullah (also Geechee) is the language spoken by rural and urban Blacks who live in the areas along the Atlantic coastal region of South Carolina and Georgia. Years ago I had the rare opportunity of meeting Mrs. Turner at an Atlanta University conference organized by linguist Richard Long in honor of her husband. According to Mrs. Turner, the Gullah study took Lorenzo Turner nearly twenty years, during which he also spent time learning West African languages. He felt that knowledge of these languages was absolutely essential to understanding the origin of and countering the myths about the Gullah form of US Ebonics. Mrs. Turner also spoke about the technical problems involved in collecting speech samples in those early years, a problem Lorenzo Turner solved by making his own phonograph recordings of Gullah speakers.

Turner's work located the history of Gullah in the languages of West Africa and created the intellectual space to examine the African linguistic history of African American speech communities outside the Gullah areas. It was while studying Turner that I learned the names of African languages – like Yoruba, Ibo, Fula, and others, which are now almost as familiar to me as my own name, but which I had never heard of or been exposed to in my entire (mis)education. Turner opened his pioneering work with these words:

> The distinctiveness of Gullah ... has provoked comment from writers for many years. The assumption ... has been that the peculiarities of the

dialect are traceable almost entirely to the British dialects of the seventeenth and eighteenth centuries and to a form of baby-talk adopted by
masters of the slaves to facilitate oral communication between themselves
and the slaves ... The present study, by revealing the very considerable
influence of several West African languages upon Gullah, will, it is hoped,
remove much of the mystery and confusion surrounding this dialect [...]
These survivals are most numerous in the vocabulary of the dialect but
can be observed also in its sounds, syntax, morphology, and intonation;
and there are many striking similarities between Gullah and the African
languages in the methods used to form words.

(1949, Preface, xiii)

I came to understand language and power through the work of
linguist Beryl Bailey, whom I had the special fortune to meet in my
youth before her untimely death stilled the voice of a great scholar
and cut short the contributions she was beginning to make to Black
Language and Black education. It was this Sista – who doesn't get
her props – who led the 1960s explosion of research on Ebonics
with her ground-breaking article, "Toward a New Perspective in
Negro English Dialectology" (1965), which reflected several years of
research and teaching. Bailey analyzed the systematic syntax of her
native Jamaican Creole – which surely would have landed her in
speech therapy too had she done her teacher training in the US. She
turned her Columbia University dissertation into a book, *Jamaican
Creole Syntax* (1966), making it the first full description of a Creole
syntax in scholarly literature. In doing this work, she became attuned
to the linkage between her native Jamaican tongue and the Black
speech she heard on the streets of New York where she taught in
the Black and Puerto Rican Studies Department at Hunter College.
In fact, it was Bailey who reintroduced the concept of a linguistic
continuum from Africa to the Caribbean and North America in the
Diaspora. (I say "reintroduced" because Turner's work had gone out
of print amid attacks on the concept of African survivals in Black
Culture, an attack led, unfortunately, by Black sociologist E. Franklin
Frazier in the 1950s.)

Bailey's work gave me the idea of tapping into the Black literary
tradition to recover the authentic linguistic nuances reproduced by
our writers crafting works of art in the Black Tradition. In the
1965 article, she had utilized the language of the novel, *The Cool
World*, to argue that African American Language was an independent linguistic system and needed to be considered as such. Not
only did Bailey do linguistic research, she immediately began to
apply her theoretical knowledge to issues involved in language and
literacy instruction for speakers of Ebonics, both at public school

and college levels. She sought to explode myths and misconceptions that teachers had about Black children's abilities and called for revisions of the language arts curriculum and Black Language-specific instructional strategies for Black children (see, for example, Bailey 1968; 1969). In her own quiet, firm, determined way, this Sista was bout it, bout it — the use of education for the empowerment of Africans in America.

Armed with this intellectual background from the Black Tradition, I readily embraced Critical Linguistics when it arrived upon the scene in the late 1970s. Arriving, though, from Europe, not America. In *Language and Control*, British linguists Fowler and Kress called for a Critical Linguistics in this way:

> [Linguistics] has been neutralized ... [there is need for a] critical linguistics ... aware of the assumptions on which it is based ... and prepared to reflect critically about the underlying causes of the phenomena it studies, and the nature of the society whose language it is.
>
> (1979, 186)

I believe with Fairclough that the interconnections of language and society "may be distorted out of vision," and therefore a critical approach to language study will "make visible the interconnections of things" (1985).

More recently, I found a kindred spirit in Austrian linguist, Wodak — winner of the million-dollar Wittgenstein Award. She calls not only for Critical Linguistics (CL), but also Critical Discourse Analysis (CDA). The "critical" nature of this line of inquiry into language demands that one go beyond the immediacy of the linguistic text to consider matters of socio-political and economic subordination and language, the perpetuation of inequality through language, and the historical backdrop against which these linguistic power-plays are enacted. Addressing the reaction against "Labovian quantitative linguistics," Wodak argues that we have to go beyond quantifying and counting. She states:

> CL and CDA may be defined as fundamentally interested in analyzing opaque as well as transparent structural relationships of dominance, discrimination, power and control as manifested in language. In other words, CDA aims to investigate critically social inequality as it is expressed, signalled, constituted, legitimized, etc., by language use (or in discourse) ... Consequently, three concepts figure indispensably in all CDA: the concept of *power*, the concept of *history*, and the concept of *ideology*.
>
> ("Critical Linguistics and Critical Discourse," 1995)

Being a critical linguist means seeking not only to describe language and its socio-cultural rules, but doing so within a paradigm of language for social transformation. Recognizing the limitations of the quantitative paradigm and number crunching does not mean abandoning research. By no means. For research expands our knowledge base, and without knowledge there is no power and no prospect for change. Being a critical linguist means recognizing that all research is about power – who has it, who doesn't – and the use of power to shape reality based on research. Which is to say that all research is political and derives from a certain ideological stance. After all, even the position that asserts that research should be "objective" is itself an ideological position. Speaking from the vantage point of an "octogenarian questioner" about the teaching of social grammatical rules (e.g., don't use "ain't," avoid double negatives), linguist James Sledd, surely deserving of membership in the contemporary Critical Linguistics camp, has argued that:

> Since the blood, sweat, and tears of generations have neither eradicated *aint* nor taught journalists either to forget *whom* or at least to use it in the proper places, teachers must ask not just the surface questions of what rules to teach and when and how to teach and test them but the deeper questions of the nature and right purpose of the whole undertaking . . . This article makes the obviously debatable suggestion that the best way to enable the teaching of grammar usage is first to learn and teach some harsh ways of the world we live in, so that eventually, political action may just possibly create the preconditions for more successful teaching.
>
> ("Grammar for Social Awareness in Time of Class Warfare," 1996, p. 59)

I am conscious that research, when filtered through the eyes of others, can come out distorted and far from the researcher's original intent. This is, I think, what happened to the work of some sociolinguists and ethnographers working on Black Language in the 1960s. Their findings were disseminated to the lay public unacquainted with sociolinguistic theory, ethnography, or historical linguistics. Often "deviant" descriptions of Black Talk were passed on to the public, and speech events such as signifyin, were caricatured as "jive talk" and "ghetto speech" used by oversexed African Americans, thus reinscribing the worst stereotypes of Ebonics speakers and Black people generally as clowning, low-life, sex-crazed ghetto dwellers. In my own work I have very consciously sought to present the whole of Black Life, and the rich continuum of African American speech from the secular semantics of the street and the basketball court to the talkin and testifyin of the family reunion and the Black Church.

From the moment I came onto the language battlefield, I was acutely conscious that people outside linguistics thought it hypocritical for linguists to argue for the legitimacy of "Black English" without ever using any of its forms or flava. I stepped to this challenge and made a decision to mix the language of school and the language of home. Thus, in the first article I wrote (though not the first I published), I tried to capture the essence of Black Language, using a mixture of academic talk and Black Talk. I titled that article, "English Teacher, Why You Be Doing the Thangs You Don't Do?" (1972). That publication led to an invitation from then-editor Stephen Tchudi to write a column for *English Journal*, which I ended up doing over a period of three years. In those columns, entitled "Soul 'N Style," I took my code-shifting and mixing even further, trying to make my points with the language arts crowd in the same voice I used with my Black professional friends when they expressed dismay over "Black English." (All of those columns are included in this volume, see pp. 405–30.) Finally, in *Talkin and Testifyin: The Language of Black America* (1977), I expanded my rhetorical experimentation to book form, taking it to the max, conflating the Language of Wider Communication (i.e., "Standard American English"), Academic Discourse, and my Mother Tongue. This work marks the height of my effort to represent (as the Hip Hoppers say). Mel Watkins, reviewing *Talkin and Testifyin* in the *New York Times* spoke on my rhetorical strategy:

> Smitherman uses many of the mannerisms of black dialect even as she explains them, a device that gives her prose a distinct and effective tone. This could be a problem for readers not familiar with black patois – somewhat like studying a French-language text in which parts of the exposition are given in French. But this lively, unorthodox approach helps make "Talkin and Testifyin" an entertaining book that persuasively extends the meaning of black English.
>
> (29 March 1978)

I confess now something I have never before put into print: this kind of writing was the hardest writing I have ever done, requiring draft after draft after draft to get it right. "Right" meaning representing Black linguistic authenticity and simultaneously making it intelligible for those lacking linguistic competence in Ebonics. Then after this Faulknerian outpouring of the agony and sweat of my human spirit, after the endless late night hours of struggle to bring forth this new Black scholarly aesthetic – after all this, on more than one occasion I would have to do battle with editors to keep the Ebonics flava in a piece. (Not Steve Tchudi though. He was very receptive to my evolving "soul 'n style." With props and thanks for his encouragement, I report with pride that I won a national award for "Soul 'N Style.")

Without reopening old wounds, let me just run one example of this linguistic gate-keeping. Publication of the first edition of *Talkin and Testifyin* in 1977 was held up for weeks while my editor duked it out with her boss, marketing folk, and some of her colleagues about leaving those "g's" off "talking" and "testifying." With the language of my title, I was making a statement, and I was adamant about the "talkin" — and the "testifyin." Over the years, I have been amused by the way references to this book are misrepresented: sometimes with both "g's"; other times with a "g" on "talking," but none on "testifyin"; and a couple of times with no "g's" followed by "sic" (like, hey, that's on Smitherman, it ain me). Exactly. Irrespective of your language politics you have to stop and think about the implications of those "g's."

In later publications, I eased up on using this rhetorical strategy because I was anxious to spread the word. Writing in two languages simultaneously demands enormous time and energy. (It took me eight years to write *Talkin and Testifyin*.)

Sista Beryl Bailey foreshadowed today's Critical Linguistics. She seemed to be speaking directly to me as she argued for research that would not bind a scholar slavishly and narrowly to one paradigm. Rather, she contended that there was a need to carve out new, uncharted routes in the quest for the truth about what we are these days calling Ebonics. Keepin it real, way back in 1965, she made the case for intellectual boldness in analyzing the speech not only of Blacks in Jamaica, but also those in the United States:

> I was compelled to modify the orthodox procedures considerably and even, at times, to adopt some completely unorthodox ones. The first problem that I had to face was that of abstracting a hypothetical dialect which could reasonably be regarded as featuring the main elements of the deep structure. This may sound like hocus-pocus, but indeed a good deal of linguistics is. A hocus-pocus procedure which yields the linguistic facts is surely preferable to a scientifically rigorous one which murders those facts.
>
> ("Towards a New Perspective in Negro English Dialectology," p. 173)

Part one

EBONICS,
LANGUAGE THEORY,
AND RESEARCH

"**A**IN WE DONE been here befo?" I kept asking myself when the Ebonics controversy first took the country by storm in late December, 1996. The Oakland, California School Board's 18 December 1996 resolution had acknowledged that Ebonics was the primary language of its African American students. The Board proposed that this language be used as a language of instruction to raise the tragically low educational-achievement level of their Black students. The Board's use of "language" to refer to the speech of African American students was a focal point in media coverage, on talk shows, in Internet jokes, in public forums, and even in supermarket chit-chat. Is the speech of Africans in America a language or a dialect? This same question was at the core of issues raised by the *King* ("Black English") case a generation ago. Same song, different verse.

INTRODUCTION
TO PART ONE

The question of whether Ebonics – which also goes by several other names, such as Black Language, African American Vernacular English – is a language or a dialect is not one that can be definitively answered by linguistics. Ultimately, this is a political, not a linguistic, question. In its resolution supporting Oakland on the Ebonics issue, the Linguistic Society of America (LSA) – the chief professional organization of linguists, with a membership of 7,000 – had this to say in January 1997:

> The distinction between "languages" and "dialects" is usually made more on social and political grounds than on purely linguistic ones. For example, different varieties of Chinese are popularly regarded as "dialects," though their speakers cannot understand each other, but speakers of Swedish and Norwegian, which are regarded as separate "languages," generally understand each other.

Perhaps the linguist Weinreich put it best when he said the difference between a dialect and a language is whoever's got the army and the navy!

Somewhere around the mid-1970s, I started using the term "language" rather than "dialect." One reason I tried to avoid the term "dialect" – a term, by the way, that is perfectly respectable among linguists – is that it has gotten a bad rap among the public and is almost always used in a pejorative sense. Because of this negative public view of anything called a "dialect," many linguists started using the term "variety."

But another, even more critical reason I began referring to Black Talk as "language" is that as I got deeper into the study of my Mother Tongue, it became starkly clear that the speech of Africans in America is so fundamentally different, in so many ways, from the speech of European Americans that it seems to get right up in yo face and *demand* that you address it as "language." How else to account for something like *signifyin*? Or the several different meanings of *nigga* (which now has its own Africanized spelling, thanks to the innovation of Hip Hop Culture)? Or the semantic inversion that made *bad* become "good"? Or the blues note in an expression like "It bees dat way sometime"? ("'What Go Round Come Round': *King* in Perspective" addresses the complexity of the language–dialect issue in greater detail.)

Even those scholars who consider African American speech a "dialect" have to concede that it is dramatically different from other "dialects" of American English. Linguist John Rickford, responding to reporter Clarence Johnson's question about the language–dialect issue, had this to say:

> a lot of subjective factors fall into place. There used to be a method where you would look at how many words are shared between two languages. If it was 80 percent or more, you'd say they were dialects of the same language rather than different languages.
>
> By those criteria, I would probably say that African American vernacular English or Ebonics is most accurately described as a dialect rather than a totally separate language. But having said that, I would have to say that it is the most distinctive dialect in the United States and the one that has gotten the attention of linguistics more than any other for the last thirty years. It's really quite different from other dialects in a number of respects.
>
> ("Holding on to a Language of Our Own,"
> 1998, pp. 59–60)

This first section tries to capture the essence of this "most distinctive dialect" – its racial semantics, its patterns, and communicative styles – as it has developed and evolved during the nearly four hundred years that Africans have been part of the American landscape. The essays in this section also reveal how differing notions of what language is affect approaches to studying and analyzing this "distinctive" speech. Further, the essays call attention to the relationship between social and political conditions and language issues in African America.

The first essay, "Introduction to Ebonics," seeks to lay out a definition of the language and to track its historical development from the enslavement era to the new millennium. This article is new and was written expressly for this book.

In the years between "White English in Blackface, or Who Do I Be?" written in 1970 but not published until three years later, and *Talkin and Testifyin: The Language of Black America*, first published in 1977, I shifted my thinking about the existence of deep-structure differences between White and Black English. In 1970, I thought that the grammatical patterns of the Black Idiom (as I often called it in those years) amounted to no more than surface differences from standard, or "White" English, as I called it back then. That is, a statement like Black English's "The coffee cold" was only minimally different from the White English version, "The coffee is cold." Such differences, as the "White English in Blackface" essay argues, could easily be accounted for by using concepts and rule specifications from the then-new Transformational–Generative grammar framework. The explanation would be that a deletion rule, which is allowable in English, had been applied, so that the speaker went from "The coffee is cold" to "The coffee's cold," to dropping the /'s/ in pronunciation, thereby producing "The coffee cold." In spite of the influence of Sista Beryl Bailey on my thinking, in those years she hadn't convinced me that the grammar was fundamentally different, that is, that Black English had a different deep structure, which would be one way of beginning to talk about Black English as a different *language*, not merely a different *dialect*.

In retrospect, though, this line of thought was obviously insufficient for my native-speaker intuition about Black English because I continued to struggle to define the uniqueness of the "dialect." Thus "White English in Blackface" argues that we have to look elsewhere, beyond syntax, to rhetorical style and communication patterns for the distinctiveness of Black English. Still this line of analysis about Black speech was not wholly satisfactory because how do you explain that there is a distinction in meaning between "The coffee cold" and "The coffee be cold"? The first statement means that the coffee is cold today, or right now, as we speak, but the second statement means that the coffee is cold on more than one occasion and perhaps most of the time.

After some years of study and research, I came to understand what the good Sista had been trying to say, namely that there are indeed deep-structure linguistic differences, in addition to "deep" differences in rhetorical style and strategies of discourse. I began to speak of the "language," not the "dialect," of Black America. In time, I came to think of this linguistic phenomenon not only as a "language," but as a language that could be a vehicle for unifying America's outsiders and consequently as a tool for social transformation. That is the framework of the 1988 "New Way of Talkin" essay, which was first presented at a conference on race and class convened at Oxford University. This essay relied on items labelled "black" or "chiefly black" from the *Dictionary of American Regional English* (DARE) to construct the Black English Assessment instrument that was administered to Black and white workers in Detroit's automobile plants. Analyzing the relationship between language and social change, "New Way of Talkin" suggests that Black Language was emerging as the *lingua franca* of the working class and calls for activists and change agents to factor language into social and political transformation paradigms.

A similar line of analysis – about language as an instrument and reflector of social change – undergirds the essay "From African to African American." This 1991 essay combines historical analysis with a five-city survey to analyze the changing racial labels that Blacks have chosen for themselves, from 1619, the period of "African" to the 1990s and beyond, the period of "African American."

The "White English in Blackface" essay reflects my early attempts at writing in the Black Idiom, to tell as well as show the power of Black speech. Putting what a 1970 recording called the "dialect of the Black American" in print, not just in a printed piece of poetry or fiction, but in print in academic, scholarly, public discourse! – this strategy had radically different effects on readers. A vivid illustration is provided by the contrasting assessments of reviewers of *The State of the Language* (1980), which reprinted "White English in Blackface" along with essays by sixty-two other contributors. Both the *London Times Literary Supplement* reviewer and the *New York Times Book Review* critic singled my essay out for special mention, one giving it short shrift in a brief condemnatory sentence, the other heaping lavish, extended praise upon it. Roger Scruton, writing in the *London Times,* said:

> Other contributors to the volume make similar efforts – often more brazen and usually far less sophisticated – to outface the critics of sloppy

habits of speech, sometimes by adopting them (as in Geneva Smitherman's affected use of Black English: "what we bees needin is teachers with the proper attitudinal orientation").

(22 February 1980)

John Russell, writing in the *New York Times*, said:

All is not lost, however. There are some wonderful pieces in "The State of the Language." You will not soon find – in fact, you will *never* find – a more brilliant case for the acknowledgment of standard black English as an alternative to standard white English than the one put forward by Geneva Smitherman in "White English in Blackface, or Who Do I Be?" Right from the opening sentence ("Ain nothin in a long time lit up the English teaching profession like the current hassle over Black English"), this long essay has an intellectual energy, a sense of style and a sense of justified scorn to which very few white contributors to the book can lay claim.

But then Professor Smitherman does not see language in terms of pure or impure usage, neologism or etiquette. She sees it in terms of privilege, and of privilege that can be legally withheld. It is, in her view, the inalienable right of black Americans to talk in their own way. The choice between standard white English and standard black English has "everything to do with American political reality, which is usually ignored, and nothing to do with educational process, which is usually claimed." "Niggers," as she says elsewhere, "is more than deleted copulas," and the right to speak as one pleases should not be subject to veto, explicit or implicit.

(6 January 1980, p. 7)

"Discriminatory Discourse on African American Speech" also received diametrically opposite assessments. The essay was first conceived in 1985 as a contribution to a collection of articles by Black scholars dealing with Black Communication. The editor of the collection asked me to write a critical review of the research literature on Black English done by white scholars in the US. The anthology, under consideration for publication by a large language arts professional organization, was sent out for review, as is typical in the academic publishing world. Although the editor, as ethics required, would not reveal the identities of the two reviewers, my prodding did get him to acknowledge the gender and racial identity of the reviewers: both white males. One of them attacked the essay for its "extensive editorializing," contending that I was guilty of "letting your politics show," and that "a scholarly article or book chapter is simply not the place to give vent to . . . anger." Even though he thought the article was "logically organized" and "well referenced," and that it "inspires additional research while it analyzes that of the past," he found it in need of "surgical removal" of my opinions and assessments of the research and discourse on African American speech. He thus slashed sentences left and right and cut out innumerable phrases that were "dreadfully editorial" and "out of place." Of course, a critical review of the literature is, in academic terms, about opinions and assessments of the work of others; it was just that the reviewer did not like my particular set of opinions and assessments. The other reviewer only had one comment: "Brilliant. Every member of [the organization] should read this paper." The essay ended up being published in 1988 in the collection, *Discourse and Discrimination*, which was conceptualized by the Dutch linguist, Teun van Dijk, who invited me to contribute this essay, and subsequently invited me to co-edit the book.

The last essay in this section, a review of Chomsky's book, *Language and Responsibility*, was written a few months after the *King* decision in 1979 (but not published until 1983). For those of us in the language-rights struggle, Chomsky's theory of language and the research tradition that he launched have been an invaluable weapon in putting the lie to notions of "inferior" languages or speakers. Rather, language is the purview of *all* men and women, and all acquire it in the same way, and go through similar stages in this acquisition process, regardless of culture, race/ethnicity, gender, nationality. As a linguist, Chomsky is interested in the relationship between "language and mind" (the title of one of his books on the subject), in how knowledge about the workings of language can illuminate the workings of human intellect – anybody's intellect, including, obviously, the intellect of the Ebonics speaker. As a scholar–activist, he was well known for his progressive work against imperialism and for his efforts in helping to expose the machinations of the FBI against the Black Panther Party in the 1960s and 1970s. So I readily accepted linguist–editor Dell Hymes's invitation to review Chomsky's latest book for the journal, *Language and Society*. In that book, Chomsky contended that his language theory, of course, applied to Black English, that the defensive posture about Black English was exactly the wrong posture because it forced you into defending the humanity of the speakers of Black English, and that issues about Black English or other language variations are basically "questions of *power*" (emphasis his).

THE EBONICS SPOKEN in the US is rooted in the Black American Oral Tradition, reflecting the combination of African languages (Niger-Congo) and Euro American English. It is a language forged in the crucible of enslavement, US-style apartheid, and the struggle to survive and thrive in the face of domination. Ebonics *is* emphatically *not* "broken" English, nor "sloppy" speech. Nor is it merely "slang." Nor is it some bizarre form of language spoken by baggy-pants-wearing Black youth. Ebonics *is* a set of communication patterns and practices resulting from Africans'

INTRODUCTION
TO EBONICS

DEFINITION

"Eve'body talkin bout Heaben ain goin dere."

appropriation and transformation of a foreign tongue during the African Holocaust.[1] Using elements of the white man's speech, in combination with their own linguistic patterns and practices, enslaved Africans developed an oppositional way of speaking, a kind of counterlanguage, that allowed for the communication of simultaneous double meanings. When an enslaved African said, "Eve'body talkin bout Heaben ain goin dere," it was a double-voiced form of speech that *signified on* slaveholders who professed Christianity but practiced slavery. This Africanized form of speaking became a code for Africans in America to talk about Black business, publicly or privately, and in the enslavement period, even to talk about "ole Massa" himself right in front of his face! Given these historical processes and the various purposes that US Ebonics serves, it is only logical that 90 percent of the African American community uses one or more aspects of the language some of the time.

Another way to get a handle on what Ebonics *is* and *is not* is to understand the larger reality of language use in the African American community. That community comprises some 35 million people who define themselves and/or are defined by American society as people of African descent, who are US citizens and descendants of Africans enslaved in the US. The following languages and dialects are spoken in the African American community:

1   US Ebonics (considered by some a dialect of American English, and by others, a language, distinct and separate from American English);
2   the US Language of Wider Communication (LWC), aka "Standard American English";
3   Nonstandard American English;
4   Arabic, Spanish, Swahili, Creole (and other foreign languages, but these are the main ones).

Depending on time, place, and circumstance, all of the above languages and dialects may be heard in a given Black community on any day of the week. The forms in (1), (2), and (3) overlap such that one speaker may use all three in the course of a conversation, or even in a single statement. Most middle-class and professional Blacks speak the Language of Wider Communication (LWC), as well as some aspect of US Ebonics at least some of the time. Most working-class Blacks speak US Ebonics, Nonstandard English, and some degree of LWC.

Nonstandard American English refers to those language patterns and communication styles that are non-African in origin and which are used by the working class. These patterns serve as linguistic borders that separate those who "carry on the affairs of the English-speaking people" from those who do not. Examples are the pronunciation of "ask" as "axe," use of double negatives, as in "They don't know nothing," and the use of "ain't." Such features of American English are often *erroneously* characterized as Ebonics. They are not.

US Ebonics refers to those language patterns and communication styles that:

1   are derived from Niger-Congo (African) languages; and/or
2   are derived from Creole languages of the Caribbean; and/or
3   are derived from the linguistic interaction of English and African languages, creating a language related to but not directly the same as either English or West African languages.

I am phrasing it this way to reflect the current debate about the precise linguistic source of today's US Ebonics (see e.g., Mufwene, 1992; Blackshire-Belay, 1996; Winford, 1997.) Significantly, though, there is fundamental agreement among linguists that US Ebonics, aka African American Vernacular English, did not completely originate in British English, nor in other white-immigrant dialects from the seventeenth century.

Examples of US Ebonics that reflect African language influence are the pronunciation "dat" (most West African languages do not have a "th" sound); the sentence "He tall" (the verb "to be" is not obligatory in such constructions in West African languages, nor is it obligatory in Creole Englishes); Playin the Dozens/Snappin, a verbal game of insult, usually about someone's mother (related to, if not directly derived from, ritual insult verbal practices in West African cultures; see "'If I'm Lyin, I'm Flyin': The Game of Insult in Black Language," this volume, pp. 223–30.)

Some folk, dismissive of Ebonics, think that all you have to do to speak Ebonics is use "incorrect grammar," by which they generally are referring to violating a rule of LWC. However, like all languages, LWC has two levels of rules: one social, the other grammatical. We may think of these two levels of grammar as G_1 (linguistic grammar) and G_2 (social grammar). For example, both an Ebonics speaker and a white nonstandard English speaker, giving a presentation in school, might say "He don't care about it," violating a social language rule in School Talk, but upholding the social language rule of the speaker's Home Talk. However, neither of our hypothetical speakers would say "Lamb little Mary a had" (for "Mary had a little lamb"), which would be a violation of a grammatical, not a social, rule inherent to the structure of English.

When people think of a different language, the first thing that usually strikes them as different is the words of the language. To be sure, Ebonics does not have a large number of words that are directly from African languages. There are, for example *okay, gorilla, cola, jazz*, to cite a few common words that Ebonics has contributed to mainstream American English (Dalby, 1969, 1970, 1972). There are also words with unique Africanized meanings, reflecting semantic strategies, such as semantic inversion – for example, *bad* used to refer to something that is actually considered "good."

While US Ebonics does not have a totally different grammatical system from European American English, there *are* some areas of profound grammatical differences. Further, there are unique rhetorical strategies and communicative practices among Ebonics speakers. These dimensions of Ebonics, while not directly like their West African counterparts, suggest a pattern of influence, or continuity (see e.g., Williams, 1993, Morgan, 1993). We may think of what Africans in America have done, and are continuing to do, to English as the Africanization of American English.

Some contemporary examples. Consider this statement, which comes from some Black women just kickin it in the beauty shop (gloss: conversational chit-chat at a hair salon):

"The Brotha be lookin good; that's what got the Sista nose open!"

In this statement, *Brotha* refers to an African American man, *lookin good* refers to his style (not necessarily the same thing as physical beauty in Ebonics), *Sista* is an African American woman, and her passionate love for the Brotha is conveyed by the phrase *nose open* (the kind of passionate love that makes you vulnerable to exploitation). *Sista nose* is standard Ebonics grammar for denoting possession, indicated by adjacency/context (rather than the /'s, s'/). The use of *be* means that the quality of *lookin good* is not limited to the present moment but reflects the Brotha's past, present, and future essence. As in the case of Efik and other West African languages, aspect is important in the verb system of US Ebonics, conveyed by the use of the English verb *be* to denote a recurring, habitual state of affairs. (Contrast *He be lookin good* with *He lookin good*, which refers to the present moment only – certainly not the kind of *lookin good* that opens the nose!). Note further that many Black writers and today's Hip Hop artists employ the spellings "Brotha" and "Sista" to convey a pronunciation pattern showing West African language influence, i.e., a vowel sound instead of an /r/ sound. The absence of the /r/ at the end of words like "Sista" parallels /r/ absence in many West African languages, many of which do not have the typical English /r/ sound. Also in these communities, kinship terms may be used when one is referring to other African people, whether they are biologically related or not.

Undeniably, there is overlap between Africanized and non-Africanized English. The commonalities often lull you into glossing over, or ignoring, the sometimes subtle, but linguistically profound differences. There are critical distinctions that separate linguistically competent Ebonics speakers from the wannabes. For example, in the colloquial speech of both African and European Americans, you may hear *gonna* or *goin to* for the prestige form *going to*. But in Ebonics the form is a nasalized vowel form, producing a sound close to, but not identical with, *gone*, thus: "What she go (n) do now?" ("What is she going to do now?") Another example is in negation patterns. While those obsessed with what linguist Donald J. Lloyd called the "national mania for correctness" often rail against the "double negatives" found in colloquial speech, Ebonics is distinctive for its *multiple* negatives. Further, the language is distinctive for its use of multiple negatives in combination with negative inversion, that is, putting the negative before, instead of after, the verb. An example from a sixty-something devout member of a Traditional Black Church: "Don't nobody don't know God can't tell me nothin!" ("Anybody who doesn't know God cannot tell me anything," that is, a person who doesn't believe in God and isn't saved has no credibility.)

In response to the question, "Is she married?" a speaker using Ebonics may answer "She been married," or "She BEEN married." If the speaker pronounces "been" without stress, it means that the woman in question was once married, and she may or may not be married now. However, if the speaker pronounces it "BEEN," i.e., with stress, it means she married a long time ago and is still married.

ADDITIONAL PATTERNS OF GRAMMAR AND PRONUNCIATION IN EBONICS

- Use of invariant *be* for future
  Example: "I be there in a minute."

- No copula *is* and *are* for equative structures and present tense actions
  Example: "She ready."
  "They laughing."

- Use of *done* for completed action (can co-occur with *been*)
  Example: "They done been sitting there a whole hour."

- Future perfective *be done* (action that will be past by the time it is completed in the future)
  Example: "She be done graduated by June." (spoken in December of the previous year)

- *Ain* as negator with base verb form (i.e., translates as *didn't*)
  Example: "They ain know what I was doing."
  "He ain come to the club that night."

- *Ain but* and *Don't but* for limited negation
  Example: "She ain nothin but a kid." (She is only a kid.)
  "Don't but two people know what really happen."
  (Only two people know what really happened.)

- Contextual signals for tense
  Example: "They *look* for him everywhere but never did find him."
  "They brother *do* the same thang they do."

- *Uhm* and *Ima* for *am, am going to*
  Example: "Uhm really tired." (I am really tired.)
  "Ima show everybody up."
  (I am going to show everybody up,
  i.e., outdo everyone else)

- *Finna* for immediate future
  Example: "We finna go."
  "Uhm finna get to it right now."

- *Here go/There go* as statives (no motion occurs)
  Example: "There go my momma in the front row."
  "Here go the poem I wrote."

- Contextual signals for plurals and, as noted earlier, possessives
  (i.e., "that's what got the Sista nose open")

    Example: "There were many thing that influence her life."

- *They* and *yall/yall's* for possessive

    Example: "The expressway bought they house." (Referring to a
    family's home demolished to make room for a freeway)
    "It's yall's bid."

- Existential *"it"* (as expletive or filler)

    Example: "Is it anybody home?"
    "It's a lot of people live there."

- *And nem* (or *'n nem/nem*) for associative plurals

    Example: "My momma nem was right behind us."
    "Kwesi 'n nem left too early."

- Redundant past tense marking

    Example: "likeded" (for "liked"); "dark skinnded" (for "dark skinned")

- *Verb + S* for recurring activity

    Example: "I *gets* my check on the first of the month."
    "They *comes* by here every day actin a fool."

- Pronominal apposition, sometimes for emphasis, sometimes as
  a kind of topic, plus comment on the topic, but not a double
  subject

    Example: "Now Robert, *he* don't know where he going."
    "That teacher, *she* mean and be hollin and stuff."

- *Steady* for continuous or persistent activity

    Example: "Them fools be steady hustlin everybody they see."
    (From Baugh, *Black Street Speech*, 1983)
    "That Sista steady on the case."

- Medial and final *l* not realized

    Example: "hep" (for "help")
    "I-ah" (for "I'll")

- Initial voiced *th* realized as *d*

    Example: "dem" (for "them")

- Final *th* realized as *f*, *t*, or *d*

    Example: "down souf" (for "down south"); "wit" or "wid" (for "with")

- *Ing* and *Ink* realized as *ang* and *ank*

    Example: "It's a Black thang"
    "You doing what? I don't thank so."

- Front shifting of stress
  Example: PO-lice; HO-tel

- Few consonant pairs
  Example: "tes" (for "test"); "des" (for "desk"); plural "tesses"
  (for "tests"); "desses" (for "desks")

- Unstressed initial affixes not realized
  Example: "bout it, bout it" (for "about it, about it")
  "member" (for "remember")

Before leaving the area of structure, let's look at a couple of examples that reveal how grammatical differences can contribute to miscommunication between teacher and student. From Los Angeles, California, Noma LeMoine reports, in her book *English for Success* (Peoples Publishing, 1999), the following interaction:

> SCENE: *Elementary school, Los Angeles*

TEACHER: Bobby, what does your mother do everyday? (Teacher apparently wanted to call Bobby's parents.)

BOBBY: She be at home!

TEACHER: You mean, she *is* at home.

BOBBY: No, she ain't, 'cause she took my grandmother to the hospital this morning.

TEACHER: You know what I meant. You are not supposed to say, "she *be* at home." You are to say, "she *is* at home."

BOBBY: Why you trying to make me lie? She ain't at home.

Of course, what Bobby is trying to convey is that his mother is not at home at this particular moment though she is generally home most days. But it is not just Los Angeles, nor for that matter, Oakland, California, where one might observe such communication failures between an Ebonics-speaking student and a teacher unfamiliar with the grammatical system of African American Language. Here is a similar interaction from a Detroit, Michigan classroom:

> SCENE: *First-grade classroom, Detroit*

TEACHER: Where is Mary?

STUDENT: She not here.

TEACHER: (exasperatedly): She is *never* here!

STUDENT: Yeah, she be here.

TEACHER: Where? You just said she wasn't here.

Question: Is Mary in the classroom? Answer: No, not at the present moment, but she is there sometimes. Therefore, the teacher's statement that Mary is "never here" is not accurate.

We turn now to the area of semantics in Black Language. There are several patterns and examples we could note. One example is the assignment of distinctively African American meanings to ordinary American English words, as in the use of forms that are "camouflaged" (Spears, 1982). In the statement, "She come tellin me I'n [didn't] know what I was talkin bout," the verb *come* does not denote motion. Rather the meaning of *come* in this context is one of indigation, like, "She had the nerve to tell me that I didn't know what I was talking about. How dare she!" Yet another pattern is that of semantic inversion. Although most non-Ebonics speakers might be aware that *bad* means "good," terms that haven't enjoyed such a high degree of crossover become problematic in crosscultural exchanges between Black and White Americans. Consider the following form of address common among many African American males: "Yo, Dog!" *Dog* is a linguistic symbol of male bonding, most likely derived from the African American fraternity tradition of referring to pledges as *dogs*. (Black women also use "dog" on occasion, but it is more common among men.) "Yo, Dog!" was used by a Brotha on lock down (gloss: imprisoned) to address his European American male psychiatrist as an expression of camaraderie. Turns out, though, that this white psychiatrist was not yet down (gloss: hip, understanding of the Black Cultural framework). He misinterpreted the Brotha's greeting and made an issue of this "insult."

In the area of linguistic–cultural practices – to a far greater extent than in the case of grammar or pronunciation – Ebonics cuts across gender, generation, and class in the African American community. Consider the speech act of *Signification*,[2] or, more commonly, *signifyin*, which can be rendered with or without the grammatical patterns and characteristic pronunciation of Ebonics. *Signification* is a ritualized kind of put-down, an insult, a way of talking about, needling, or *signifyin on* someone else. Sometimes it's done just for fun, in conversations with friends and close associates. Other times, the put-down is used for a more serious purpose. In this communicative practice, the speaker deploys exaggeration, irony, and indirection as a way of saying something on two different levels at once. It is often used to send a message of social critique, a bit of social commentary on the actions or statements of someone who is in need of a wake-up call. Malcolm X once began a speech with these words: "Mr. Moderator, Brotha Lomax, Brothas and Sistas, friends and enemies." Now, one doesn't usually begin a speech by addressing one's enemies. Thus Malcolm's signifyin statement let his audience know that he knew inimical forces were in their midst. Or like one of the deacons at this Traditional Black Church, who complained that his preacher would never deal with the problems and issues folk were facing on a daily basis. Rather, he was always preaching about the pearly gates and how great "thangs was gon be at dat home up in the sky." So one day this deacon said to the preacher, "Reb, you know I got a home in Heaven, but I ain homesick!"

Signifyin is engaged in by all age groups and by both males and females in the Black community. To fully appreciate the socio-linguistic complexity involved, let us analyze in some detail a conversational excerpt involving two Sistas in a group of several at a wedding shower:

LINDA: Girl, what up with that head? [*Referring to her friend's hairstyle.*]
BETTY: Ask yo momma. [*Laughter from all the Sistas on the set.*]
LINDA: Oh, so you going there, huh? Well, I *did* ask my momma. And she said, "Cain't you see that Betty look like her momma spit her out?"
              [*Laughter from all, including Betty.*]

Betty and Linda signify on each other. Instead of answering Linda's question directly, Betty decides to inform Linda that the condition of her hairstyle is none of Linda's business by responding with "Ask yo momma." The usual expectation in a conversation is that a speaker's question will be answered honestly and sincerely; thus Betty's unexpected indirection produces laughter from the listeners.

Speech–act theory indicates that communication succeeds or fails as a result of the illocutionary (that is, intended) and perlocutionary (that is, received) effects of a message. The surface meaning of "yo momma" for those outside the Ebonics-speaking community is simply "your mother/mom." However, within that community, the utterance immediately signals that an insult has been hurled. The intended and received meaning of *yo momma* is invective; the game of ritual insult begins with participants creating the most appropriate, humorous, spontaneous, creative, exaggerated/untrue retorts that they can come up with.

The source of the retort "Ask yo momma" probably stems from family patterns in which mothers are consulted ("asked") about all kinds of things, great or small. Fathers may even respond to their children's questions or requests by saying "Ask your mother." The Ebonics speaker does not intend the literal, direct meaning, "You should go and ask your mother about this situation." Rather, given the conversational context, the speaker is indirectly saying, "Let the game of The Dozens begin." Linda clearly recognizes the entry into this game as indicated by her response, "Oh, so you going there, huh?" Unskilled players, lacking a spontaneous, on-target, humorous retort, would have let the conversation end at this point. However, Linda shows adeptness in playing the game. She regroups momentarily ("Oh, so you going there, huh?") and fires back skillfully. In fact, she *caps* (wins) this exchange with a more clever retort. Although Betty's use of the common Ebonics expression, *Ask yo momma*, is humorous and sets up a challenge, it is formulaic, simplistic and stylized. In this instance, it cannot, and does not, beat: "Well I *did* ask my momma. And she said, 'Cain't you see that Betty look like her momma spit her out?'" (Smitherman and Troutman: see Smitherman, 1997d).

ORIGIN OF THE TERM "EBONICS"

One month after the Oakland School Board passed its Ebonics resolution in December of 1996, the term "Ebonics" turned twenty-four years old. That's right, despite the widespread controversy and the media distortions of the Ebonics controversy, this label for the speech of the descendants of African slaves is over two decades old. However, the term did not catch on among linguists and never became the label of choice in the dominant American mainstream. (I have never been happy with the term "Black English," and I tried using "Ebonics" for a period. But I got tired of having to explain it, and after it didn't seem to be catching on, I finally settled on "Black Talk" and "Black Language," but on occasion, I still used "Black English.")

"Ebonics" was coined by a group of African American scholars, chief among them, clinical psychologist, Robert L. Williams, at a conference, "Language and the Urban Child," convened in St. Louis, Missouri, in January of 1973. Now Professor Emeritus at Washington University, Williams published the conference proceedings in 1975 as a book, entitled *Ebonics: The True Language of Black Folks*. In the Preface and Introduction to this work, Williams captures the thinking of that historical moment:

> A significant incident occurred at the conference. The Black conferees were so critical of the work on the subject done by white researchers, many of whom also happened to be present, that they decided to caucus among themselves and define Black Language from a Black perspective. It was in this caucus that the term *Ebonics* was created. [The term refers to] linguistic and paralinguistic features which on a concentric continuum represent the communicative competence of the West African, Caribbean, and United States slave descendant of African origin. It includes the various idioms, patois, argots, ideolects, and social dialects of Black people, especially those who have been forced to adapt to colonial circumstances. "Ebonics" derives its form from ebony (black) and phonics (sound, the study of sound).

Somehow or other (*somehow?*) the concept of a linguistic continuum from Africa to the "New World," and the terminology to express that concept, as created by these Black scholars, never caught on in the academic world, nor in the educational establishment. After only a few years, Williams's book went out of print, and the linguistic–cultural practices of US slave descendants continued to be referred to as "Black English" or "Black Vernacular English," updated in the 1990s to "African American English" or "African American Vernacular English." Nonetheless, it is fortunate that Williams had the wisdom and vision to write it all down, to publish the spirit and essence of those Black scholars' thinking and the conference proceedings, to preserve the historical record in the Black voice.

It seems clear that these scholars conceived of Ebonics as a superordinate term, covering all the African–European language mixtures developed in various African–European language contact situations throughout the world – e.g., Haitian Creole, a West African–French language mixture; the Dutch Creole spoken in Suriname; the English-based Creole spoken in Jamaica; West African Pidgin English; the West African–English mixture spoken in the US – all would be dimensions (varieties or dialects) of Ebonics, not of any European language. This superordinate concept thus symbolizes the linguistic–cultural unity of the global Black World and locates Black American speech, or "US Ebonics" within an African linguistic–cultural framework. Since December 1996, when the Oakland resolution on Ebonics was passed, the term "Ebonics" has come to be used loosely to refer to "US Ebonics," and used interchangeably with "Black/African American (Vernacular) English," a practice I also follow. But we should keep in mind that the original conception encompassed more languages than African American Language and was, in fact, a rejection of the term "Black English" and the concomitant subordination of this Africanized language under the categorical heading, "English." (See Smith (1998) and Blackshire-Belay (1996) for a fuller discussion of the political implications of language classification.)

HISTORICAL OVERVIEW OF EBONICS

The history of Ebonics can be best understood against the backdrop of the long-standing controversy about the existence and role of Africanisms in the Black Experience. Much of the late nineteenth (e.g., Harrison, 1884) and early twentieth-century commentary and research literature on Black speech were historical in nature, reflecting the dominant paradigm in linguistic science of the times. Language study concerned itself with reconstructing the origin of languages, demonstrating kinships in language families, etymology and other types of philological studies. When the tools of historical linguistics focused on "Negro English" (as it was often referred to in this era), the critical issue was the question of African survivals in African America. Two schools of thought emerged: (1) the Anglian-based tradition, aka Anglicist and dialectologist (e.g., Krapp, 1924, 1925; Kurath, 1928), and (2) the African-based tradition (e.g., Herskovits, 1941; Turner, 1949), aka "Creolist."

The Anglian tradition of scholarship asserted that what was called "Negro" or "Black" English is really "*White* English," traceable to British dialects spoken in remote areas. (This position has resurfaced in the 1990s; see e.g., Schneider (1993). This school of thought argued that Africans in enslavement picked up their English from white immigrants from places like East Anglia, that is, from whites speaking various dialects of the British Isles, who had settled in the South during the Colonial era in US history. Thus, according to this line of reasoning, Black speech is simply outdated or archaic white speech, and these old-fashioned forms of English have persisted in the African American community because of racial, and consequently, linguistic isolation. Over time, Blacks have not participated in the language changes taking place in the white mainstream because they have not been part of that mainstream. Seen from another vantage point, however, one might say that this line of thinking simply replaced the theories of biological determinism which had explained Black speech and other cultural differences on the basis of physiognomy and genetics. Whether archaic and old-fashioned, or genetic and biological, we are led to the view that the African still has not caught up with the European in the scheme of things, and in post-modern twentieth century-America, the shift has simply been from biology to sociobiology (see e.g., Herrnstein, 1994). See "Discriminatory Discourse on African American Speech" for a more detailed analysis of this issue, this volume, pp. 67–92.)

The Anglicist origins theory about Black speech is the linguistic version of the socio-historical school that argues that most everything African was eradicated during the hardship of the Middle Passage and the aftermath of slavery. What was left was a cultural *tabula rasa*, that is, a blank slate, filled with European American culture. Even one of the notable, highly respected Black scholars, E. Franklin Frazier (1966) attributed the cultural differences of African Americans to the degradation of poverty and hard times, rather than to African linguistic and cultural influence.

One problem that confronts all scholars in quest of the linguistic origins of US Ebonics is the lack of an empirical record of the language in its incubation period, i.e., the period dating from 1619 up until the Revolutionary War era. While a few writings by whites make reference to some kind of linguistic phenomenon they call "speaking Negro," there is no written record of the language used by African Americans – or, more precisely, enslaved Africans in those days – until the late eighteenth century when we get representations of slave speech in literature. Further, there are only a few written examples of speech from enslaved Africans in other parts of the "New World" during this early period. However, analysis of the historical linguistic evidence from enslaved Africans, scant though it may be, reveals language patterns that are still in use by today's slave descendants, that is, speakers of twentieth-century Ebonics. Further, there are patterns dating from this early period, still in use today, which are *not* found in older British English (the source of the early English dialects brought to Britain's American colony in the "New World"). One example is the pattern of making a statement without an obligatory copula (the verb "to be"). This is also a feature of a number of West African languages, but it is not a pattern of older British English dialects. Consider this statement from an enslaved African in America in 1776:

Me massa name Cunney Tomsee.
(My master's name is Colonel Thompson.)

The grammar of this construction, with no mandatory form of the verb "to be," parallels a similar statement made by an enslaved African from the island of Barbados in the British West Indies. The statement was recorded by Justice Hathorne at the Salem witch trial in 1692:

He tell me he God.

Yet another example of the same construction, that is, a sentence without a form of the verb "to be," which is required in English, is provided by an enslaved African from the Dutch colony of Suriname in South America in 1718:

Me bella well (I am very well).

Parallels such as these lend support to the older Turner–Herskovits thesis about a linguistic continuum throughout the African Diaspora. That is, the way the African grammatical rules were applied to the European words was the same regardless of the European language. This was possible because of the underlying similarities in the grammatical systems of the various West African languages. Further, such linguistic parallels were undoubtedly what Dr. Robert Williams and his colleagues had in mind when he coined the term "Ebonics" back in 1973 to capture the linguistic commonalities of the "West African, Caribbean, and United States slave descendants of African origin" (Williams, 1975). (Readers interested in examining the intricacies of this historical reconstruction and linguistic analysis in greater detail should consult the history of Black English done by Dillard (1972), a pioneering piece of scholarship that has become a classic. Important, later sources include Alleyne, 1980; DeBose and Faraclas, 1993; Spears and Winford, 1997; Bailey and Cukor-Avila, 1991.)

The important point for those who want to have a general, informed understanding of the Ebonics origin issue is this: there is general consensus among contemporary linguists that the Anglian tradition *does not fully* account for the historical development of Ebonics. And while not all of these scholars embrace the African language origins – some arguing, for instance, that US Ebonics reflects the influence of Caribbean Creole and that not all Creole features themselves are Africanisms – all clearly reject the view that Ebonics is simply a dialect of English which enslaved Africans learned from white speakers of various British English dialects. (See Rickford (1998) for a recent, thorough overview and analysis of this issue. Morgan (1993) and Williams (1993) also provide creative and interesting perspectives on this issue.)

The African-based tradition of Ebonics, then, asserted that "Negro English" was a kind of Africanized English developed during the slave trade. One version of this view, an older but still highly plausible theory promulgated by Dillard (1972) and Stewart (1972), argued that this Africanized English most probably began as Pidgin English, which later evolved into Plantation Creole, which subsequently became de-creolized over time. The terms "pidgin" and "creole" refer to language mixtures developed in situations where speakers of different languages had extended contact that required them to communicate with one another. Many linguists make a distinction between a pidgin and a creole. With just a few exceptions, most pidgins are simpler than creoles. Further, a pidgin is spoken on a limited basis since the people who use the pidgin have other, fully developed languages that they speak on a more regular basis, as in the case of Africans who spoke several African languages as well as one of the pidgin languages. A pidgin evolves into a creole when it becomes the *only* language of a community, a situation created when the children of pidgin speakers grow up using the pidgin as their first and only language. Since the creole is used widely and frequently, it becomes more developed grammatically and has a more extensive vocabulary than its parent, the pidgin.

In the African–European language contact situation, both in the Motherland, and in the "New World," the Pidgin/Creole combined the vocabulary of a given European language – English, Dutch, French, etc. – with the grammatical and pronunciation patterns of African languages. While the words might have been derived from the European language, the way the Africans used the words was distinctly African, reflecting systems of syntax and communicative styles that were not found in the European languages. In the US, despite the variety of West African language groups (deliberately mixed on the plantations so as to foil communication and rebellion), a common language evolved because the enslaved Africans shared two linguistic denominators: (1) the English vocabulary ; and (2) the structure and meaning systems of the African languages. This process created the Africanized English, which became the *lingua franca* of the enslavement communities as well as the language used to communicate with the Europeans in the British colony in America.

The line of thinking that Ebonics reflects African-language origins is the linguistic version of views put forth by Woodson beginning in the 1920s and by DuBois beginning in 1903 – long before it was fashionable or socially acceptable to speak of Afrocentricity. These Black scholars argued that African American cultural distinctiveness resulted from retentions and adaptations of African culture to new circumstances and conditions. They disavowed the cultural *tabula rasa* theory as a logical impossibility for any human group, even one under the siege of enslavement and post-Emancipation poverty and degradation, because culture is not just things, objects, or material artefacts. More importantly, culture is ways of thinking, behavioral habits, patterns of conduct – and language – none of which can simply be wiped out by a journey across the Atlantic or harsh living conditions.

Over the past two decades, as more historically based research has been done on US Ebonics and on Pidgins and Creoles in the Caribbean and elsewhere, linguists have developed variations on the older (1960s-1970s) Pidgin–Creole–De-Creolization Hypothesis in an effort to account for the tremendous complexity in the development of all the Ebonic languages over time. For example, some scholars now question whether there was ever a Pidgin stage in US Ebonics, arguing that it rapidly creolized, probably within a generation; thus, it was *Creole* English, not *Pidgin* English that was spoken in the early years of enslavement in North America (e.g., Rickford, 1998). Others argue that US Ebonics was a kind of "semi-creole" (e.g., Holm, 1992). Some assert that the African languages were probably heard for a long time, much longer than a generation, and that these languages greatly influenced the developing Creoles throughout the "New World" (e.g., Alleyne, 1980). Still others sketch a historical scenario of the development of a common tongue in the early period, one that reflected settler dialect, spoken by both African slaves and the Southern white working class for the first few generations (e.g., Winford, 1997). Insights to be gained from current work on the history of US Ebonics, Pidgins, and Creoles, by such linguists as Rickford, Spears, Mufwene, Winford (to cite just a few), will be a welcome addition to the scholarly literature about these complex phenomena.

US EBONICS AND THE BLACK EXPERIENCE

The linguistic origin of Ebonics is one significant part of the history of the language. The other crucial dimension is the social and political experience of enslaved Africans and their descendants. The Black Experience is a narrative of resistance, of an on-going struggle to be free, perhaps the motive force in African American history. Since language is inextricably interwoven with a group's culture and history, US Ebonics would have been affected/continues to be affected by the concrete historical conditions of Africans in America. Figure 1.1 on page 36, attempts to capture key events, social forces, and modal experiences that influenced the development of Ebonics. The figure also charts the changing terms of racial reference among Africans in America. (Racial semantics is discussed more fully in "From African to African American", this volume, pp. 41–56) What this kind of historical examination demonstrates is the interrelationship between the language and the status of Africans and later, African Americans. Stated more succinctly, if somewhat oversimplified: in historical moments of racial progress, the language is less Ebonified; in times of racial suppression, the language is more Ebonified.

We begin with 1619, the year marking the introduction of slavery into the British colony that would become the United States of America. The place was Jamestown where a Dutch ship unloaded twenty Africans. In this early period, the enslaved Africans would have been speaking their own African languages as well as a Pidgin (or Creole) language, that enabled them to talk with the white settlers, as well as among themselves in instances where there was no shared African language they could use. The Pidgin/Creole formation may have been introduced by enslaved Africans from the Caribbean (where slaves would be taken for "seasoning" and "breaking"), and/or it may have been formed on the West Coast of Africa, in slave-trading transactions, in the British colonization of West Africa, and during the long periods of time when captured Africans were held in the slave "castles" awaiting transport to the "New World."

During these years in Colonial America, some Africans could buy themselves out of enslavement; that is, they had the status of indentured servants like many of the white workers of that time. Further, even those Africans who were enslaved enjoyed a certain mobility and freedom of movement. This situation did not last long. The colonists became concerned about controlling the growing (and often rebellious) African slave population, and it was both dangerous and costly to continue invasions of Africa and the transport of slaves across the Atlantic. They began to institute laws and policies to deal with the developing slave crisis.

The repressive Black Codes (also known as Slave Codes) were launched before the end of the seventeenth century, after only two generations of enslavement. These laws were designed to restrict the movements of the enslaved African population, to bring it under control, and to ensure that there would be a large pool of free slave labor. No longer was it possible to buy oneself out of bondage. The Codes mandated that once a slave, you were a slave for life. The laws circumscribed the movements and activities of slaves – for instance, passes were required for slaves to leave the plantation. It became illegal to teach slaves to read and write. The possibility of "flying away" back to Africa (rooted in the belief that there were Africans who could fly) became increasingly remote. To build up the slave-labor force internally, certain male slaves were encouraged to be breeders in their own slave communities, and sometimes hired out to other plantations, to impregnate as many female slaves as possible. The linguistic consequence of this new set of conditions would have been children born into slave communities in which African languages were heard and used less and less. At the same time, there would have been an increase in the use of the Africanized language (Pidgin/Creole English) for communication and solidarity among the enslaved.

Class distinctions began to be refracted through the linguistic prism of the enslavement community. Although all were enslaved, some Africans worked in ole Massa's house, others worked in the fields. The "house" slaves had more exposure to Massa's language and to what writer Langston Hughes once called the "ways of white folk." These slaves used a version of English that was less Africanized than that of their fellow slaves working in the fields.

Initially, *De-creolization*, that is, the linguistic de-Africanization of Black speech, would have been more prominent in the speech of house slaves and among free Blacks. As the late eighteenth- and early nineteenth-century Anti-Slavery Movement gained momentum, the De-Creolization process would sweep the entire enslaved community because the dream of freedom and citizenship – as an

1557	1619	1661	1808	1863	1877	1914–45	1966	1990s
Beginning of African use of English[1]	20 African slaves/ indentured servants arrive at Jamestown on a Dutch ship	Beginning of slave codes circumscribing activities and lives of slaves	Outlawing of Slave Trade; rise of Anti-Slavery Movement	Emancipation	Reconstruction ends; institutionalization of "separate but equal"	World Wars I & II; vast urban migration of Blacks out of South	Black Power Movement; push for integration comes to a halt	Capitalist, post-industrialist crises creating severe problems for some Blacks; unparalleled prosperity for others
Pidgin		Creole	De-creolization De-Africanization		De-creolized forms solidify, especially among underclass/ "field" slave descendants	De-creolization continues	Recreolization Re-Africanization De-creolization halted; conscious attempt to recapture earlier Black Language forms and create new ones	Emergence of bilingual conciousness; linguistic experimentation
	African		Colored		Negro		Black	African American

Figure 1.1 US Ebonics and the Black Experience

[1] An Englishman, William Towerson, takes five Africans to England in 1554 to learn English and serve as interpreters in the slave trade and in Britain's colonization campaign on the West Coast of Africa. Three of them returned to the African Gold Coast in 1557. "It is reasonable to accept this as the date from which the African use of English began." (Dalby, 1970, pp. 11–12.)

American, not an African – loomed on the horizon. The thinking was that a citizen would need to speak the standard English of European American citizens, not an Africanized version of English. The date of 1808 as the historical marker of this new phase (see Figure 1.1) in the development of US Ebonics is somewhat arbitrary. The historical record is clear that Africans in America resisted enslavement long before the passage of any antislavery laws. Nonetheless, 1808 was the effective date of the *Federal* law that finally banned the importation of human cargo into the US, which would have given renewed impetus to the resistance movement and the possibility of citizenship in the not-so-distant future.

Langston Hughes once posed the rhetorical question, "What happens to a dream deferred? Does it dry up like a raisin in the sun?" If not dried up, the dream of Black equality and full participation in American life seems to have been deferred indefinitely. Certainly freedom and citizenship did not result from Emancipation and the Civil War. Instead, in 1877 when the Federal Government pulled its troops out of the South and ended Reconstruction, enslavement was re-enacted in another form, laws and policies that created a separate and unequal world for Africans in America. The linguistic effect of the institutionalization of US-style apartheid, which was the model for South African apartheid, was to halt the De-creolization that had begun during the Anti-Slavery Movement. The de-Africanized forms solidified, particularly among field slave descendants.

Each of America's global wars to make the world "safe for democracy" were wars in which Blacks fought with the belief that they too would finally enjoy the fruits of US democracy. In the World War years, Black hopes for full citizenship took a leap forward – only to be crushed when the end of World Wars I and II resulted in yet another dream deferred. Linguistically, the war years re-energized the forces of De-creolization as Blacks sought to demonstrate that "I too sing America." Although this Americanization was not granted in the postwar era, the de-Africanization of the language continued as Black Americans went through a period of the denial of Africa.

The Black Freedom Struggle that began in the late 1950s with protest marches and boycotts in the South signaled a new way of thinking – and talking – in African America. Black Pride replaced Black inferiority. A reassertion of and reconnection with the pre-enslavement past replaced the denial of Africa. The Black Power wing of the Freedom Struggle, during the mid-1960s and beyond, played a particular role in bringing a halt to De-creolization. Black Power intellectuals and activists sought to speak the language of the people, tapping into the Black Oral Tradition, using its metaphors, images, and rhetorical stances. Black Arts/Black Power writers sought to capture the idioms, nuances, and speaking styles of the people and represented Ebonics in their work , seeking to make the medium the message. This phase of the Black Experience launched a kind of *Recreolization* (Smitherman, 1989): a conscious attempt to accentuate the uniqueness of Ebonics, to recapture and reconfigure earlier forms of Black speech, to carve out a distinctly African-in-America linguistic identity. The process of Recreolization continues today and is most evident in Hip Hop Culture and in the works of Black women writers, such as Walker, Morrison, and McMillan. Simultaneously, there is an emerging sense of a bilingual consciousness among middle-class Blacks (particularly those who are not yet middle age) and a developing level of linguistic experimentation as they incorporate the Ebonics flava into dialog and discourse. The Recreolization efforts of Black women writers and the Hip Hop Nation, in concert with the linguistic experimentation of (young) Black professionals, should eventuate in a new linguistic form, reflecting a dynamic blend of traditional and innovative language patterns, as US Ebonics enters the twenty-first century. Stay tuned.

In the meantime, there remain deep and widening educational and linguistic contradictions in African America, as well as a great cultural divide (e.g., Spears, 1998), unparalleled in Black American history. While the Black middle class is generally bilingual, their Brothas and Sistas in the working and Un-working classes are generally monolingual. The educational system continues to fail the youth from these monolingual groups, rejecting and/or stigmatizing their culture and background and making them linguistic outcasts. For their part, the youth see no reason to add another language to their communication toolbox and thus only half-heartedly accept, or may even outright reject, the Language of Wider Communication. Yet, this is the language of literacy, commerce, politics, and education, and it is a necessary addition to most people's linguistic repertoire. (Yes, Black youth need to learn the LWC; there has never been any argument against this policy, though I for one have been accused of this position. My argument has to do with when, how, for what purposes, and at what cost. For instance, plumbers − very well paid these days, by the way − certainly don't need the LWC.)

It is not difficult to see how Black youth − and some Black adults, for that matter − come to reject the LWC. Historically, Standard American English was the language of the oppressor, hence a lingering association of Standard American English with "talkin white." For an older generation of Blacks, who came of age at a time when the Black middle and working classes shared the same neighborhood and attended the same schools, the linguistic role models for working-class Blacks were middle-class, professional Blacks, not whites. Your homiez might have accused you of trying to sound like Dr. Thompson, the local Black internist, but not of "talkin white." That concept has come into widespread use with the contemporary isolation of the Black working and under classes in the cities. The Black models and speakers of LWC, the Dr. Thompsons, are now living outside the hood.

Still very much in existence are the "two separate societies," one Black, the other white, which the National Advisory Commission on Civil Disorders (aka the "Kerner Commission") warned the Nation about in the wake of the rebellions of the 1960s. As Hacker's study (1992) demonstrated, there is continuing racial injustice and economic inequality between Blacks and whites. The growth of prisons is "approaching the nearly-complete racial homogeneity of concentration camps . . . Nationwide 6% of the population – African American men – provides nearly 50% of the prison population . . . and are incarcerated in jails and prisons at a far higher rate than are whites, 3,109 as compared to 426 per 100,000 population" (Buck, 1999, 6–7). Compounding the Black condition, the African American community itself is subdividing into two separate societies, an expanding middle-class group of "have's," who *do* have command of LWC (which is often perceived as "talkin white" these days, as noted above), and a very large and troubled group of "have nots," who *do not* have command of LWC.

Can these contradictions be resolved? We certainly know enough to do it. But can we do what we know? A major step in addressing the educational and linguistic contradictions would be to formulate a language policy for the African American community, with the simultaneous goal of formulating a progressive multi-faceted language policy for the entire Nation.

The language policy for the Black community must be one of multilingualism as I noted over a decade ago (Smitherman, 1984). We need a multilingualism policy not only as Williams (1982) noted, to "protect the interests of the Black community," but also to prepare African American youth for world leadership. Such a policy would call for official recognition of US Ebonics and for its use as a co-equal language of instruction in schools with large numbers of Ebonics-speaking students. It would reinforce the need for the Language of Wider Communication, the acquisition of which would be achievable throughout the Black student population if there were full recognition, not lip-service phoniness, of Ebonics. As Williams's research demonstrated, the more understanding there is about the Mother Tongue, and the more secure one is about its legitimacy, the greater is one's willingness to learn another language. He called this the Language Consciousness Hypothesis (1982). Finally, the language policy for the Black community must include one or more languages from Africa and/or other parts of the so-called "Third World" (Smitherman, 1984). African Americans need to be able to carry on independent dialog with Africans and other persons of Color — the majority population in the global community. Possibly Spanish would be one of the "Third World" languages because of its large number of speakers both in the US and the Caribbean as well as in other parts of the Western Hemisphere. Such a language policy would chart a new, unprecedented course in the history of US Ebonics. Its time will come.

2

THE RELATIONSHIP OF Black
Americans to "Mother Africa" is being
raised anew and in a broad public
forum as the national Black community struggles with the call to move
from the racial designation "Black" to
"African American." Because of
Reverend Jesse Jackson's widespread
popularity, many have assumed him
to be the catalyst for the current
linguistic change. However, it was
actually Dr. Ramona Edelin, President
of the National Urban Coalition, who,
in late 1988, proposed that the
upcoming 1989 summit be called the
"African American Summit" because
the semantics "would establish a cultural context for the new agenda"
(quoted in Lacayo and Monroe,
1989). Taking up Edelin's call at the
December 1988 news conference to
announce the Summit, Jackson indicated that "just as we were called
colored, but were not that . . . and
then Negro, but not that . . . to be
called Black is just as baseless," and
further, like other groups of Americans, African Americans want to link
their heritage to the land of their
origin (quoted in Page, 1989).

FROM AFRICAN TO AFRICAN AMERICAN [1991]

What is Africa to me
Copper sun or scarlet sea,
Jungle star or jungle track,
Strong bronzed men, or regal black,
Women from whose loins I sprang
When the birds of Eden sang?

*One three centuries removed
From the scenes his fathers loved,
Spicy grove, cinnamon tree,
What is Africa to me?*
(Countee Cullen, 1925)[1]

The issue of racial semantics set in motion by Edelin, Jackson,
and others has generated far greater national publicity and media
attention than the Summit itself. In addition to extensive coverage
by *The New York Times*, articles have appeared in *Time, The Chicago
Tribune, The Washington Post*, several metropolitan dailies across the
country, and in *Ebony, Essence*, and other African American media.
CBS "Nightwatch" News hosted an hour-long panel discussion on

the issue.[2] Even Ann Landers (1989) devoted attention to the question, publishing responses in one column and indicating in another column that African American "seems appropriate because it gets away from color and designates origin instead. I hope it catches on." As recently as 28 October 1990, *The Washington Post National Weekly Edition* featured the issue in a column by Michael Specter headlined "Men and Women of Their Word: But should that word be 'Black' or 'African American'?" (p. 10). And in December, 1990, as I was writing this article, Rosemary Bray dealt with this topic in a special section of *Essence*.

Inasmuch as the current linguistic movement is complexified by the dynamics of race, there are bound to be cases of uncertainty as well as confusion. Lexicographers, such as those at Random House, and the mainstream press, such as the Associated Press and *The New York Times*, are waiting for a consensus among speakers and writers before establishing a policy decision on *Black* versus *African American*. Although the US Census Bureau did not use "African American" as a category on the 1990 Census Bureau did not use "African American" as a category on the 1990 census form – reportedly because the call for change was issued too late to be included (Wilkerson, 1989) – the Bureau did add special instructions to the form indicating that "Black" or "Negro" includes "African Americans." Humorous instances of linguistic confusion are starting to crop up, as these two examples indicate:

> We, the Black African American people will soon rise to our God-given greatness – if we just hold on to His unchanging hand.
>
> (Banquet speaker at an African American church 22 September 1990, Detroit)

> An item in Thursday's *Nation Digest* about the Massachusetts budget crisis made reference to new taxes that will help put Massachusetts "back in the African American." The item should have said "back in the black."
>
> (The Fresno Bee, 21 July 1990, p. 12A)

This article seeks to illuminate the age-old question of a name for the enslaved African population of the United States and its emancipated descendants. [See Figure 1.1, page 36] Two dimensions of the question will be presented: (1) the history of racial labelling from the perspective of the changing material conditions of Blacks; and (2) contemporary opinions about the use of African American based on the author's five-city survey of public opinion about language matters.

WHAT'S IN A NAME?

This study is informed by the paradigm, in linguistics, of "language as social semiotic" (Halliday, 1978) and the theoretical framework, in sociology, of the "social construction of reality" (Berger and Luckmann, 1966). Following Berger and Luckmann's contention that language constitutes the most important content and instrument of socialization, I will here summarize an argument I've made extensively elsewhere (Smitherman, 1980, 1983, 1989): reality is not merely *socially*, but *sociolinguistically* constructed. Real-world experience and phenomena do not exist in some raw, undifferentiated form. Rather, reality is always filtered, apprehended, encoded, codified, and conveyed via some linguistic shape. This linguistic form exists in a dialectical relationship with social cognition and social behavior. While Humboldtian linguists (and most Whorfians, for that matter) overstate the case for language as the determiner of thought, consciousness and behavior, nonetheless, language does play a dominant role in the formation of ideology, consciousness, and class relations. As Voloshinov put it, "ideology is revealed in a word" (1929, p. 70). Thus my contention is that consciousness and ideology are largely the products of what I call the *sociolinguistic construction of reality*.

For African Americans, the semantics of race have been recurring themes in our sociolinguistic constructions of reality since 1619, when the first cargo of African slaves landed at Jamestown. The societal complexity of the Black condition continues to necessitate a self-conscious construction of identity. Notwithstanding historical, cultural and cosmological linkages with Continental and Diasporic Africans and, further, notwithstanding similarities between American slavery and slavery in other historical epochs, the African American, as James Baldwin once put it, is a unique creation. Whereas other African peoples lay claim to national identity in countries where the population is "Black" – e.g., Jamaicans, Ghanaians, Bajans, Nigerians – African Americans claim national identity in a country where most of the population is non-Black. After being emancipated and granted citizenship, there were (and continue to be) profound implications for a group with a lifetime suntan trying to forge an identity and a life in the midst of the European American population which for decades had found them lacking the necessities of intellect and morality.[3]

From 1619 and right up until Emancipation, in fact, the identity question was complexified by the widely divergent statuses of Blacks. Because of the commonality of skin color, it was impossible to distinguish permanent from "temporary" African slaves (i.e.,

those who, like the European indentured servants, were working
to purchase their freedom), or either of these from those Africans
freed by their masters or those born to free parents. None of the
aforementioned groups, by virtue of "blackness" alone, could be
distinguished from escaped/"fugitive" slaves. And what about the
products of miscegenation, where one parent was European (and
therefore free), the other was an African slave, and the skin color
was light black?

AFRICAN

Europeans in Colonial America used racial labels based on what was
for them the critical category of enslavement. Thus, depending on
status, Africans were referred to as "free" or "slave" (Franklin, 1969).
Where enslavement status was unknown, or where there was
occasion to use a collective term for all Africans, they used "nigger"
(not a racial epithet until the late nineteenth century) or "negro"
(Portuguese and Spanish adjective "black"; used by fifteenth-century
Portuguese slave traders; lowercased until the 1920s).

   Although the small number of "free" Africans tended to refer to
themselves as "colored," the most frequently used label, for "free"
and "slave" alike, was African (Drake, 1966). The first church was
called the African Episcopal Church. The first formally organized
self-help group was designated the Free African Society, followed by
the African Educational and Benevolent Society, the Sons of Africa
Society, and the African Association for Mutual Relief. The first
Masonic Lodge was called African Lodge No. 459. And the writer
of one of the first slave narratives referred to himself as "Olaudah
Equiano, or Gustavus Vassa, the African" (1789).

   The sociolinguistic reality these early Africans constructed
reflected a distinct African consciousness. Since the African experience was still very immediate for most Blacks, regardless of their
status, the possibility of returning to Africa haunted them constantly.
Two years before the signing of the Declaration of Independence,
a group of African slaves formally petitioned the British governor
of Massachusetts for permission to return to Africa (Drake, 1987).
The legendary folk hero Solomon (also of Toni Morrison's novel
Song of Solomon) was believed to have the capacity to fly back to
Africa – and hence, freedom. In fact, according to Asante (1988),
what some scholars refer to as the African American pre-generic
quest myth of freedom speaks originally to escape to Mother Africa
out of bondage, with Canada and the northern United States
coming in at a later historical stage. In any case, the ideological
function of the label *African* served as a logical rallying point, since

all Blacks had current or ancestral ties to Africa, whether they were temporary or permanent slaves, free men/women, fugitives, or mixed-bloods (albeit if the mother was a slave – the usual case – the offspring was also classified as a slave). *African* symbolized a common heritage, thus becoming a focal, unifying semantic for socially divergent groups of Africans, both creating and reinforcing the social construction of group solidarity and commonality.

COLORED

The Black condition became even more complexified after England's colonies became the United States. For one thing, slavery was *not abolished*, as the enslaved African population had anticipated, and as the free Africans – such as the leader Prince Hall, who fought at Lexington, Concord, and Bunker Hill – had believed. The Black Codes passed in the seventeenth and eighteenth centuries had abolished temporary slavery and instituted the "slave-for-life" status for all enslaved Africans, including their offspring, thus differentiating African slaves from the European indentured servant population (Franklin, 1969). But 1776 brought about neither a repeal of these laws nor universal emancipation. Further, the costly, inefficient method of importing shiploads of human cargo across the abyss of the Middle Passage was gradually supplanted by the greater cost benefit system of local slave (re)production (enhanced on some plantations by the designation of certain males as breeders).[4] Yet the importation did not cease altogether, even after passage of the 1808 Slave Trade Act outlawing this transportation of human chattel. Then there were the free men/women who, though not slaves, were denied full citizenship and equal rights in the newly formed United States. Finally, the processes of individual manumission and miscegenation continued, each adding another layer of complexity to the status of people of African descent during the era between the Revolutionary and the Civil Wars. Could the same racial label be used for slaves fresh from Africa as for slaves born in the United States, some of whom were fifth and sixth generation descendants of Africans? (In some of the advertisements for runaway slaves, recently captured Africans were referred to as "*new* negroes" (Read, 1939).) And if freed men/women of African descent were not full citizens of the newly-created American State, what should they be called? (Surely not African AMERICANS?!)

In the nineteenth century, the era of *colored* began, and the semantics of *African* declined in use and significance. By this era several generations of Blacks had been born on American soil, and with fewer arrivals from Africa, there was decreased cultural infusion into the slave community. Further, although colonization societies and movements to resettle the slaves in Africa persisted right up until the Civil War, the huge Black population – well over one million by 1800 – made wholesale emigration of Blacks to Africa impractical, if not impossible. Most critically, both the free and the enslaved African populations were developing a new understanding of their role in the making of America (Frazier, 1966). They had helped build the country through nearly two hundred years of free labor, and free Africans had participated both in the Revolutionary War and the War of 1812. The possibility for emancipation and citizenship was being created through their agitation and struggle, as well as through the efforts of European American Abolitionists. The Africans reasoned that the European American-dominated movements to resettle them in Africa would effectively disinherit them of their share of the American pie whose ingredients included not only their own blood, sweat, and tears, but that of many thousands gone.

Although *colored* had been used in the earlier period by some "free" Africans, it re-emerged in the nineteenth century as a racial referent for the entire Black group, now united in its collective move toward emancipation. There was the formation of the Pennsylvania Augustine Society "for the education of people of colour." There was the publication of David Walker's radical *Appeal* (1829) calling for open rebellion against enslavement, which he addressed to the "Coloured Citizens of the World, but in Particular and very Expressly to Those of the United States of America." Abolitionist leader Frederick Douglass used *colored* (as well as *negro*) in his speeches and writings. Oral histories and folk narratives indicate the widespread use of *colored* among everyday Black people (Bennett, 1961). Even into the early twentieth century, *colored* was the preferred racial designation. The oldest Civil Rights organization, founded in 1909, was (and still is) called the National Association for the Advancement of *Colored* People.

NEGRO

The shift away from *colored* to *negro*, and the subsequent campaign for its capitalization, began at the turn of the century and hit its full stride during the period of the two world wars. The initial signs of linguistic change were the American Negro Academy, founded in 1897, and the National Negro Business League, founded in 1900. Booker T. Washington and other leaders of this period used "negro" frequently in their speeches (Bennett, 1967). The ideological vision was that with the spotlight on Europe and global struggles for freedom against fascism, and with "colored" soldiers (albeit in segregated regiments) shedding their blood for America, surely the still-unrealized quest for first-class citizenship and racial equity would at last be fulfilled. The appropriate conceptual label to usher in this new phase was *negro*, which had come into widespread linguistic currency among European Americans, especially those in the North, the seat of capital and political power. The new language was needed to construct a new identity of dignity, respect and full citizenship, all of which had been lacking in the past.

Negro leaders of the 1920s launched a massive, Nation-wide campaign for the capitalization of *negro* in order to elevate the Portuguese slavery-time adjective to the symbolic level of dignity and respect accorded a racial label. The NAACP sent out over 700 letters to European American publishers and editors. Dr W. E. B. DuBois wrote numerous editorial "Postscripts" in *Crisis*. Significant efforts were launched on local community and grass roots levels (e.g., the biweekly newsletter published by the Paul Laurence Dunbar Apartments in Cincinnati, Ohio). Finally the European American press capitulated: "In our Style Book, *Negro* is now added to the list of words to be capitalized. It is not merely a typographical change, it is an act in recognition of racial self-respect for those who have been for generations in the 'lower case'" (*New York Times*, 7 March 1930, p. 22). Although some Negroes continued to use *colored*, and although some Negro leaders and intellectuals – DuBois among them – balanced *Negro* with *Black* (Smitherman, 1986), *Negro* became the label of choice, dominating discourse by and about Negroes for over forty years.

BLACK

In 1966, Negro activist and leader Stokeley Carmichael issued a call for "Black power," and Negroes began to create a new sociolinguistic construction of reality. Several local and national conferences were held under the rubric of "Black Power" in 1966 and 1967 (Walters, 1993). Symbolizing a new ideological phase in the Negro Experience, these conferences and their leadership called upon Negroes to abandon the "slavery-imposed name" (Bennett, 1967).

The move from *Negro* to *Black* signaled an ideological shift, a repudiation of whiteness and the rejection of assimilation. The failure to embrace Blackness and to capitalize on the strengths of Black Culture and the Black Experience was reasoned to have stagnated the progress of the Civil Rights Movement. Only by being true to themselves and their heritage would Black people be able to harness the necessary power to liberate themselves. Freedom could not be achieved without a healthy racial consciousness, underscored by a strong belief in the collective Black Will to change the conditions of oppression. Thus it was imperative that Blacks eradicate the negativity and self-hatred of the Coloracracy, exemplified in the folk ditty, "If you white, you all right, if you brown, stick around, if you Black, git back."

The choice of a label that had traditionally been a way of calling a Negro "outa they name" now was being employed to purify Negroes of the idealization of white skin, white ideas, and white values. Spreading throughout the national Black community, the newly constructed reality was captured in the popular, best-selling 1968 song by James Brown, "Say it loud: 'I'm Black, and I'm proud.'" It was a profoundly classic case of the semantic inversion characteristics of Black English Vernacular speakers.[5] Bad was truly turned on its head and made good as the celebration of "Black" – Black Culture, Black skin color, the Black Experience – became a rallying cry for unity, empowerment and self-definition.

Negro History Week, in existence since its founding by Dr Carter G. Woodson in 1926, became *Black* History Week (and eventually Black History Month). The language announced Black people's right to chart their destiny; it conveyed their determined will for freedom and equity on their own terms. Most critically, the new racial semantics served a cathartic function as the national Black community purged itself of age-old scripts of self-hatred and denial. This period of catharsis was necessary, for it enabled African Americans to come to grips with centuries of much ado about the nothingness of skin color.

AFRICAN AMERICAN

In 1977 (in the first edition of *Talkin and Testifyin*), I stated:

> The semantic designations 'Afro-American' and 'African American' accompanied the 1966 rise of 'Black' but have yet to achieve its widespread general usage in the Black community ... The ... terms denote the reality of the double consciousness and dual cultural heritage of Black folk: part Africa, part America. Perhaps the more frequent use of Afro-American and African American awaits the complete healing of the psychic wounds of the Black past.
>
> (pp. 41–2)

That healing has now been completed. It is time to evolve to a new ideological plateau.

The call for *African American* is a call for a new paradigm in the unceasing quest for freedom. The hard-won progress of the previous generation of struggle is being eroded by national policies and court decisions that would turn back the hands of time. At the same time, the freedom struggle on the Continent – e.g., South Africa – and in the Diaspora outside of the United States – e.g., Grenada – has taken center stage in the world. It is time to redefine and reconceptualize the identity of the African in North America.

Though minimizing the significance of language, Dr. Manning Marable, prolific African American scholar and newspaper columnist, addresses the domestic issues that have triggered the current call for a new racial semantic:

> The important question, therefore, is not the terminology per se, but why the phrase has emerged now ... The decade of the 1980s is ... bleak: ... the massive white electoral mandates for the Reagan/Bush administrations, which campaigned successfully on programs of thinly veiled racism; the growth of urban youth violence, Black-on-Black homicides, high unemployment and drug proliferation; and the fragmentation of many Black social institutions such as the Black Church ... The combination of destructive socio-economic and political forces from without and the social decay and chaos from within have prompted a looking inward ...
>
> (1989, p. 72)

Writer Gloria Naylor, addressing the internationalist domain evoked by the call for *African American*, notes that "to call ourselves that, we would have to forge true ties with other people of color" (quoted in Anon, 1989, p. 80). Dr. Dorothy I. Height, President of the National Council of Negro Women, makes a similar point when she says "It is a recognition that we've always been African and American, but we are now going to ... make a unified effort to identify with our African brothers and sisters" (quoted in Anon, 1989, p. 80). Perhaps Jesse Jackson made the most eloquent and succinct statement about the international scope of the new label when he said "Black tells you about skin color and what side of town you live on. *African American* evokes discussion of the world" (quoted in Wilkerson, 1989). In this period of reassessment and reevaluation of the rapidly deteriorating Black condition, the new semantic constructs an identity of unified global struggle against race domination, linking Africans in North America with Continental Africans and with other Diasporic African groups. For a people grappling with disempowerment and its tragic effects on entire Black communities across the Nation, the term provides the security of "I am somebody" by reaffirming the origin and cultural continuity of our African heritage. At the same time, *African American* calls attention to four hundred years of contributions to the making of America and legitimates the political and economic demand for equity. The "American" identity of African Americans has been sustained and continues to be embraced in the form that Walker articulated over a century and a half ago, stating in his *Appeal*, "Men who are resolved to keep us in eternal wretchedness are also bent on sending us to Liberia . . . America is more our country than it is the whites – we have enriched it with our BLOOD AND TEARS" ([1829] 1965, p. 65).

The call for *African American* has been issued. What has been the response?

There are several noteworthy institutional examples of its use. Atlanta, Chicago and Detroit, three urban school districts with predominantly African American student populations, have adopted the term in their curricula and are encouraging teachers to use it. Tennis great Arthur Ashe titled his 1988 book *A Hard Road to Glory: A History of the African American Athlete*. WWR and WLIB, both large Black-oriented radio stations in New York City, use the term, as well as New York's first African American mayor, David Dinkins. According to Joseph Hollander, Director of Publications for The Modern Language Association, *African American* is used in most cases, but Black and other terms are acceptable as long as they are appropriate (personal communication 1991). Three of the largest African American newspapers in the country now use the term: New York's *Amsterdam News*: Chicago's *Daily Defender*; and Detroit's *Michigan Chronicle*. In the November 1990 Motown television special, in which Motown celebrated its thirty-year history in the recording and entertainment industry, all of the entertainers who participated in the narration used *African American* consistently throughout the entire program (a few doing so quite self-consciously).

The NAACP, which was in the forefront of the movement from *colored* to *Negro* in the 1920s, has adopted a wait-and-see posture on the current linguistic movement. According to Dr. Benjamin Hooks, Executive Director, ". . . we will neither oppose nor endorse the use of the term 'African-American.' This does not indicate a lack of concern, but rather an abiding respect for the sound judgment of our people, who, on their own, will reach a consensus, just as they have done in the past" (quoted in *Ebony*, July 1989 in an article "African American or Black: What's in a Name? Prominent Black and/or African Americans Express Their Views," pp. 76–80).

THE PEOPLE SPEAK: FIVE-CITY PUBLIC OPINION SURVEY

SAMPLE AND METHOD

In an attempt to assess the "sound judgment of our people," I included a question about *African American* in a language attitude instrument designed to elicit opinions about foreign language teaching in the public schools and "English-Only" legislation (Smitherman, 1992a). This survey research project involved five cities with large African American populations. It was conducted between May and September, 1989. The cities were Atlanta, Chicago, Cincinnati, Detroit, and Philadelphia. The 667 respondents included both African and European Americans, 512 of whom answered the *African American question.*

In Chicago, Cincinnati, and Philadelphia, the data (hereafter C1), were collected using written questionnaires which the respondents completed themselves. They were selected using a sample-of-convenience approach. Thus while the results are informative, the power of the claims we could make is somewhat limited by the sampling procedures.[6] The Detroit and Atlanta surveys (hereafter C2) were administered to scientifically selected samples, using census data, ZIP codes, and computer-generated telephone numbers. These data were collected through telephone surveys by a staff of interviewers trained in survey research techniques. Thus there is greater confidence in these results.

The *African American* question was posed in the following form: "There is a lot of talk about what different racial and ethnic groups should be called. Do you think the term 'African American' should replace the term 'Black' as the name for Black people in the United States?" Respondents were then asked to explain their answers.

RESULTS

When all respondents are considered, results show that anywhere from slightly more than one-third to one-half favor the shift to *African American.* In the C1 sample (n = 210), opinions were split exactly evenly, whereas in the C2 sample, the scientifically selected group (n = 302), only 33 percent favored the shift.

When we consider only the African American respondents, results are somewhat, but not significantly, different from results for all respondents. In the C1 group, 43 percent favored the shift, and in the C2 sample, 37 percent favored the shift. (See Table 2.1.)

African Americans gave three broad explanations for approval of the proposed change: (1) identification with Africa/dual heritage, for example "It tells our origin and cultural identity"; (2) inadequacy of a color label (e.g., "Black is a color, not a race" and "Colors belong in a crayon box"); (3) aesthetic quality of *African American* (e.g., "I can't explain it, it just has a better sound to it").

Three types of explanations were given for *disapproval* of the linguistic shift: (1) lack of identification with Africa (e.g., "Blacks are not African" and "We are more American than African; we have been here too long"; (2) syllabic density of *African American* (e.g., "It takes too long to say it and it's too much trouble"); (3) semantic change unnecessary and irrelevant (e.g., "Every ten to fifteen years it's something new. However you want to say it, we are still Black").

As anticipated, the most frequently given reason in support of *African American* was its reflection of the African past (46.4 percent). Also as anticipated, the negative version of this same reason was given by a large percentage of those who did not favor the term (26.3 percent). Typical responses were, "I wasn't born in Africa, I was born in Illinois" and "What do they mean about African American? By now we have no African in us." However, among those who said "No," a far larger number (55.8 percent) indicated that a name change was insignificant and irrelevant to changing the Black condition. (See Table 2.2.)

If we look at the results by age and sex, some significant inter-actions emerge. In the C1 sample, respondents 21 and under were more favorably disposed to the shift than those over 21. (See Table 2.3.) Although age was not significant in the other cities, I think the results are indicative of a trend among African American youth. The semantic movement parallels the re-emerging 1960s-style nationalism and Afrocentric consciousness taking place in youth culture. Witness the Malcolm X revival, the political messages of popular rap groups like Public Enemy, the wearing of medallions embossed with the map of Africa, African-style haircuts, and rein-vigorated campus activism.

Sex was also significant, but only in Detroit. In that city, African American women were more overwhelmingly opposed to the semantic shift than African American men. (See Table 2.4.) Although I can offer no definitive explanation to account for this difference, recent scholars in both African American and Women's Studies (e.g., Gates, 1988; Spillers, 1983) have made a convincing case for the uniqueness of the African American woman's consciousness and experience. They have advanced the need for research to dis-aggregate what Toni Morrison has called the "invented lives" of

Table 2.1   Opinions about use of African American (African Americans only; n = 264)

	C1 Sample	C2 Sample
YES	43%	37%
NO	57%	63%

Table 2.2   Approval/disapproval of linguistic shift (C2 sample, African Americans only; n = 194; figures in percentages)

Reasons for approval of shift	
1 Identification with Africa/dual heritage	46.4
2 Inadequacy of a color label	17.4
3 Aesthetic quality of African American	36.2
Reasons for disapproval of shift	
1 Lack of identification with Africa	26.3
2 Syllabic density of African American	9.5
3 Semantic change unnecessary and irrelevant	55.8
4 Other	8.4

Table 2.3   Opinions about use of African American by age (C1 sample only; p < .02; figures in percentages)

	21 & under	*22–30*	*31–40*	*Over 40*
YES	55	24	37	29
NO	45	76	63	71

African American women from the work done on African Americans and European American women (quoted in Giddings, 1984). The finding from this survey lies in this general direction and suggests the need for further study of the views of African American women.

Although the focal point of this analysis was to get an index of the "sound judgment of our people" on the semantic issue, to the extent that race may be a significant factor in my results, it deserves comment. In the C2 sample, African Americans *approved* of the semantic shift more than European Americans, but not to as great a degree as we had predicted. (See Table 2.5.) One explanation for this difference is that African Americans have a lot more at stake in the naming controversy. Some European Americans might simply object to the change because it makes their lives slightly more complicated (in that they have to learn something new which is personally unimportant to them). These differences between European and African Americans notwithstanding, the Black group clearly has the power to define and name itself and to *compel* mainstream acceptance and usage for any label it chooses as has been demonstrated both in the shift from *colored* to *Negro* (with the capital, no less) and from *Negro* to *Black*. In fact, the general response to the issue by European Americans in the survey is typified by the following statement from one respondent: "If that's what they want to be called, it's okay with me." However, for African Americans the issue is about the construction of identity through *Nommo*, an African concept that has survived in African American culture as a belief in the power of the word – "the awareness that the word alone alters the world" (Jahn, 1961, p. 125). Racial group identity, whatever the paradigm that emerges, will dictate strategies, tactics, policies, programs, and, in general, shape the direction of the struggle in the twenty-first century. This is no small matter; one does not make such a fundamental shift without internal debate, deliberation, and struggle. Edelin, Jackson, and others in national leadership have sounded the clarion call for the debate to begin.

As far as I was able to ascertain, no other survey of the current naming issue has been reported in the literature to date, although at least three opinion polls have been undertaken by the popular press.[7] *Time* reported that, although its survey was too small to be

Table 2.4 African American males and females on the linguistic shift (Detroit only; p < .01; figures in percentages)

	Females	Males
YES	28	51
NO	72	49

Table 2.5 Opinions about use of African American by race (C2 sample only; p < .05; figures in percentages)

	African Americans	European Americans
YES	36.6	25.3
NO	63.4	74.7

statistically valid, it did show that the "name change has made some headway," with 26 percent of the Blacks polled favoring *African American* (Lacayo and Monroe, 1989). *The Washington Post–ABC News* poll indicates that only 34 percent of the Blacks surveyed approved of *African American* (Specter, 1990). However, Specter also notes "in the late 1960s, a majority of both races also favored Negro over Black." Finally, *The Michigan Chronicle* reports on a small sample survey of students attending historically Black colleges, indicating that a majority favor the shift from *Black* to *African American* (17 June 1989, p. 3A). This compares with the results of the present survey in terms of the positive responses from young (age 21 and under) respondents, most of whom were college students.

CONCLUSION

Given insufficient empirical data on African American views on the proposed terminological shift, the results of the five-city survey are a significant beginning. We can conclude that at least one-third of African Americans are in favor of the name change and that support is perhaps strongest among African American youth, particularly those in college. However, that support is probably weakest among African American women, who continue, as they have historically, to be a potent factor in social change. The obstacles to be over-come to broaden the base of terminological change are the lack of a feeling of connectedness to Africa and the perception that, as one Sista put it, "this language thang ain bout too much."

Further empirical studies are warranted to assess the impact of the current linguistic movement and its relationship to the histor-ical semantics of race. African American historians and political theorists contend that, in times of severe racial crisis, the name issue re-emerges as a call for re-examination of the status of African Americans. This reassessment forces a necessary and widespread discussion of the question, "Where do we go from here?" Bennett states: "In periods of reaction and extreme stress, Black people usually turn inward. They begin to re-define themselves and they begin to argue seriously about names" (1967, 50). The current period is a singularly dramatic manifestation of this "turning inward," paralleled, perhaps, only by the post-Reconstruction period, "one of the whitest times in American history" (Bennett, 1967, 50). Thus the linguistic debate raised by Edelin, and carried forth into the popular press by Jackson, is an appropriate and historically logical call to action.

Baldwin (1981) and others have argued that the semantics of *Black* are a unique – and historically inappropriate – American-style invention. The ethnic identities of Africans in North America were eradicated so that Ibos, Yorubas, Hausas, and other African ethnic groups were robbed of their distinctiveness, and everybody just became "Black." By the same token, all Europeans just became "white." While this analysis fits the Black condition, it fails to recognize that the "white" race created in America retained its European ethnic identity. In fact, "Black" as a name for African Americans is asymmetrical with naming practices for all other groups in the United States. For these other groups, the term employed denotes land of origin – Polish Americans, Italian Americans, Hispanic Americans, German Americans, Asian Americans, and so on. *African* American brings the "Black" race into semantic line with these other ethnolinguistic traditions.[8]

Our survey results and the press polls, with the promising exceptions of the African American college students in *The Michigan Chronicle* survey, and the 21 and under group in Philadelphia, Cincinnati, and Chicago, indicate that current leaders have their work cut out for them. As with the shift from *Negro* to *Black*, it is the everyday people who must rise to the semantic challenge and rally around the new paradigmatic shift. Yet as the lexicosemantic history presented here indicates, the current issue of racial labelling is but a variation on a familiar theme: the unfinished business of forging an identity and a life for Africans in North America.

As an African American womanist linguist, it is clear to me that this is not a debate about semantics at the expense of addressing the plight of the community, as some intellectuals fear. Rather, this new racial designation can lead to the construction of an identity to facilitate the creation of policy, tactics, strategies, and programs to redress that plight – that is, the use of language to create a new theory of reality. As Ramona Edelin so eloquently put it (quoted in Anon, 1989, p. 76):

> It is our obligation to reconstruct our culture at this critical point in history so that we can move forward and not be satisfied with one or two people rising to the surface ... Calling ourselves African American is the first step in the cultural offensive. Our cultural renaissance can change our lot in the nation and around the world.

3

AIN NOTHIN IN a long time lit up the English-teaching profession like the current hassle over Black English. One finds beaucoup sociolinguistic research studies and language projects for the "disadvantaged" on the scene in nearly every sizable black community in the country.[1] And educators from K-Grad. School bees debating whether: (1) blacks should learn and use only standard white English (hereafter referred to as WE); (2) blacks should command both dialects, i.e., be bi-dialectal (hereafter BD); (3) blacks should be allowed (??????) to use standard Black English (hereafter BE or BI). The appropriate choice having everything to do with American

WHITE ENGLISH IN BLACKFACE OR, WHO DO I BE? [1973]

political reality, which is usually ignored, and nothing to do with the educational process, which is usually claimed. I say without qualification that we can not talk about the Black Idiom apart from Black Culture and the Black Experience. Nor can we specify educational goals for blacks apart from considerations about the structure of (white) American society.

And we black folks is not gon take all that weight, for no one has empirically demonstrated that linguistic/stylistic features of BE impede educational progress in communication skills, or any other area of cognitive learning. Take reading. It's don been charged, but not actually verified, that BE interferes with mastery of reading skills.[2] Yet beyond pointing out the gap between the young brother/sistuh's phonological and syntactical patterns and those of the usually-middle-class-WE-speaking-teacher, this claim has not been validated. The distance between the two systems is, after all, short and is illuminated only by the fact that reading is taught *orally*. (Also get to the fact that preceding generations of BE-speaking folks learned to read, despite the many classrooms in which the teacher spoke a dialect different from that of her students.)

For example, a student who reads *den* for *then* probably pronounces initial /th/ as /d/ in most words. Or the one who reads *doing* for *during* probably deletes intervocalic and final /r/ in most words. So it is not that such students can't read, they is simply employing the black phonological system. In the reading classrooms of today, what we bees needin is teachers with the proper attitudinal orientation who thus can distinguish actual reading problems from mere dialect differences. Or take the writing of an essay. The only percentage in writing a paper with WE spelling, punctuation, and usage is in maybe eliciting a positive *attitudinal* response from a prescriptivist middle-class-aspirant-teacher. Dig on the fact that sheer "correctness" does not a good writer make. And is it any point in dealing with the charge of BE speakers being "non-verbal" or "linguistically deficient" in oral communication skills – behind our many Raps who done disproved that in living, vibrant color?[3]

What linguists and educators need to do at this juncture is to take serious cognizance of the Oral Tradition in Black Culture. The uniqueness of this verbal style requires a language competence/performance model to fit the black scheme of things. Clearly BI speakers possess rich communication skills (i.e., are highly *competent* in using language), but as yet there bees no criteria (evaluative, testing, or other instrument of measurement), based on black communication patterns, wherein BI speakers can demonstrate they competence (i.e., *performance*). Hence brothers and sisters fail on language performance tests and in English classrooms. Like, to amplify on what Nikki said, that's why we always lose, not only cause we don't know the rules, but it ain't even our game.

We can devise a performance model only after an analysis of the components of BI. Now there do be linguists who supposedly done did this categorization and definition of BE.[4] But the descriptions are generally confining, limited as they are to discrete linguistic units. One finds simply 10–15 patterns cited, as for example, the most frequently listed one, the use of *be* as finite verb, contrasting with its deletion: (A) *The coffee be cold* contrasts with (B) *The coffee cold*, the former statement denoting a continuing state of affairs, the latter applying to the present moment only. (Like if you the cook, (A) probably get you fired, and (B) only get you talked about.) In WE no comparable grammatical distinction exists and *The coffee is cold* would be used to indicate both meanings. However, rarely does one find an investigation of the total vitality of black expressive style, a style inextricable from the Black Cultural Universe, for after all, BI connects with Black Soul and niggers is more than deleted copulas.[5]

The black idiom should be viewed from two important perspectives: linguistic and stylistic. The linguistic dimension is comprised of the so-called "nonstandard" features of phonology and syntax (patterns like *dis heah* and *The coffee be cold*), and a lexicon generally equated with "slang" or hip talk. The stylistic dimension has to do with *rapping, capping, jiving*, etc., and with features such as cadence, rhythm, resonance, gestures, and all those other elusive, difficult-to-objectify elements that make up what is considered a writer or speaker's "style." While I am separating linguistic and stylistic features, I have done so only for the purpose of simplifying the discussion since the BI speaker runs the full gamut of both dimensions in any given speech event.

I acknowledge from the bell that we's dealing with a dialect structure which is a sub-system of the English language; thus BE and WE may not appear fundamentally different. Yet, though black folks speak English, it do seem to be an entirely different lingo altogether. But wherein lies the uniqueness? Essentially in language, as in other areas of Black Culture, we have the problem of isolating those elements indigenous to black folks from those cultural aspects shared with white folks. Anthropologist Johnnetta Cole suggests that Black Culture has three dimensions: (1) those elements shared with mainstream America; (2) those elements shared with all oppressed peoples; (3) those elements peculiar to the black condition in America.[6] Applying her concepts to language, I propose the following schematic representation as shown in Table 3.1.

Referring to the first column, contemporary BE is simply one of the many dialects of contemporary American English, and it is most likely the case that the linguistic patterns of BE differ from those of WE in surface structure only. There's no essential linguistic difference between *dis heah* and *this here*, and from a strictly linguistic point of view, *God don't never change* can be rewritten *God doesn't ever change* (though definitely not from a socio-cultural/political perspective, as Baraka quite rightly notes.)[7] Perhaps we could make a case for deep-structure difference in the BE use of *be* as finite verb (refer to *The coffee be cold* example above), but we be hard pressed to find any other examples, and even in the case of *The coffee cold*, we could posit that the copula exists in the deep structure, and is simply deleted by some low-level phonological deletion rule, dig: The coffee is cold . . . The coffee's cold . . . The coffee cold. My conclusion at this point is that despite the claims of some highly respected Creole linguists (with special propers to bad Sistuh Beryl Bailey),[8] the argument for deep structure differences between contemporary BE and WE syntax can not pass the test of rigorous transformational analysis.

Table 3.1   Cultural dimension: Language

Features shared with mainstream America	*Features shared with all oppressed peoples*	*Features unique to Black Americans*
Linguistic	**Linguistic**	**Linguistic**
1 British/American English lexicon	1 Superimposition of dominant culture's language on native language, yielding	Unique meanings attributed to certain English lexical items
		Stylistic
2 Most aspects of British/American English phonology and syntax	2 Pidginized form of dominant culture's language, subject to becoming extinct, due to	Unique communication patterns and rhetorical flourishes
	3 Historical evolution, linguistic leveling out in direction of dominant culture's dialect	

Referring to the second column, we note the psychological tendency of oppressed people to adopt the modes of behavior and expression of their oppressors (also, during the African slave trade, the functional necessity of pidginized forms of European languages). Not only does the conqueror force his victims into political subjugation, he also coerces them into adopting his language and doles out special rewards to those among the oppressed who best mimic his language and cultural style. In the initial language contact stage, the victims attempt to assemble the new language into their native linguistic mold, producing a linguistic mixture that is termed *pidgin*. In the next stage, the pidgin may develop into a Creole, a highly systematic, widely used model of communication among the oppressed, characterized by a substratum of patterns from the victim's language with an overlay of forms from the oppressor's language. As the oppressed people's identification with the victor's culture intensifies, the pidgin/Creole begins to lose its linguistic currency and naturally evolves in the direction of the victor's language. Reconstructing the linguistic history of BE, we theorize that it followed a similar pattern, but due to the radically different condition of black oppression in America, the process of *de-creolization* is nearly complete and has been for perhaps over a hundred years.

The most important features of BI are, of course, those referred to in the third column, for they point us toward the linguistic uniqueness and cultural significance of the Oral Tradition in the Black Experience. It should be clear that all along I been talkin bout that Black Experience associated with the grass-roots folks, the masses, the sho-nuff niggers – in short, all those black folks who do not aspire to white-middle-class-American-standards.

Within this tradition, language is used as a teaching/socializing force and as a means of establishing one's reputation via his verbal competence. Black talk is never meaningless cocktail chit-chat but a functional dynamic that is simultaneously a mechanism for acculturation and information-passing and a vehicle for achieving group recognition. Black communication is highly verbal and highly stylized; it is a performance before a black audience who become both observers and participants in the speech event. Whether it be through slapping of hands ("giving five" or "giving skin"), Amen's, or Right on's, the audience influences the direction of a given rap and at the same time acknowledges or withholds its approval, depending on the linguistic skill and stylistic ingenuity of the speaker. I mean like a Brother is only as bad as his rap bees.

TOWARD A BLACK LANGUAGE MODEL

LINGUISTIC

While we concede that black people use the vocabulary of the English language, certain words are always selected out of that lexicon and given a special black semantic slant. So though we rappin bout the same language, the reality referents are different. As one linguist has suggested, the proper question is not what do words mean but what do the users of the words mean? These words may be associated with and more frequently used in black street culture but not necessarily. *Muthafucka* has social boundaries, but not *nigger*.

Referring to the lexicon of BI, then, the following general principles obtain:

1   The words given the special black slant exist in a dynamic state. The terms are discarded when they move into the white mainstream. (Example: One no longer speaks of a "hip" brother, now he is a "togetha" brother.) This was/is necessitated by our need to have a code that was/is undecipherable by foreigners (i.e., whites).

2   In BI, the concept of denotation vs. connotation does not apply.

3   What does apply is shades of meaning along the connotative spectrum. For example, depending on contextual environment, the word "bad" can mean *extraordinary*; *beautiful*; *good*; *versatile*; or a host of other terms of positive value. Dig it: after watching a Sammy Davis performance, a BI speaker testified: "Sammy sho did some *bad* stuff," i.e., *extraordinary* stuff. Or upon observing a beautiful sister: "She sho is *bad*," i.e., *beautiful, pretty,* or *good-looking*. Or, noticing how a brother is dressed: "You sho got on some *bad* shit," i.e., *good* shit = *attractively dressed*.

Note that the above examples are all in the category of *approbation*. It is necessary to rap bout *denigration* as well, since certain words in the black lexicon can frequently be used both ways. Consider the word "nigger," for instance. "He's my main nigger" means my best friend (hence, *approbation*); "The nigger ain't shit," means he's probably lazy, trifling, scheming, wrongdoing, or a host of other *denigrative* terms, depending on the total context of the utterance.

4   *Approbation* and *denigration* relate to the semantic level; we can add two other possible functions of the same word on the grammatical level: *intensification* and *completion*. Slide back to "nigger" for a minute, and dig that often the word is void of real meaning and simply supplies the sentence with a subject. "Niggers was getting out of there left and right, then the niggers was running, and so the niggers said . . ." etc., etc., my point being that a steady stream of overuse means neither denigration nor approbation. Some excellent illustrations of this function of the word are to be found in *Manchild in the Promised Land* where you can observe the word used in larger contexts.

To give you a most vivid illustration, consider the use of what WE labels "obscenities." From the streets of Detroit: (a) "That's a bad *muthafucka*." Referring to a Cadillac Eldorado, obviously indicating *approval*. (b) "He's a no-good *muthafucka*." Referring to a person who has just "put some game" on the speaker, obviously indicating *disapproval*. (c) "You *muthafuckin* right I wasn't gon let him do that." Emphasizing how correct the listener's assessment is, obviously using the term as a grammatical *intensifier*, modifying "right." (d) "We wasn't doin nothing, just messin round and *shit*." Though a different "obscenity," the point is nonetheless illustrated, "shit" being used neutrally, as an *expletive* (filler) to *complete* the sentence pattern; semantically speaking, it is an empty word in this contextual environment.

Where I'm comin from is that the lexicon of BI, consisting of certain specially selected words, requires a unique scheme of analysis to account for the diverse range and multiplicity of meanings attributed to these words. While there do be some dictionaries of Afro-American "slang," they fail to get at the important question of: what are the psycho-cultural processes that guide our selection of certain words out of the thousands of possible words in the Anglo-Saxon vocabulary? Like, for instance, Kochman[9] has suggested that we value *action* in the black community, and so those words that have action implied in them, we take and give *positive* meanings to, such as *swing, game, hip, hustle,* etc.; whereas words of implied *stasis* are taken and given *negative* connotations, such as *lame, square, hung-up, stiffin and jivin,* etc. At any rate, what I've tried to lay here are some suggestions in this particular linguistic dimension; the definitive word on black lexicon is yet to be given.

I shall go on to discuss the stylistic dimension of black communication patterns, where I have worked out a more definitive model.

STYLISTIC

Black verbal style exists on a sacred–secular continuum, as represented by the schematic matrix in Figure 3.1.

The model allows us to account for the many individual variations in black speech, which can all be located at some point along the continuum.

The sacred style is rural and Southern. It is the style of the black preacher and that associated with the black church tradition. It tends to be more emotive and highly charged than the secular

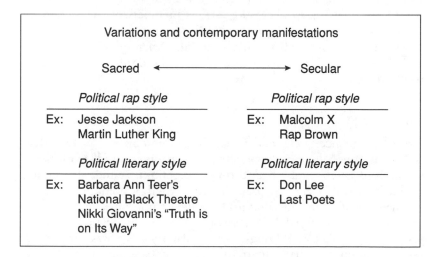

Figure 3.1 Oral Tradition in Black Culture: Stylistic dimensions

style. It is also older in time. However, though I've called it "sacred," it abounds in secularisms. Black church service tends to be highly informal, and it ain nothin for a preacher to get up in the pulpit and, say, show off what he's wearing: "Y'all didn't notice the new suit I got on today, did y'all? Ain the Lord good to us . . ."

The secular style is urban and Northern, but since it probably had its beginnings in black folk tales and proverbs, its *roots* are Southern and rural. This is the street culture style; the style found in barbershops and on street corners in the black ghettos of American cities. It tends to be more cool, more emotionally restrained than the sacred style. It is newer and younger in time and only fully evolved as a distinct style with the massive wave of black migration to the cities.

Both sacred and secular styles share the following characteristics:

Call and response

This is basic to black oral tradition. The speaker's solo voice alternates or is intermingled with the audience's response. In the sacred style, the minister is urged on by the congregation's Amen's, That's right, Reverend's, or Preach Reverend's. One also hears occasional Take your time's when the preacher is initiating his sermon, the congregation desiring to savor every little bit of this good message they bout to hear. (In both sacred and secular political rap styles, the "Preach Reverend" is transposed to "Teach Brother.") In the secular style, the response can take the form of a back-and-forth banter between the speaker and various members of the audience. Or the audience might manifest its response in giving skin (fives) when a really down verbal point is scored. Other approval responses include laughter and phrases like "Oh, you mean, nigger," "Get back, nigger," "Git down, baby," etc.

Rhythmic pattern

I refer to cadence, tone, and musical quality. This is a pattern that is lyrical, sonorous, and generally emphasizing sound apart from sense. It is often established through repetition, either of certain sounds or words. The preacher will get a rhythm going, conveying his message through sound rather than depending on sheer semantic import. "I-I-I-I-I-Oh-I-I-Oh, yeah, Lord-I-I- heard the voice of Jesus saying . . ." Even though the secular style is characterized by rapidity, as in the toasts (narrative tales of bad niggers and they exploits, like Stag-O-Lee, or bad animals and they trickeration, like the Signifying Monkey), the speaker's voice tone still has that rhythmic, musical quality, just with a faster tempo.

Spontaneity

Generally, the speaker's performance is improvisational, with the rich interaction between speaker and audience dictating and/or directing the course and outcome of the speech event. Since the speaker does not prepare a formal document, his delivery is casual, non-deliberate, and uncontrived. He speaks in a lively, conversational tone, and with an ever-present quality of immediacy. All emphasis is on process, movement, and creativity of the moment. The preacher says "Y'all wont to hear dat, so I'm gon leave it lone," and his audience shouts, "Naw, tell it Reverend, tell it!," and he does. Or, like, once Malcolm mentioned the fact of his being in prison, and sensing the surprise of his audience, he took advantage of the opportunity to note that all black people were in prison: "That's what America means: prison."

Concreteness

The speaker's imagery and ideas center around the empirical world, the world of reality, and the contemporary Here and Now. Rarely does he drift off into esoteric abstractions; his metaphors and illustrations are commonplace and grounded in everyday experience. Perhaps because of this concreteness, there is a sense of identification with the event being described or narrated, as in the secular style where the toast-teller's identity merges with that of the protagonist of his tale, and he becomes Stag-O-Lee or Shine; or when the preacher assumes the voice of God or the personality of a Biblical character. Even the experience of being saved takes on a presentness and rootedness in everyday life: "I first met God in 1925 . . ."

Signifying

This is a technique of talking about the entire audience or some member of the audience either to initiate verbal "war" or to make a point hit home. The interesting thang bout this rhetorical device is that the audience is not offended and realizes – naw, expects – the speaker to launch this offensive to achieve his desired effect. "Pimp, punk, prostitute, Ph.D. – all the P's – you still in slavery!" announces the Reverend Jesse Jackson. Malcolm puts down the non-violent movement with: "In a revolution, you swinging, not singing." (Notice the characteristic rhythmic pattern in the above examples – the alliterative poetic effect of Jackson's statement and the rhyming device in Malcolm's.)

An analysis of black expressive style, such as presented here, should facilitate the construction of a performance instrument to measure the degree of command of the style of any given BI speaker. Linguists and educators sincerely interested in black education might be about the difficult, complex business of devising such a "test," rather than establishing linguistic remediation programs to correct a non-existent remediation. Like in any other area of human activity, some BI rappers are better than others, and today's most effective black preachers, leaders, politicians, writers are those who rap in the black expressive style, appropriating the ritual framework of the Oral Tradition as vehicle for the conveyance of they political ideologies. Which brings me back to what I said from Jump Street. The real heart of this language controversy relates to/is the underlying political nature of the American educational system. Brother Frantz Fanon is highly instructive at this point. From his "Negro and Language," in *Black Skin, White Masks*:

> I ascribe a basic importance to the phenomenon of language . . . To speak means . . . above all to assume a culture, to support the weight of a civilization . . . Every dialect is a way of thinking . . . And the fact that the newly returned [i.e., from white schools] Negro adopts a language different from that of the group into which he was born is evidence of a dislocation, a separation . . .

In showing why the "Negro adopts such a position . . . with respect to European languages," Fanon continues:

> It is because he wants to emphasize the rupture that has now occurred. He is incarnating a new type of man that he imposes on his associates and his family. And so his old mother can no longer understand him when he talks to her about his *duds*, the family's *crummy joint*, the *dump* . . . all of it, of course, tricked out with the appropriate accent.
>
> In every country of the world, there are climbers, 'the ones who forget who they are,' and in contrast to them, 'the ones who remember where they came from.' The Antilles Negro who goes home from France expresses himself in the dialect if he wants to make it plain that nothing has changed.[10]

As black people go moving on up toward separation and cultural nationalism, the question of the moment is not which dialect, but which culture, not whose vocabulary but whose values, not *I am* vs. *I be*, but WHO DO I BE?

4

INTRODUCTION

THIS CHAPTER CRITICALLY reviews academic discourse on African American speech in the United States from the perspective of the reproduction of racism in that discourse. Although examples from the academic literature will be presented, our concern here is not to analyze specific texts, but to overview and broadly assess the *tradition* of American schol arship on the black language question. For it is this tradition, *qua* tradition, rather than the work of any single scholar, that sets the stage for public decision making and social policy formulation that govern the lives and ultimately the survival of black Americans. Racism in this tradition is rarely blatant, as it is with the "outright" racists (e.g., the Ku Klux Klansmen). Nor is the racism generally attributable to the idiosyncratic quirks of an individual scholar's personality. Rather, racism among scholar-elites exists within an institutionalized tradition based on a set of assumptions — virtually always implicit — about human nature, race, and social behavior. The fact that scholarly racism is subtle, rather than blatant, and institutional, rather than individual, makes it all the more an insiduously oppressive and effective dimension of the ideological apparatus that justifies and supports patterns of

DISCRIMINATORY DISCOURSE ON AFRICAN AMERICAN SPEECH [1988]

Darlene trying to teach me how to talk ... Every time I say something the way I say it, she correct me until I say it some other way. Pretty soon it feel like I can't think. My mind run up on a thought, git confuse, run back and sort of lay down ... She bring me a bunch of books. Whitefolks all over them, talking bout apples and dogs. What I care bout dogs? ... But I let Darlene worry on. Sometimes I think bout the apples and the dogs, sometimes I don't. Look like to me only a fool would want you to talk in a way that feel peculiar to your mind.

(Celie, the young black mother in Alice Walker's Pulitzer Prize-winning novel, *The Color Purple,* 1982)

racist thought and behavior in the public domain and in the socioeconomic macrostructure. (Van Dijk's forthcoming treatise on "elite
discourse and racism" in the Netherlands is illuminating in its compa-
rability with the United States.)

The degree to which racism in American linguistic discourse
may be materially explicit is governed by changing paradigms in
American consciousness. The path of racist expression in linguistic
scholarship must be charted simultaneously by the sociohistorical
development of "race relations" (as it has traditionally been referred
to in the American academy), and by changing paradigms in the
human sciences research tradition. Black language research was
affected by this century's global sociopolitical upheavals, which influenced black thought on white people and white thought on black
people. Concomitantly, shifts in the philosophical bases of science
and knowledge over the past century led to fundamental changes
in the emerging discipline of what has become linguistics and thus
to correspondingly differing approaches to the study of black speech.
Taken together, these two motive historical forces constitute the
ideological content of academic discourse about African American
speech.

Although the focus here is racism in linguistic scholarship,
scientific racism can be found in all disciplines and fields of American
intellectual endeavor. And it remained virtually unchecked until the
Black Liberation Movement of the past generation. There is an old
proverbial tale about a son who asked his father why it was that in
all the stories he read about lions and men fighting in the jungle, the
lion always loses. The father replied, "Son, it will always be that way
until the lion learns how to write." As a result of the struggles of
black people, beginning about 1955 with black seamstress Rosa
Parks's refusal to give up her seat to a white man and stand in the
back of a racially segregated bus in the American South, many "lions
learned how to write." According to Blackwell (1981), over 80 percent of all black Ph.D.s in the four-hundred-year existence of blacks
on the North American continent were produced between 1960 and
1980. These "lions" responded to the call of the Elders – scholars
such as W. E. B. DuBois (e.g., 1896, 1899, 1903), J. A. Rogers (e.g.,
1917, 1934), Carter G. Woodson (e.g., 1915, 1936) – who, because
there were so few black scholars in their time, worked in virtual isolation, almost single-handedly forging the research tradition of
African American Studies. Out of the 1960s quest for freedom and
literacy in the national black community, a cadre of scholars, armed
with the legacy of DuBois–Rogers–Woodson, emerged to challenge
the racist assumptions and paradigms of American scholarship in virtually every field and academic discipline (e.g., McWorter, 1969;

Williams, 1973, 1974; Blassingame, 1972; Staples 1971; Bailey, 1965, 1968; Smitherman, 1971, 1973a,b; Ladner, 1973; Wilson, 1972).

A central target of the challenge was the insidious assumption that American science was "objective," "pure," and somehow beyond the vagaries of politics and racism. Since the 1960s, it has been fairly well documented that knowledge is socially constructed and that the scholar's social position influences what he/she recognizes as "knowledge," "truth," or "science" (e.g., Berger and Luckmann, 1966). (I also contend that knowledge is *sociolinguistically* constructed (Smitherman, 1980b)). Even Myrdal, the Swedish scientist imported to do an "objective" study of America's "Negro problem" in the 1940s, had asserted that "biases in social science cannot be erased simply by 'keeping to the facts' and by refined methods of statistical treatment of the data . . . handling of the data sometimes show themselves even more pervious to tendencies towards bias than does pure thought" (1944). However, American scholarship has historically conceptualized and produced research on black people as if there were no dialectical relationship between ideology, politics, and science. Consequently, such scholarship has reinforced the ideological bias towards "Anglo conformity" (Gordon, 1964) in the academy, in social policy, and in the American consciousness. Further, it has generally reaffirmed the perspective that the problem is not racism but the victims of racism and their failure to conform to the Anglo ideal. This has been the case in racially oriented research in the human sciences in general. The black English research tradition is but a specific manifestation of this general phenomenon in American scholarship.

The central focus of this critical overview will be historical and center on the work of white scholars on black speech. It has only been in very recent years that a body of research and scholarship by black linguists has emerged. Moreover, although blacks may internalize racist mythology about blackness, racism depends for its existence and perpetration on unequal power relations between blacks and whites in society. In the 1960s, this view was popularly expressed as "Blacks can't be racist because they don't have any power." The structure of this inequality was created by a system of oppression (i.e., slavery and Jim Crow), and it continues to be legitimated and reinforced by institutional patterns and practices (e.g., discriminatory laws and employment policies). This framework for the analysis and understanding of racism and its machinations is at least as old as American chattel slavery itself, and it has been articulated by DuBois (1896–1914), Carmichael and Hamilton (1969), Davis (1981), Higgenbotham (1978), and a host of other scholars. Our focus here will be heavily historical, for scholars became more cautious, or at least, racism went under-ground, as a result of the Black Liberation Struggle of the 1960s and 1970s. However, as I shall argue, American racism, newly legit-imated by the national ideology of Reaganism and the rise of the Right, is re-emerging and threatens to take some scholars back to from where they ain never left.

We turn now to trace the historical development of academic discourse about African American Language and to illuminate the mechanisms through which racism has been reproduced and main-tained in this discourse.

THE ORIGIN OF BLACK SPEECH AND THE "ORIGIN OF THE SPECIES"

The first cargo of African slaves to be deposited in what would become the United States of America arrived at Jamestown in 1619. (Actually, these twenty Africans were indentured servants, who could eventually buy back their freedom; it was not until the eighteenth century that black servitude would be made a permanent condi-tion; see, e.g., Franklin, 1967.) From that point until the beginnings of the movement to abolish slavery in the nineteenth century, whites, by and large, perceived of America's African slave popula-tion as beasts of burden, exotic sexual objects, or curious primitives. There was little research interest in aspects of life in the slave community. To be sure, there was some notion that the slaves talked differently. For example, in Sarah Kemble Knight's journal of 1704–5, there is a notation about a justice "speaking Negro" in interrogation proceedings during a trial (Dillard, 1972). And in newspaper advertisements for their runaway slaves, owners might include some description of the kind of English the slave used as an identifying characteristics; for example, this 1760 ad from the North Carolina *Gazette:* "Ran away . . . a negro fellow named JACK . . . about 30 years of age, and about 5 feet high, speaks bad English" (Read, 1939). Though such commentaries do not consti-tute academic discourse, they do demonstrate that there was some awareness among eighteenth-century whites of linguistic differences between themselves and the African slave population.

Clearly, however, it was not until America was on the brink of the "War between the States" that American science and research turned its attention to the black enslaved population. The motiva-tion behind this scientific attention was the power struggle between northern and southern capitalists vying for control of the burgeoning American political economy. The slaves became pawns in this struggle (Bond, 1966). In American scholarship, this period marks the beginnings of the cultural deviant perspective, premised on the ideology of biological determinism. The deviant model views black speech (and black culture, generally) as deficient and pathological. The conception is not simply one of African *differentness* but African-derived *deficiency*. In the years just before the Civil War (roughly the 1840s and 1850s), scientific theories of racial superiority located social and behavioral differences between members of the human species in genetic factors, which became the basis of studies of black slaves (Lewontin *et al.*, 1982). Using African physiognomy and other racial characteristics to establish black "inferiority," the American South employed the ideology of biological determinism as a weapon in its struggle to preserve slavery (Fishman and Wainer, 1982).

To keep the record straight, however, it should be noted that the American North, grounded in a free labor system of production, in contrast with the South's slave labor economy, stood to gain from the emancipation of the slaves. In any case, it is clear that even northern whites of the nineteenth century were ambivalent on the question of black equality. For example, ex-slave and abolitionist Frederick Douglass broke with the white abolitionists because they were demanding that he stick to his personal story of enslavement and leave to them the "philosophy" and ideological attacks on slavery; Douglass split, stating that he "was growing and needed room" (1881). And in an 1858 speech, President Abraham Lincoln, reluctant author of the Emancipation Proclamation freeing America's slaves, perhaps articulated this white nineteenth-century ambivalence best:

> There is a physical difference between the white and black races which, I suppose, will forever forbid the two races living together upon terms of social and political equality; and inasmuch as they cannot so live, that while they do remain together there must be a position of the superiors and the inferiors; and that I, as much as any other man, am in favor of the superior being assigned to the white man.
>
> (quoted in Zinn, 1970)

When the Civil War ended and America's black slaves were freed and granted citizenship rights – at least theoretically – the ideological warfare waged by American science against the former slaves intensified to protect the developing alignment of the southern master class and northern capitalists into a national technological elite united in its exploitation of both black freedmen and white displaced agricultural and industrial workers in the South and North. This alignment was signaled by the end of Reconstruction in 1877, the passage of "separate but equal" laws, and the institutionalization of racism throughout the North as well as the South.

In this American sociohistorical context, the first "scientific" study of African American speech appeared, Harrison's "Negro English" in 1884. Harrison presents "an outline of Negro language-usage," based on his "life-long residence in the Southern States of North America." Though linguistically unsophisticated by today's standards. Harrison's "outline" is akin to a grammar, complete with verb conjugations, vowel and consonant pronunciation lists, grammatical paradigms for the parts of speech, and several pages of "specimen Negroisms" (e.g., "to make yo'se'f skace = to run away"). Although he attributes the origin of many forms to various "Old" dialects (e.g., English, Norse, Scottish) Harrison seems quite conscious of the uniqueness of black English:

> Fertility of the Negro dialect indeed is really wonderful, not only in the ingenious distortion of words by which new and startling significance is given to common English words (e.g., a *hant* in Negro means a *ghost*), but more especially in the domain of imitative sounds, cries, animal utterance.

In accounting for this uniqueness, however, Harrison is operating within the framework of the linguistic deviant model. Despite attributions of the "Strikingly poetic and multiform messages" in black speech and accolades about its "really wonderful fertility" (whatever that is!), it is clear that Harrison is coming from a position of Black Language differences based on African genetic inferiority. Although he acknowledges that aspects of the speech are unique, that is, African-derived, the Africanness is perceived as pathological.

> The humor and naivete of the Negro are features which must not be overlooked in gauging his intellectual calibre and timbre; much of his talk is baby-talk ... the slang which is an ingrained part of his being as deep-dyed as his skin ... the African, from the absence of books and teaching, had no principle of *analepsy* in his intellectual furnishing by which a word, once become obscure from a real or supposed loss of parts or meaning, can be repaired, amended, or restored to its original form ... Negro speech-organs are becoming slowly and with difficulty accustomed to the sound *th*.

The supposed intellectual inferiority and childlike mentality of blacks, to which Harrison alludes above, were widely publicized by American science from the turn of the century throughout the 1920s. Tillinghast (1902) is illustrative:

> The entire absence ... of higher things ... in Africa ... means something deeper ... than a mere lack of education for the living generation ... the

psychic nature has never been enlarged and refined by selection in response to a progressive environment, and so remains inferior to that of peoples long subjected to the stress and struggle of rapidly advancing standards ... Our knowledge of certain of the relations between the mind and its physiological basis in the brain may be taken as fairly established ... Cranial capacity ... offers one not so open to objection ... in this respect the Australian aborigines stand lowest, Africans next, Mongolians next, and highest of all, Caucasians.

Quoting Keane and other scholars with approval, he contends that:

The convolutions in the negro brain are less numerous and more massive than in the European ... the black is a child ... and will remain so ... the sudden arrest of the mental faculties at the age of puberty is attributed to the closing of the sutures ... In whatever aspect ... we consider the physiological basis of mental power, whether as to size of brain, or its inner structure, or the length of its plastic period, the natives of Guinea are at a grave disadvantage in comparison with the Caucasian.

(See also Odum, 1910; Dowd, 1926.)

Blinded by the science of biological determinism, early twentieth-century white linguistic scholars followed Harrison's lead, taking hold of his baby-talk theory of African American speech and widely disseminating it in academic discourse.[1] The child language explanation of Black Language is linguistic racism that corresponds to the biological determinist assumption that blacks are lower forms of the human species whose evolution is incomplete. For example, in the first study of Gullah (rural and urban black speech communities in the coastal regions of the American Southeast), there is the following conclusion:

To express other than the simplest ideas, plain actualities, is, however, difficult ... Intellectual indolence, or laziness, mental and physical, which shows itself in the shortening of words, the elision of syllables, and modification of every difficult enunciation ... It is the indolence, mental and physical, of the Gullah dialect that is its most characteristic feature.

(Bennett, 1908; 1909)

Even so important a piece of academic discourse as H. L. Mencken's *The American Language* ([1919] 1937) reveals subtle signs of the child language black inadequacy position. Vacillating between describing black speech as "simplified," on the one hand, or "at least different," on the other, Mencken asserts:

> But its [i.e., Gullah's] vestiges are also to be found in the speech of the
> most ignorant Negroes of the inland regions, which still shows grammat-
> ical peculiarities seldom encountered in white Southern speech, however
> lowly, e.g., the confusion of persons, as in 'I *is*,' '*Do* she?' '*Does you?*' '*Am*
> you de man?' and 'He *am*'; the frequent use of present forms in the past,
> as in 'He *been die*' and 'He *done show* me'; the tendency to omit all the
> forms of *to be*, as in 'He *gone*' and 'Where you *at?*'

Obviously, because persons in the black speech community used
the above forms regularly in communication, they were not
"confusing" or "peculiar" to them, however "lowly" the speakers
might have been. Otherwise there would have been mass unintel-
ligibility. In a later edition of his work, Mencken was not so subtle,
alleging that "Black slave language . . . may be called the worst
English in the world" ([1919] 1936).

The possibility of African provenience, of course, could well
account for these "confusions" and "peculiarities," as Turner was to
show some years later (1949). However, the ethnocentric bias of
Anglo conformity worked hand in hand with the doctrine of genetic
inferiority to dismiss this possibility from consideration. The writer
Gonzales (1922) in his collection of folk stories from the Georgia–
Carolina area illustrates this combination of racist discourse:

> The [Gullah] words are, of course, not African, for the African brought
> over or retained only a few words of his jungle-tongue, and even these
> few are by no means authenticated as part of the original scant baggage
> of the negro slaves . . . Slovenly and careless of speech, these Gullahs
> seized upon the peasant English used by some of the early settlers and
> by the white servants of the wealthier Colonists, wrapped their clumsy
> tongues about it as well as they could, and enriched with certain expres-
> sive African words, it issued through their flat noses and thick lips as so
> workable a form of speech that it was gradually adopted by the other
> slaves . . . With characteristic laziness, these Gullah Negroes took short
> cuts to the ears of their auditors . . .

Krapp's "English of the Negro" (1924) and his significant study,
English Language in America (1925), attributed the origin of black
English to baby talk between master and slave and firmly established
the East Anglian origins theory of African American speech that
would not be challenged in mainstream linguistics until the 1960s.
Although a scholar, he, like Gonzales and their contemporaries, was
obviously influenced, on the one hand, by biological determinism,
which had become institutionalized in American scholarship, and on
the other, by the ethnocentric bias and linguistic chauvinism of Anglo
speech as the ideal source from which black American speech (and,
by extension, other minority speech variations) had sprung. Yet,

though English was the source, because it was being emitted from childlike beings, the "English of the Negro" was of necessity an "infantile English." Krapp's discourse, then, though more scholarly than that of Gonzales, is, at bottom, just as racist:

> From the very beginning the white overlords addressed themselves in English to their black vassals. It is not difficult to imagine the kind of English this would be. It would be a very much simplified English – the kind of English some people employ when they talk to babies ... Difficult sounds would be eliminated, as they are in baby-talk. Its vocabulary would be reduced to the lowest possible elements ... As the Negroes imported into America came from many unrelated tribes, speaking languages so different that one tribe could not understand the language of another, they themselves were driven to the use of this infantile English in speaking to one another ... It is reasonably safe to say that not a single detail of Negro pronunciation or Negro syntax can be proved to have any other than an English origin.

Present-day scholars are generally agreed that black linguist Lorenzo Dow Turner (1949) conclusively demonstrated that there is a significant African linguistic dimension to Gullah speech, as well as strong possibilities of links to African languages in the speech of black Americans outside the Gullah region. Turner's work is represented by his monumental fifteen-year study of blacks in the speech communities on the Sea Islands and in other areas along the Atlantic coastal region of South Carolina and Georgia. Even the name "Gullah" was determined to be an African survival, from "gula, name of the tribe in Liberia." (However, see also Vass 1979, who attributes the term to "Ngola" in Angola, the source of significant numbers of slaves imported into South Carolina.) Further, Turner's data indicated that "the Gullahs ... have used the same methods as their African ancestors in naming their children ... names of the periods of the day, week, and year, names indicating whether the child is ... the first, second or third born ... etc." Because he was fluent in several West African languages, he was able to uncover over six thousand West African words in frequent use, fundamental African survivals in sound and syntax, and ultimately to counter the baby-talk myths. Turner states:

> The sounds of Gullah show many striking resemblances to those of several West African languages. When the African came to the United States and encountered in English certain sounds not present in his native language, he did what any other person to whom English was a foreign language would have done under similar circumstances – he substituted sounds from his own language which appeared to him to resemble most closely those English sounds which were unfamiliar to him.

And in what sounds like a direct response to Harrison, Turner explains:

> The English inter-dental fricative *th* does not exist in Gullah nor in the West African languages included in this study. In pronouncing English words containing this sound, both the Gullah speaker and the West African substitute [d] and [t], respectively, for the voiced and voiceless varieties of it.

Several years before Turner's work appeared, white anthropologist Melville Herskovits, in his *Myth of the Negro Past* (1941), had quoted extensively from Turner's then–unpublished manuscript in Herskovits's scholarly quest to prove that blacks did indeed have a past – their African cultural and linguistic heritage – and that that past continued to survive in the present. Moreover, the linguists Hall (1950) and McDavid (1950, 1951) had issued laudatory reviews of Turner's work. Although McDavid, often referred to as the "Dean of American dialectology," would later retract his strong support for the African-based tradition of Black English (McDavid 1967), his praise of Turner was lavish:

> Turner's book ... should inaugurate a new approach to the study of American Negro speech ... The prevailing interpretation of Gullah has been one which minimizes the features derived from African languages and attributes most of the characteristic features ... either to 17th century British dialects or to some form of baby talk used by plantation overseers to the simple-minded representatives of undeveloped primitive cultures, who in turn distorted ... the language through their ignorance, laziness, or physical inability to reproduce the sounds of English ... [Turner] has identified several thousand items in Gullah with possible African sources – a mass of evidence which should go far towards correcting ... previous investigators ... The presentation in the ... book is soberly factual, the conclusions are conservative, even the details are rarely questionable ... The fact that these phenomena occur in white speech in and near the Gullah country, in a region marked by large early slaveholdings, suggests borrowing; linguists can not afford to be cocksure that all borrowing ... was in one direction ... Turner's book is one which no student of American English can afford to ignore.

Turner's influence was to be short-lived and his work largely ignored until its revival by Creolists in the 1960s and 1970s (e.g., Bailey 1965). American race relations in the 1940s entered its period of the denial of differences (which may be viewed as yet another manifestation of racism, that is, to deny the existence of differences, in the face of overwhelming objective data to the contrary, is to imply that something is *wrong* with the differences).

Although Turner's focus was a comparison between West African language structures and black Gullah English, his work implicitly addressed the issue of differences between black and white American English. Thus his scholarship could not enjoy the scientific recognition it deserved. In this era of black–white relations, roughly 1940–60, social science was busily trying to resolve the "American dilemma" by demonstrating that blacks were just like whites – only darker. And given Anglo bias and racism, certainly whites were not about to acknowledge that there had been borrowings into white American speech from African languages, as Turner's work implied and as McDavid noted in his review of Turner. Additionally, in American mass media and popular culture of this era, images of the "dark continent" were dominated by Tarzan and apelike Africans in wild, barbaric jungles, surely a cultural link to be disavowed and discredited, regardless of what the science demonstrated. Turner's work, then, which could have put the lie to a half century of racist mythology in the African American English research tradition, was cast aside in this denial of differences phase. (Ironically, a prominent black scholar of this era, the sociologist E. Franklin Frazier, soundly denounced the African origins work of Herskovits; see his review of Herskovits's *Myth of the Negro Past* in Frazier, 1942.)

AFRICAN AMERICAN SPEECH AND THE "LINGUISTICS OF WHITE SUPREMACY"

After the hiatus of the 1940s and 1950s, there was a virtual explosion of research on Black English amid the social and political upheavals of the fire this time in the Black Power era of the 1960s and 1970s. The research was characterized by less attention to the origins of black speech and greater focus on its contemporary characteristics and its social, educational, and other implications within Americas' political economy. As for American linguistics, it had shifted from historical to synchronic research studies (e.g., Francis, 1958) and had yet to break completely free of a behaviorist conceptualization of language (e.g., Bloomfield, 1933) resulting from American science's shift to empiricism. In Black English research, the stage was set for the emergence of a decidedly more subtle form of racist ideology premised on assumptions about environmental and social conditioning. If language were the consequence of response conditioning to environmental stimuli, and if there were no basis for African provenience in Black Language, then the differences between black and white speech must result from the depressed social and environmental conditions of blacks. In point of fact, it was argued that Black English is just as linguistically and functionally systematic as white English. However, the "problem" is that Black English is socially and economically inadequate.

The evolving ideology was accelerated by social and political developments in black communities worldwide, spearheaded by liberation movements in Africa. On American shores, the Black Power era ushered in sit-ins, marches, demonstrations, and other forms of civil disobedience and protest. As white America grappled with this massive black energy in its streets, academic elites were sought to assemble research and data that could be used to co-opt America's marching, fist-raising, loud-talking, Molotov-cocktail-throwing black minority into the majority ideology (capitalism, consumerism, and Americanism). In this context, academic discourse about Black Language shifted from a biological/racial focus to an environmental/social focus. The reasoning was that the linguistic differences between black speakers and the white middle class was a matter of socioeconomic, educational status. Blacks could thus be brought "up from the ghetto," as they had come "up from slavery" with language modeled on that of the middle class, and America's streets would become safe to walk once again. The academic establishment split over the question of whether the language differences were social or "cognitive," with the latter group coming to be labeled "deficit theorists." (However, a deficit is a deficit by any other name, and at bottom, there was little difference in the racism inherent in the discourse of social- and cognitive-based theorists.)

The deficit theory, stemming primarily from psychologists, contended that because many blacks lived in impoverished environments, the debilitating physical surroundings adversely affected the acquisition and development of language among them, leading to a state of "verbal deprivation." Terms used to describe the language were "language retardation," linguistic "impoverishment," and verbal "underdevelopment." At best, African American English was deemed to be an "underdeveloped version of standard English . . . a non-logical mode of expressive behavior . . . lacking the formal properties necessary for formulating cognitive concepts" (Bereiter, 1965; Bereiter and Engelmann, 1966). At worst, it was dismissed as "no language at all" (Deutsch, 1963). The widely quoted psychologist Arthur Jensen is also illustrative:

> Language in the lower class is not as flexible a means of communication as in the middle class. It is not as readily adapted to the subtleties of the particular situations, but consists more of a relatively small repertoire of stereotyped phrases and expressions which are used rather loosely without much effort to achieve a subtle correspondence between perception and

verbal expression. Much of lower-class language consists of a kind of incidental "emotional" accompaniment to action here and now.

(1968)

The argument of the deficit theorists borders on the biological
determinist position inasmuch as they contend that verbal skills
are conditioned responses reflecting underlying cognitive structure.
For example, a stimulus word (e.g., *fat*) is presented to a "subject,"
for his/her verbal association, which "normatively" would be *thin*.
Because the normative responses are conditioned by the scholar's
Anglo conformity perspective, linguistically divergent responses are
considered deviant (e.g., for many black speakers, the verbal association with *fat* would be *skinny*.) In this way, then, the discourse
of such scholars comes close to recapitulating the biological determinist position.

The social deficit theorists disassociated themselves from the
cognitive deficit theorists, contending that the Black Language question has to do with social inadequacy, not cognitive–linguistic
inadequacy. One of the first language programs premised on this
ideological base was financed by the federal government and established in Detroit in 1959. It espoused the following philosophy:

> It must be acknowledged that standard language is a key that will open
> many doors, and conversely, many doors may be closed to those with
> nonstandard language ... In other words, if they wish to progress in
> Northern and Midwestern urban communities, they must speak as we do
> ... Negro students of a low socio-economic level in Detroit [must] change
> their patterns of speech.

(Golden, 1959)

(Ironically, in 1967, Detroit was the scene of the most extensive
and most damaging "civil disturbance" of all urban rebellions in
that historical period.)

Ten years later, in a supposedly more enlightened approach,
the discourse acknowledges that middle–class speech has little to do
with "comprehensibility" and that "people who speak standard
English do not always and invariably communicate any more clearly
or forcefully than speakers of nonstandard dialects do." However,
the value assigned to nonstandard speech is tantamount to the difference between going to the front door and the back door, the usual
entrance to white establishments that blacks were forced to use
before segregation laws were struck down in the 1960s.
"Undemocratic and unfair as it may seem, the fact is that standard
English is 'front door' English ... a command of standard English
is vital to any American (particularly any 'minority-group' American)

who aims to associate with speakers of the standard dialect on anything like an equal footing" (Allen, 1969).

Both cognitive and social deficiency theories are premised on the assumption of black linguistic inadequacy, so much so that a few scholars called for the eradication of Black Language. (How that was to be accomplished without the eradication of black people was unclear.) Most scholars, however, put forth "bi-dialectalism," that is, the philosophy that blacks needed to master two dialects, their own and the language of wider communication (i.e., "standard English"). The underlying assumption was that even if all dialects are equal, some are more equal than others. Blacks, then, would have to learn white English although whites would not have to learn Black English. Thus, the term "bi-dialectalism" was a misnomer, which obfuscated the racism of policies and practices that would discriminate against blacks because of the blackness of Black English. Instead of focusing on racism and acts of discrimination, which created the social and environmental conditions of blacks, scholars, in effect, blamed the victims for their failure to conform to white linguistic (and/or cognitive) standards. Through this kind of academic discourse in the Black Power era, racism was reproduced in another form. As white linguist James Sledd argued (1969), bi-dialectalism was, at bottom, the "linguistics of white supremacy."

BLACK SPEECH AND "BENIGN NEGLECT"

There was another important set of academic discourse on black speech that emerged during the 1960s. Produced largely by sociolinguists and ethnographers, all with presumably good intentions, this research, nonetheless, must be taken to task not so much for *what it did do* as for *what it did not do*. Although the scholars were apparently well meaning and concerned to right the linguistic record on Black English, their focus was on black *language*, not on the language of black *people*. They avoided the arena of public policy and the national spotlight in public debates and discussions over the black language question. Confining themselves to ivory towers, such scholars pursued what they perceived as their "work" and "pure" research, seemingly oblivious to the political ramifications and potential impact of this "work" on public attitudes and policy decisions about a historically disenfranchised and oppressed people. Within the paradigms of American science and the scholarly traditions of the American academy, this position of noninvolvement in politics and public policy is implicitly justified on the grounds of scientific "objectivity," "distance," and "letting the data speak for themselves." Yet America's political elites readily raid research centers

and selectively choose research that will produce ideological justification to support public decision making, laws, and policy that
adversely affect the lives and struggles of African Americans.

Obviously at this stage in American race relations, the discourse
qua discourse seldom revealed racism. Rather, it was located in the
dominant institutionalized patterns of reproducing knowledge and
science in the American academy and in American intellectual circles.
Scholars, researchers, and academics work within a system that legitimates social and political noninvolvement. Particularly is this stance
encouraged in racially oriented research. (In point of fact, blacks
doing research on blacks have often been accused of biases resulting
from being black and a part of the black experience. Yet, no similar
charge has been leveled against white scholars who, somehow mirac-
ulously, can do research on whites without any biases creeping into
their work.) In the case of the Black English research tradition (as
with other research in the social sciences, arts, and humanities),
voluminous resources were expended in the 1960s era. Scholarly
reputations were made, hundreds of books and articles published,
and millions of dollars for grants and research awarded for study
on the speech of black Americans. On the one hand, scholars could
safely retreat to ivory towers and do their "work." On the other,
had it not been for the massive social upheavals created by Myrdal's
"American dilemma" – the "Negro problem and modern democracy" – there would have been neither research "work" nor the
consequent awards to the scholars who did the work. Furthermore,
though they retreated from the real world of racism to study
linguistic phenomena created in and by that world, their research
results and data, in a distorted and racially negative form, were
disseminated to that racist world by the popular press, the media,
and through other forms of public communication. The consequence of this scholarly "distance" in Black English research can
be characterized as a sin of omission, a subtle mechanism through
which racism is reproduced by the academic elite. We may call this
"racism through 'benign neglect.'"[2]

The body of work on Black English produced by sociolinguists
in the 1960s and 1970s focused on structural features of language
abstracted from social context. In accounting for the nature of these
features, neither Turner's Creolist nor Krapp's Anglian position was
supported. The issue of origins was simply ignored; the concentration of the research was strictly synchronic and heavily statistical
(e.g., Labov *et al.* 1968, 1972; Wolfram, 1969; Fasold, 1964; Fasold
and Wolfram, 1970). The "blackness" of black language was shown
to derive from the linguistic features that black speakers share with
other speakers of English, but realize at a higher frequency of

occurrence. For example, all speakers of English tend to delete the final member of some consonant clusters at the ends of words. In the phrase *west side*, for instance, there is a tendency for speakers to reduce the final *st* in *west* to *wes'side*, but the deletion rule operates at a higher frequency for blacks. The sociolinguists did not posit different underlying meanings between black and white speech systems, but the same syntactical and phonological rules with differing frequencies. For instance, copula deletion in black English (as in "The coffee cold") exists only in environments where contraction is possible in white English (e.g., "The coffee's cold"). But neither black nor white English speakers delete the copula in tag questions (i.e., subject–verb contraction not possible, as in "The coffee's cold, *isn't it?*").

It should be noted that there was a re-emerging Creolist theory which challenged such interpretations of the African American English verb system. In the example cited above, the Creolist theory would posit that the copula in black English functions within an aspectual meaning system, in which distinctions are made – as Turner had demonstrated in several West African language systems – between static and continuous actions. Hence, "The coffee cold" roughly conveys the meaning, *The coffee is cold today*, whereas "The coffee be cold" roughly equivalent to *The coffee is usually cold*. However, the Creolists among conventional scholars (e.g., Stewart, 1967; Dillard, 1972) were at the time a distinct minority working outside the scholarly mainstream and generally outside the resource support network of linguistic scholarship. This was also sadly true of the pioneer black woman linguist, Beryl Bailey (e.g., 1966), whose brilliant scholarly potential was cut short by her extended illness and untimely death.

For the sociolinguists to demonstrate that black and white speech systems were not substantively diverse in their "deep" semantic essence, but only quantitatively different in their surface manifestations, set up an intriguing paradox. On the one hand, it came close to reinvoking the 1940s and 1950s denial of linguistic differences between blacks and whites. On the other, it raised the question of *why* there were these linguistic frequency differences between black and white speech. The lack of attention to the cause of the differences and what was to be made of them was a serious shortcoming in this scholarship. Explanations were rarely advanced, and when they were forthcoming, generally in passing, they were delivered in the form of inadequacy, such as "the social distance between white and black Americans [is a] contributing factor [to] Negro dialect" (Fasold and Wolfram, 1970). The sociolinguists' failure to address the reasons for black–white speech differences in *linguistic* terms unwittingly served to rekindle racial determinism arguments and left open the possibility for the public to supply reasons in *racist* terms. (William Labov is an outstanding exception to his peers in this tradition. He is heavily involved in educational and social policy formulations and in media explanations[3] of his work, e.g., 1970, 1985. Further, he has reversed his earlier rejection of the Creole origin of black speech, crediting the emerging body of work by black linguists, particularly the Creolists – e.g., Rickford, 1979; Baugh, 1979 – for this reversal; see, e.g., Labov, 1982.)

The academic discourse on black language that came from ethnographers was significant as a corrective to the obsession with the quantitative paradigm that characterized the work of the socio-linguists. Contending that language cannot be abstracted from the sociocultural context, ethnolinguists focused on the use and users of black language – their history, culture, values, worldview, and social structure. Emphasis was on the types of speech events and interaction processes (e.g., signifying, shucking, marking, call–response) and on the cultural norms that shape the forms of black speech and determine the rules governing who will speak to whom, when, where, in what way, and for what outcomes (e.g., Kochman, 1972, 1981, Abrahams, 1964, Jackson, 1974). For example, if a young Blood meets a friend and shifts from his normal greeting routine ("Hey man, what's happenin'?") to an overly formal form ("Well, Mr. Jones, how do you do?"), he may do so to mark humor, to maintain social distance, or to convey a subtle put-down. It is not the new greeting form that conveys the message, but the shift away from the regular routine. Ultimately, the significant contribution of ethnographic research on Black English was that it reinforced the dimension of culture and all its ramifications in Black English research and broadened our knowledge and understanding of why blacks "be doing the thangs they don't do."

As mentioned, the work of both sociolinguists and ethno-graphers received widespread public attention in the media, in the educational arena, and in public life. This work was disseminated to the lay public unacquainted with sociolinguistic theory, ethno-graphy, or historical linguistics. Rather than writing and speaking to the people, the scholar elites communicated among themselves and allowed their descriptions of black speech to be reproduced through lay channels, such as the media, to audiences lacking the "objectivity" of the "scientist." In the American mind-set, these descriptions served to reinforce the worst stereotypes of black people as clowns, low-life, and sex-crazed.

For sociolinguistic descriptions, features of Black English were passed on to students, teachers, and later to general audiences in

stilted, stereotypic formats. An illustrative example is Seymour's article (1971) in *Commonweal*, a highly conservative (if not reactionary)
magazine, in which she presents "deviant" black English constructions in contrast with "standard" translations. Such descriptions conveyed the impression that black English was the "dem, dat, dose"
lingo of Amos 'n Andy and what Morse (1973) scathingly denounced
as the "shuffling speech of slavery." Understandably, then, in some
quarters in the black community, black English was rejected as "not
a valid concept" and as "Black Nonsense" (Curry, 1971), and its study
was virtually outlawed by the NAACP (Wilkins, 1971).

For ethnographic descriptions, black speech events, such as
signifying, shucking, and joke telling were caricatured as "jive talk"
and "ghetto speech" in "Dyn-O-Mite" television shows and in the
local and national press. Books like Abrahams's *Deep Down in the
Jungle* (1964), Jackson's *Get Your Ass in the Water and Swim Like
Me* (1974), and Folb's *Runnin' Down Some Lines* (1980) — the titles
themselves tell you something — conveyed the impression that black
speech was the lingo of criminals, dope pushers, teenage hoodlums,
and various and sundry hustlers, who spoke only in "muthafuckas"
and "pussy-copping raps."

Overwhelmingly, the black "subjects" of the research were
predominantly male, and the content of their speech data primarily
sexual. For example, several of the toasts in Jackson's collection
were narrated by black ex-convicts, and most were collected at
prisons. In the introduction, we are told that the toasts "contain
much violence, some of it sexual," which is explained thus:

> Sexual conquest of the female is . . . important . . . The object of the con-
> quest has significance only insofar as it is there to be conquered . . . One
> does not conquer the female to have sex; it is *with* sex . . . one negotiates,
> executes, and terminates the conquest . . . In the toasts, verbal agility is often
> the basis of contest between the pimp and whore: he first bests her in an
> insult or bragging session, and then superfucks her into adulating respect
> for "that too."
>
> (Jackson 1974)

There is no denying that the "toast world" is a dimension of black
linguistic tradition; the point, however, is that a slice of black folk
character was presented as the whole. This is invariably the conclusion drawn by the lay reader unfamiliar with other aspects of African
American community life and folklore, particularly when the reader
is told that "it would be difficult to underestimate the power of verbal
skill, not only in the toasts but *in the culture using them*" (this in the
context of pimp–whore speech and social interaction; emphasis mine).
Further authentication of the "toast world" as reflective of the reality

of black life is suggested by the interpretation that the toast characters are simply "exaggerations of roles known on the street."

We are dealing here with subliminal messages conveyed by the selection of material, the selection of "subjects," and the style of presentation. In the absence of countervailing positive images of black folk life in mainstream culture, the ethnographic research data confirmed racist stereotypes. For instance, Folb's work on black teenage language and culture (1980) overwhelmingly focuses on hustling and male–female sexual interaction, and from a distinctly male viewpoint – of her over three hundred informants, only fifty were women. The following passage is characteristic of the presentational style of this body of research:

> The various strategies used to rank someone's play are highly creative and sometimes totally outrageous (and very funny). Sometimes two people will try to outwait each other – with the result that neither one gets over: "Like somebody wanna do they thing and neither one o' you gonna give up. Ain't neither one gonna move. So you both jus' gonna set dere and cock block and neither one o' you gonna get nothin." At other times one person will try to outwit or outmaneuver the other: "Like you rappin' to some fine stuff, dude come up, say, 'Hey, man, so-'n-so got some bad weed. Yeh, in d' john. Better get some 'fore it gone.' Go dere, nothin' happenin'. Come back, dude mackin' on d' young lady. Nigger done ranked yo' play." Sometimes the cock block is more overtly disruptive: "Like dude talkin' to a young lady and you say, 'I'ma rank the nigger, take his stuff from 'im.' Come up 'n tell d'broad, 'Dat dude, you know what? He mess wid a dog.' Gonna make d' young lady kin'a look at you kinda funny. Or like if she older, den you say, 'Ah, man you aint' but so-'n-so age.' Or tell broad he married. Say somethin' wrong about 'im like, 'You still got dat clap?' Fuck up his pussy. Intrude rudely."

Figure 4.1 "Kudzu" cartoon, by Doug Marlette

Source: Reprinted by permission of Tribune Media Services

(Interestingly, both Folb and Jackson were published by the prestigious Harvard University Press, affording them yet another "seal of approval" in public perception.)

It is significant that one of the most important scholars in this tradition, a pioneer who was widely quoted and who became the model for several ethnographic studies of black speech, repudiated the sensationalism and racism of this approach in his "belated apology to . . . neighbors and friends" who had served as informants in his research. In Abrahams's introduction to his second edition (1970) of *Deep Down in the Jungle*, he writes:

> Since the publication of *Deep Down* . . . in 1964, I have been hoping for the chance of this second say . . . I may be hiding behind my academic objectivity in saying that I emphasized the matrifocal family in the first edition because of the scholarly fashion of the time . . . This document [i.e., *Deep Down*] was crucial in working out my own problems in relation to women . . . It is clear to me now that my personal situation at the time had a great influence on my interpretation of the life around me . . . I make my *mea culpas* now only to make the record a little clearer. Objectivity in a field situation is only an ideal toward which we strive; but focus of interest will always be determined, at least in part, by personal problems.

On the question of African origins in African American folklore and life, he acknowledges yet another shortcoming in his original work:

> Another limitation . . . was the insularity of the approach . . . The patterns of performance and their uses were not unique to Negro Philadelphia or to lower-class black Americans . . . Field work in the British West Indies [has shown] that the approach to words and word use and creative performance is shared throughout the two culture areas . . . Recent ethnographic works on Negro groups throughout Africa and the New World give indications that this attitude and pattern is an African cultural retention in its New World situations, subject to reinterpretation.

The most crucial statement in Abrahams's "second say" is his stunning acknowledgment of the institutional character of racism in academic scholarship and the internalization of it by individual scholars:

> I sensed from the beginning of the writing [i.e., in 1964] that I was not capturing the spirit of my experiences and the essentials of my observations and thus was unwillingly playing into the hands of racists. It wasn't until the era of black militancy . . . that I was able to see how my *ex post facto* judgments had been conditioned by my reading of the scholarship on black life rather than by the life style I had observed and experienced.

Although Abraham's admission represents a rare display of scholarly courage, within the body of conventional research and scholarship on black people, this research framework is all too common. It is rare to admit the wrong, but it is not rare to commit it.

BLACK ENGLISH AND THE "GOOD OLD DAYS" REVISITED

Although there was a virtual explosion of social "uplift" programs and race-oriented research in the human sciences in the black power era, these efforts did not succeed in assimilating the masses of blacks into the socioeconomic mainstream. Only the most talented of the DuBoisian "talented tenth" gained entry into the system, and now in the 1980s, the ranks of the black underclass have swelled as a consequence of America's declining industrial base and technological explosion and the concomitant worldwide crisis in capitalism. Conservative and reactionary forces are trying to address the massive unemployment, crime, and other social crises of the black (and minority) underclass by turning back the hands of time. Once again, segments of American science are in complicity (again "unwillingly"?) with the forces of racism. The manifestation in linguistic scholarship is evidenced in movements to make English the official national language of the United States and in the re-emergence of linguistic–cognitive deficit theory.

The campaign for English as the only officially recognized national language has taken the form of an organizational movement, "US English," whose goal is to amend the Constitution to reflect the legal institutionalization of American English as the official language. It is spearheaded by semanticist Hayakawa, whose important work on semantics (1940) helped revolutionize the field. A linguistic corollary to the reactionary mood of conservatism sweeping across America, US English is a national, well-financed, increasingly mass movement head-quartered in Washington, DC. The Constitutional amendment that Hayakawa introduced into the Senate is currently being refined in a Senate committee that has done a significant amount of work on the proposed amendment already. US English is undoubtedly primarily responsible for the legal proposal approved by the voters in the state of California, which will effectively overturn the tradition of printing election ballots in languages other than English, thus effectively disenfranchising many Spanish-speaking voters on the verge of becoming the dominant population in that state. Further, linguistic forces, such as US English, provide yet another justification for cutbacks in federal spending for the language-based educational programs for blacks and other minorities struggling to achieve freedom and literacy in the United States.

The reappearance of linguistic–cognitive deficit theory may be seen in some of the scholarship emanating from the literacy movement and from composition theorists. In the scholarship on literacy, a prevailing theme is the inadequacy of oral tradition cultures to perform abstract thinking and problem solving that require the written code. Olson's widely quoted, ground-breaking article (1977) is illustrative. He notes that "in oral speech, the interpersonal function is primary . . . In written text, the logical or ideational functions become primary . . . The emphasis, therefore, can shift from simple communication to truth, to 'getting it right.'" Of course, at this stage in race relations and Third World peoples' quest for liberation, the scholarship must concede the communicative ability of oral language, the scholarship must concede the communicative ability of oral language, as Olson does. However, he cautions us that it is "an instrument of limited power for exploring abstract ideas." Ultimately, such scholarship in the literacy movement reveals not only the re-emergence of Anglo conformity, but a racial bias in favor of Western culture writ large. The argument in capsule form is that alphabetic writing invented by the Greeks made possible the literacy necessary for modern abstract thinking. Further, this development from speech to literacy is evolutionary for both individuals and cultures. Positing that the move is from language as utterance to language as text, Olson asserts "speech makes us human and literacy makes us civilized."

Although the racism has indeed become imbedded in subtleties, it is clear who ain evolved yet. And if there is any doubt, Farrell (1983) makes it plain: one group comprises the users of Black English who score low on standard intelligence tests in great measure because they lack command of the verb "to be" and other features of standard English. In a piece entitled "IQ and Standard English," Farrell articulates this resurfacing linguistic deficit theory:

> Another result is the emergence of the verb "to be," which affords a far more flexible sense of time than what was previously possible conceptually when action verbs alone dominated the language. The development of the copulative verb is very important because a language with only action verbs is not likely to develop propositional thinking . . . The cognitive differences manifested on these different tests grow out of differences in grammar. Of course, people in functionally oral cultures use languages, and the languages they use have grammars. But those grammars differ from the grammars of literate languages.

Once again, however, the differences are not simply differences, but as in the racist scholarship of biological and social determinism of years past, the differences amount to deficits.

> The non-standard forms of the verb "to be" in various regional forms of Black English may affect the thinking of the users . . . Black ghetto children do not use the standard forms of the verb "to be" . . . Many of those same black ghetto children have difficulty learning to read, and they do not score highly on measures of abstract thinking.

Finally, although he says he rejects the genetic theory of IQ differences, this is implicitly contradicted by the following line of analysis:

> The syntax of thought that [Vygotsky] is referring to is abstract thought, which developed historically with the interiorization of literacy . . . Literate thinking is abstract thinking, the kind of thinking used in both deductive and inferential reasoning, the kind of thinking measured by various non-verbal tests of mental ability . . . Literate thinking is . . . propositional, oral thinking . . . appositional . . . Appositional thinking is association with one hemisphere of the neocortex, propositional with the other . . . Since both hemispheres are present in the neocortex of all normal . . . human beings, normal persons have the "brain potential" to learn propositional thinking. One begins to learn propositional thinking by mastering . . . the hypotactic grammatical structures of the sort Vygotsky mentions. In this country, that means learning the grammar of standard English. This is easier said than done for functionally oral people, however, because their thinking is characterized by parataxis.

STEADY ON THE CASE

As the black liberation struggle was being suppressed and destroyed by the forces of racism and American intelligence (see, e.g., Chomsky on *Cointelpro* 1975), a cadre of black linguists was being produced and forming itself into what has become a critical community of scholars as of this writing in 1987. In part, because of their contributions (see, e.g., reference to Labov above) and, in great measure, because of the legacy of black people's struggles in the black pride–Black Power era, there is an emerging positive perspective on black language. Empirical studies by Williams (1982) and Linn (1982) are among the body of scholarship beginning to document these new language attitudes. In the public domain, there has been recognition of the contributions of black speech to American mainstream language, as exemplified, for instance, by Safire in his *New York Times* column on language (see, e.g., 1981). And in the educational arena, the internationally publicized *King* federal court case of 1979 (popularly known as the "Black English Case") advanced the case for broad-based institutional changes in the education of Black English speakers (Smitherman, 1981 [a], [b]).

Yet, as discussed above, racism is creeping back into academic discourse on black speech. Black English researchers must challenge these moves to take us back to from where some folk ain never left. In particular, the newly developing cadre of African American linguists must exert leadership in this struggle and remain steady on the case. For all those commited to advancing the research tradition of black language and the continuing struggle for black liberation, I present the following outline for a program of what I call "macroethnolinguistics" as the next necessary phase in the black English research tradition.

First, there is the area of testing. The linguistic bias in IQ and other standardized tests has been more than sufficiently documented (e.g., Williams, 1972; Green, 1975; Williams, Rivers, and Brantley, 1975; Vaughn-Cooke, 1980; Bliss and Allen, 1978). For example, standard speech articulation and language assessment tests measure forms and distinctions that do not exist in Black English (e.g., distinction in articulation between *Ruth* and *roof*, which in African American speech are pronounced the same; singular/plural distinction signaled by morphological change, as in *The Cat is playing* vs. *The cats are playing*, which in Black English would be rendered *The cat playing*, with the singular/plural distinction established through contextual signaling).

Despite the body of literature challenging these tests; despite the Association of Black Psychologists' call for a moratorium on testing; notwithstanding several states' requirement of training in minority cultural patterns by psychiatrists seeking clinical licenses; although the courageous stand of black speech pathologists (e.g., Taylor, 1971) resulted in the American Speech Language and Hearing Association's rigorous policy governing the training and licensing of pathologists working with black and other minority language groups – despite all this, standardized tests of all varieties continue to be used to the detriment of blacks. These tests results track blacks in learning disability and speech pathology classrooms, as was done to the students involved in the *Larry P. vs. Riles* (1979) and in the *King vs. Ann Arbor* (1979) court cases; justify black exclusion from employment opportunities, entry into professional schools, participation in the media; and in general become the basis for rationalizing black people's differential access to social and economic power.

(When, as a consultant for Bliss and Allen's 1978 multiyear federally financed project on speech and language assessment for

black and Spanish-speaking children, I pushed for a policy challenge to the existing battery of tests, such as the Northwestern
Syntax Screening Test and the Carrow Elicited Language Inventory,
and the establishment of new tests, or at least new clinical procedures to replace those biased instruments, I was informed that the
federal government would only allow for patching up the current
tests and further, that the researchers could only do research, they
were not permitted to get into policy issues. Well, the testing
industry is, after all, a multimillion dollar capitalist enterprise; e.g.,
Stone, 1975. I subsequently withdrew from the project.)

Black English researchers, with the support of the black lay
community, must call a halt to the use and misuse of standardized
tests. So long as we continue to be "subjects" of these instruments,
the cognitive deficit label will stand.

A second critical area is in educational policy and practice.
Despite so-called bi-dialectal programs and lip service to the systematicity of black English, the language of instruction in black education
is not, as DuBois urged us fifty years ago, "that variety of the
English idiom which Negroes understand" (1933); it is not the
"mother tongue" that Bamgbose (1976), Bokamba (1981), and others
have argued for in African education; it is not the "dialect of
nurture" as the Students' Right to Their Own Language (1974)
termed it. No, it is none of the above. Standard white English
continues to be the only language acceptable in the teaching–learning
process. Rejecting the bourgeois sociolinguistic character of the
schools, the rate of force-outs among black underclass youth is
accelerating faster than the Concorde. Thus their sole "passport to
literacy" (Bamgbose, 1976) is withdrawn as they traverse the painful
journey from school to street to slammer. Black English researchers,
again with the support of the black lay community, must push for
Black Language as an alternative, co-equal language of instruction,
particularly among black children and pre-adolescents, where the
greatest potential for linguistic impact exists.

Third, and possibly most complex, is the need for public
language awareness campaigns and the simultaneous promotion of
the legitimacy of black English. Despite the turn toward positive
images of black speech, there remains some residual linguistic
"push–pull" (Smitherman, [1977] 1986) to be overcome. In this
connection, there is a need for additional research conceptualized
within the ideology of black liberation – we can no longer afford
"pure" research of the kind that was done in the past. Specific areas
of investigation include: the phenomenon of code-switching; how
does one learn to do this? Most bilingual blacks certainly did not
learn this skill in school, for the schools have not been able to

teach even the language of wider communication, let alone the more complex skill of code-switching. Another area of needed research is on the sociolinguistic rules governing conversation, information processing, the use of social rituals, such as greetings, farewells, compliment-giving, forms of address, and other discourse features. What are the black community's standards in these speech interactions? Further, it would be very important to ask who are the linguistic role models in the black community, that is, the "ideally competent" Black English speakers? Finally, we need feasibility studies that would guide researchers and policymakers in selecting the most effective strategies to promote language awareness and Black English legitimacy throughout the national black community.

Finally, researchers of African American speech need to formulate a national language policy (e.g., Smitherman, 1986), or at the very least, a language policy to protect the interests of the black community (e.g., Williams, 1982). Such a policy would govern language teaching and language use throughout the United States and ultimately be beneficial to all communities. (Thus, as has always been so throughout American history, whenever blacks have pioneered social change, the result has been change and betterment throughout the American social reality.) I propose a tripartite language policy:

1   Reinforcing the need for and teaching of the language of wider communication;
2   Elevation of Black English and other minority languages and dialects on co-equal status with the language of wider communication; and
3   Promotion of one or more foreign languages spoken by Third World persons, such as Spanish, so that future generations can carry on independent dialog with persons of color – the majority population in today's world.

In remaining steady on the case, I am putting forth language as the basis for preparation in world leadership by blacks. The lions have learned to write. Our time has come.

5

LET US BEGIN, as writer Amiri Baraka would say, "in the Tradition."

I looked at my hands and they
   looked new
I looked at my feet and they did too.
I got a new way of walkin'
And a new way of talkin'.

          (Traditional Black Gospel Song)

In traditional Black Church theology a person who has been "saved" is one whom God has rescued from the travails of sin and transformed into a new being. This transformation involves a revolutionary process whereby the "saved" individual's status is symbolized not only by a new physical essence — new hands and new feet — but also by new behaviors — "a new way of walkin' and a new way of talkin'".

"A NEW WAY OF TALKIN'": LANGUAGE, SOCIAL CHANGE, AND POLITICAL THEORY[1] [1989]

Next we turn to Celie, heroine of Alice Walker's Pulitzer Prize novel, *The Color Purple*:

> Darlene trying to teach me how to talk ... Every time I say something the way I say it, she correct me until I say it some other way. Pretty soon it feel like I can't think. My mind run up on a thought, git confuse, run back and sort of lay down ... She bring me a bunch of books. Whitefolks all over them, talking bout apples and dogs. What I care bout dogs? ... But I let Darlene worry on. Sometimes I think bout the apples and the dogs, sometimes I don't. Look like to me only a fool would want you to talk in a way that feel peculiar to your mind.
>
> (Walker, 1982; pp. 183–4)

At this point in her life, Celie has at last been freed from the oppressive stranglehold, brutality and sexual exploitation of her father and husband. She has had to struggle against what Toni Morrison (1984) might refer to as "the profound desolation of her reality." In the process, she has been transformed into a new, empowered woman. Thus having finally found her voice — "a new way of talkin'" — she wisely admonishes us that only fools talk in ways peculiar to their minds.

My central thesis is this: language plays a dominant role in the formation of ideology, consciousness, behavior and social relations; thus contemporary political and social theory must address the role of language in social change. I seek here to present a theory of language within the framework of social and revolutionary trans-formation using the linguistic situation of US society where race, class, and sex have historically, and often successfully, been manip-ulated in the consolidation of power. Borrowing from many sources and traditions, I am less concerned about theoretical neatness than about an explanatory framework that accounts for the observed phenomena. The theoretical formulations are grounded in an analysis of the historical formation of black English, non-standard English and white English and in empirical research in the African American speech community and among black and white automobile factory workers in Detroit.

Let me clarify my use of "language." I refer, in a holistic sense, both to language as abstract structure and language in speech interaction, and to a symbolic system rooted in social formations. I view language and speech — that is, individual and social expres-sion, structure and use — as a unified behavioral dialectic govern-ing the cognitive and social life of men and women. I thus depart from prevailing tendencies in US mainstream linguistics which is dominated by two scholarly camps: sociolinguistics and Cartesian or Chomskyan linguistics. The former camp focuses on social and ethnic language, the latter on "ideally competent" language, devoid of social influence. Neither is adequate to formulate a theory of language for social transformation as both schools — including black English studies — fail to locate language within the historical struc-turing of society and the class system. As Fowler and Kress put it:

> [Linguistics] has been neutralized . . . [there is need for a] critical linguistics . . . aware of the assumptions on which it is based . . . and prepared to reflect critically about the underlying causes of the phenomena it studies, and the nature of the society whose language it is.
>
> (1979, p. 186)

LANGUAGE, IDEOLOGY, AND CONSCIOUSNESS

The issue of the relationship between language and thought contin-ues to be an enduring one. (One is tempted to call it "timeless.") What is the nature of reality? Is it only existent in what we name?

For instance, given the differing types and numbers of colors in various languages, how many colors actually – materially – exist? Is language what I often call a "marked deck of cards"? For example, given the historical oppression of people of color in western societies, is the white boss lady's reference to her fifty-year-old black maid as "my girl" a revelation of racist ideology? Do speakers of different grammatical systems have different conceptions of external and social reality? For instance, do "Standard Average European" languages (Whorf, 1956), with their structural reliance on the duality of agent action utterances, force their speakers to conceptualize their physical and social worlds into bi-polar entities? Or is language neutral because it "'produces' nothing or 'produces' words only" and is thus irrelevant in social and revolutionary change (Stalin, 1951)?

In the beginning was Work and Word. As Marx said, "speech is as old as consciousness" (1844). In the evolution of human society, Work provided the impetus for the Word, and thus Marx was undoubtedly accurate in asserting that speech was the product of labor. However, once language started forming, Work and Word had mutually reinforcing effects on each other. Over historical time, the language–speech dialectic came to play a dominant role in the formation of ideology, consciousness and class relations. This dialectic acts as a filter through which material conditions and the struggle to change them is apprehended. Without the medium of language, real-world experience is encoded as undifferentiated phenomena. As Vygotsky says, "reality is generalized and reflected in a word" (1962, p. 122).

Only in the most idealist sense can language be considered neutral because once it is employed in speech interaction, that is, in social dialog, it is "filled with content and meaning drawn from behavior or ideology" (Volosinov, [1929] 1973, p. 70). Notwithstanding the existence of "inner speech" and talking to oneself, language is *social* behavior. The language–speech dialectic represents a society's theory of reality. As Fowler and Kress put it, the "society . . . impregnate[s] its language with social meanings . . ." (1979, p. 196).

Can "syntax code a world view" (Fowler and Kress, 1979, p. 185)? Both von Humboldt in the nineteenth century and Whorf in this one argued the point convincingly. Von Humboldt asserted that "every language sets certain limits to the spirit of those who speak it; it assumes a certain direction and by doing so, excludes many others" ([1810] 1963, p. 245). Further, he contended that "thinking is not merely dependent on language in general, but up to a certain degree on each specific language . . ." ([1810], p. 245).

Whorf devoted most of his unfortunately short life to analyses of Native American languages, contrasting their grammars and the cultural and social patterns they gave rise to with languages of the western world. He posited that "meaning will be found to be intimately connected with the linguistic: its principle is symbolism, but language is the great symbolism from which other symbolisms take their cue . . ." Throughout all of his work – even during the time he was a fire investigator for an insurance company – he insisted on the power of language to shape and control thought and behavior:

> the grammar of each language is not merely a reproducing instrument for voicing ideas, but rather is itself the shaper of ideas, the program and the guide for the individual's mental activity . . . Formulation of ideas is not an independent process, strictly rational in the old sense, but it is part of a particular grammar and differs, from slightly to greatly between grammars.
>
> (1956: 26)

For real-world evidence, we are given, for example, the morphology of Hopi verbs, which are marked not for time, but for the nature or source of validity. Hopi is thus a "timeless" language. Because of Hopi grammar, Whorf argued, the culture conceives of time as fluid, in process, rather than static or fixed, and dialogic assertions about reality are to be weighed not by temporal standards but by truth criteria. (Kress and Hodge (1979, p. 6) joked that we would want to buy a used car from a Hopi salesman, rather than from an Englishman.)

Although von Humboldt and Whorf may have overstated the case for language as *the* determiner of thought, consciousness, and behavior, language *is*, as Volosinov asserted, "implicated in the current ideology" ([1929] 1973, p. 70), and thus it *does* "constitute[s] the most important content and the most important instrument of socialization" (Berger and Luckmann, 1966, p. 133). From this vantage-point, it is my contention that ideology and consciousness are largely the products of what I call the "sociolinguistic construction of reality." Let us consider a few examples.

In US popular culture, the number 13 is considered symbolic of bad luck, and so in high-rise hotels in the USA, marketing strategies require that there be no "13th floor." The elevator goes from the 12th floor to the 14th, and hotel guests stay and sleep soundly in $200.00 rooms located on the 14th floor, which is, of course, floor 13, sociolinguistically constructed as nonexistent.

As another example, consider the language that marks power relationships. Although English does not have formal and informal forms of the second-person pronoun which govern forms of address – e.g. *du–Sie* in German, *tu–vous* in French, *ty–vy* in Russian – US English speakers do have access to other linguistic forms reflective of the class system. Peers and subordinates are sociolinguistically differentiated through the use of titles and first and last names. As a sociolinguistic class marker, maids receive first name but in return must give the boss lady or man last name – hence "Rita Smith" becomes simply "Rita", but "Phyllis Stein" is "Mrs. Stein", or occasionally, "Stein" (Smitherman unpublished manuscript). As sociolinguistic markers of social subordination based on race and sex, note the import of titles and their omission in the following exchanges:

> [A scene on a public street, white policeman, black physician]
> "What's your name, boy?" the policeman asked.
> "Dr. Pouissant. I'm a physician."
> "What's your first name, boy?"
> "Alvin."
>
> (Pouissant, 1967, p. 53)

> [A scene in a law office, two males, one female]
> "This is Dr. Johnson; she's a new physician on our staff over at General," the chief surgeon said.
> "How do you do, Ms. Johnson," the senior partner in the law firm replied.
>
> (Smitherman, 1995d)

These sociolinguistic markers of address reflect historically constituted patterns of classism, racism and sexism in the USA. From among the available linguistic options in English, each of the above speakers has chosen a form that sociolinguistically constructs and reproduces exploitation based on class, race, and sex.

A sharp illustration is provided by various meanings assigned to the epithet "nigger." In the following dialog, two workers at a Chrysler plant in Detroit are talking about the large number of Vietnamese – the "boat people" as US citizens derisively called them – who attempted to enter the US in 1975–6:

> J.T.:   The Viet Nam who didn't git off the boat, they was gon be the new nigguhs – for the whiteys and us.
> SAM: . . . I wish they hadda come on out there to work cause I'm tired of being the nigguh.
>
> (Smitherman, 1976)

The racial epithet is taken beyond the historical oppression of African slaves and their descendants. On the automobile assembly line, the "nigguh" is *any* exploited worker.

In a similar vein, during the social movements of the 1960s white counter-culture youth groups, mostly university students, and emerging white feminists used "nigger" to characterize their social oppression and exploitation. They viewed their status as akin to the historical enslavement of Africans and the oppression of their descendants, who typically work at the lowest and meanest jobs (in the car factories as elsewhere). Hence phrases such as the "student as nigger" and the "woman (or wife) as nigger." Students are constructed as "niggers" because not only are they subservient and powerless, their intellectual labor is expropriated by professors in pursuit of their own self-interest (e.g. research grants, promotion, tenure). Women are "niggers" by virtue of the domestic and sexual labor expropriated in their enslavement by men.

What we see illustrated here is extension and sociolinguistic reinterpretation of the semantic range of a verbal symbol rooted in slave labor and subsequent racial exploitation. Contrary to *Oxford English Dictionary* lexicographers, who attest that the term "nigger" is "incorrectly applied to members of other dark-skinned races", the language usage of black car-workers and progressive whites *correctly* reconstructs "nigguhs" as both black and white, male and female, or *any* group whose labor is exploited.

Among power elites, the sociolinguistic construction of reality is linguistic "trickeration" writ large. Operating at the macro-structural level, with the powerful, pervasive force of the media to aid in the reproduction of thought control, US elites promote a national doublespeak which makes "the bad seem good . . . the negative positive . . . [the] unpleasant . . . attractive, or at least tolerable" and "which does not extend thought but limits it" (Lutz, 1987, p. 10). When the US State Department decides, as it did in 1984, that "killing" in US-supported countries would be replaced with "unlawful or arbitrary deprivation of life;" when US nuclear strategists use "countervalue attacks" to refer to the destruction of entire cities (Elias, 1986, p. 10); and when, in this age of nuclear weapons, President Reagan discourses about Russia as an "evil empire", Marxism as a "virus", and communism as a "cancer", thus inviting extermination of these "microorganisms and demons" (Bosmajian, 1984, p. 5) – such language is designed to "distort reality and corrupt the mind" (Lutz, 1987, p. 12).

Not only is the pernicious use of language evident in words, *qua* words, but also in syntactical contouring and discourse style we can witness evidence of language to conceal, obfuscate and distort reality. Yes, syntax can code a world view (van Dijk, 1988; Sykes, 1988). Objects of action are nominalized rather than objectified resulting in a reversal of the reality of who does what to whom, as in the newspaper headline "Rioting Blacks Shot Dead." "Thus someone who has something done to him by another can be made responsible for his own suffering . . ." (Fowler and Kress, 1979,

p. 41). Actors and agents are buried in the passive voice so respon-sibility for action cannot be assigned. Thus "pain exists, but seldom blame" (Kozol, 1975, p. 25). The passive voice is particularly prob-lematic because of its rampant use in US academic discourse as well as in the national doublespeak, both of which have become discourse models for student writers and young learners. In a statement like "The invasion of Grenada was officially approved", a deletion trans-formation has been employed permitting the escape of the agent, "President Reagan." Further, the statement displaces the theme topic (in English utterances, generally found at the beginning of a state-ment), thus shifting the emphasis from Reagan to Grenada.

To recapitulate, language represents a society's theory of reality. It not only reflects that theory of reality, it explains, interprets, constructs, and reproduces that reality. In the global struggle for social and revolutionary change, there must be concomitant linguistic change. The first to go should be the old adage, "sticks and stones may break my bones, but words can never hurt me."

BLACK–WHITE–NON-STANDARD ENGLISH IN THE US

The sociolinguistic construction of reality in the class system of the US is made more complex by the contradiction of black and white English which are the same and not the same. White English (aka standard English) is that language spoken by power elites and those who aspire to upward social mobility; non-standard English is that language spoken by working-class whites; black English is that language spoken by African Americans. Significant and profound social and economic distinctions accompany each of these three linguistic phenomena.

White English (hereafter WE) is a class dialect derived from the speech of power elites. Because this group comprises white upper-class males, WE reflects and reproduces the classism, racism, and sexism of the US. Linguistic correctness is a function of ruling-class white male hegemony manifested in the historical development of WE, concomitant with capitalist formation in US history. Let us take a closer look at this sociolinguistic development.

Early US linguists (e.g. Webster, [1784] 1984; Murray, [1795] 1819; Brown, 1851) were primarily school-orientated grammarians intent upon the linguistic socialization of the new masses, particu-larly impressionable youth, into the linguistic conventions and rules of correctness of the emerging US bourgeoisie, rapidly consolidating itself into a capitalist formation on the basis of race and sex. These linguists – like their counterparts in England (e.g. Lowth, [1762] 1979 and France (e.g. the Port-Royal School, 1660, see e.g. Arnauld and Lancelot, 1975) – viewed their mission as that of "purifying the dialect of the tribe" which had been unleased by the demise of feudalism and the rise of capitalism and expanding technology. Models of correct speech were developed, based on *Pax Romana*, on the speech forms of the emerging capitalist elite, and on the *ipse dixit* pronouncements and preferences of the grammarians themselves. Although they were not above biting the hand that was feeding them by criticizing the elites, the primary purpose of these grammarians was to lay down the linguistic law to the white masses and their children in the schools. (Remember, black literacy and schooling were forbidden in this era.) In this way, the new social "hordes" would be "civilized" and brought into the language "family" of the ruling class.

Twentieth-century grammarians have abandoned all pretensions to Latinate norms and have come straight out with the doctrine that "standard English is that dialect used by those who carry on the affairs of the English-speaking people" (Fries, 1940). Thus it behoves those wishing to partake of the American Dream to master this class dialect (e.g. Golden, 1960; Allen, 1969). For both blacks and whites, such linguistic mastery is touted as a *sine qua non* of upward mobility. Blacks who lack this mastery are speakers of black English; whites who lack it are speakers of non-standard English. Since the norms of WE fluctuate according to the linguistic whims of those in power, an entire school of US linguists devotes significant amounts of time and state capital to chronicling the linguistic whereabouts of contemporary pace-setters. The products are voluminous guides to contemporary usage which become tools of linguistic (and hence ideological) indoctrination in our nation-wide public and university educational systems.

Whereas WE and NSE are *class* dialects in US society, BE, by contrast, is a *racial* dialect within the class system. That is, BE is spoken across the class spectrum among African Americans; middle-class blacks develop code-switching skills (i.e. from black to white English) which the black working and *unworking* classes generally do not possess.

BE is a product of the free labor system of the African slave trade. It arose as a result of two sets of factors: (1) the need for a *lingua franca* in the US slave community where it was the practice of slavers to intermingle linguistically diverse African ethnic groups so as to impede communication and hinder escape, and (2) the need for a linguistic code intelligible to slaves but unintelligible to slave masters. In its formalistic dimensions, BE reflects a combination of British/US English with West African deep structure. Its lexicon is largely English, its syntax, semantics and phonology a mixture of both linguistic traditions. For example, BE has elements of a surviving aspectual verb system which facilitates the expression of continuous versus static action, as in *The coffee be cold* (i.e. habitually, frequently) versus *The coffee cold* (i.e. today, now) (see, e.g., Dillard, 1972; Alleyne, 1980; Labov, 1982). Although there are some few words of direct African origin that have survived in BE (e.g. Dalby, 1969, 1970; Turner, 1949), the African component is revealed more in the ethnographic realm. For example, the application of distinct meaning to WE words, often resulting in "semantic inversion" (Holt, 1972), thus generating an utterance like "Black English is so good it's bad." Similarly, "nigguh" can be used in affectionate, positive contexts, as in "He my main nigguh," i.e. *He is my best friend*, and "She is a shonuff nigguh," i.e. *She is culturally black and rooted in the experiences and aspirations of black people*. (Note that whites never use "nigger" with these meanings.) Other significant examples can be found in norms of discourse and dialogic interaction. For instance, in the pattern of call–response, which obliges listeners to participate verbally and actively in speakers' messages and delivery (ritualized in the preacher's sermon style in the traditional Black Church); in the speech acts of signifying, testifying, rapping, toast-telling and proverb use (see, e.g., Smitherman, 1986; Daniel, 1974; Mitchell-Kernan, 1969; Kochman, 1972, 1981).

BE is related to other African–European language mixtures – pidgins and creoles – that developed in the slave trade. The development of BE reflects the modal experiences of African Americans and the continuing quest for freedom and literacy. For instance, black struggles for literacy have caused BE to de-creolize considerably since the seventeenth century – i.e. blacks have de-Africanized BE linguistic structure and moved it in the direction of WE. Yet continuing US racism (i.e. as manifested in *de facto* racial segregation, economic and other forms of discrimination) creates the need for black solidarity and thus results in the maintenance of sufficient distinctiveness in BE deep structure to render aspects of it unintelligible to WE speakers – that is to say, de-creolization remains incomplete. Thus BE and WE are the same but not the same.

It is necessary to account for the linguistic contradiction of black–white English in order to grasp the sociolinguistic construction of reality in the US. This contradiction is a function of and helps to reproduce patterns of labor exploitation. During slavery, white workers had to relinquish wage demands in the face of competition from free (slave) labor. When slavery became non-profitable, culminating in the Emancipation Proclamation, US society was faced with the potential time-bomb of its newly emancipated African workers joining forces with white workers. Racism was the ruling class's tool to prevent this alliance. Blacks were assigned the lowest-paying and meanest jobs in the society and relegated, in disproportionate numbers, to the marginal working class and the unemployed. In language use, it was − and is − the practice to designate the race of a worker. And the term "nigger" added to its semantic features the conceptual discourse "at least I ain't no nigger" as ideological compensation for the exploitation of the white working class. Further, although NSE is denigrated in the class system, BE remains at the very bottom of the US sociolinguistic hierarchy.

BLACK ENGLISH − A CLASS SOCIOLECT?

As is the nature of contradictions, the language at the bottom appears to be rising to the top. If we analyse languages-in-contact at the point of production, in particular in automobile manufacturing, there is evidence to suggest that BE is emerging as the *lingua franca* of the US industrial workplace. Given that language usage reflects social network and solidarity, if US black English is indeed an emerging class sociolect, it points towards a linguistic index of shifting social relations and compels us to re-examine the traditional model of race relations in the US.

Seeking empirical validation of the hypothesis that BE is the language of US workers, particularly those in automobile manufacturing, Botan and Smitherman (1983) devised the Black English Assessment, a language questionnaire (see Figure 5.1) to assess knowledge of BE semantics among production workers and nonproduction workers (i.e. professionals, plant supervisors, managers, etc.), both inside and outside the car factories. The questionnaire consists of ten items drawn from the *Dictionary of American Regional English* (DARE). The items chosen have been designated by DARE as "black" or "especially black" based on the frequency with which a certain meaning was given by blacks (see Table 5.1). Informants were asked to select the correct definition of each item from a set of five definitions per item. The usage given by DARE informants was always one of the five options.

DARE (Cassidy, 1985, continuing) presents the advantage of a national probability sample of US citizens from every state, interviewed by trained fieldworkers, who provided language data on a variety of topics of general interest: foods, religion, attitudes towards others, social activities, etc. The number of informants in each state reflects that state's proportion of the total US population; the number of blacks in the sample is relative to the proportion of blacks in each state. Altogether, the DARE sample consists of 2,752 informants in 1,002 communities across the US who were interviewed

Please do not put your name or any other personal identification on this paper.

Below are ten (10) terms which are underlined. After each item are four possible definitions; choose the most correct one. If you do not know the meaning of the term, use the "I do not know" answer.

1. Bid whist
   (a) a bid made in an auction
   (b) a kind of dress
   (c) the habit of paying bills on time
   (d) a kind of card game
   (e) I do not know

2. Call the hogs
   (a) shout very loudly
   (b) snore
   (c) get angry and yell at someone
   (d) celebrate
   (e) I do not know

3. Bo dollar
   (a) a dollar owed a brother
   (b) silver dollar
   (c) last dollar you have to your name
   (d) a kind of hubcap
   (e) I do not know

4. Chicken eater
   (a) a Baptist preacher
   (b) a city dweller
   (c) a weasel or mink
   (d) one who raises chickens
   (e) I do not know

5. Crack a rib
   (a) eat spare ribs (or share them)
   (b) stomp someone in a fight
   (c) a kind of block in football
   (d) laugh very hard
   (e) I do not know

6. Dead cat
   (a) something suspicious
   (b) when a criminal is killed
   (c) to be badly beaten in a game of luck
   (d) a ringer in horseshoes
   (e) I do not know

7. Jackleg
   (a) a good high jumper
   (b) a kind of spider
   (c) unprofessional or dishonest preacher
   (d) well tailored slacks
   (e) I do not know

8. Nose wide open
   (a) injured in a fight
   (b) being openly and strongly in love
   (c) smelling nice flowers
   (d) just getting over a cold
   (e) I do not know

9. Ig
   (a) a dance
   (b) to get a promotion
   (c) ignorant
   (d) ignore
   (e) I do not know

10. Gall shirt
   (a) undershirt
   (b) army uniform shirt
   (c) work shirt
   (d) spicy food
   (e) I do not know

The following information will be kept confidential but is very important for the study. Are you: White _____ Black _____ Hispanic _____ Latino _____ Middle Eastern _____ Other _____ . Your age is _____ . Where were you raised? Eastern US _____ Western US _____ Southern US _____ Midwestern US _____ . If not US, where? Your occupation is (if unemployed, give last job) _____

Figure 5.1   The Black English Assessment Questionnaire

Table 5.1 Black responses per item in
Black English Assessment

Item	%
Bid whist	82.7
Call the hogs	61
Bo dollar	79
Chicken eater	100
Crack a rib	60
Dead cat	66.6
Jackleg	63
Nose wide open	100
Ig	100
Gall shirt	85.7

Source: *Dictionary of American Regional English* (see
also Hirshberg, 1982).

between 1965 and 1970. Two and a half million responses were
obtained from informants, computer analyzed and, thus far, dictionaries released in two or three alphabetic sequences each year,
beginning in 1985.

For the Detroit survey, informants were randomly selected from
the Detroit metropolitan area, using assembly-line workers to admin-
ister surveys in the car plants, and university research assistants for
survey administration outside the plants. The results reported here
have been extrapolated from two surveys conducted five years apart.
While age and section of the US, where raised, were analyzed, it
is the analysis of responses by race and occupation that are of primary
interest. In the 1982 data (reported in Botan and Smitherman, 1983),
the comparison of production workers with supervisors/professionals
confirmed our predictions. White car-workers scored higher
than did white professionals and managers – i.e. the production
workers exhibited greater familiarity with BE semantics. However,
black workers did not score significantly higher than black professionals – as expected, given the linguistic homogeneity of the
black community and the phenomenon of code-switching among
black professionals.

For the 1987–8 data (to be reported in Smitherman, work in
progress), we have done a preliminary item analysis of surveys
from a subsample of production workers. Results reflect a trend
towards white knowledge of "especially black" terms – "chicken
eater" "bid whist", and "nose wide open". And although the
percentages of whites familiar with "ig" (a 100-percent black term)

Table 5.2 Black–White correct responses (%) per item in Black
English Assessment (production workers only)

Item	Black responses in DARE (%)	Black correct Detroit (n = 56)	White correct Detroit (n = 47)
Bid whist	82.7	94	45
Call the hogs	61	67	17
Bo dollar	79	73	12
Chicken eater	100	64	37
Crack a rib	60	73	37
Dead cat	66.6	27	15
Jackleg	63	79	17
Nose wide open	100	97	51
Ig	100	24	23
Gall shirt	85.7	15	13

Source: Smitherman, unpublished manuscript.

and "gall shirt" (85.7 percent black) are lower, those percentages
are almost identical to the percentages of black workers who knew
these two terms (see Table 5.2).

Of course there are possible limitations to this kind of language
survey. The Black English Assessment is a *written* survey of an *oral*
language. We can glean an index of receptive competence only;
the question remains to what degree, if any, white workers use BE
and in what contexts. Related to this limitation is the effect of
limited literacy skills on both black and white workers' performance
on the Assessment. And finally, there remains the question of the
extent of white workers' knowledge of BE beyond semantics.
On the other hand, we can pose several challenges to the question
of limitations. It is entirely possible that white workers exhibit
greater familiarity with BE in natural language environments. When
they returned their surveys, many of the workers, including whites,
indicated recognition of some items when they heard them pronounced; hence oral reading of the surveys might have produced
a greater number of correct responses from whites. Although it
would be valuable to compare white workers' knowledge of BE
with their use of BE, and although the fully competent speaker
possesses both receptive and productive competence in a given
language, it remains an open question whether the ideological
process requires competence in *both* linguistic dimensions. Conceptualizing language in a social change model raises the possibility that
one could be indoctrinated into a speech community's theory of
reality solely on the basis of one's *comprehension* of that community's language. Finally, while it might also be of some value to

assess white workers' knowledge of BE beyond semantics into the realms of morpho–syntax and phonology, such an investigation is premised on the assumption – widely held among linguists in the Chomsky school – that the semantic component of language is subordinate to its syntactical and phonological dimensions. If we accept the principle that "ideology is revealed in a word", a compelling case can be made for conceptualizing a model of language with semantics as the primary component.

CONCLUSIONS AND IMPLICATIONS

Language should be assigned a central place in models of social change and in political and revolutionary theories. The language– speech dialectic represents habitual, systematic social behavior. Its linguistic forms, embodying the world view of the society, are encoded in childhood in natural, developmental socialization pro- cesses. These forms construct and reproduce the society's theory of reality and become embedded in the socio-cognitive structure of speakers, who in turn use their language in spontaneous, virtually reflexive ways largely inaccessible to consciousness. This language acquisition process is universal, transcending cultural space and societal time. In fact it is this process which gives validity to Cartesian assumptions about language as an inherent human trait. On these grounds, there is no quarrel with the Chomsky school. *Dico, ergo sum*. However, the "I speak" and the "I am" are functions of the class system. Through repetitive language use and social reinforce- ment in class relations, negative social meanings and class-biased sociolinguistic patterns come to sound common and innocuously "natural." Because speakers thus become oblivious to underlying deep structure, in the process of social transformation, we are all challenged to a new level of linguistic consciousness. We must learn to attend to habitual, socially encoded patterns of speech, that construct and reproduce classism, racism and sexism.

As a personal example, I had never given thought to referring to the US as "America" until a comrade in Chicago linguistics called it to my attention. Even as I critiqued "America" for its participation in the repression of the people of Nicaragua and else- where in the "Americas," I was unconsciously reinforcing US cultural chauvinism and its regressive ideology. The underlying social meaning conveyed by reference to the US as "America" was that it was the only region among the "Americans" worthy of the title "America," the others being referred to as "Central America," "South America," "Latin America." I have thus consciously sought, throughout this article, to use the term "US." Such linguistic awareness has its practical problems. For example, the metaphorical construct "American Dream" is a linguistic register with immediate social familiarity, whereas "US Dream" is not. However, the crucial point is that attention to language use re-raises social consciousness and ideological awareness each time speakers must consciously select a linguistic option from their sociolinguistically constructed communication repertoire. Ultimately, "natural" sounding negative language will come to sound as "unnatural" and oppressive as race, class, and sex exploitation.

An analysis of black–white–non-standard English calls into question the traditional model of race relations in the US. There is a need to redefine the semantics of race and class. Assumptions about who is black, who is white and about racial solidarity (i.e. all blacks versus all whites) must be re-examined. A critical lesson of the Black Movement of the 1960s and 1970s is that the verbal concept "Black" could not automatically be marked with the semantic features (+socially progressive), (+for the people), (–competitiveness), (–labor exploitation). As the National Organization for an American Revolution asserts:

> the Black Power movement degenerated into "piece of the action" politics ... blacks ... resist engaging in the principled political struggles with other blacks that would force them to recognize how deeply blacks have been incorporated into the values of the capitalist system. So they cling to the illusion that changing the color of those in city government will solve their problems, despite the mounting evidence that black mayors, black police chiefs and black school superintendents are only overseers on the corporate plantations and reservations that our big cities have become.
>
> (1982, p. 37)

There is little evidence that the black middle class decries the machinations of capitalism. Many, if not most, seem to have bought into it as the pathway to the Good Life, the only obstacle to which is white racism. While they have racial consciousness, there is little evidence of class consciousness. For example, though they use the concept "nigguh" in the cultural ways in which working-class blacks use it (see examples cited earlier), they do not use it to refer to exploited labor as do black workers and progressive whites.

The paramount role of black labor is underscored by black carworkers' verbalizations of class and in the emerging linguistic cross-over of BE in the workplace. Though susceptible and often succumbing to the temptations of capitalist consumerism, the workers evidence a linguistic sense of class consciousness coexistent with their sense of racial consciousness. In analyzing verbalizations of class in his 1960 study of black and white workers in Detroit, Leggett (1968) found strong evidence of class consciousness among the blacks in his study. In our interviews with black car-workers, there emerged distinctions between whites who are members of the power elite and those of the working class. Phrases such as "Whiteys with the shonuff money" and "White boys with big paper" differentiate "Po'ass Whiteys" and "Howard Beach suckers" who "ain't in charge of nothin" (Smitherman, unpublished manuscript). And there is evidence of an understanding of the manipulations of race by white elites:

> Nigguhs know the real thang is bout money, so they sik them pecks [lower-class whites] on the nigguhs to keep them from gittin too far ... They [whites] live out there in them lil funky shacks, driving them lil biddy funny rides, stay on E [empty, no money] and happy as a sissy [male homosexual] in Jackson [State prison for men] long as they got nigguhs to fuck wit ...
>
> (Smitherman, 1976b)

The linguistic evidence from white workers indicating a trend toward the adoption of BE as the *lingua franca* in the workplace suggests the emergence of BE as a class sociolect and raises the possibility of capitalizing on the resources of the language for social transformation. Not only is BE the workers' *lingua franca*, it is all US outsiders' language of choice. The ideological function and sociolinguistic status of BE is reminiscent of (though not identical to) an "anti-language" (Halliday, 1976). This is a linguistic system that reinforces group solidarity and excludes the Other. It is speech characteristic of a group which is *in* but not *of* a society. As an anti-language, BE emerges as a counter-ideology; it is the language of rebellion and the symbolic expression of solidarity among the oppressed. For whites and blacks outside the working class (i.e. in the US not the Marxist sense), it is a language which permits progressives to commit "class suicide" by sociolinguistically reconstructing themselves. One may well question whether this is not too great a claim for BE, and the answer may well be "yes." But one thing is certain: if we are to speak the truth to the people and usher in societal transformation, we must have "a new way of walkin' *and* a new way of talkin'."

6

REVIEW OF
NOAM
CHOMSKY'S
*LANGUAGE AND
RESPONSIBILITY*[1]
[1983]

THE ENGLISH VERSION of *Language and Responsibility* arrived on the American scene at a propitious moment in the history of black people during our four-hundred-year travail in this land of the free. For 1979 was the year of *King* (also known as the "Ann Arbor Black English Case"), marking the legitimation of the language of black people in judicial annals and confirming the possibilities of linguistic theory and research in our quest for self-definition and literate vision.[2] Arousing passionate debate and re-raising questions of nationalism and community development throughout black America, the legal precedent established in *King* directly resulted from the labor of linguists cognizant of social responsibility and the role of critical linguistics in the *sine qua non* quest for global understanding.

Chomsky's book also came at a propitious moment in my personal history. Having been the dominant figure orchestrating the linguistic strategy of *King* for two years prior to and during the trial, I began work on *Language, Politics and Ideology*, for *King* had moved not only myself but other black linguists, scholars, intellectuals, and countless others in the national black community to confront anew DuBois's challenging question: "Whither now and why?" ([1930] 1973). It was during this historical moment that I approached Chomsky's work, keenly attuned to *his* personal history as a dues–paying linguist–intellectual who had supported student activist struggles in the 1960s, who had campaigned vigorously against the Vietnam war, who had unceasingly challenged Western imperialism on many fronts, and who had helped rip the covers off American intelligence operations against the Black Panthers and other social progressives (Chomsky, 1975).

Read on one level, the work *appears* to disavow the connection between linguistics (and the human sciences in general) and politics. This is, after all, the standard line among American academics. However, above and beyond his brilliance, Chomsky is also a clever kind of fellow. The *reality* is that *Language and Responsibility* is the product of an alienated white American intellectual assuming the posture of contradiction for maximum rhetorical effect. As a controlling strategy for the work, it is akin to the high art of Signification in the Black Tradition (e.g., Smitherman, [1977] (1986); Mitchell-Kernan, 1969) and serves to exemplify, in the field of linguistics, writer–critic Harris's point that "the greater the degree of alienation, the more likely is the white intellectual to identify with and even assume the perspective and modality of blacks" (personal communication). Functioning like the tricksters and signifiers in the Black Tradition, Chomsky employs the rhetorical strategy of figuring and configuring, saying one thing but meaning and doing another. It is Signification of the highest order. This rhetorical posture allows him to demystify science and academic scholarship, to demonstrate the power of social and political action over empty rhetorical platitudes, and to throw down, rhetorically "trope-a-doping"[3] critics, rivals, and various and sundry detractors.

The work is the result of a series of conversational-style interviews of Noam Chomsky conducted by French linguist Mitsou Ronat in January of 1976. The resulting tape-recorded dialogs, with Chomsky speaking in English, Ronat in French, were first published in French in 1977. The English version, published in 1979, thus represents a retranslation of Chomsky into English – without benefit of the original tapes, which were no longer available. Nonetheless, we can be assured of the work's authenticity regarding Chomsky's views since he aided Viertel in the reconstruction of the text, elaborating, modifying, and even making substantive changes.

There are nine chapters, divided into two sections. Part I, Linguistics and Politics, deals with social and ideological issues. Part II, Generative Grammar, focuses on the evolution of generative grammar within the context of the "scientific revolution" of our era and serves to update Chomsky's "Standard Theory." As an explanatory theory with observational adequacy, Chomsky's formulation of generative grammar, with its continuing refinements and modifications, is, by now, almost a household word among scholars. So, too, is his powerfully correct opposition to the reconstruction of the human sciences on the basis of technological concepts, his attacks on Skinner and company, and his analysis of the limits of empiricism, in particular his demonstration of how empiricism created an intellectual and ideological climate favorable to racism and cultural and linguistic hegemony. Thus, there is little having to do with linguistics, *per se*, or Chomsky's antibehaviorist leadership not already well-known and dealt with more fully and in greater depth elsewhere (for instance, Chomsky, 1959, 1972, 1979).

What *is* fascinating and intriguing is the historical portrait of Chomsky's developing intellectual consciousness. As a Harvard student in the early 1950s, he found himself struggling against "behaviorist concepts of human nature" because of their "link to potentially quite dangerous political currents." Yet he remained trapped in the paradigm of descriptive linguistics: "I was completely schizophrenic at that time. I still thought that the approach of American structural linguistics was essentially right." If the discovery procedures of structuralism did not work, he felt that "the mistake was mine, due to wrong formulations." What emerges is a picture of Chomsky continuing to attempt to fix up a linguistic paradigm which did not accord with his intuition nor with the observable facts. He even disagreed with his friend Morris Halle, the only one of Chomsky's contemporaries opposing American structuralism and thus, encouraging Chomsky's generative grammar. Then finally, and quite suddenly and dramatically, "aided by a bout of seasickness" – well, the Lord do work in mysterious ways, and wonders do perform! – he became convinced that it was time for a new paradigm (pp. 128–31).

Still, as is the case with all challenges to existing scientific paradigms, the community of scholars rushes to the cause of the prevailing framework and rejects or ignores the interloper. Thus, the world took little note of what Ronat has titled "the birth of generative grammar," and the Standard Theory was nurtured at MIT because, having none of the problems of academic turf relative to the humanities and social sciences, it was "outside the American university system" (p. 134). The list of the midwives of this heretical birth and the child-care providers reads today like a who's who in generative and theoretical linguistics: in addition to Halle, Robert Lees – the first student in the graduate linguistics program, though he received his degree in engineering (he had written a review of Chomsky's *Syntactic Structures* for *Language* in 1957) – G. H. Matthews, Edward Klima, Fred Lukoff, Jerry Fodor, Jerry Katz, Paul Postal, and John Viertel, the translator of the present work.

In both Parts I and II, Ronat, critically aware of vying schools of thought within American linguistics, poses questions about sociolinguistics. Chomsky, with a curious broad stroke, dismisses, rather than discusses, sociolinguistics. Curious because his contribution is profoundly valuable and poses no rival to sociolinguistics as both perspectives are needed to form a unified, holistic view of language and human nature. While Chomsky's Cartesian formulations point us toward our linguistic and human commonalities, "socially constituted" formulations (e.g., Hymes, 1974) point us toward our linguistic and human differences. From the standpoint of a philosophy of science, Chomsky virtually acknowledges as much in discussing Marxist intellectuals (although he has some profound disagreements with them. To sociolinguists, though, he ain bout to concede nothin!). Commenting on the question of human nature in his discussion with Michel Foucault on Dutch television, Chomsky tells Ronat: " . . . we were climbing the same mountain, starting from opposite directions . . . scientific creativity depends on two facts: on the one hand, on an intrinsic property of mind, and on the other, on a combination of social and intellectual conditions. There is no question of choosing between these. In order to understand a scientific discovery, it is necessary to understand the interaction between these factors" (p. 75). Throughout, Chomsky employs the strategy of contradiction to say what he believes while simultaneously conceding nothing to what he perceives to be his opposition among linguists and intellectuals.

Chomsky's dismissal of sociolinguistics for its "theoretical pretensions," rather than a brutal attack, is more akin to what I would call a taunting "trope-a-dope" (following the literary analysis of Gates [1988b]) to bait sociolinguists into his rhetorical trap. The counter-strategy, of course, is not to be a gofuh. Two points should be made on the subject. First, the fruit of sociolinguistic labor in the educational and social progress of disenfranchised people and women speaks for itself and requires no defense (e.g., Hymes, 1956, 1961 on Amerindians; Labov 1970, 1972 on blacks; Peñalosa, 1972, 1980 on Chicanos; Kramarae 1974, 1981 and Lakoff 1975 on women; and most recently, the work of the friends of *King*, 1977–81).

Second, dismissing Bernstein (whose "restricted code" was used against many of the groups cited above to demonstrate their supposed linguistic and genetic inferiority) as a "reactionary" and his work as "hardly worth discussing as a specimen of the rational study of language" (p. 56), Chomsky points out that it hardly seems necessary to have to defend the language of the urban ghetto as a real language. Agreed. By implication, he is indicting not only the social order but also the intellectual activity of those working on behalf of the dispossessed. To raise up a question about, say, Black English as a linguistically legitimate language system is really to raise up a

question about the humanity of Black English speakers and by extension, black people generally. The key word here is "defend." All
too often, the scholarship and writing on Black English (as well as
other forms of language variation) have been conceptualized from
a defensive paradigm, a posture in reaction to, often even an
apologia, rather than a celebration and affirmation of the language
and humanity of those who are "linguistically diverse." There is a
lesson for socially responsible, committed linguist–intellectuals in all
of this. So, too, is there a lesson in Chomsky's final parting shot
at sociolinguistics, that questions of linguistic variability are "basically questions of *power*" (p. 191, emphasis his).

As Chomsky whips along, rapidly slaying generative semantics
and sociolinguistics in one fell swoop, Ronat, sharply attuned to
the schisms in American intellectual life and culture, is ever on the
case, prodding and posing in various forms the fundamental question of the relationship between intellectual work and social
responsibility. At one point, the question takes the form of whether
the idealization of language is legitimate; at another, it takes the
form of a scientific distinction between a language and a dialect (an
issue also raised in discussions of *King*; see, for example, Smitherman,
1981a), and the relationships among linguistic theory, multilingualism, and national development. Perhaps the question is most
succinctly put when Ronat asks: " . . . there are many divergences
over the definition given to the activity of linguists. The analyses,
the theories they present, are these simply intellectual games or do
they seek to establish the truth (even partially) of an objective law
imposed upon something real?" (p. 118). Chomsky's response
throughout these conversations emphasizes the significance of theoretical formulations and linguistic activity that describe and express
a "psychological reality" rather than the work of simply compiling
taxonomies.

It has always been clear to me that his psychological reality is
not a metaphysical idealist abstraction but is manifest in the material,
concrete world. We are all trapped in our own historical moment
and wish to understand that; to the extent that general laws of
"language and mind" help with that effort, we should gladly embrace
them. Still, it is understandable that there is no interest in studying
the general or universal purely for the sake of the general/universal.
Yet there is a dialectical relationship between the general and the
particular – and between speech and language. While each of us
is imbedded in the present moment, the historical past is simultaneously imbedded in us. Both human differences and human
commonalities are factors in the equation of the new man/woman.
While dialects are "interesting" (both in and of themselves and for

what they reveal about mankind), language is equally "interesting." Dialects vary and will continue to do so, responding to changing material conditions. But *language*, that is, the "bioprogram language" (Bickerton 1981), the *language* of *Cartesian linguistics* (Chomsky 1966), remains the fullest embodiment of human essence, transcending cultural boundaries and space–time dimensions.

Using ages-old "rules" to arrive at the "representations" of the other, one can, in essence, read another's mind. I have always felt that Chomsky was interested in language as a doorway to the human mind and subsequently to unlocking the keys to the riddle of the universe. And I continue to think that he, and we, are − or should be − after bigger game than transformational deletions − or copula deletions, for that matter.

That the Transformational–Generative (TG) school has trivialized a profoundly complex phonomenon that is the foundationstone of human nature, and the Standard Theory has degenerated into a focus on low-level, inconsequential − and yes, uninteresting − problems of grammatical representation is a commentary on the vulgarization of the Standard Theory and the provincialism and intellectual pretensions of American academics (though they bees callin theyselves "scholars"). DuBois ([1930] 1973) said that the "object of education was not to make men carpenters but to make carpenters men."[4] But what is the ideal man/woman? On what basis do we construct this ideal? The vision must not be constrained by the here and now, but by a search for universal truths and timeless moral laws. Chomsky pushes us toward this vision by forcing an examination of the essence of human nature through language. Thus, as a linguist in the TG school, he remains in a class by himself precisely because he has kept his eye on the target, which is the "question whether distinct cognitive structures can be identified, which interact in the real use of language and linguistic judgments, the grammatical system being one of these" (p. 153), because at bottom, "the linguist is interested in the real nature of human beings" (p. 48).

It is clear, in Chomsky's practice, if not expressly articulated in his linguistic theory, that he sees a clear obligation of intellectuals to work in the sociopolitical vineyards (see, for example, his most recent work, *Towards a New Cold War*, 1982). It is legitimate, then, for Ronat to keep pressing Chomsky for his ideological line about the sociopolitical relevance of linguistics and the social responsibility of linguists, academics, and intellectuals. And Chomsky does have a position, but it is articulated in his own wily, signifyin way. (Why, my man Noam, you old sly fox, are you attempting to be the Ishmael Reed of linguistics?)

Rightly lambasting "state capitalist intellectuals" for their rampant "ideological uniformity," Chomsky contends that critical analysis in the ideological arena is a "fairly straightforward matter." He argues that he is not special in this regard and that no high level academic training is necessary to unveil the "modes of distortion" in the arena of political activity – just "Cartesian common sense, which is quite evenly distributed . . ." (I mean!!!)

While the operation of ideology is often inaccessible to consciousness, as Ronat correctly asserts, and while there is an intricate interrelationship between consciousness, ideology, and material conditions, through Chomsky we can see that language provides an avenue of escape from the deterministic box. Whether one agrees that ideology is revealed in language (e.g., Vološinov [1929] 1973) or with the position that language is outside both base and superstructures (e.g., Stalin, 1951), undeniably, scrutiny of linguistic form enables one to uncover contradictions between appearance and reality. Such a contradiction can be found, for example, in the *Washington Post*'s use of "we as a people" in reference to America's role in Vietnam, which Chomsky righteously challenges: "Was it 'we as a people' who decided to conduct the war . . . ?" (p. 40) As a linguist engaged in political activity, Chomsky is his own example, exposing the deep meaning of the language and discourse of America's liberal intelligentsia and its liberal press.

The educator Hall once remarked, "for one who knows linguistics, language is a marked deck of cards" (personal communication). Agreed. Yet Chomsky is quick to assert that people who are not linguists, academics, or professionals can take control of their lives; that they must not allow themselves to be awed by the intelligentsia and "experts"; that they need no special scientific or technical training to be able to "remove the masks" (p. 8) – including those that are linguistic and rhetorical – that disguise social reality. On one level, then, Chomsky is addressing the "ordinary citizen concerned with understanding social reality" (p. 8). On another level, he is addressing the academic intellectuals who have not extricated themselves from the capitalist ideological trap. In their elitism, they pass themselves off as experts on social issues and on the problems of "the people." But in fact, they have been socialized to accept the contradictions of their petit-bourgeois status such that they fail to present the "logical possibility of a third position" and thus "fix the limits of possible thought" (p. 36–8).

Ultimately, Chomsky forces us to confront the glaring contradiction between show and tell: Unlike him, most American academics and intellectuals – including linguists and sociolinguists – fail to take an active part in the lifeblood of the sociopolitical arena, confining themselves to ivory – or in the case of blacks, ebony – towers. Working the conjuration of Signification to the max, *Language and Responsibility* thus propels us toward the precipice of truth.

Part two

LANGUAGE AND THE EDUCATION OF AFRICAN AMERICANS

EDUCATION IS A household word in the African American community. Blacks continue to believe in and promote schooling (yes, even Blacks from the working and underclass). However, schools don't always return the favor, particularly in this post-modern era. It is well known these days, but little talked about openly, that for many, if not most, urban Black kids, the longer they stay in school, the farther behind they get. During the 1997 Congressional hearings on Ebonics, data were presented demonstrating this fact in one of the – if not *the* – most critical basic skill: reading. Students who lack this skill are seriously hampered in their education. At age nine, African American students are 27 points behind in reading. At age seventeen, they are 37 points behind in reading.

Language is the foundationstone of education and the medium of instruction in all subjects and disciplines throughout schooling. It is critical that teachers have an understanding of and appreciation for the language students bring to school. The motivation for the first article in this section, "English Teacher, Why You Be Doing the Thangs You Don't Do?" stemmed from observations of teaching practices across the country, particularly those classrooms that are full of Black Language speakers. In these classrooms, there is emphasis on surface correctness, but little or no emphasis on critical thinking and critical literacy and language use. "English Teacher . . ." sought to use Black Language, as Toni Morrison would put it years later, ". . . like a preacher's [language]: to make you stand up out of your seat, make you lose yourself and hear yourself" (1981). The essay was written for the *English Journal* and initially addressed teachers of middle/junior and high-school students. However, as I became more familiar with what was happening in college and university English classrooms, I began to realize that inadequate language and literacy instruction for African American students was pervasive throughout the entire educational system. I then revised the essay to include a scenario I had observed in a college writing course.

A major problem in this mis-education of Black Language speakers is the education of English professionals (at the Bachelor's as well as the Ph.D. level). Most are trained in literature and have insufficient knowledge about language and language diversity. Thus, they hold some of the same myths and misconceptions about languages and dialects – and Ebonics – that we find among the lay public. That was the situation when "English Teacher" was published back in 1972. Today, some institutions of higher education include language and language diversity courses in the curricular training of English professionals. However, old in-grained attitudes and myths die hard, and unfortunately, knowing the right thing doesn't always translate into doing the right thing.

Not surprising, then, that back in 1977, a group of parents took the Ann Arbor School District to court. Reading was the major concern of these parents. The fact that their kids had spent several years at the Martin Luther King, Jr. Elementary School (located in the upscale college town of Ann Arbor, Michigan), but still could not read defied all logic. And it made these single-parent Black females, some on welfare, mad enough to take their case to Federal court. The literacy issue was overshadowed by the language issue in the case. Although Black English was there in the case from the Git-Go, it ended up taking center stage because of technicalities that forced us to shift our legal strategy. Federal legislation addresses the issue of "language barriers" in the educational process, but not reading. Ann Arbor's response to the different language system the Green Road housing project kids brought to King School had taken the form of labeling them "learning disabled." But the parents weren't having it. "'What Go Round Come Round:' *King* in Perspective," written a few months after Judge Charles Joiner's decision in the parents' favor, chronicles the case from the summer of 1977, when the lawsuit was filed, through July of 1979, when the final decision was issued. This essay also analyzes the language issue and situates it within the context of the education of Black children and youth. It was published in the *Harvard Educational Review*, in a special 1981 issue, entitled "Education as Transformation: Identity, Change, and Development." (An earlier, slightly different version of this essay was published as the introduction to the book I edited, *Black English and the Education of Black Children and Youth: Proceedings of the National Invitational Symposium on the*

King *Decision*. This book, published in 1981 by what was then the Center for Black Studies at Wayne State University in Detroit, is a collection of papers, reports, and other proceedings from the national conference I convened in February 1980, a few months after Judge Joiner's ruling in the court case.)

In spite of the *King* case, and despite some advances over the years, we still ain home free, as I argue in "Ebonics, *King*, and Oakland: Some Folk Don't Believe Fat Meat is Greasy." This essay was first published in the *Journal of English Linguistics* in June of 1998. The version included here has been substantially revised for this book. The essay points to the historical continuity of the "national mania for correctness," from the 1917 "Better Speech Week" campaign through *King* and the Ebonics controversy today. It focuses on the relationship between language and education, presents data from two experimental research studies involving Black students, and seeks to demonstrate how language is integral to the African American struggle for empowerment through education, a continuing motif in the Black Experience. Drawing on the wisdom of the Elders in the Black Intellectual Tradition, "Ebonics, *King*, and Oakland" concludes with a four-point platform for the education of African American youth.

Continuing to explore the link between language and education, the last essay, "The Blacker the Berry, the Sweeter the Juice," rounds out this section on a hopeful note. The essay collapses two research articles based on my study of national writing samples from Black 17-year-old students over a twenty-year time frame (1969–88/89). A total of 2,764 essays, written for the National Assessment of Educational Progress, were analyzed to assess the status of written literacy in Black youth, to ascertain whether the use of Ebonics in their writing had increased or decreased over time, and to determine what role, if any, Ebonics played in the way their writing was scored by teachers. The current Ebonics controversy notwithstanding, this essay concludes that progress has been made over the past twenty years, both in terms of a higher quality of Black student writing and in terms of more pedagogically sound teacher ratings of this writing. For their part, the national teacher-raters of the essays demonstrate, over twenty years, an increased sensitivity to matters of language diversity and an awareness of the need for critical thinking in African American youth. For instance, it has become more difficult to get a high score on an essay that uses standard American English grammar but doesn't say anything, or says it in a disorganized, incoherent style. For their part, Black youth at the school-leaving age (i.e., 17 years old) exhibit a higher quality of writing over the years, and in one period –

1969 to 1979 – their writing improved twice as much as that of whites. However, the writing scores of Black students still are not on par with those of their white counterparts. So English teachers, yall been doin some thangs right, but we ain reached the promised land yet! Lastly, this study indicates that Black students may be learning how to tap into the dynamic richness of Black Rhetorical Discourse as a resource to aid them in the production of high quality writing – hence "the blacker the berry, the sweeter the juice."

7

LET ME SAY right from the bell, this piece is not to be taken as an indictment of ALL English teachers in inner-city Black schools, for there are, to be sure, a few brave, enlightened souls who are doing an excellent job in the ghetto. To them, I say: just keep on keepin' on. But to those others, that whole heap of English teachers who be castigating Black students for using a "nonstandard" dialect – I got to say: the question in the title is directed to you, and if the shoe fit, put it on.

In all fairness, I suppose, one must credit many such correctionist English teachers for the misguided notion that they are readying Black students for the world (read: white America). The rationale is that this world is one in which Black kids must master the prestige dialect if they are to partake of that socioeconomic mobility for which America is world renowned – an argument which linguist James Sledd, for one, has completely devastated.[2] And so the student who submits a paper with frequent "I be's" and multiple negatives is forced to "correct," write and rewrite towards the end of achieving a grammatically flawless piece. In this painstaking and almost always useless and insignificant process, little else is stressed. (Besides, as the overworked, underpaid English teacher knows only too well, it's a lot simpler and easier to correct the Black English of a theme than to read

ENGLISH TEACHER, WHY YOU BE DOING THE THANGS YOU DON'T DO? [1972]

& then it was hip – it was hip
to walk, talk & act a certain
    neighborhoodway,
we wore 24 hr sunglasses & called our
    woman *baby*, our woman,
we wished her something else,
& she became that wish.
she developed into what we wanted,
she not only reflected *her*, but reflected
    us,
was a mirror of our death-desires.
we failed to protect or respect her
& no one else would,
& we didn't understand, we didn't
    understand.
why,
she be doing the things she don't do.[1]

and really analyze that theme.) As a daughter of the Black ghetto myself, don't seem like it's no reason the teacher be doing none of that correctin' mess. (After all, what do you want – good grammar or good sense?) I contend that the size of the above-mentioned shoe fully exceeds the magnitude of the problem, for language power is a function not of one's dialect but of larger linguistic structures skillfully and effectively employed. In the following dialog,[3] Langston Hughes's character, Jesse B. Simple, that swingin' Black folk hero, combines Black English with linguistic wit and forceful repartee both to win his woman and to demonstrate to us how trivial the "dialect problem" actually is.

SIMPLE   What're you doing with all those timetables and travel books, baby?

JOYCE   Just in case we ever should get married, maybe I'm picking out a place to spend our honeymoon – Niagara Falls, the Grand Canyon, Plymouth Rock . . .

SIMPLE   I don't want to spend no honeymoon on no rock. These books is pretty, but, baby, we ain't ready to travel yet.

JOYCE   We can dream, can't we?

SIMPLE   Niagara Falls makes a mighty lot of noise falling down. I likes to sleep on holidays.

JOYCE   Oh, Jess! Then how about the far West? Were you ever at the Grand Canyon?

SIMPLE   I were. Fact is, I was also at Niagara Falls, after I were at Grand Canyon.

JOYCE   I do not wish to criticize your grammar, Mr. Simple, but as long as you have been around New York, I wonder why you continue to say, I were, and at other times, I was?

SIMPLE   Because sometimes I were, and sometimes I was, baby. I was at Niagara Falls and I were at the Grand Canyon – since that were in the far distant past when I were a coachboy on the Santa Fe. I was more recently at Niagara Falls.

JOYCE   I see. But you never were "I were"! There is no "I were." In the past tense, there is only "I was." The verb *to be* is declined, "I am, I was, I have been."

SIMPLE   Joyce, baby, don't be so touchous about it. Do you want me to talk like Edward R. Murrow?

JOYCE   No! But when we go to formals I hate to hear you saying, for example, "I taken" instead of "I took." Why do colored people say, "I taken," so much?

SIMPLE   Because we are taken – taken until we are undertaken, and, Joyce, baby, funerals is high!

JOYCE	Funerals are high.
SIMPLE	Joyce, what difference do it make?
JOYCE	Jess! What difference does it make? Does is correct English.
SIMPLE	And do ain't?
JOYCE	Isn't — not ain't.
SIMPLE	Woman, don't tell me *ain't* ain't in the dictionary.
JOYCE	But it ain't — I mean — it isn't correct.
SIMPLE	Joyce, I gives less than a small damn! What if it aren't?

(*In his excitement he attempts to sit down, but leaps up as soon as his seat touches the chair*)

JOYCE	You say what if things aren't. You give less than a damn. Well, I'm tired of a man who gives less than a damn about "What if things aren't." I'm tired! Tired! You hear me? Tired! I have never known any one man so long without having some kind of action out of him. You have not even formally proposed to me, let alone writing my father for my hand.
SIMPLE	I did not know I had to write your old man for your hand.
JOYCE	My father, Jess, not my old man. And don't let it be too long. After all, I might meet some other man.
SIMPLE	You better not meet no other man. You better not! Do and I will marry you right now this June in spite of my first wife, bigamy, your old man — I mean your father. Joyce, don't you know I am not to be trifled with? I'm Jesse B. Simple.
JOYCE	I know who you are. Now, just sit down and let's spend a nice Sunday evening conversing, heh?
SIMPLE	(*Sits down, but it hurts him*) Ouch!
JOYCE	Oh, Sweety! Let me make you a nice cool drink. Lemonade?
SIMPLE	Yes, Joyce, lemonade. (JOYCE *exits. Suddenly* SIMPLE *realizes what he has agreed to drink and cries in despair*) Lemonade! (*He sits dejected until* JOYCE *returns*) Baby, you ain't mad with me, is you? (JOYCE *smiles and shakes her head no*) Because I know you know what I mean when I say, "I is" — or "I are" or "was" or whatever it be. Listen, Joyce, honey please. (*He sings*)

> When I say "I am" believe me.
> When I say "I is" believe me, too —
> Because I were, and was, and I *is*,
> Deep in love with you.
> Damn if I ain't![4]

Simple's message and its many ramifications seem to have been heeded in suburbia at least, for in recent years the trend in English teaching in white middle-class schools has been away from grammatical overkill and toward emphasis on critical thinking, creativity, analytical processes, and the like. (Yes, I know there are still some linguistic purists hovering about in such schools, but the number is dwindling, and I'm gon give the rest of you your propers.) Yet when it comes to the Black English classroom, English teachers are working out of the same old traditional bag of eradicationist (attempting to obliterate Black English) or, more recently, bidialectalist (attempting to teach Black students the skill and necessity of being versatile in both they dialect and "the Man's"). Of course, when you get right down to the nitty-gritty, it ain't no essential difference between the two inasmuch as both bees operating on a difference equals deficit model; the latter is simply more sneaky about making this assertion. (Dig it: white middle-class kids don't have to be "versatile" in Black English.) Bees that as it may, there is no need to reiterate the many sociopsychological/pedagogical arguments against either of these approaches. As I mentioned earlier, this has already been done by Sledd – beyond, I think, anyone's power to "add or detract." (Anyway, Black folks is always in the position of *reacting* rather than *acting*.) Rather, I wish to propose a Five-Point Program for teaching English in the inner-city – a program based on the *real* needs of the Black ghetto student. Over and beyond girding this student to deal with racism – an established given in the American context – these needs have to do with initiating Black students into a confusing, turbulent society of power politics and nearly incredible complexity.

I Examination of alternative lifestyles

It is now a cliché to speak of the identity crisis of contemporary Americans, yet for Black youth particularly, the crisis is very real since in many significant dimensions, Black culture is diametrically opposed to white middle-class culture. Witness, for example, the ghetto culture's hair styles, mannerisms, patterns of dress, dance, etc. (many of which, of course, have been adopted by white youth as a mark of rebellion). On a larger scale, note the conflict between value systems wherein the ghetto's pimps, hustlers, and sundry other brothers into an "illegit" thang are idealized and respected. The Black youth must decide is he gon square up and join the mainstream or get super-hip and remain in the street thang?

A for instance. In my study of 28,000 words of data collected from a group of Black junior high students, one young man wrote a letter glorifying the status of pimp, maintaining that the pimp's life was a "life of ease. All you have to do is eat and sleep." Finding the statement and the student's attitude "horrendous," the teacher made the student rewrite the letter. Yet any pimp that you can get into a deep and truthful rap with, as well as writers such as Baldwin, Brown, or Iceberg Slim (author of *Pimp*), will all attest to the difficulties and anxieties of this way of life. Thus this young brother's analysis was not so much "offensive" as grossly oversimplified. Here, then, would have been a good place for the English teacher to step in, not as legislator of morality or proponent of *either* status quo but as a sort of intellectual gadfly, prodding the student to treat and research this complex lifestyle (and others as well) in a sophisticated and deeply analytical manner.

II Emphasis on reading

The literature on Black "culturally deprived" students is shot through with statistical information on the reading disabilities of Black ghetto youth. Of the students from whom the aforementioned data were gathered, only one was reading on grade level. In fact, though "reading problems of the disadvantaged" is now a cliché in educational circles, no one can deny the excruciating reality of the problem. While, admittedly, English teachers are not trained remedial reading specialists, I have seen inexperienced teachers do some rather effective things with, for instance, an SRA kit. In point of fact, the gravity of the literacy problem is such that I feel virtually ANY activity geared in this direction is preferable to frittering away valuable classroom time on "correct" usage drills or rewriting the "mistakes" on a composition.

III Emphasis on oral work

McLuhan has alerted us to the disappearance of our print-oriented culture (though, with reference to II above, obviously we'll always need functional literacy), and anyone who has carefully observed people in the world of work, professional or otherwise, has noticed the paucity of writing jobs. Let's face it: writers and English majors aside, once students leave academia, they probably ain't gon never write another theme. Furthermore, Black culture is an oral culture, and here's where the rappin' ability of our students enters in. One eighth-grade student wrote the following theme about the "civil disturbance" of Detroit '67:

> I don't like riots because they destroy things that have taken people life times to build. It leaves some homeless without food, and cause man thier good health or their lives.

In a taped interview with this student, he responded to the question about the riots by not only filling in more details but also using several sophisticated words and linguistic structures that did not appear in the theme.

> Everybody stole them something. Everybody was looting. Everybody was looting last year. I seen a boy get – a policeman – get shot in a pawn shop. But he – the three boys – broke in the pawn shop and climbed down through the skylight. So the police came and they knew the police was gon shoot 'em if they caught 'em. So they waited, they waited for one of 'em to come down the skylight, and they took them rifles and all three of them opened up on them. Dead on hits. They hit him with so much force, he just popped out that chimney dead. He just popped out that skylight dead. They ain't – they just – they hit him with a barrage of bullets and rifles.

Other researchers, for example, Kochman[5] and Labov,[6] have described similar findings, attesting to the high verbal ability of Black students in they own dialect. This strength, coupled with the fact that the future will demand far more speaking than writing of our students, suggest that oral work should be substituted for much of the written work in the English classroom. This could be done through improvisational drama, panel discussions, debates, short speeches, etc.

IV Intensive study of language and culture and both social and regional dialects

What students need (and here I would say both Black and white students) is not models of correctness – they have their own anyway – but a broader understanding of the intricate connection between one's language and his cultural experience, combined with insight into the political nature and social stratification of American dialects. They need to see how language is not something decreed from on High but an evolutionary dynamic, fluctuating according to the dictates of its users; those users of words, who, to paraphrase LeRoi Jones,[9] have the power to define reality; those dialect pace-setters, who in America happen to be white and middle class. It is axiomatic that if Black people were in power in this country, Black English would be the prestige idiom. This is a point which cannot be stressed too often, for frequently we find even Black students themselves with a negative image of they speech. They too have been

Figure 7.1   "Herb & Jamal cartoon", by Stephen Bentley

Source: Tribune Media Services

brainwashed about the "inherent and Absolute rightness" of white, middle-class dialect and do not realize that language can be/has been for Black people in America a tool of oppression. On the other hand, while the Black junior high students I interviewed all conceded that their speech was "wrong" according to school standards, none said that they would change their dialect nor that of their parents and peers. It is obvious, then, that only educational institutions – English teachers in particular – and the dominant culture, which, unfortunately, schools reflect rather than lead, make Black ghetto students feel that their language and experience are negative and inconsequential.

Of course, here too, as with my point on reading, I recognize that English teachers frequently are not trained in linguistics, but inservice programs and workshops could be one way of providing such vitally needed knowledge. (After all, we did it for the "new math.") In the meantime, there are several one-shot sort of language lessons that could be used. One idea would be to excerpt passages from a book like *Manchild in the Promised Land* (New American Library, 1965), particularly those in which Claude Brown, the "linguist," is at work – for instance, his explanation of the import of the Black use of the word "baby," or his comments about achieving gang status through his own rappin' ability (pp. 171–2, 79–80). Other ideas are suggested by Neil Postman and Charles Weingartner in *Teaching as a Subversive Activity* (Postman and Weingartner, 1969). For instance, they describe a classroom discussion in which the students come to understand the relative meaning of the word "right" in reference to language matters (pp. 70–5). Still another idea would be to combine language study with that of literature by letting your students dig on some of the new Black poetry, most of which is highly oral and written in the Black. I highly recommend super-bad Don Lee's *Don't Cry, Scream* (Detroit:

Broadside Press, 1969). There is a $5.00 very excellent tape that can be purchased from Broadside and used with the book.

V Emphasis on content and message, logical development, use of supporting details and examples, analysis and arrangement, style, specificity, variation of word choice, sentence structure, originality, etc.

I am referring here to the *real* components of rhetorical power. If we recognize rhetoric as the art of persuasion and the aim of composition, both oral and written, as communication of that art, we can readily see that we're talking about elements which have nothing to do with the English teacher's "mania for correctness." Audiences are moved by message and style of delivery, not correct spelling, lack of copula deletion, or the addition of the s-morpheme to third-person-singular-present-tense verbs. For instance, in the themes I analyzed, the students compared quite favorably with other writers of American English in terms of the ratio of adjectives to verbs – i.e., they used a significantly higher proportion of adjectives than verbs. Such a degree of modification and qualification is generally considered to make for a lively, clear, and precise style. Yet, on a word-variation analysis scale (i.e., measurement of the ratio of *different* adjectives to the total number of adjectives), the students' scores were disappointingly low by comparison to other writers. One student used the word "big" to denote largeness of size seven different times in a one-paragraph theme. Note also the fact that simple sentence patterns of the N V and N V N type occurred with heavy preponderance in most of the themes. Or consider the following theme, by one of the ninth-grade girls in the study, which is weak in many of the areas I mentioned under the heading of this section – though the mechanics are probably at least passable, even to the most rigorous correctionist. (I've highlighted certain phrases and sentences in italics that I'll comment on following the theme.)

[**Assignment**: If everybody knew what war was like, would we still have war?]

No! Some people just don't understand the *hardship* of a war. *Some* say lets keep fighting and we still are fighting. *More people are being killed and the poor are starving to death. To me war is a terrible thing to happen in any country. The causes of a war maybe very simple, one side* will disagree on a subject that is brought up. Like the poor should have money or better conditions to live in. The people should put in money for the poor. *The other side* may not agree. Instead they think *the government should do the work. This may cause a war. Little things* like this and more can destroy the world.

1   Nature or kinds of hardships not specified.
2   "Some say . . ." who?
3   "More people are being killed . . ." should follow the next
     statement since the former explains why the writer thinks war
     is a "terrible thing."
4   The statement beginning "the causes . . ." diverges off in another
     direction, although in the writer's mind, it may be related to
     what precedes; if so, the connection should have been clearly
     established.
5   "One side . . ." again lack of specificity; who or what category
     of people is being referred to here?; similarly with the phrase
     "the other side," no clear identification of opposing forces being
     alluded to here.
6   ". . . the government should do the work." Aren't the "people"
     the government? In the context of American politics, this is a
     profound question, not to be dismissed so lightly.
7   "This may cause a war." No example or when or how such
     a disagreement leads to war.
8   "Little things . . ." LITTLE?????!!!!

Do you see where I'm coming from with my Five-Point Package?
Fundamentally, I am talking about survival strategies that extend far
beyond the classroom. I am talking about the acquisition of those
tools essential for thinking through a situation and making decisions. I am talking about telling it like it T. I. IS so effectively and
persuasively that your audience will move in whatever direction
you desire. I am talking about teaching Black students that language
can be/is power, that they can/must develop that power, and that
ultimately in the struggle for Black liberation, the pen may be/is
mightier than the Molotov cocktail.

     In conclusion, lest it seem that I am taking to task only elemen-
tary and secondary school English teachers, consider the following
paper, written by a Black college freshman at Wayne State.

> [**Assignment**: Take a position on the war in Viet Nam
> and present arguments to defend your position.]
> I think the war in Viet Nam bad. Because we don't have no business over
> there. My brother friend been in the war, and he say it's hard and mean.
> I do not like war because it's bad. And so I don't think we have no busi-
> ness there. The reason the war in China is bad is that American boys is
> dying over there.

     The paper was returned to the student with only one comment:
"Correct your grammar and resubmit." Now, I ask you, English
teacher, why you be doing the thangs you don't do?

8

"WHAT GO ROUND COME ROUND": *KING* IN PERSPECTIVE [1981]

That teacher, he too mean. He be hollin at us and stuff.
Browny, he real little, he six, and he smart cause he know how to read ...

(Two of the plaintiff children in *King*)

THE CHILDREN ARE the future and hope of Black America. Therefore, it is fitting and proper to begin with the words of those children who brought the federal lawsuit in the nationally prominent but widely misunderstood case of *Martin Luther King Junior Elementary School Children* v. *Ann Arbor School District Board*. Although this case has come to be known as the "Black English Case," it was as much a case about black children as about Black English. As Judge Charles W. Joiner himself said: "It is a straightforward effort to require the court to intervene on the children's behalf to require the defendant School District Board to take appropriate action to teach them to read in the standard English of the school, the commercial world, the arts, science and professions. This action is a cry for judicial help in opening the doors to the establishment ... It is an action to keep another generation from becoming functionally illiterate" (Reference note 1).

The precedent established by the *King* decision represents the first test of the applicability of 1703(f), the language provision of the 1974 Equal Educational Opportunity Act, to Black English speakers. The case suggests new possibilities for educational and social policies in our struggle to save the children and develop future leadership. As the plaintiff children's chief consultant and expert witness during the two years of litigation. I shall provide an analysis of *King* and its implications for public policy and black community development in light of the stark reality of white racism and class contradictions among blacks in the United States.

Briefly, the background facts of the case are as follows. On 28 July 1977, Attorneys Gabe Kaimowitz and Kenneth Lewis of Michigan Legal Services filed suit in Eastern District Court located in Detroit, Michigan on behalf of fifteen black, economically deprived children residing in a low-income housing project on Green Road in Ann Arbor, Michigan. By the time the case came to trial in the summer of 1979, one family with four children had moved out of the school district, leaving eleven plaintiff children to litigate the case.

Initially, the plaintiffs' action was directed against the State of Michigan, the Ann Arbor School District, and officials at Martin Luther King Junior Elementary School, where black children comprised 13 percent of the school population of predominantly white, upper-class children. The allegation was that the defendants had failed to properly educate the children, who were thus in danger of becoming functionally illiterate. Specifically, plaintiffs charged that school officials had improperly placed the children in learning disability and speech pathology classes; that they had suspended, disciplined, and repeatedly retained the children at grade level without taking into account their social, economic, and cultural differences; and that they had failed to overcome language barriers preventing the children from learning standard English and learning to read. Actions taken by school officials, such as labeling the children "handicapped" and providing them with museum trips and other types of "cultural exposure," had failed to solve the academic problems of the children. The attitude of school officials was that the school had done its job, and that perhaps the children were uneducable. Yet close scrutiny of the academic records and psychological and speech–language evaluations failed to uncover any inherent limitation in the children's cognitive or language capacities. Further, the children's mothers were not persuaded that the academic and behavioral problems were due to slowness or mental retardation. The mothers' intuition was corroborated by professional judgment: their children were normal, intelligent kids who could learn if properly taught.

During the pre-trial stages of King, Judge Joiner tried to settle the case out of court, perhaps wary of the precedent that would be set. The "friends of King," as we, the children's advocates, came to call ourselves, prepared a reading program which the school officials rejected.[1] The Complaint was revised and amended several times to comply with Joiner's orders. For the course of future litigation in this area, the most critical revision was that all claims relative to economic, social, and cultural factors were dismissed. Joiner contended that there is no constitutional provision guaranteeing the right to

educational services to overcome unsatisfactory academic performance based on cultural, social, or economic background. To put it
more pointedly, the US Constitution can provide protection on the
basis of being black, but not on the basis of being poor.

In Judge Joiner's reasoning, it was necessary to focus the issues
in *King* on a decidedly narrow set of arguments. He dismissed all of
the plaintiffs' claims except one which forced the lawsuit to be tried
solely on 1703(f), which reads in part: "No state shall deny equal
educational opportunity to an individual on account of his or her
race, color, sex, or national origin, by . . . the failure to overcome
language barriers that impede equal participation by its students in its
instructional programs." Restricting the case to the issue of language
barriers, Joiner instructed plaintiffs to specify the nature of the
barriers, the lack of appropriate action to overcome them, and the
resulting denial of educational opportunity based on race. What
began as much more than a "Black English Case" would now focus
narrowly on language issues, and its outcome would depend on the
interpretation of a single sentence. For the plaintiffs and the friends
of *King*, it was clear that the trial would depend on expert testimony.
During the four-week trial, a bi-racial team[2] of expert witnesses in
the fields of psychology, education, linguistics, and reading testified
on behalf of the plaintiff children. The members of this team advised
the court of the extensive research in their respective fields, the
relationship of this knowledge to language barriers, and the obligation of schools to overcome these barriers.

Significantly, the defendant school board called no expert witnesses. Its attorneys simply relied on cross-examination of the plaintiffs' experts – a strategy consistent with the community posture of
self-righteousness. Ann Arbor prides itself on being a liberal community, and ranks among the country's top six public school systems
in academic achievement. It is also the home of the prestigious
University of Michigan and a multi-million dollar research program
that has included the study of race, language, teaching, and learning.
Indicative of its presumed enlightenment, Ann Arbor had decided
to promote racial and economic integration by opting in the 1960s
for scattered-site, low-income housing; poor blacks live in the same
neighborhood and attend the same schools as affluent whites and
blacks. The Ann Arbor defendants, reflecting a blame-the-victim
mythology, contended that their school district could not possibly
have failed to practice equal educational opportunity. Although
apparently confident about being vindicated, the school district
nevertheless employed the expensive Detroit law firm that had
successfully defended Detroit's suburbs before the US Supreme
Court in the *Bradley* v. *Milliken* school desegregation case.[3]

The trial proceedings established that the school district had failed to recognize the existence and legitimacy of the children's language, Black English. This failure of the teachers to recognize the language as legitimate and the corresponding negative attitudes toward the children's language led to negative expectations of the children which turned into self-fulfilling prophecies. One critical consequence was that the children were not being taught to read. On 12 July 1979, Judge Charles W. Joiner, a resident of Ann Arbor himself, issued what he later described as a "rather conservative" ruling: on the basis of failing to overcome language barriers, the Ann Arbor School District had violated the children's right to equal educational opportunity. Though Black English was not found to be a barrier *per se*, the institutional response to it was a barrier. In short, this ruling affirmed the obligation of school districts to educate black children and served to establish, within a legal framework, what has been well documented in academic scholarship: Black English is a systematic, rule-governed language system developed by black Americans as they struggled to combine the cultures of Africa and the United States. The district was given thirty days to devise a remedy.

The intent of the Equal Educational Opportunity Act (EEOA) is fairly clear. Initiated by President Nixon and passed by Congress at the height of the antibusing crusades, the EEOA shifted the policy emphasis from desegregation to quality education, and thus, in classic US fashion, attempted to reconcile the two contradictory forces of white racism and black aspirations. Therefore, much of the impetus behind the new legislation was related to racial issues. Because bilingual legislation had already been in existence for four years, however, the inclusion of 1703(f) within the EEOA raises the question of whom this obscure language provision was originally designed to protect. In fact, once Joiner had ruled this a language case, the Ann Arbor School District immediately filed a motion to dismiss on the grounds that 1703(f) did not apply to Black English speakers but only to those with foreign language backgrounds. Had this reasoning prevailed, of course, there would have been no case, since this was the only remaining claim of the plaintiffs that Joiner had allowed to stand. Emphasizing former HEW Secretary Elliott Richardson's interpretation that the statute protected the "legal right of any child [with] a language handicap" (Reference note 2), Joiner denied Ann Arbor's motion and issued the following ruling that represented our first victory in the case:

> The President's [Nixon's] list of persons covered by his proposal is only merely illustrative but could well include students whose "language barrier"

results from the use of some type of non-standard English ... The statutory language places no limitations on the character or source of the language barrier except that it must be serious enough to impede equal participation by ... students in ... instructional programs. Barring any more legislative guidance to the contrary, 1703(f) applies to language barriers of appropriate severity encountered by students who speak "Black English" as well as to language barriers encountered by students who speak German.

(Reference note 3)

The court's ruling in this regard meant that the case would not have to be based on the theoretical problem of differentiating a language from a dialect, nor consequently, on specifically determining whether Black English is a language or a dialect. Yet it was an issue that really was not − and, in fact, cannot be − dismissed, for the lack of theoretical clarity and intellectual consensus on the question presented serious difficulties in formulating our legal arguments and pedagogical remedies. Further, this confusion serves to account, in part, for the broad misinterpretations of *King* and the continuing ambivalence about Black English in the lay community.

In categorizing linguistic phenomena, a commonly applied test is that of mutual intelligibility. If speech data from Community A can be understood by Community B, and vice versa, with relative ease, requiring only slight adjustment on the part of each group of speakers, we can generally conclude that the two sets of speech data derive from the same source, that is, they are variations of the same language. Since there is an overlap between Africanized (Black) English and Euro-American (white/standard) English, mutual comprehension exists between blacks and whites, suggesting that Black English is a dialect. There are also areas of significant linguistic differentiation between the two speech communities, however, which can lead to lack of understanding and confusion, and can contribute to the conceptualization of Black English as a language. (See Dillard, 1972; Fasold and Shuy, 1970; Labov, 1971, 1972b; Smitherman, [1977] 1986, [1973] 1980, Valdman, 1977.)

A few examples will serve to more fully illuminate the nature of the language–dialect controversy. An often-cited characteristic of Black English, strikingly distinguishing it from standard white English, is the use of *be* as a full verb form, as in our opening quote: "He be hollin at us and stuff." This use of the verb "to be" derives from an aspectual verb system that is also found in many African languages, in Creole language forms of the Caribbean, in West African Pidgin English, and in the Gullah Creole spoken by blacks living on the Sea Islands along the southeastern seaboard of the United States. Its use conveys the speaker's meaning with reference to the qualitative character and distribution of an action over time. In the case of "He be hollin at us," the speaker indicates habitual action. The standard English verb system of past, present, and future tenses cannot accommodate this type of construction, while the Black English usage has captured all three tenses simultaneously. The closest standard English equivalent would be: he is always (or, constantly) hollering at us; he frequently (or often) hollers at us; or, he sometimes (or occasionally) hollers at us. Other examples of aspectual *be* collected from taped interviews with the plaintiff children are: *When school is out dis time, uhma be going to summer school; They be hitting on peoples;* and *I like the way he be psyching people out.* Black English also allows for sentences without any form of the copula, as in *He real little; He six; My momma name Annie; She my teacher;* and *They always fighting.*

In Black English, possession does not require the inflectional *z* (written as *s* preceded or followed by an apostrophe), but rather, is indicated by juxtaposition, as in these examples from the children: *She took him to his grandmother house; Popeye girlfriend;* and *My daddy name John.* Consider the potential for linguistic confusion to the non-Black English speaker that can result from the co-occurrence of two or more features of Black English within a single statement, as in the following item from the "Black Language Test" (Reference note 4): "*She the girl momma.*" Does this mean that she is the mother of the girl in question; that she is a very young girl who is the mother of a child; or, that she is a girl being pointed out to somebody's mother?

It is not only in phonology (sound) and morpho-syntax (grammar and structure) that critical differences between the black and white speech communities occur. Intelligibility can be affected by the lack of familiarity with the rhetorical and semantic strategies of Black English. For example, Muhammad Ali, hero and rapper *par excellence* to virtually the entire Black English-speaking community, nearly caused an international diplomatic disaster by using the rules of "talkin black" when he said: "There are two bad white men in the world, the Russian white man and the American white man. They are the two baddest men in the history of the world." Although the Tanzanians, to whom Ali was speaking at the time, apparently understood his meaning perfectly well, the standard white English-speaking world did not. He was castigated for using a term interpreted in the Websterian tradition as evil, wicked, negative, or not good. In the semantics of inversion used by the descendants of African slaves, however, "bad" can mean powerful, omnipotent, spiritually or physically tough, outstanding, wonderful, and, with emphasis, very good. For this feature of language use in Black English, Dalby (1969, 1972) cites linguistic parallels in Mandingo and several other African languages. His work remains the most rigorous treatment of the lexico-semantic system of black language from a diachronic perspective. (See also Dillard, 1977; and Major, 1970.)

I have deliberately chosen the example of Muhammad Ali because the contrasting black and white American interpretations of his verbal showmanship place the language–dialect controversy in bold relief. Although Ali's language appears to be English – and fairly standard English at that – the correct interpretation of his meaning requires the listener to have access to sociocultural data outside the realm of standard English. Ali represents the bad man of words in the black oral tradition. Through boastful talk, pungent rhymes, verbal repartee and clever "signifyin" (indirect language used to tease, admonish, or disparage), the rapper establishes himself or herself (but more generally himself) as a cultural hero solely on the basis of oral performance. Preachers, politicians, and other black leaders reflect this tradition. A clever rapper can talk himself out of a jam, and in sessions of ritual insult such as "playing the dozens" (talking about somebody's momma and/or other kinfolk), tension is relieved and fights often avoided. Those who are verbally adept at the art of "selling woof (wolf) tickets" (boasting) often do not have to prove anything by action. It is believed that the African concept of Nommo, word power, can indeed "psych your opponent out." Thus, when Ali engages in the art of black braggadocio, the louder and badder he talks, the more blacks applaud him, but the more whites, lacking cultural experience in this tradition, censure him. Ali symbolizes a cultural value manifested in black language behavior, suggesting that we are dealing with more than surface dialect differences.

The Black English language–dialect controversy reflects a fundamental contradiction within linguistics itself as to how language is to be defined, conceptualized, and studied. The classic dichotomy between *langue* and *parole* (loosely, speech and language) is evident in the differences between Chomskyian theoretical linguistics and Hymesian "socially constituted" linguistics. The Chomsky school (1966, 1972) abstracts language from social context and focuses on its structure – sound patterns, grammatical structure, and vocabulary. The Hymes school (1974) more broadly conceptualizes language within the framework of culture and society, and focuses on the use and users of language: their history, culture, values, world views, and social structure are considered basic to understanding a given language. The former is the more popular view of language and that taken by Judge Joiner when he demanded that we identify language barriers without reference to the children's cultural characteristics, which he deemed "irrelevant to a cause of action under the language barrier statute" (Reference note 5).

Elsewhere (Smitherman, 1980a), I detail the relationship of this general controversy in linguistics to study and research on Black English. The point is that the semantics within which one formulates a general theory of language can determine whether one views the issue as black language or as black dialect. If one considers only words, grammar, and sounds as the essence of language, then black speech data might tend to look more like a dialect of English. If one also considers the history and social rules that govern the use, production, and interpretation of the words, grammar, and sounds, then black speech data more nearly resemble a different language. Applying this to *King*, if Black English is a dialect, then the language barriers are mere surface differences that do not impede communication between teacher and student, nor between student and material written in standard English. If the barriers are not in the language *per se*, we must look elsewhere for impediments to the children's access to equal educational opportunity. In this case they were found in attitudes of teachers and other school personnel toward language. On the other hand, if we are dealing with a language, then the barriers reside not only in attitudes, but also in actual linguistic interferences that hamper communication. Since linguistics cannot offer the definitive word on language–dialect differentiation, it ultimately comes down to who has the power to define; or as Max Weinreich once put it, the difference between a language and a dialect is who's got the army (1931).

With the *King* case clearly, if narrowly, focused on the language issue, Joiner outlined four areas to be covered in our final amended complaint. We were to identify the language barriers confronting the plaintiff children, specify how these barriers had impeded the equal participation of the children in the instructional program of King School, set forth the appropriate action that defendants had allegedly failed to take, and identify the connection between the defendants' failure to take appropriate action and the race of the plaintiff children.

The several versions of the complaint had consistently highlighted structural and nonstructural interference phenomena as constituting the basis of the language barriers confronting the plaintiff children at King School. These, we argued, represented essentially a languages-in-contact interaction (Weinreich, 1963). Structural interferences derive from the structural differences between two languages – a mismatch of linguistic structures on the levels of phonology, lexico-semantics, and/or morpho-syntax. Nonstructural interference phenomena refer to differing attitudes and conflicting values about the two speech systems and the individuals who use them. The analysis of Muhammad Ali's speaking style illustrates both structural and nonstructural interference phenomena in operation. These phenomena are actually inextricable, though they are often expressed as a dichotomy to create an analytically convenient, if artificial, schema that readily lends itself to empiricism.

Because the language–dialect conflict remains unresolved, there is no consensus among language scholars as to whether there are both structural and nonstructural interferences between Black and standard/white English ("What go round come round"). Some black psychologists (Simpkins, 1976; Simpkins, Holt, and Simpkins, 1976; Williams, 1972; Williams, Rivers, and Brantley, 1975; Wilson, 1971) contend that the points of mismatch between standard and Black English constitute cognitive barriers to meaning for Black English-speaking children; that is, they have to translate standard English input data. Such mismatches seem to occur on the larger level of rhetorical patterning and discourse rather than in being simple points of interference, as suggested in the contrast between *He look for me last night* and "He looked for me last night." This is not the cognitive–linguistic deficit argument espoused by Deutsch (1963), Bereiter and Engelmann (1966), and others, but a postulation that the two different speech communities employ differing thought patterns and conceptions of reality and that these differences are reflected in different styles of discourse. Cooper (Reference note 6), for example, suggests that standard English speakers employ a more impersonal style with greater distance from the material of their discourse.

Although the evidence is not definitive, the best available data and expert judgment, particularly from black psychologists, seem to suggest that Black English speakers have language-based problems, and only those who master code-switching make it through the educational system successfully. With inconclusive research data at this point, coupled with the inadequacy of current language models to account for differences in discourse structure, the friends of *King* were unsuccessful in persuading the court that structural linguistic barriers existed. Although Joiner conceded that "there was initially a type of language difference," he reasoned that "it did not pose a communication obstruction" in teacher–student interaction (Reference note 1).

Research on sociolinguistics in the education process has been most fruitful and convincing in uncovering underlying attitudes about language. Specifying the nature of these nonstructural barriers proved to be our most powerful legal strategy. In the educational context, negative linguistic attitudes are reflected in the institutional policies and practices that become educationally dysfunctional for Black English-speaking children. Research on language attitudes consistently indicates that teachers believe Black English-speaking youngsters are nonverbal and possess limited vocabularies. They are perceived to be slow learners or uneducable; their speech is unsystematic and needs constant correction and improvement (Esselman, 1977; Shuy and Fasold, 1973; Williams, 1972; Williams, Whitehead, and Miller, 1971). These beliefs, though linguistically untenable, are essentially those held about Black English speakers.

Myths and misconceptions about language and negative attitudes toward language diversity are fostered in the school and perpetuated in the general populace by the public school experience (Pooley, 1974). Schools and teachers are seen as guardians of the national tongue. Condemned as immoral, ignorant, and inferior are all those who depart from the idealized norm of standard English which, as Pooley's research (1969) so powerfully demonstrates, teachers themselves preach but do not practice. It was this type of mental set that led King School teachers to correct constantly, to the point of verbal badgering, some of the plaintiff children's speech, thereby causing them to become truly nonverbal; to exclude them from regular classes in order to take speech remediation for a nonexistent pathology; to give them remedial work since "that's the best they can do"; and to suspend them from class for trivial and inconsequential acts of so-called misbehavior.

The use, or rather misuse, of standardized tests is a prime example of institutional policy detrimental to the educational success of Black English-speaking children. Intelligence tests and other diagnostic and assessment tools used in the schools have been normed on white, middle-class, standard English speakers and are obviously linguistically and culturally biased against poor black children. For example, standard speech articulation and language assessment tests measure forms and distinction between *Ruth* and *roof*, which in Black English are pronounced the same. Examples of this feature of Black English in the speech data from the King School children include: *maf* ("math") work; *birfday* ("birthday"); *bof* ("both"). Another set of test items calls for the singular/plural distinction to be made by changing the verb form, as in the task requiring children to match pictures with the examiner's spoken sentences: "The cat is playing" vs. "The cats are playing." In Black English, each sentence would be expressed without the verb and without the morphemic indication of plural. Plurality is generally realized by context in Black English. Examples from the plaintiff children include "two captain," "a few cartoon," and "two year." In sum, what we were able to show is that these linguistically biased instruments of educational institutions cannot possibly validate the problems nor the promise of a Black English-speaking student (Bliss and Allen, 1978; Green, 1975; Taylor, 1971; Williams, 1972; Williams, Rivers, and Brantley, 1975).

This impressive array of social science research on attitudinal language barriers led the court to conclude that "if a barrier exists because of the language used by the children in this case, it exists . . . because in the process of attempting to teach the students how to speak standard English the students are made somehow to feel inferior and are thereby turned off from the learning process" (Reference note 1).

Since Black English is viewed so pejoratively by standard English-speaking teachers, it is not difficult to reconstruct the process whereby this language barrier impeded the educational success of the plaintiff children. King School teachers denied that the plaintiff children even spoke Black English, contending that "they talk like everybody else." In contradiction, however, were their own formal commentaries on the children's school records indicating the use of Black English forms, test data showing low verbal ability in standard English, and the taped samples of the children's speech, excerpts of which were cited in the final amended complaint and detailed during the trial. Because teachers did not even acknowledge the existence, much less the legitimacy, of the plaintiff children's language, they obviously failed to "take it into account" in teaching standard English. It is not, then, black language in and of itself that constitutes the barrier, but negative institutional policies and classroom practices relative to Black English that were, and are, key causes of black children's reading problems. Since reading is crucial to academic achievement in all school subjects, the inability to read at grade level prevents equal participation in the educational programs of the school.

What, then, was the appropriate action the defendant school board had failed to take? It had not instituted policies to assist King School teachers and personnel to handle the linguistic and educational needs of the plaintiff children. As Joiner indicated: "The court cannot find that the defendant School Board has taken steps (1) to help the teachers understand the problem; (2) to help provide them with knowledge about the children's use of a 'black English' language system; and (3) to suggest ways and means of using the knowledge in teaching the students to read" (Reference note 1).

In his *Opinion*, Joiner refers to the crucial data from social science research on effective schools for poor black children (Brookover and Beady, 1978; Edmonds, 1979; Weber, 1971;

Edmonds and Frederiksen, Reference note 7). This research has established that appropriate action by schools can result in educational achievement despite pupil characteristics. Educational climate is the critical variable, not the race or class of the children.

Finally, the relationship between the district's lack of appropriate action and race lies in the manner in which Black English has developed and is maintained as a unique speech system. The speech patterns of Black Americans developed from an African linguistic and cultural base which was transformed by their experience in the United States, and reinforced and sustained by racial oppression and segregation, on the one hand, and by the response to racism, in the form of ethnic solidarity, on the other. The institutionalization of racism in America, through both *de facto* and *de jure* mechanisms, has meant exclusion of blacks from participation in the dominant culture, and has resulted in the continuance of two separate societies and two distinct, if not entirely separate, languages.

Blacks, however, have been differentially affected by white racism, and that has created class distinctions within the black community. Differing degrees of competence in standard English is one way these distinctions are manifest. Not all black children suffer from language barriers. Indeed, at King, the only black children having great difficulty were those from the Green Road Housing Project, who were both black and poor. The other black children attending King were from middle-class, professional families. Though these middle-class children spoke Black English, they were also competent in standard English: they were skilled at code-switching and, hence, "bilingual." This is precisely the case among those blacks who have successfully negotiated the educational system and become middle class. Thus, it may be said that a black speaker's ability to code-switch is a behavioral manifestation of the interaction of race and class. Not being adequate code-switchers, the economically deprived plaintiff children experienced language-based problems in school. The language barriers for the Green Road children were thereby directly related to racial, as well as economic, discrimination, but Joiner had ruled out the latter as a consideration.

Put more succinctly, negative language attitudes are directed toward the "blackness" of Black English; the attitudes and the language itself are the consequences of the historical operations of racism in the United States. To the extent that the district failed to take appropriate action, such failure was connected to the race of the plaintiff children by virtue of their speaking Black English, and the barriers created are therefore directly related to race. This, in turn, obligates the district to take appropriate action under the Equal Educational Opportunity Act of 1974 to eliminate the discrimination. Such action would consist of an educational plan designed to help teachers identify Black English-speaking children and to help these children learn to read standard English.

The educational plan approved by Joiner, however, falls far short of the mark. As Attorney Kenneth Lewis (1980) noted, the plan "amounts to no more than yet another shot in the arm of teacher inservice programs [which] only travels halfway to a full solution to overcome language barriers impeding learning" (Lewis, Reference note 8). Clearly a teacher inservice program is desirable and needed to alter teacher attitudes toward Black English. Programs of this nature are not uncommon, particularly among school districts undergoing desegregation. Yet such programs are pitifully inadequate as a remedy to eliminate barriers to equal educational opportunity. Inservice training should simply be a component of a more comprehensive education remediation plan that would have as its central theme the teaching of reading and other communication skills. In sum, with no assessment of teacher behavior and actual classroom practice, the Ann Arbor approach is premised on the theory that benefits will accrue to the children after teachers are properly trained and thereby develop new attitudes. This remedy is too slow and too limited for the immediate educational crisis facing poor black youth in schools in the United States.

Based on the procedural strategy and the outcome of *King*, there are several additional approaches to the formulation of public policy that would address this crisis. First, judicial processes are critical in shaping educational policy and practice. Joiner was reluctant to tread these waters, and partly for that reason. Ann Arbor's education management of social institutions, the judiciary can promote the just and humane administration of large social bureaucracies that seem incapable of righting themselves. As the custodian and protector of values, the judiciary should be more involved, not less in social management. The public school, more so than any other institution, directly involves and affects every citizen of the United States. Education is everybody's business − including the judge's.

Second, we need a school effectiveness policy monitored and enforced by the courts and by appropriate citizens' bodies. Accountability must be demanded and delivered. Race and class cannot be used to justify miseducation. There is now an overwhelming body of data to demonstrate that, as Edmonds put it, "some schools work, and more can" (1979). Further, schools must be willing to adopt policies to overcome cultural and economic handicaps. This is a basis for future litigation since this claim was dismissed early on in

King. An argument could be made that culture and class are handicaps just as are physical infirmities. As Kaimowitz (1981) later put it, "Economic, social, and cultural factors, as well as the racial factors . . . and the language factor, must be taken into account."

Third, there should be a national moratorium on tests – standardized, employment, and other such assessment instruments. All evidence points to the cultural and linguistic biases of such tests. *King*, along with *Larry P.* v. *Riles* (1979), attests to the inadequacy of tests for evaluating and diagnosing black children. These rulings reinforce the call for such a moratorium, already issued by a number of professional and concerned citizens' groups.

Fourth, one outcome of Joiner's ruling was clearly to give legalistic legitimacy to a speech form spoken at times by 80–90 percent of the black community in the United States (Dillard, 1972; Smitherman, [1977] 1986). As a corollary to *King* and coincident with the goals of the Bilingual Education Act, we need a national public policy on language that asserts the legitimacy of languages and dialects other than standard English. As recommended by the Task Force on Language Policy and National Development (1981), a parallel tactic might be the development of awareness campaigns on Black English conducted in communities throughout the country.

Fifth, just as *King* reaffirms the viability and appropriateness of Black English, it also demands that students gain competence in standard English. As sociolinguists have maintained, effective speakers, writers, and readers have a highly developed level of communicative competence, that is, using language forms in socially appropriate contexts. Such competence allows one to manipulate a variety of speech forms, adapted to various audiences, media of communication, intention, and other social variables. There is not simply one form of standard English, but varieties of standard English – formal, informal, and colloquial. Similarly, there are varieties of Black English conducive to communicating in various social situations; black church language, proverbs, and street raps are examples. The recognition of Black English alongside standard English reinforces the call for a curriculum policy that would mandate and facilitate the teaching of communicative competence.

Sixth, because of the distortions of *King* perpetrated by the media, a potential weapon for black child advocacy has been grossly misunderstood. There were over three hundred newspaper and magazine articles and editorials (Bailey, 1981) along with numerous television and radio broadcasts. Yet media sensationalism prevented the issues from being clearly and fully delineated. There was a persistent attempt to discredit the plaintiffs' mothers and to exonerate the school district, and survey results indicate that many people received negative views of Black English from media coverage of *King* (Wilks, 1981). Black and other non-mainstream communities have traditionally been the victims of biased media coverage. Communities must rally to force the media to adhere to a standard of ethics and to establish media clearinghouses to counter the dissemination of inaccurate and distorted information (Task Force on Media and Information Dissemination, 1981).

Seventh, in some circles it has become fashionable to disavow the need for and utility of academic research. *King*, however, reaffirms the need for more, not less, research, of the kind that is responsive to the needs of black and other similarly dispossessed communities. Joiner also commented in his ruling on the value of research in informing the court (Reference note 1).

He noted the efficacy of the personal appearance and involvement of experts as advocates for the children. Research efforts of this kind should be encouraged, and blacks should be involved from the beginning. Creative ways must be found to encourage the allocation of funds for research on black children and youth. At the very least, blacks should vigorously monitor all such research to insure that only projects with policy implications for improving the education of black children and youth receive top priority.

To complete our analysis of *King*, I shall briefly examine the issues of black double-consciousness and class contradictions which were raised during the legal proceedings. "Double-consciousness" was first described by DuBois when he said:

> After the Egyptian and Indian, the Greek and Roman, the Teuton and Mongolian, the Negro is a sort of seventh son, born with a veil, and gifted with second-sight in this American world – a world which yields him no true self-consciousness, but only lets him see himself through the revelation of the other world. It is a peculiar sensation, this double-consciousness, this sense of always looking at one's self through the eyes of others ... One ever feels his twoness – an American, a Negro: two souls, two warring ideals in one dark body ... The history of the American Negro is the history of this strife – this longing to attain self-conscious manhood, to merge his double self into a better and truer self. In this merging, he wishes neither of the older selves to be lost.
>
> ([1903] 1961, p. 44)

With respect to black speech, I describe the manifestation of double-consciousness in language as "linguistic push–pull": the push toward Americanization of Black English counterbalanced by the pull of its Africanization (Smitherman, [1977] 1986). Both linguistic forms have been necessary for black survival in white America – standard English in attempts to gain access to the social and economic mainstream, Black English for community, solidarity, deception, and "puttin on ole massa." In "If Black English Isn't a Language, Then Tell Me What Is?," written shortly after the *King* trial, Baldwin (1979, p. 19) spoke eloquently of the role of Black English in the black experience: "There was a moment, in time, and in this place, when my brother, or my mother, or my father, or my sister, had to convey to me, for example, the danger in which I was standing from the white man standing just behind me, and to convey this with a speed, and in a language, that the white man could not possibly understand, and that, indeed, he cannot understand, until today."

With the beginnings of education for blacks in the late nineteenth century, linguistic push–pull became more pervasive in the Afro-American community. As Woodson ([1936] 1969) tells us, that education has always been away from – not toward – black culture, language, and community. Relating his critique specifically to language, Woodson ([1933] 1969) noted that: "In the study of language in school, pupils were made to scoff at the Negro dialect as some peculiar possession of the Negro which they should despise rather than directed to study the background of this language as a broken down African tongue – in short to understand their own linguistic history, which is certainly more important for them than the study of French Phonetics, or Historical Spanish Grammar" (p. 19).

This ambivalence about a dimension of blackness so close to personal identity explains the mixed reactions of blacks to *King*. Despite the decidedly forward advancement in black pride during the 1960s, there continues to be a lingering self-consciousness about the value of black culture and black language, even among those who speak it most frequently and who, in their more culturally chauvinistic moments, decry "nigguhs who talk all proper and white."

This linguistic push–pull also serves to account, in part, for the paucity of research on black speech by contemporary black scholars. Seeing the value and distinctive African character of Black English, white researchers have produced a sizable body of data attesting to the systematicity, use, and functions of Black English. Not all of this research has been to our betterment. In particular, blacks have decried treatments such as Folb's *Runnin' Down Some Lines* (1980) and Jackson's *Get Your Ass in the Water and Swim Like Me* (1974) because they focus on the sensational words and phrases in black speech. Black language is, after all, more than the "jive-ass" lingo of ghetto teenagers or the "pussy-coppin" raps of prisoners. The "more than" awaits the treatment of black scholars who can continue in the black intellectual tradition of Frederick Douglass, W. E. B. DuBois, Carter G. Woodson, and Lorenzo Turner. All wrote positively about — and in Turner's case, thoroughly analyzed — Black English long before post-1960 white scholars. In fact, Turner's *Africanisms in the Gullah Dialect* (1949) was quoted, while still in manuscript form, by white anthropologist Herskovits in *Myth of the Negro Past* (1941), surely one of the rare instances in which a white scholar acknowledges an intellectual debt to a black scholar.

Black teachers and educators are often more negative toward Black English-speaking children than are white educators. This reaction of educators and other black leaders to *King* serves to remind the black community that our class contradictions were never resolved in the 1960s era of black progress ("What go round come round"). Briefly, their fear is that black speech will prevent blacks from getting a share of the rapidly shrinking pie — a treat, as Baldwin indicated in his keynote speech to the National Invitational Symposium on Black English and the Education of Black Children and Youth, that is no longer in the power of the United States to give, as the Third World continues to cut off America's historically free and ready access to resources (Baldwin, 1981). Several editorials by noted black columnist Rowan (1979) are representative of the disturbing reaction of many members of the black middle class. Stating that *King* was one of the "silliest and potentially most destructive" cases to affect the education of black children, he argued that this approach would "consign millions of ghetto children to a linguistic separation [as if it doesn't already exist!] which would guarantee that they will never make it in the larger US society." Note that it is not high unemployment, or the shifting balance in world economic power, or the crises caused by a highly advanced, technological capitalist society in the United States but "linguistic separation," mind you, that will keep black children and youth from making it in the United States.

The language, education, and other public policies typically proposed by black middle-class leadership will not serve the needs of the black underclass. Their programs only ensure that a few blacks slide past the gatekeepers. Limited by an analysis based solely on race, without considering issues of class, they are unable to propose solutions that address the broader structural crises that affect all groups in United States society, but affect poor blacks with disproportionate severity. While *King* reminds us that standard English is a *sine qua non* of survival in our complex society, the harsh reality is that if all blacks commanded the language of textbooks and technocracy, the system, as it is presently constructed, could not accommodate all of us. Further, if our society could solve the problem of black unemployment – and that's a big if – it would only shift the burden to some other group. It would do nothing to address the fundamental cause of unemployment.

There are no spoils to the victors in *King*. Though the ruling set a legal precedent establishing that Black English falls within the parameters of the statutory language of 1703(f), it is an acknowledged reformist strategy. But it is a tool now available to other communities for manipulating the legal system to obtain a measure of redress from our continuing oppression.

The fate of black children as victims of miseducation continues to be the bottom line in the "Black English Case." *King* gives us yet another weapon in our struggle to save the children and develop future leadership. The case began with a claim of institutional mismanagement of education for children from the Green Road Housing Project. It ended with a claim of institutional mismanagement of the children's language. For those who know that language is identity, the issue is the same: *the children's language is them is they mommas and kinfolk and community and black culture and the black experience made manifest in verbal form.*

REFERENCE NOTES

1   473 F. Suppl. 1371 (E. D. Mich. 1979).
2   118 Congressional Record 8928 (1972).
3   451 F. Supp. 1332 (E. D. Mich. 1978).
4   Smitherman, G. Black language test. Unpublished manuscript, 1975.
5   Edmonds, R., and Frederiksen, J. R. "Search for effective schools: The identification and analysis of city schools that are instructionally effective for poor children," unpublished manuscript, 1978.
6   Lewis, K. "Analysis of the *King* case," unpublished manuscript, 1980.

9

EBONICS, *KING*, AND OAKLAND: SOME FOLK DON'T BELIEVE FAT MEAT IS GREASY¹

[1998]

O<small>N</small> 18 DECEMBER 1996, the Oakland, California School Board passed a resolution calling for the recognition of Ebonics as the primary language of its Black students and for use of this language in teaching these students. That resolution read in part:

RESOLVED that the Board of Education officially recognizes the existence, and the cultural and historic bases of West and Niger-Congo African Language Systems, and each language as the predominantly primary language of African-American students ... BE IT FURTHER RESOLVED that the Superintendent in conjunction with her staff shall immediately devise and implement the best possible academic program for imparting instruction to African-American students in their primary language for the combined purposes of maintaining the legitimacy and richness of such language whether it is known as "Ebonics," "African Language Systems," "Pan-African Communication Behaviors," or other description, and to facilitate their acquisition and mastery of English language skills.

The impetus for Oakland's policy was the extremely low level of literacy and the poor academic performance of Oakland's African American students. For instance, these students had a collective grade point average below "C." Further, although they were 53 percent of the Oakland School District's population, they comprised 71 percent of the students in special education. Oakland's contention was that the students' dismal levels of educational achievement were attributable, in great measure, to the significant linguistic mismatch between the home and school communication systems. To reduce this mismatch and its consequent impact on literacy and academic performance, Oakland proposed to implement a bilingual/bicultural language pedagogy, and thus to intervene in the tragic narratives of African American students.

> We have had pronouncements on Black speech from the NAACP ...
> from highly publicized scholars ... from executives of national corpora-
> tions ... from housewives and community folk. I mean, really, it seem like
> everybody and they momma done had something to say on the subject!

These words were NOT written in the wake of Oakland's resolution. Rather this quotation comes from my first book on Black
Language, *Talkin and Testifyin: The Language of Black America*, which
was published more than twenty years ago (1977, p. 1). As in the
past, recent negative pronouncements on Ebonics reveal a serious
lack of knowledge about the scientific study of language, as well
as galling ignorance about what the "language of Black America"
is (more than "slang") and who speaks it (at some point in their
lives, 90 percent of African Americans use some aspect of US
Ebonics). Further, these pronouncements and the accompanying
condemnations of the Oakland resolution represent an appaling
rejection of the language of everyday Black people. See, when you
lambast the home language that kids bring to school, you ain jes
dissin dem, you talkin bout they mommas! Check out the concept
of *"Mother* Tongue."

LANGUAGE, EDUCATION, AND POWER

In 1917, the National Council of Teachers of English (NCTE),
then in its organizational infancy, led a national promotion of "Better
Speech Week." Recounting this history, Gawthrop writes:

> This movement [for "Better Speech Week"] had originated in Montevallo,
> Alabama, the year before. It was patterned after "Better Babies Week,"
> "Fashion Week," and similar festivities of the time. Its aim was to improve
> speech through such devices as posters, parades, newspaper articles,
> student elections of classmates who used the best speech, and short skits
> of the type in which "Mr. Dictionary" defeats the villain "ain't." ... Better
> Speech Week became something of a national phenomenon for the next
> ten or twelve years.
>
> (1965, p. 9)

One of the hallmarks of this national phenomenon was a pledge
that students across the Nation recited with regularity:

> I love the United States of America. I love my country's flag. I love my
> country's language. I promise:
> 1   That I will not dishonor my country's speech by leaving off the last
>   syllable of words.
> 2   That I will say a good American "yes" and "no" in place of an Indian
>   grunt "um-hum" and "nup-um" or a foreign "ya" or "yeh" and "nope."

3   That I will do my best to improve American speech by avoiding loud rough tones, by enunciating distinctly, and by speaking pleasantly, clearly, and sincerely.

4   That I will learn to articulate correctly as many words as possible during the year.

(quoted in Gawthrop, 1965, pp. 9–10)

Over half a century after "Better Speech Week" swept the country, New York Public Schools Chancellor, the late Dr Richard Green, teaming up with then-Mayor Edward Koch, focused on a list of twenty "speech demons." Green was dedicated to eliminating these "demons" from the speech of New York students. Here go the Green-Koch list of "demons possessing student tongues" (underlining theirs):

May I <u>axe</u> a question?
Hang the <u>pitcher</u> on the wall.
He's <u>goin</u> home.
He <u>be</u> sick.
I <u>ain't got</u> none.
<u>Can</u> I leave the room?
I was <u>like</u> tired, <u>you know</u>?
Where is the ball <u>at</u>?
What-<u>cha doin'</u>?
I'll <u>meetcha</u> at the <u>cau-nuh</u>.
What do <u>youse</u> want?
Let's go to <u>da</u> center.
I <u>brang</u> my date along.
The <u>books is</u> in the <u>liberry</u>.
<u>Yup</u>, you <u>betcha</u>!
<u>Pacifically</u> . . .
I don't know <u>nuttin</u> about it.
I'm not the <u>on'y</u> one.
We <u>was</u> only <u>foolin 'round</u>.
So I <u>says</u> to him.

(Lewis, 1989, p. 5B)

During the first few months of the Ebonics controversy, my email was on jam with messages about the issue. Here is an excerpt from a lengthy letter that a young Black male teacher sent me. (I've deleted a few identifying details to protect his identity.)

Presently, I am finishing up my M.S. degree in Education . . . I also received a B.S. in Education, majoring in English with a reading endorsement . . . I am currently teaching [at-risk] high school students . . . Since I strongly believe that my students should be privileged [the same as those in] English honors classes, I taught them how to write poetry ... and entered their poems in [a national poetry contest]. Two girls in my class won and had their poems published. [My] principal was impressed since they were two of the biggest troublemakers in the school ... My life was not supposed to take this course. I remember a few of my professors encouraging me to drop out of the education program because I did not fit their image of a professional Black male educator. One professor told me that Blacks had enough stigma against them already and needed a positive role model like Bryant Gumbel in the teaching field. I was given the impression that I would be doing the Black race a favor if I didn't go into teaching. I didn't talk right. Not only did I use the Black Vernacular, I talked fast and when I tried to slow down, I would stutter at times ... I was raised in a low [socio] economic single parent household. And I had the nerve to want to be an English and reading teacher ... There were so many teachers whose ideology [about] us students ... prohibited them from under-standing where we kids were really coming from.

(Private communication, 28 February 1997)

That "Better Speech Week" pledge of the 1920s, the speech "demons" campaign of New York City Schools, and stories like that of the young Black male teacher who sent me the email demon-strate how those who have the power to define seek to force others to conform to their own *ipse dixit* notions of language. And although People of Color more often feel the wrath of language dominance, even white folk can get caught up in the hegemonic crossfire of linguistic oppression. All too often the powerless internalize the linguistic and cultural norms of the powerful and denigrate their own native language and culture. In the case of Ebonics, ambiva-lent and/or negative attitudes toward the language reflect deep generational and class conflicts in the national Black community. Younger Blacks – particularly the Hip Hop community, writers, students – embrace the language. On the other hand, older, estab-lished Blacks – some of whom are perceived as "leaders" – reject Ebonics – even as some of them unknowingly speak it! In addi-tion to the Hip Hop Generation, the Black working and unworking classes continue to speak Ebonics. As a linguistic minority, the Black so-called "masses" are continuously exposed to the Language of Wider Communication (aka "Standard American English") – in school, in the mass media, etc. Further, they have the cogni-tive–linguistic capacity to eradicate Ebonics if they desired to do so. Clearly, much of current African American leadership is out of touch with what is happening on the ground.

There is a fundamental, dialectical relationship between language and power, between language and oppression, and between language and liberation. Surely it is only the unwise who consider language a "mere" instrument of communication. In a dialog/interview in 1985, Freire argued that "language and thinking . . . are a dialectical unity" (187). He goes on to state that

> language variations (female language, ethnic language, dialects) are intimately interconnected with, coincide with, and express identity. They help defend one's sense of identity and they are absolutely necessary in the process of struggling for liberation . . . Certain cultural behavior patterns that were forbidden by the colonizers, including language . . . [reappear] . . . People walk without having to bow any longer. They now walk upright, looking up. There is a pedagogy of walking in this new behavior . . . these issues constitute a new way of thinking and a new way of speaking . . .
> (1985, pp. 186–7)

Language is critical in talking about the education of a people because it represents a people's theory of reality; it explains, interprets, constructs and reproduces that reality. It is well to remember that the inextricable relationship between language and power applies to languages and societies throughout human history. For instance, those who study the history of English will find that the English language was once considered "barbaric" and in need of "regularizing and purifying" since it was the "dialect of the tribe." This state of affairs existed because British English was striving to come into its own in the face of the great power and prestige of the Latin language. The American version of the English language did not achieve high prestige until the emergence of America as a world superpower after World Wars I and II. From this historical vantage point, note that the particular variety or dialect of American English that became the US dialect of power, was NOT that version spoken by the white working class, but the American English used by the elites, those who "carry on the affairs of the English-speaking people."

In the education of Black youth, and in the struggle for social change, there must be concomitant linguistic change. The first to go should be the old adage, "sticks and stones may break my bones, but words can never hurt me." The Ebonics debate reaffirms the power of words to hurt, reminds us of the potential of language to maim and destroy. Thus the repair of the linguistically maimed psyche of Blacks requires a "reappropriation of [one's] culture, which also includes . . . language" (Freire, p. 1985, 183).

FROM *KING* TO OAKLAND

What became known internationally as the "Black English Case" was launched in the summer of 1977 when a group of Black parents, acting on behalf of their young children, filed *King v. Ann Arbor* in Federal court. These parents lived in the Green Road housing project in the upscale college town of Ann Arbor, Michigan (home of the prestigious University of Michigan). The school in which the children were being linguistically and educationally destroyed was named, ironically, the Martin Luther King Jr. Elementary School. The parents' complaint against the Ann Arbor School District was that it had failed to educate their children and had dealt with the problem of the linguistic mismatch between the school language and the children's home language by simply classifying the children as "learning disabled." Judge Joiner's decision acknowledged the legitimacy of the children's Mother Tongue, citing the linguists and educators who had testified during the four-week trial in the summer of 1979, and also citing some of the voluminous research that had been done on Ebonics since the 1960s. He mandated that the language had to be recognized as legitimate and that the School District had to come up with a remedy to train King teachers to take the language into account in teaching the children.

> Researchers and professionals testified as to the existence of a language system, which is a part of the English language but different in significant respects from ... standard English ... it has as its genesis the ... pidgin language of the slaves, which after a generation or two became a Creole language ... It ... is used largely by black people in their casual conversation and informal talk ... It is clear that black children who succeed, and many do, learn to be bilingual. They retain fluency in "black English" to maintain status in the community and they become fluent in standard English to succeed in the general society. They achieve in this way by learning to "code switch" from one to the other depending on the circumstances ...The evidence supports a finding that ... the failure [of the Ann Arbor School Board] to develop a program to assist their teachers to take into account the home language in teaching standard English may be one of the causes of the children's reading problems ... no matter how well intentioned the teachers are, they are not likely to be successful in overcoming the language barrier caused by their failure to take into account the home language system, unless they are helped ... to recognize the existence of the language system used by the children in their home community and to use that knowledge as a way of helping the children to learn to read standard English.

Legal technicalities prevented us from realizing all our objectives in the case – for example, our goal of teacher training for the entire Ann Arbor School District and the legal recognition of the *King* children as a "class," representative of Black children across the Nation, as indeed they were (the legal ruling against class action

status notwithstanding). Nonetheless, *King* was significant because
it was the first legal action filed about the language of a people
who have relied on the courts and hundreds of court cases, filed
by them or their advocates, to achieve justice and equity for nearly
four hundred years. Thus, what started out in July of 1977 as an
obscure Federal court case, had, by the time of Judge Joiner's final
ruling in July of 1979, generated a voluminous amount of written
material and public outcry. Not only were there numerous academic articles, there were over 300 newspaper and magazine articles,
some of them in the foreign press. (See Bailey's bibliographic compilation of press coverage in Smitherman, 1981a.) There were dozens
of local and national radio and television programs about the case.
In community forums, churches, school meetings, and other local
and national gatherings, there were intense and heated debates as
well as occasional outbursts of hysteria. Seven months after Judge
Joiner's final ruling, on the campus of Wayne State University in
Detroit, I convened a national invitational symposium on the case
and its implications for the education of Black children and youth.
The British Broadcasting Corporation sent a film crew to Detroit
to shoot footage at the symposium and in Ann Arbor, Michigan,
some 40 miles from Detroit. They subsequently produced a film
about the case.

The critical issues raised by *King* have been integral to the
struggle of African Americans throughout our history: language,
education, literacy, and power. These are the same issues surrounding
the Ebonics controversy a generation later. (See "'What Go Round
Come Round'", in this volume, pp. 132–49, for a more thorough
analysis of the *King* case and attendant issues.) In each of these
historical moments, we have been confronted with a symbolic issue
which goes beyond some narrow conception of teaching "correct"
English. Negative reactions against Ebonics in 1996–7, like those
against "Black English" in 1977–9, reflect racist assumptions about
the language and educational needs of Black working and unworking
class people. In *King*, for instance, one well-known Black journalist
had asserted that the children in the court case could learn to read
if their mothers would get the books in and the boyfriends out!
Assault on the language of African America is a way of reinscribing
the subordination and powerlessness of Black youth and Black
working-class people. One member of the Hip Hop generation put
it this way:

> Most of the people who have been opponents of Ebonics are the same
> ones who have been dismissive of Hip-Hop. There is a segment of the
> older Black generation, the middle class, civil rights leadership, that is anti-

youth. Most of them have no idea if Ebonics works as a method of reaching Black students. But because they are so busy being reactive to anything that mainstream white politicians are against, once again they are speaking out. And they haven't scratched the surface in understanding how the Hip Hop Generation views the issue.

(Stephney, quoted in Kelly, 1997, p. 26)

The Oakland School Board's proposal for using Ebonics as the instructional avenue to literacy in the Language of Wider Communication accords with the pedagogical approach that has become fairly standard around the world, namely using the Mother Tongue as the medium of teaching and learning. However, here in the US, Oakland's action not only ignited a national controversy, it motivated anti-Ebonics legislative proposals, and it even gave renewed impetus to the English Only campaign.

Within days after the Oakland resolution, Secretary of Education, Richard Riley, representing the US government's position, issued a public policy statement indicating that Ebonics is a "nonstandard form of English and not a foreign language." In 1997, just weeks after Oakland's resolution, five states formulated anti-Ebonics legislation: Florida, California, Georgia, South Carolina, and Oklahoma. Three of these states passed the legislation: Georgia, South Carolina, and Oklahoma. (See Richardson (1998) for a brilliant analysis of the anti-Ebonics legislation.) Paradoxically, as the English Only and anti-Ebonics campaigns gain momentum, there is a major national push for foreign language study for white, monolingual students, particularly those from the families who "carry on the affairs of the English-speaking people." Clearly, the children of the elite are being prepared to govern and rule in the just-around-the-corner twenty-first century global, multilingual world.

The call for recognition of US Ebonics as a language in its own right and for funding to support bilingual/bicultural instruction for its speakers is being manipulated to threaten the developing, fragile alliance of Blacks and Latinos. Hopefully, both the Latino community and my people will be able to see through this divide-and-rule trickeration, will have the wisdom to peep through muddy water and spy dry land, and rather than fight over pieces of the present pie, will have the courage to struggle to enlarge the pie in the future so that all youth of Color will be empowered with language and literacy skills.

WHERE TO FROM HERE? THE WISDOM OF THE ELDERS

Over three decades ago, Fanon analyzed the dilemmas and contradictions faced by Blacks under the linguistic and cultural domination of Europeans. In his "The Negro and Language" (1967), he argued that "every dialect, every language, is a way of thinking. To speak means to assume a culture." Therefore, to foster the psycho-social well-being and liberation of Blacks, Fanon's contention was that those Blacks who get educated and return to the community that gave them birth must express themselves in the community language to make it plain that nothing done change. In 1933, DuBois called for what we are these days labeling "African-Centered" education – and for instruction to be conducted in the Mother Tongue. Woodson taught that Black children need to study our language as an African tongue that had been broken down by the conditions of enslavement, and that we need a system of education to serve OUR needs, because "even if . . . Negroes do successfully imitate the white, nothing new has . . . been accomplished. You simply have a larger number of persons doing what others have been doing" ([1933] 1973, p. 7).

Building on the wisdom of the Elders, I here put forth several proposals relative to language and education to address the educational crises facing African American youth.

MULTI-LINGUAL POLICY

The goal of such a policy is to prepare Black (as well as all) youth not merely to be citizens of the US, but citizens of the world. This policy should include:

1   the Language of Wider Communication here in the US because English may eventually become the global *lingua franca*;
2   a foreign language, either an African language spoken widely on the Continent – where the everyday people do not speak English and French – or Spanish because of the large number of Spanish speakers not only in the US, but also in the Caribbean, and in other parts of the Western hemisphere; and
3   preservation and enhancement of competence in the Mother Tongue, the base of one's cultural identity. Since the policy being proposed here would be for ALL students, not just African Americans, this multilingualism could also be a way for European Americans to develop greater fluency in the Mother Tongues that are part of their heritage – e.g., Polish, Lithuanian, German, Italian, etc. – Mother Tongues that were hastily and foolishly shed in their push to become "Americans."

EDUCATION FOR WHAT?

We need a socially responsible educational philosophy. Time out for an education just for individual "gittin ovah," to enter the mainstream and continue with business as usual. We need education for social change. We need to promote a vision of community and social responsibility, that infuses youth – ALL youth, regardless of race or ethnicity – with a sense of "I am because we are."

INTERROGATION OF THE SOCIAL AND CULTURAL CONTEXT OF LANGUAGE, INCLUDING "STANDARD ENGLISH"

Like the old slave said, you can teach me the law, but not what justice is. In their critical examination of the socio-historical situatedness of language, students would discover, for instance, that standards of language correctness correlate with power, race, and status, and that exceptions are made for the linguistic lapses of those who "carry on the affairs of the English-speaking people" – [e.g., "between you and I," which is used by many middle-class speakers of "standard English"]. In the process of interrogation, students would also discover that the present bias against Ebonics speakers (like that against the young Black male English teacher who sent me the email) is not new, but dates back to scholars like George P. Krapp – his name tells you something – who declared that Blacks spoke "baby talk" English (1924; 1925) and to nineteenth-century scholars like Harrison (1884) who railed against the "pathological" Africanness in Black speech.

CAPITALIZE ON THE ORAL TRADITION

Black youth bring a rich oral tradition, knowledge, and linguistic skills into the classroom. They are not starved for language, and they are far from *tabula rasa* zombies in need of linguistic nourishment. Freire was critical both of the nutrition metaphor in education as well as the "banking" concept which assumes that students are empty vessels or "accounts" into which teachers make deposits. Rather, students have a wealth of "lived experience" that we can capitalize on. Linguistic competence in their Mother Tongue – Ebonics – is a fundamental aspect of this experience. That competence can be tapped into in the teaching of language and literacy. This is where Bailey was headed in her work in the mid-1960s with Black pre-freshmen at Tougaloo College in Mississippi. She worked for a summer with 100 students, analyzing their speech and writing. Consistently and systematically, the students used language patterns "directly traceable to a dialectal substratum" which had been unaffected by the piecemeal corrections and irrelevant drills of language arts classrooms; patterns, I might add, still in use among Ebonics speakers today – e.g., "Nearly all my instructors white" and "This occur over a period of two and a half hours" (Bailey, 1968, p. 22). She contended that teachers needed to recognize that such language patterns were not "sporadic deviations," but structured and rule-governed parts of a system that was "only partially similar to that of standard English" (p. 24). Thus pedagogical intervention had to take the form of a "systemic approach to the teaching of the language arts" to speakers of Ebonics. Bailey concluded that:

> These observations may appear to some as no more than a rehashing or recataloging of well known facts of language usage, not only in the writing of Negro students in Mississippi, but throughout the country. It is my contention, however, that *like effects do not necessarily spring from like causes* [my italics] ... Recognition of this fact *should* and *must* [Bailey's italics] lead to a revision of our classroom techniques.
>
> (1968, pp. 23–4)

Only a few studies applying the conceptual framework outlined by Bailey have been conducted, owing, in great measure, to the undue negative influence of Black so-called "leaders." (One wishes they would check out some of the linguistic research literature before jumping out there sounding like know-nothings.) One important study dealt with written literacy. It was conducted by Hanni Taylor, a native-German speaker, fluent in English, who worked with Black students from Chicago enrolled at Aurora University, a short drive from the City. Taylor developed an ethno-linguistic curriculum for teaching writing that reflected targeted recognition and work with the systematic patterns of the students' native Ebonics. Her rationale was that such an approach would lead to a reduction in the frequency and amount of Ebonics forms in the students' written essays, and thus to a greater command of Academic Discourse. To test the efficacy of her theory, she set up experimental and control classes. The experimental group used Taylor's ethnolinguistic curriculum and pedagogical approach; the control group used the traditional rhetoric and language curriculum approach, i.e., with no recognition of the systematic nature of the students' language, and with mere piecemeal correction. At the end of the term, the total occurrence of features of Ebonics in the essays of the experimental group was *reduced by 59.3 percent*. However, in the control group, the total occurrence of Ebonics features *increased by 8.5 percent* (1989, p. 149).

In the area of reading, a critically important research project was conducted by Simpkins, Holt, and Simpkins (1974) for the reading series, *Bridge*, that they developed. Capitalizing on stories from the Folk, combined with original stories the authors wrote, they developed a curriculum to teach decoding and reading-comprehension skills using readers in two different languages, "Black Vernacular" and "Standard English." The Simpkins team supervised 14 teachers and 27 classes, involving 540 students, in grades 7–12, in both experimental and control groups, over a four-month period, in five areas: Chicago, Illinois; Phoenix, Arizona; Washington, DC; Memphis, Tennessee; and Macon County, Alabama. The control groups were taught reading via the traditional method, with no focus on the students' home language. Using the standardized Iowa Test of Basic Skills in Reading Comprehension to assess gains in reading, the researchers found that the experimental/Bridge groups made a gain of *6.2 months* in their reading over the four-month period, whereas the control/non-Bridge groups only gained *1.6 months* in the four months of instruction, i.e., these kids lost ground. Today, as we approach the millennium, it's the same song, just a different verse. The longer Black kids stay in school, the further behind they get! This is exactly what the Oakland, California School District was (and still is) struggling against, and which was behind the impetus for their Ebonics resolution.

Now, don't nobody go trippin cause ain none of dese proposals suggesting that schools shouldn't teach "standard English," or more precisely, the US Language of Wider Communication – note I said "wider," not "whiter" communication. *All* students need to know this language if they are going to participate fully in the global world of the twenty-first century. In a similar fashion, Freire argued that it "would be very foolish" and "made no sense . . . for the Cape Verdians [and other colonized people] to cut themselves off from the language of the colonizer" (p. 183). My point has to do with how you teach the LWC and the social and political messages that should accompany language and literacy instruction. My further point is that mastery of the LWC is necessary, but insufficient to be a citizen (or, especially, a leader) in the global, diverse world of the twenty-first century and beyond.

CONCLUSION

Change is blowing in the wind. Progressive educators on all levels must step up and chart a course to help the next generation rise to the social and political challenges facing them. For, as Fanon said, "Each generation must out of relative obscurity discover its mission, fulfill it, or betray it" (1963, p. 206). Multilingualism and celebration and promotion of linguistic diversity must be part of the language and literacy training of youth and of their preparation for world citizenship in the twenty-first century. This vision recognizes the foolishness and dangerous folly of continuing to do more of the same that has not worked well in the past, a deplorable pedagogy and way of thinking about language that has only added thousands of African American and other students of Color to the marginal underclass. In putting forth its Ebonics resolution, the Oakland California School Board was trying to learn from past wrongs and educational tragedies cause they know that fat meat do be greasy.

10

THE TWO ARTICLES which follow are research reports of a major study of writing by 17-year-old African American students in the National Assessment of Educational Progress (NAEP), from 1969 to 1988/89. My study was funded by grants from the National Council of Teachers of English. NAEP is a Federally-funded decennial evaluation program, mandated by Congress and initiated in 1969. The last full-scale, national Writing Assessment was done in 1988–9, the last year of my study. Since that time, focus has shifted gradually to state writing-assessment systems.

This twenty-year study, conducted with the assistance of colleagues and student research assistants, analyzed a total of 2,764 essays, which had been scored by teacher-raters trained by NAEP. My goal was to develop a profile of the written literacy accomplishments of African American youth, at the school-leaving age, over the span of a generation, at three different time periods – 1969, 1979, 1988–9. The first research report, "Black English, Diverging or Converging?" published in 1992, focuses on rater scores and syntax in the essays; the second report, "The Blacker the Berry, the Sweeter the Juice," published in 1994, focuses on rater scores, syntax, and discourse styles.

AFRICAN
AMERICAN
STUDENT
WRITERS IN
THE NAEP,
1969–88/89
[1992]
AND
"THE BLACKER
THE BERRY,
THE SWEETER
THE JUICE"
[1994]

NATIONAL ASSESSMENT OF EDUCATIONAL
PROGRESS (NAEP)

NAEP is a federally funded survey of the educational attainments of youth and adults at four age levels: nine, thirteen, seventeen, and twenty-six to thirty-five. Its purpose is to measure growth or decline in educational achievement in ten subject areas: writing, reading, literature, science, mathematics, citizenship, music, art, social studies, and career and occupational development. Administered at five- and ten-year intervals since its inception in 1969, NAEP offers the advantage of a scientifically selected national representative sample, uniform scoring procedures and guidelines, a nationally administered, standardized test format, and a high degree of reliability and validity.

For example, the percentage of exact agreement on the rating of the 1984 papers from seventeen-year-olds ranged from 89 percent to 92 percent, with corresponding reliability coefficients of .89 and .91 (Applebee, Langer, and Mullis 1985, p. 68). The writing task time is fifteen or sixteen minutes, depending on the task, and students submit first drafts. Previously administered by the Education Commission of the States, NAEP has been under the purview of the Educational Testing Service since 1984.

The students assessed reflect national, representative groups, in a random sample, stratified by race–ethnicity, social–educational class, region of country, urban–rural, gender, and other demographics. From 1969 to 1979, approximately 8,100 students were assessed. From 1984 to 1988–9, approximately 18,000 students were assessed.

NAEP's essay tasks represent three types of rhetorical modalities: (1) imaginative–narrative, (2) descriptive–informative, and (3) persuasive. For the *imaginative* modality, in the 1969 and 1979 NAEP, students were given a picture of a stork and told to make up a story about it. The prompt was comprised of three possible opening lines: (1) "I'm telling you, Henry, if you don't get rid of that thing, it's going to eat up the cat!"; (2) "But mother, I *am* telling the truth! It laid an egg in the Chevy"; and (3) "Last night a very odd-looking bird appeared in the neighborhood." In 1984, students were given a picture of a box with a hole in it and an eye peering out. They were told to "imagine" themselves in the picture, to describe the scene and their feelings about it, and to make their descriptions "lively and interesting." There was no imaginative task in 1988.

For the *descriptive–informative* task, the 1969 and 1979 students were asked to describe something they knew about, a familiar place or thing, in such a way that it could be recognized by someone reading the description. For 1984 and 1988, they were given the topic "Food on the Frontier" and asked to write an essay discussing reasons for the differences between food on the frontier and food today. Finally, for the *persuasive* modality, in 1984 and 1988 the students' task was to write a letter to the recreation department in their city or town, trying to convince the head of that department to buy either an abandoned railroad track or an old warehouse to create recreational opportunities. (We were unable to obtain the persuasive essays for 1969 and 1979; thus this longitudinal comparison was not possible.)

BLACK ENGLISH: DIVERGING OR CONVERGING?

During the decades of the 1960s and 1970s, African Americans made great strides in educational and community development. The years from 1960–80 produced 80 percent of *all* the African American doctorates in our entire history in North America (Blackwell, 1981). Since 1960, we have witnessed a burgeoning Black middle class without parallel or precedence in the Black Experience. And finally, in an area closer to the subject of this article, the writing of African American students improved *twice* as much as that of their white counterparts in the decade from 1969 to 1979, as measured by the National Assessment of Educational Progress (NAEP, 1980). Thus William Labov's mid-1980s announcement that Black English was diverging from Standard White English shocked the scholarly and lay communities across the nation (Labov and Harris, 1986).

What has come to be called the 'Divergence Hypothesis' posits that Black English Vernacular (BEV) is charting a separate course of development from that of white dialects in this post-modern era. Contrary to predictions about the impact of racial integration, of the media, of increased educational development and enhanced literacy, Black speech has not continued to de-creolize as we had anticipated back in the 1960s and 1970s – or so the divergence argument goes. Labov attributes divergence to racial isolation and foreshadows serious negative consequences for African American students who are now facing a language of instruction even more drastically different from their own language than was the case in their parents' day. While rebuttals to the Labovian Divergence Hypothesis have employed counter-examples from *speech* (e.g. Vaughn-Cooke, 1987; Wolfram, 1990), this article examines the issue from the vantage point of *writing*; using national samples of 17-year-old African Americans in the National Assessment of Educational Progress (NAEP), from 1969–88/89. This study seeks to illuminate the question of the frequency and distribution of Black English Vernacular in writing over a generational time span. If Labov is right and there has been divergence from Standard English (SE) in speech, has there been concomitant divergence in writing?

ISSUES IN THE STUDY

I first began this line of research in early 1981, with the release of the 1979 NAEP writing results. The test results indicated that the writing of African American students had improved *twice* as much as that of their white counterparts in the decade from 1969 to 1979. I sought to investigate whether these higher writing scores were accompanied by a decline in Black English Vernacular over the decade and a concomitant greater control of Edited American/ Standard English. Results from this earlier research did indeed indicate a significant decline in BEV over the decade in the case of the imaginative–narrative essays. However, there was no parallel decrease in the descriptive/informative essay modality from 1969 to 1979 (Smitherman and Wright, 1983).

The question of the relationship between writing scores and the distribution of BEV in writing is a logical issue given assumed negative teacher attitudes and the stigma attached to features of Black English in writing. This earlier research shed some light on this question in that the narrative essays, which showed significant declines in BEV features from 1969–79, also were the essays which demonstrated the dramatic improvement in writing scores over the same time frame. Thus we concluded that the decrease in BEV in the narrative essays and the corollary increase in rater scores spoke 'favorably for our efforts at teaching EAE' (Smitherman and Wright, 1983 NCTE Research Report). Further, we noted that the lack of increase in the descriptive essay scores and the concomitant lack of decline in BEV suggests that while writers may produce Standard English prose for one type of writing assignment, they may not exhibit the same level of control over SE in other types of assignment (p. 9).

Although the 1988 writing assessment did not result in significantly increased writing scores from 1979–88/89, the issue of Black English in the essays was a natural outgrowth of discussions about divergence which first emerged in 1985 among national media accounts about the direction of BEV. Extending the analysis and methods of the first research, our recent study sought to examine not only the co-variation of BEV and rater scores. More critically, it examined the question of divergence vs. convergence over a 20-year time span.

SAMPLE AND METHODS

The data set consists of 2,764 essays written by 17-year-old African Americans in NAEP for 1969, 1979, 1984, and 1988/89. Each essay has been given a primary trait and/or a holistic score by NAEP teacher-raters trained and experienced in holistic scoring and general writing assessment. A holistic score is an assessment of overall writing competency, what NAEP describes as 'a global view of the ideas, language facility, organization, mechanics, and syntax of each paper taken as a whole' (Applebee *et al.*, 1990, p. 84). Further, with holistic scoring, papers are evaluated relative to one another, rather than against specific criteria, as is the case with primary trait scoring. In 1969 and 1979, NAEP raters utilized a four-point scale for holistic scoring, and in 1984 and 1988, they used a six-point scale.

In primary trait assessment, papers are evaluated according to features of specific writing tasks. This score reflects the measure of student success of accomplishing the specific assigned purpose of the writing task. Here matters of mechanics, grammar, and syntax are subordinated to fluency and execution of the assignment. In all years under analysis here, NAEP raters utilized a four-point scale for primary trait scoring (although not the same scale across the 20-year span) (see Tables 10.1 and 10.2 for sample scales).

The method for analyzing BEV in the essays was as follows. Each of the linguistic variables comprising Black English was analyzed and coded, based on the presence or absence of the variable in a specified environment (see Table 10.3). The percent of realization for each variable was computed. Then the data were statistically analyzed using analysis of variance. Pearson correlation was used for determining the co-variation of rater scores and BEV. Significance level was set at 0.05.

Although the same linguistic variables were analyzed across all four assessments, rating scales, as mentioned, differed from 1969/79 to 1984/88. Additionally, topics were different, and some differences in test administration and procedures occurred after NAEP moved to Educational Testing Service (ETS) in 1983. To adjust for these differences, comparisons were made from 1969 to 1979 and from 1984 to 1988. The 1969–79 results were then juxtaposed with the 1984–88/89 results.

RESULTS

First, one of the most significant results is that the frequency of BEV in *all* essays for *all* years is generally low. This finding matches other studies of African American student writing in that BEV

Table 10.1   NAEP primary trait scale

Score	
4	**Elaborated**. Students providing elaborated responses went beyond the essential, reflecting a higher level of coherence and providing more detail to support the points made.
3	**Adequate**. Students providing adequate responses included the information and ideas necessary to accomplish the underlying task and were considered likely to be effective in achieving the desired purpose.
2	**Minimal**. Students writing at the minimal level recognized some or all of the elements needed to complete the task but did not manage these elements well enough to assure that the purpose of the task would be achieved.
1	**Unsatisfactory**. Students who wrote papers judged as unsatisfactory provided very abbreviated, circular, or disjointed responses that did not even begin to address the writing task.
0	**Not Rated**. A small percentage of the responses were blank, indecipherable, or completely off task, or contained a statement to the effect that the student did not know how to do the task; these responses were not rated.

speech patterns are only minimally reproduced in writing (see, e.g. Scott, 1981; Chaplin, 1987). Further, certain prevalent BEV speech patterns occur very infrequently in writing, for example, the classic *be* aspect, as in *They be tired*.

Now to summarize the results of the 1969–79 comparison reported in Smitherman and Wright (1983 NCTE Research Report).

1   Black English *did decline* in the narrative essays from 1969 to 1979; however, this was not the case with the descriptive/ informative essays.
2   In fact, with some features of BEV – e.g. irregular verbs, subject–verb–agreement–past – there was an *increase* in the 1979 descriptive essays.
3   Copula patterns – strong indications of the African substratum that characterizes Black English – remained exactly the same over the ten-year period – i.e. 6 percent in both years.
4   There was a significant positive correlation between the amount of BEV and the rater score, even in the case of primary trait scoring (i.e., if the rater is following the scale, there should be minimal or no penalties for BEV).

Table 10.2   NAEP holistic scale (imaginative essay modality)

Score	
6	A 6 story demonstrates a high degree of competence [appropriate for grade level] in response to the prompt but may have a few minor errors. A story in this category generally has the following features: • is well developed with a clear narrative structure • contains considerable detail that enriches the narrative • clearly demonstrates facility in the use of language • is generally free from errors in mechanics, usage, and sentence structure
5	A 5 story demonstrates clear competence in response to the prompt but may have minor errors. A story in this category generally has the following features: • is developed with a clear negative structure • contains details that contribute effectively to the narrative • demonstrates facility in the use of language • contains few errors in mechanics, usage, and sentence structure
4	A 4 story demonstrates competence in response to the prompt. A story in this category generally has the following features: • is adequately developed but may have occasional weaknesses in narrative structure • contains details that contribute to the narrative • demonstrates adequate facility in the use of language • may display some errors in mechanics, usage, or sentence structure but not a consistent pattern or accumulation of such errors.
3	A 3 story demonstrates some degree of competence in response to the prompt but is clearly flawed. A story in this category reveals one or more of the following weaknesses: • is somewhat developed but lacks clear narrative structure • contains few details that contribute to the narrative • demonstrates inappropriate use of language • reveals a pattern or accumulation of errors in mechanics, usage, or sentence structure
2	A 2 story demonstrates only limited competence and is seriously flawed. A story in this category reveals one or more of the following weaknesses: • lacks development and/or narrative structure • contains little or no relevant detail • displays serious or persistent errors in use of language • displays serious errors in mechanics, usage, or sentence structure
1	A 1 story demonstrates fundamental deficiencies in writing skills. A story in this category reveals one or more of the following weaknesses: • is undeveloped • is incoherent • contains serious and persistent writing errors

Table 10.3   Black English variables

Variable	Example from NAEP essay
ED MORPHEME:	
Main-Verb Past (MV + Ø)	Frontier *use* corn and meat for there basic food.
Main-Verb-Perfect (Have/Had + MV + Ø)	They have *work* hard . . . to keep the crops growing good to eat.
Verbal Adjective (V + Ø)	I am writing because I am *concern* of the recreational project . . . in our town.
Passive (Be + MV + Ø)	I am *lock* in an apartment with darkness looking through this little hole.
S-MORPHEME:	
Noun-Plural (N + Ø pl)	Pioneers didn't have such *thing* . . . to keep their foods.
Noun-Possessive (N + Ø poss)	*Today* way is . . . easier.
Third Person-Singular (V + Ø)	But our environment of today *do* have refrigeration and things . . . can be stored.
HYPERCORRECTION	
(N pl + s)	But today *peoples* are able to get refrigeraters and food still spoil.
COPULA:	
Be + Main Verb (Ø + MV)	I feel like someone __ *watching* me throwing at me.
Be + Noun (Ø + N)	He __ a real good *citizen*.
Be + Adjective (Ø + Adj)	I think it __ *great* to have some place to play.
Be + Preposition (Ø + Prep)	I feel really good about what __ *around* me.
Be + Adverb (Ø + Adv)	But it *out door*.
SUBJECT–VERB AGREEMENT-PRESENT (Subj pl + is)	*A bird and egg is* in that car.
SUBJECT–VERB AGREEMENT-PAST (Subj pl + was)	The pioneers then *was* no different than what we do today.
PERFECTIVE DONE/HAVE (Ø have/has/had + MV)	. . . the food to mostley allready __ been cooked and caned for you . . .

Table 10.3   cont.

Variable	Example from NAEP essay
IRREGULAR VERBS:	But back then they *eat* a lot of heath food.
	So I *have gave* my opinions about what I think you should do.
MULTIPLE NEGATION	Last night there was a straight-looking new bird in the neighborhood *no one never* seen before *nowhere*.
IT EXPLETIVE (It + V + N)	*It* is a lot different things that would brighten up our community.
UNDIFFERENTIATED THIRD-PERSON PLURAL PRONOUN	. . . soon are later they will quiet that job because they will have a lot of money in the bank for *they family* and *they self*
PRONOMINAL APPOSITION (N Subj + P subj)	People in the old day *they* do not have refrigeration . . .

In the 1984–8 comparison, juxtaposed with the 1969–79 results, the evidence emerges more clearly and unambiguously for convergence, not divergence. Significant results were found with the following linguistic variables:

1   *copula*;
2   *ED morpheme*;
3   *S morpheme*;
4   *it-expletive*.

All of these variables declined from 1984 to 1988 (see Table 10.4). Finally, in terms of the total sum of *all* Black English variables, the period from 1984 to 1988 showed a clear decline, unlike the unevenness of the 1969–79 decade (see Table 10.5).

One other interesting result was made possible in 1988, a test of the interaction of essay modality and production of Black English.

Table 10.4   BEV patterns compared, 1984–88/89

Variable	Essay type and year	BEV mean
Copula	1984P	0.05
	1988P	0.04★
	1984I	0.06
	1988I	0.03★★
–ED Morpheme	1984P	0.13
	1988P	0.10★
	1984I	0.18
	1988I	0.08★★
–S Morpheme	1984P	0.10
	1988P	0.05★★
	1984I	0.12
	1988I	0.07★★
IT-Expletive	1984P	0.008
	1988P	0.04★
	1984I	0.06
	1988I	0.00★★

P = Persuasive
I = Informative
★ = Not statistically significant
★★ = Statistically significant at 0.05 or lower

In the 1969–79 comparison, there was a trend toward a difference in the distribution of Black English in imaginative and informative essays. The imaginatives tended to have less Black English, both within and across years. The informatives had more BEV, and as mentioned, it actually increased in some subvariables and overall from 1969 to 1979 (see Table 10.5). We concluded then, and the statistical analysis supported this conclusion, that there is a correlation between essay modality and the production of BEV. We theorized that when the writer is familiar with the form, as in the case of the imaginative story-telling tradition in African American culture, he/she produces less Black English than is the case with culturally 'foreign' essay forms. With ETS' innovation in the 1988 NAEP of having the same writers write on both the informative and persuasive topics, we were able to test this correlation further.

Results comparing the same writers' essays on 'food' (informative/ descriptive) and 'recreation' (persuasive) were conflicting. That is,

Table 10.5 Overall BEV patterns compared, 1969–88/89

1969–79 Essay type	Year	BEV mean
Imaginative	1969	0.11
Imaginative	1979	0.09★
Informative	1969	0.10
Informative	1979	0.44★★
Persuasive	Not available	Not available

1984 88/89 Essay type	Year	BEV mean
Imaginative	1984	0.11
	Not given in 1988	
Informative	1984	0.10
Informative	1988	0.06★★
Persuasive	1984	0.09
Persuasive	1988	0.05★★

★ = Not statistically significant
★★ = Statistically significant at 0.05 or lower

with some subvariables of Black English, there were *more* in the persuasive modality ('recreation') than in the informative ('food'), as in the case of the *ED morpheme*, for example. With others, as in the case of *It-expletive*, the Black English form occurred only in the informative (see Table 10.6). The results seem to suggest that modality might have no effect on BEV production. By using the same writers on two different tasks, NAEP's 1988 administration allowed for an analysis controlling for the effect of the writer, which we were unable to do in our 1969–79 analysis, where the writing was done by different writers on two different tasks. Yet the question of the interaction of essay modality and BEV production still remains

Table 10.6 BEV patterns compared, same writer, persuasive and informative essays, 1988

Variable	Persuasive	Informative
ED	0.22	0.11★★
S	0.08	0.10★
COPULA	0.08	0.05
IT-EXPL	0.00	0.09★
OVERALL BEV	0.09	0.08★

★ = Not statistically significant
★★ = Statistically significant at 0.05 or lower

Table 10.7 Correlations between BEV syntax and holistic or
primary trait scores, 1984 and 1988

Essay year and type	Scoring method	R-value	P-value
1984 Informative	H	−0.3192	0.006★★
1988 Informative	P	−0.0526	0.170★
1984 Persuasive	H	−0.3248	0.000★★
1988 Persuasive	H	−0.1591	0.03★★
1984 Imaginative	H	−0.2748	0.000★★
	P	−0.0802	0.10★

H = Holistic Scoring
P = Primary Trait Scoring
★ = Not statistically significant
★★ = Statistically significant at 0.05 or lower

open because we do not yet have a comparison of the same writers
performing both *imaginative and informative (or persuasive)* tasks (the basis
of comparison that led to our conclusion about the 1969–79 NAEP
essays). That is, it may very well be that the imaginative story-telling
rhetorical style is the ideal form for BEV writers. Certainly, this
proposition should be tested in future research.

We turn now to the results of rater evaluations and BEV distribution and frequency in 1984 and 1988. With holistic scores, there
continues to be what we found in 1969–79, a significant correlation between the amount of BEV and the rater score. As expected,
it was a negative correlation (see Table 10.7). That is, the more
BEV, the lower the holistic score. This finding is not surprising,
given the holistic method, which includes assessment of grammar,
mechanics, and syntax. With primary trait scores, however, a significant difference emerges in the 1984 and 1988 NAEP that we did
not see earlier, no statistically significant correlations between BEV
and primary trait scores. In the 1980s, only holistic scores proved
to significantly correlate with the frequency of BEV. Further, the
1984 imaginatives, which were rated both holistically and with
primary trait scoring, provide a good indication of how the same
essay fares under two different rating scales. The amount of BEV
syntax had a significant adverse effect on rater score only when
holistic, but not primary trait, scoring was used to rate the essay
(see Table 10.7). As mentioned, this contrasts sharply with the 1969
and 1979 results where BEV grammar had a significantly negative
effect on rater score, *even in the case of primary trait scoring*. Ideally,
if raters are assessing task accomplishment for specific features of
discourse production, then features of grammar and syntax would

count minimally or not at all in whether a writer accomplished the rhetorical demands of the task. This ideal was not achieved in either 1969 or 1979, but 1984 and 1988/89 NAEP raters accomplished this goal.

Finally, unlike the period from 1969 to 1979, writing scores of African American students did not exhibit any dramatic improvement over the decade from 1979 to 1988/89. However, if we look at 1984–1988, according to NAEP, 'Black and Hispanic students appeared to show consistent improvements at all three grade levels, although the changes were not statistically significant' (Applebee et al., 1990, p. 9).

CONCLUSIONS AND IMPLICATIONS

This analysis of Black English Vernacular in essays by African American 17-year-olds over a generational time span yields two significant conclusions: (1) BEV does not presently affect rater score in primary trait scoring; and (2) the use of BEV in writing has significantly declined since 1969.

The fact that writers are not penalized for BEV in terms of their accomplishment of specific writing tasks is testimony to the various educational and social forces that have served to sensitize teachers about dialects. We can note such movements and policies as the 1974 CCCC "Students' Right to Their Own Language"; language diversity seminars and training workshops and programs in teacher education and in school districts across the country, beginning in the 1970s; the internationally-publicized King ('Black English') Federal Court Case in 1979; the numerous convention programs and presentations on linguistic diversity and nonstandard English since the 1970s; and the voluminous scholarly and lay publications and media attention to language issues over the past fifteen years. All of these forces and events have had an impact on the linguistic liberation of African American students in the nation's schools and classrooms. The clear implication is that teachers now seem comfortable with and demonstrate the competence to divorce success in writing modality from attention to features of grammar.

The fact that there is a pattern of decline in BEV in the NAEP essays raises questions about the Divergence Hypothesis, at least in Black *writing*, over the past twenty years. Although there was a slight, but not statistically significant, increase from 1969 to 1979, in the informative essay modality, this increase did not hold for the imaginative essays where the trend was toward a decline. More importantly, there were significant decreases in both essay types from 1984 to 1988. In the informative category, BEV *decreased* from 10 percent to 6 percent ($p = 0.0004$), *interestingly the exact number of percentage points of the increase from 1969–79*. Although NAEP raters did not code for specific BEV variables, as this study did, NAEP's conclusions about Black students' grammar may be considered as matching the general direction of the present findings. NAEP states: "For the nation as a whole, students' control of the mechanics of written English was comparable in 1984 and 1988. However, Black students showed small gains in grammar, punctuation, and spelling relative to their White counterparts" (Applebee *et al.*, 1990, p. 9). This result, in combination with the present study's findings about the decline in Black English production over time, strengthens the case for BEV convergence in the direction of Edited American/ Standard English over the past twenty years, at least in writing, if not in speech.

Objectively, empirically, there seems to be a case for convergence. What is the explanation for this? One possibility is today's students' increased facility in code switching, i.e. from Black to Standard English, as the situation warrants, in comparison to their counterparts in the previous generation. African American students seem to have become more adept in their command of Edited American English [standard US English that has been edited for errors in grammar, punctuation, etc.] perhaps due to increased literacy, schooling, media exposure, and heightened awareness of the importance of education. Thus the predictions of the 1960s and 1970s about eventual complete *de-creolization* (i.e. the de-Africanizing of BEV in the direction of Standard English) were not so far off the mark, as Divergence theorists have argued. It may simply be that the manifestation of de-creolization is to be found in *writing* (and other school-based language tasks), not in the oral repertoire of the African American speech community. Here the rich verbal and linguistic traditions are thriving, changing, even "diverging", and charting new paths in American popular culture forms (e.g. BEV in Rap music). I see this as a healthy state of affairs.

"THE BLACKER THE BERRY, THE SWEETER THE JUICE"[1] [1994]

Written literacy among African American students continues to be of major concern to educators, policy makers, researchers, and the lay community. African American students have consistently scored lower than their European American counterparts in all rounds of the National Assessment of Educational Progress (NAEP) since its inception in 1969 (NAEP 1980; Applebee, Langer, and Mullis 1985). And even in that decade of remarkable progress for African American student writers, 1969 to 1979, where 1979 NAEP results indicated that they had improved *twice* as much as their white counterparts, African American students still were not writing on a par with white students, as the 1979 NAEP results also indicated.

The upward surge first evidenced in 1979 continued in the 1980s, though not with the same dramatic level of improvement. According to NAEP, from 1984 to 1988, "Black and Hispanic students appeared to show consistent improvements at all three grade levels, although the changes were not statistically significant" (Applebee *et al.* 1990, p. 9). Although black students' scores still do not parallel those of whites, there is some slight encouragement in NAEP's finding, particularly in light of their conclusion that generally in 1988 the nation's students "continued to perform at minimal levels on the . . . writing assessment tasks, and relatively few performed at adequate or better levels" (Applebee *et al.,* 1990, 6).

The topic of the African American Verbal Tradition – both its discourse modalities and its grammar – is frequently at the heart of discussion and concern about African American student writing. Of particular significance is the extent to which Black English Vernacular (BEV) patterns of syntax and discourse are reproduced in writing. A significant related issue concerns the potential correlation between a student's use of such BEV patterns and evaluation of his or her essay by writing instructors. This aspect of the study addresses both issues by focusing on BEV *discourse* patterns.

ISSUES IN THE STUDY

Work by researchers such as Whiteman (1976), Scott (1981), Wright (1984), Chaplin (1987), and my own earlier work on NAEP (Smitherman, 1985 NCTE Research Report) raised issues concerning comparisons of African American and European American student writers, methodological concerns about differential topics, audiences, task conditions for speech and writing, the importance of BEV discourse over BEV syntax in writing, and the relationship between the "students' right to their own language" and teacher ratings of student writing. The following crucial questions are examined here:

1   Can black student writing be characterized by an identifiable discourse style rooted in the African American Verbal Tradition?
2   If so, does use of this discourse style correlate with use of patterns of BEV grammar?

3   What effect, if any, does use of an African American discourse
    style have on teacher ratings of black student writing?
4   Given writing with *both* BEV discourse and BEV grammar, does
    one dimension have greater effect on teacher ratings than the
    other?

Some responses to these questions emerged from the research
of Scott (1981) and Chaplin (1987). Scott controlled for the methodological shortcomings in earlier studies (for example, unequivalent
topics, modalities, and audiences) by using African American college
freshmen's speeches and essays on identical topics, produced under
identical conditions. The essays were edited by freshman composition instructors for BEV, mechanics, spelling, and punctuation.
Scott then asked the writing instructors to evaluate edited and
unedited versions of the students' essays. When she compared the
ratings of edited essays with ratings of corresponding unedited essays,
no significant difference was found. Scott concluded that other
factors such as discourse patterns were probably influencing the
ratings.

Chaplin used 1984 NAEP essays for her work. (Hers is believed
to be the only other research on African American student writing
in NAEP.) She compared African American and European American
eighth- and ninth-grade students in NAEP and African American students in the 1986 New Jersey High School Proficiency
Test in an attempt to identify discourse patterns differentiating
black and white students. She focused on the construct of field
dependency–independency, that is, the thinker's–writer's relationship to the event, idea, phenomenon, or "field" under discussion.
The field dependent thinker's–writer's style demands involvement
with and a lack of distancing from the phenomenon being studied,
analyzed, or communicated about. There is a tendency to see things
whole, rather than segmented. The field independent thinker's–
writer's style demands distance from and a lack of involvement with
the field. There is a tendency to view things in parts or segments.

African American psychologists have long theorized that African Americans employ a field dependent style and European
Americans a field independent style (e.g., Wilson 1971; Williams
1972; Simpkins, Holt, and Simpkins 1976). Cooper (1979) did the
pioneering research on linguistic correlates of field dependency,
bringing together the insights of African American psychologists and
communication scholars. While the notion of differing cognitive
styles, varied along racial–cultural lines, has caused controversy, it is
imperative to understand that we are not talking about cognitive style
in the "genetic inferiority" sense used by Bereiter and Engleman
(1966) or Jensen (1980). Rather, field dependency–independency

emanates from different cultural orientations and world views, a view in concert with the theoretical frameworks of Von Humboldt (1841), Sapir (1929), Vološinov ([1923] 1973), Whorf (1956), Vygotsky (1962), and more recently Hymes (1974). It can be argued that we may not sufficiently understand the exact nature of the field dependency–independency constructs, yet a great deal of research substantiates that these constructs are reliable indicators of differing cultural experiences and cosmologies. Critically, and futuristically as US society becomes increasingly diverse, we must arrive at a genuine acceptance of the fact that difference does not mean deficiency.

Chaplin used black and white teacher raters to assess the African American and European American students' use of field dependency–independency as a discourse style in their essays. Her analysis led to the following observation: "[F]or more of the Black than White student writers, there was an identifiable field dependent style" (Chaplin, 1987, p. 26). Without being given an imposed structure or racial identification of the student writers, Chaplin's readers identified two discourse features in the black student writing that marked field dependency: cultural vocabulary–influence and conversational tone. According to Chaplin, cultural vocabulary–influence represented culture-specific words, idioms, and phrases, the language that has "helped them to shape reality" and thus "become a part of their writing" (p. 48). Conversational tone she defined as producing an essay that reads like "recorded oral language or a conversation" (p. 37). Although Chaplin states that there were more similarities than differences in the black and white students' writing, she does conclude that "conversational tone, cultural vocabulary and Black Vernacular English were used more often by Black . . . students" (1990, p. 18).

In terms of implications for writing instruction, Chaplin advises that, since "Black students . . . seemed . . . less able to distance themselves from cultural influences," such instruction "should be conceived within the context of an understanding and appreciation of the Black experience" if we are to "maximize the potential that Black students have for writing development" (1990, p. 21). Chaplin's work has buttressed my own claims about a discernible African American discourse style of writing which I began to explore in analyzing the 1969 and 1979 NAEP essays. Those explorations were extended and developed, and the use of a black discourse style became the focal point in the present study.

SAMPLE AND METHODS

In developing the methodology for this study, I felt it critical to compare African American student writers with one another, rather

than with European American student writers. The research literature is quite definitive about the existence of an African American
Verbal Tradition, with varying degrees of survival within the race
(see e.g., Herskovits 1941; Dillard 1972; Lincoln 1990; Thompson
1983; Labov 1972; Asante 1990; Smitherman [1977] 1986; Gates
1988b). Our focus here was to analyze the degree to which this tradition survives in the writing of black students across a generational
time span, rather than to assess the degree of borrowing from this
tradition by European American students. Further, although black
students are often disproportionately represented in "basic" writing
courses, I felt it imperative to analyze a variety of black student
writers, not just those deemed "basic" or "remedial." Because there
is diversity of performance within race, writing norms can be derived
from African American student performance.

In our study of 1969 and 1979 NAEP essays, we analyzed black
discourse, using holistic scoring for field dependency. The discourse
analysis involved only the sample of imaginative–narrative essays
and employed general, impressionistic ratings of field involvement
by a social psychologist, a graduate student in English, and me. We
rated the essays holistically using a "field involvement score" based
on the rater's assessment of the degree of distance of the writer
from his or her subject matter. Some of the stylistic–linguistic features
that this measurement involved were the presence of interaction
between the writer and others, dialog in the essay that clearly
involved the writer, the attribution of human qualities to nonhuman
things, and other signals that the writer was in the environment of
the communication context he or she created.

For the present work, using 1984 and 1988/89 NAEP essays,
we extended and refined that earlier methodology. Several writing
instructors experienced in teaching African American students
and one other sociolinguist, who specializes in Black English
Vernacular studies, worked with me to construct a model of
African American discourse to use in analyzing the essays. First, all
became conversant with work on field dependency–independency,
including Cooper's and Chaplin's studies and my 1985 NAEP
study. Then each instructor independently read the same 25 essays,
noting any features that struck him or her as discernibly African
American. Next, the group members came together to discuss
and compare our lists. We repeated this same procedure twice,
thus ending up with a model based on independent assessment,
discussion, and 85 percent agreement about the black discourse
features in 75 essays in the NAEP sample. Each time we came
together for discussion, we found ourselves coming up with similar

concepts, different labels and terminology to be sure, but essentially the same characteristic conceptual features. We established the following set of criteria for African American discourse in black student writing:

1   Rhythmic, dramatic, evocative language. *Example:* "Darkness is like a cage in black around me, shutting me off from the rest of the world."

2   Reference to color–race–ethnicity (that is, when topic does not call for it). *Example:* "I dont get in trouble at school or have any problems with people picking on me I am nice to every one no matter what color or sex."

3   Use of proverbs, aphorisms, Biblical verses. *Example:* "People might have shut me off from the world cause of a mistake, crime, or a sin ... Judge not others, for you to will have your day to be judge"

4   Sermonic tone reminiscent of traditional Black Church rhetoric, especially in vocabulary, imagery, metaphor. *Example:* "I feel like I'm suffering from being with world. There no lights, food, water, bed and clothes for me to put on. Im fighten, scared of what might happened if no one finds me But I pray and pray until they do find me."

5   Direct address–conversational tone. *Example:* "I think you should use the money for the railroad track ... it could fall off the tracks and kill someone on the train And that is very dangerius. Don't you think so. Please change your mind and pick the railroad tracks. For the People safelty O.K." [From letter-writing, persuasive task]

6   Cultural references. *Example:* "How about slipping me some chitterlings in tonite"

7   Ethnolinguistic idioms. *Example:* ". . . a fight has broke loose"; "It would run me crazy . . ."

8   Verbal inventiveness, unique nomenclature. *Example:* "[The settlers] were pioneerific"; "[The box] has an eye look-out"

9   Cultural values–community consciousness. Expressions of concern for development of African Americans; concern for welfare of entire community, not just individuals, as for example several essays in which students expressed the view that recreational facilities would have to be for everybody, "young and old, and the homeless among Blacks"

10   Field dependency. Involvement with and immersion in events and situations; personalizing phenomena; lack of distance from topics and subjects.

The research team used holistic scoring to rank each essay in terms of the degree of African American discourse in the essay. We used a 4-point Likert-type scale, from 1 ("highly discernible African American style") to 4 ("not discernible African American style"). Each of the 1984 imaginative essays ($N = 432$) and a subsample ($N = 435$) of the 1984 and 1988 persuasive essays were coded independently by two members of our research team. In the case of a discrepancy in coding, a third member coded the essay. The total number of essays coded was 867. For 780 of the essays, or in 90 percent of the discourse sample, the two raters agreed independently on the discourse score assigned to the essay. (For sample essays from 1969 through 1988, see Sample essays, pp. 187–9.)

Each of the essays had also been given a primary trait score or a holistic score, or both by NAEP teachers – raters trained and experienced in holistic scoring and general writing assessment. A holistic score is an assessment of overall writing competency, what NAEP describes as "a global view of the ideas, language facility, organization, mechanics, and syntax of each paper taken as whole" (Applebee et al. 1990, p. 84). Further, with holistic scoring, papers are evaluated relative to one another, rather than against specific criteria, as is the case with primary trait scoring. In 1969 and 1979, NAEP raters used a 4-point scale for both types of scoring. In 1984 and 1988, NAEP rates used a 6-point scale for holistic and a 4-point scale for primary trait scoring.

In primary trait assessment, papers are evaluated according to features of specific writing tasks. This score reflects the measure of student success in accomplishing the assigned purpose of the writing (Applebee et al. 1990, p. 6). Here, matters of mechanics, grammar, and syntax are subordinated to fluency and execution of the writing task.

For analysis, our team's discourse scores and NAEP's rater scores were compared to ascertain the degree of correlation, if any, between use of an African American discourse style and the primary trait and holistic scores assigned to an essay by raters.

Next, the discourse scores were analyzed to examine the correlation, if any, between the production of BEV syntax and the use of a black oral discourse style. BEV syntax was measured by the percentage of realization of patterns established in the literature as BEV grammatical patterns.

RESULTS

Let us begin with a summary of the findings relative to discourse analysis and primary trait and holistic scores in NAEP 1969 and 1979. Analysis indicated the following:

1 There was no statistically significant decline in field dependency from 1969 to 1979. This finding contrasted with the significant decline in BEV syntax in the narrative mode over the decade (Smitherman and Wright, 1983a).

2 There was no correlation between use of BEV syntax and field dependency; that is, high users of BEV syntax do not necessarily use field dependent style, nor are those writers who use low BEV syntax predictably field independent.

3 There was no correlation between rater score and field dependency. By contrast, BEV syntax correlated significantly and negatively with rater score for both primary trait and holistic scoring. Even when all variables (sex, year, essay type, field dependency score) were factored into equation, BEV syntax remained the most significant predictor of rater score.

Next, we turn to the 1984 and 1988 results of discourse analysis, BEV syntax, and rater scores. As detailed above, our present NAEP study used a fully developed, explicit set of criteria for identifying varying degrees of black discourse in the 1984 imaginative essays and the 1984 and 1988/89 persuasive essays. Correlations were run between (1) the discourse score and BEV syntax, and (2) the discourse score and holistic and primary trait scores.

In the case of the first relationship, results tend to support the tendency we observed in 1969 and 1979, namely, that BEV syntax and BEV discourse are *not* co-occurring variables. No correlation was found between a discernibly African American discourse style and the production of BEV syntax. In fact, of the three sets of essay data subjected to discourse analysis, *correlations were found between BEV grammar and non-African American discourse style*. Although only one of these analyses reached statistical significance, it is interesting to note that the correlations are all positive. That is, when overall BEV syntax was high, the discourse scores tended to be high also. A high discourse score on our rating scale indicated an essay that *did not have a discernibly African American discourse style*, thus suggesting that the production of BEV grammar goes up as the writing becomes less "black" rhetorically. Although we must propose this as an observed trend, not a conclusion (see Table 10.8), it is interesting to note that this observation coincides with that of researchers who posit that "talking black" does not have to encompass features of BEV grammar (e.g., Taylor, 1992; Hoover, 1978; Smitherman, 1986).

In the second possible relationship — between discourse score and holistic and primary trait scores — results for 1984 and 1988/89 were highly significant, in contrast to the 1969 and 1979 findings. In the 1980s, *the more discernibly African American the discourse, the higher the primary trait and holistic scores; the less discernibly African*

American the discourse, the lower the primary trait and holistic scores.
This finding was statistically significant for all three data sets and
for both holistic and primary trait scoring (see Table 10.9). What
the negative correlations in Table 10.9 indicate is that the higher
the discourse score, the lower the rater's score. As mentioned, a
high discourse score indicates an essay written in a non–African
American discourse style. As it turns out, these essays were assigned
lower rater scores, whether assessed by using primary trait of holistic
scoring criteria. This finding held regardless of the degree of BEV
grammar in a given essay, at least with primary trait scoring.

As an illustration of this finding, note the opening sentences
in the two essays below. The writers are responding to NAEP's
1984 imaginative essay prompt, a picture of a box with a hole in
it and an eye looking out, requiring the writers to "imagine" themselves in the picture and to describe the scene and their feelings in
a "lively and interesting" way. Essay 582200 begins this way (see
Sample essays for entire essay):

> Well, a boy is in a box outside, may be in his or her back and looking
> through a square hole. He or she look like hear she is hiding from someone.
> Maybe he or she is 5 year old and some one is trying to find him/her to
> beat him or her up.

In terms of its degree of African American discourse, we rated this
essay a 4, that is, distinctly non-black style. NAEP raters gave the
essay a primary trait score of 1, and a holistic score of 2, both low
scores. By contrast, essay 590877 begins this way (refer to Sample
essays, p. 189 for entire essay):

> I see little kids playing around me some on the swings, and some on the
> sliding bord. The kids are enjoying themselfs. As for me I'm in this box
> because I'm afraid of all of the other kids in the park.

We gave this essay a black discourse score of 1, that is, distinctly
black style. NAEP raters gave the essay a primary trait score of 3
and a holistic score of 5, both high scores.

Table 10.8 Correlations between BEV syntax and discourse style,
1984 and 1988

Essay year and type	R-value	P-value
1984 Imaginative	.0361	.45★
1984 Persuasive	.1436	.05★★
1988 Persuasive	.0044	.95★

★ = Not statistically significant.
★★ = Statistically significant at .05 or less.

Table 10.9   Correlations between BEV discourse and holistic and primary trait scores, 1984 and 1988

Essay year and type	Scoring method	R-value	P-value
1984 Imaginative★	P	−.1660	.001★★
	H	−.1783	.000★★
1984 Persuasive	H	−.3260	.009★★
1988 Persuasive	P	−.1967	.002★★
	H	−.3924	.000★★

P = Primary trait.
II = Holistic.
★ = Imaginative task not given in 1988.
★★ = Statistically significant at .05 or lower.

Now, clearly both of the above essays begin with departures from Edited American English. Yet the latter essay exhibits greater fluency and power, and it is clear that this writer is on her or his way somewhere towards a product that will be rhetorically effective. In sum, what our analysis of essays by several hundred African American student writers indicates is this: given a paper with both BEV grammar and BEV discourse, the greater the degree of black discourse, irrespective of the degree—amount of BEV grammar, the higher will be the rating in primary trait scoring, that is, scoring for fluency—accomplishment of the rhetorical task.

Finally, the imaginative—narrative essay continues to be black students' strong suit. These essays were consistently assessed higher by NAEP raters than were the 1984 or 1988 persuasives. Further, the imaginatives also exhibited higher levels of African American Verbal Tradition style, as indicated by the fact that greater numbers of these essays received discourse scores of 1 or 2 by our research team than was the case with our discourse rating of persuasives.

CONCLUSIONS AND IMPLICATIONS

The title of this essay contains an age-old black proverb whose message speaks to the power of blackness in skin color, rhetorical fluency, and cultural affinity. For 1984 imaginative and 1984 and 1988 persuasive NAEP essays, a team of experienced writing instructors was able to identify a discernible black discourse style and establish criteria for rating the "blackness" of student essays. The team achieved a 90 percent agreement for 867 essays. Results indicated that students who employed a black expressive discourse style received higher NAEP scores than those who did not. In the case of primary trait scores, this finding held regardless of the frequency of BEV syntax (fairly low anyway, and continuing to decline over time; see Smitherman, 1992d).

There are several clear implications here for writing instructors and others concerned about African American students' written literacy. First, capitalize on the strengths of African American cultural discourse; it is a rich reservoir which students can and should tap. Second, encourage students toward the field dependency style, which enables them to produce more powerful, meaningful, and highly rated essays. Third, design strategies for incorporating the black imaginative, storytelling style into student production of other essay modalities. Fourth, de-emphasize your and your students' concerns about BEV grammar; overconcentration on these forms frequently suppresses the production of African American discourse and its rich, expressive style.

As cultural norms shift focus from "book" English to "human" English, the narrativizing, dynamic quality of the African American Verbal Tradition will help students produce lively, image-filled, concrete, readable essays, regardless of rhetorical modality – persuasive, informative, comparison–contrast, and so forth. I am often asked "how far" does the teacher go with this kind of writing pedagogy. My answer: as far as you can. Once you have pushed your students to rewrite, revise; rewrite, revise; rewrite, revise; and once they have produced the most powerful essay possible, then and only then should you have them turn their attention to BEV grammar and matters of punctuation, spelling, and mechanics.

Finally, if you are worried about preparing your students for the next level ("Well, that might be okay in *my* classroom, but then what about when they pass on to Mrs. X's class . . ."), consider the NAEP results reported here from the perspective of the teacher-raters of the 1980s and beyond. They contrast sharply with those teacher-raters in the 1969 and 1979 NAEP, where African American discourse style had no effect on rater scores. The fact that rater scores in 1984 and 1988 *positively correlated with black discourse styles* speaks favorably for the social and educational efforts of groups such as the Center for Applied Linguistics, the National Council of Teachers of English, the Conference on College Composition and Communication, and others who, over the past twenty years, have worked to sensitize teachers to the linguistic–cultural norms of the African American speech community. Many people now appear to be receptive to and subliminally aware of the rhetorical power of the African American Verbal Tradition, and in some quarters they even consciously celebrate it. Public schools and college teachers, too, now appear to understand that "the blacker the berry, the sweeter the juice."

SAMPLE ESSAYS

INFORMATIVE, 1969

Essay 344

I remember going to the mounment when in washington. It was a tall building in which the class walk up the way up to the top. and look out the window which was somewhat very small, I didn't mind because I saw washington as it really was. After being up there for a long period of time and the teacher felt that the class had had plenty of rest, we decide to walk down the stairs. Then we went to the capital and just happen that congress was in section that day. So we listen to them for about 10 minutes. From the capital we went to the white house where the guide give us a guide the house.

INFORMATIVE, 1988

Essay 540770

The unquestionable difference between food on the frontier and food today is technology. All of today's conveniences: microwaves, food processors, and even refrigeration have made food preparation and food usage far different from that of early American pioneers.

As our nation developed, so did its innovative and technological ideas. The pioneers settled on undeveloped land that yielded on certain crops and livestock. Now, we are living in a nation where almost any food is available For instance, pioneers would have never thought of eating kiwi fruit from Australia or even Lobster from Alaska.

With the increase in technology came the modernization of transportation. With varied uses of travel many type of food are now available that were unthinkable in early American life. Also with the increase in technology came, convenient methods of preseration or food, namely refrigeration.

In short, the reasons for the vast array of differenes between foods on the frontier and food today are modernization and technological advances.

IMAGINATIVE, 1969

Essay 32

> But, mother I am telling you the hole truth about Henry laid egg in the Chevy May be he not that kind of thing that go around eat of little thing you were say, But also you doesn't like him.

Essay 53

> I am a sad sad bird. Nobody wants me because I am so weird-looking. But some day just like the Negro they will realize that I am something. May be I do have a long beck. They shouldn't juge me that way. I might look dumb to them but I have some sense. They just wont give me change to show it. They just left me out here all by myself. The don't realize. that I'm blood and skin. I'm just as good as any other bird.

Field dependent essay, a discernible black style; NAEP rater score (2), low score.

IMAGINATIVE, 1979

Essay 148

> Last night a very odd-looking bird appeared in the neighborhood. Then suddenly upon seeing this odd-looking bird a kaos arose before serveral families. This was one of the biggest controversies in several years due to the fact that this town almost became a ghost town. It came to be that the appearance of this bird in the town was a runaway from the California state zoo. And their authorities had come to search for this bird and was offering a reward well over the town's income for a whole year. This incident was news making in more than thirty-eight states throughtout the country. The reason the odd bird's valuability was that it was the only of its kind left in existence. And it was carrying youn'g ready for a full life in a matter of two to three weeks. Nevertheless money to those authorities who were searching for this odd looking bird, was no object. Although the bird wich was last seen in the small village was not found there, the town's fame and popularity rose to everyone. The town was far away from being a ghost town.

Field independent essay, not a discernible black style; NAEP rater score (3), high score.

Essay 149

It was the last of its kind, the only one left. The Ornithologists did not know what to do. Cloning? No, it had only been accomplished with lower forms such as frogs and othe amphibians. Cryogenics? That won't work either, complete cell preservation is still a mystery. What can be done? The scientists thought, discussed and tried to brainstorm their way to an answer. Nothing. 'So this is what our road to the future is. A road to destruction is what it is. So this is where technology is taking us. We are the only species of animal blessed with the gift of creative thought. We are given the responsibility of life on this planet And this what we do. We can't leave well enough alone. One by one we're wiping out the inhabitants of this planet. Well gentlemen, I've come to my decision.' With that Dr Avers PhD, naturalist, etc., etc., steps over to the window, throws it open, and releases the bird. Everyone watches in silence, with mixed feeling as the last of a dying species comes to grips with freedom and with powerful wing strokes gracefully drifts into the horizon.

IMAGINATIVE, 1984

Essay 582200

Well, a boy is in a box outside, may be in his or her back and loking through a square hole. He or she look like hear she is hiding from someone. Maybe he or she is 5 year old and some one is trying to find him/her to beat him or her up. There for a hour the person in the box stay there and it is getting dark. The person looking for the kid in the box knows where the kid is a waiting for that person to come out.

NEAP primary trait score (1), holistic score (2), both low; discourse score (4), not a discernible black style.

Essay 590877

I see little kids playing around me some on the swings, and some on the sliding bord. The kids are enjoying themselfs. As for me I'm in this box because I'm afraid of all of the other kids in the park. In a distinance I see a baseball field and some men playing and over by the park is a Basketball court where other kids are playing. And in the picnic grounds theirs a family having a picnic. The kids are playing catch with their father while the mother I think is setting up the picnic area. In another section of the park theirs a crowd of people watching these two guys "break" dancing. "Break" dancing is a new form of dance combining some gymnastics with some regular dance moves. It is a real sight to see. Also I see some girls on the sidewalk jumping rope double dutch style that's when you use two ropes. The girls are very good to. It is a hot day so I see that the swimming pool is doing good today. I would be over their myself If I wasn't shy. It's a very hot in this box but I'm so afraid to come out. I see that a fight has broke loose by the swings. Two little kids are fighting over one see all the other kids have already taken all the other swings and their two kids and only one swing left. I think that the kids have settled their argument now.

Now here comes a big black man over by me now. He says that my mother is here to pick me up so I could go home By.

NAEP primary trait score (3), holistic score (5), both high; discourse score (1), a highly discernible African American style.

PERSUASIVE, 1984

Essay 050238

I think that If the ABandoned RailRoad track was not there. that we can use the money that we have saved could go on the things we need for the community center. So that the children can have many & more things to do. The RailRoad could Be destroyed so that they can make a play ground out of It. And the warehouse could have some toys In It Also Just in case It get cold or Rain. Therefore they could have toys Inside and outside.

NAEP holistic score (2), low score; discourse score (4), not a discernible black style.

PERSUASIVE, 1988

Essay 520462

How are you doing? Fine I hope!

I'm writing you this letter in reference to you making your purchase in buying the warehouse.

I think that in buying the old warehouse, we could paint it and fix it up and make it out of a gym for the kids during the week and on week-ends and on Fridays we could have bingo and maybe once or twice a month on Sundays we could give a super.

During the week we could have the children come here after school and do their homework and then let them play a little basketball, until about 5:30 p.m.

On Fridays at about 7:00 we could set up for Bingo and sell the cards 8 for $10 and that way we could help pay for the pot and have 14 games and cherry betts.

Every first or last Sunday in the month we could give a super for the community and sell each plate for $3 to $5.

If you have any questions, please feel free to call me at 288–8263.

Sincerely,

Ms. Zenitta

NAEP holistic score (4), high score; discourse score (1), a highly discernible black style.

Essay 541082

I live about one mile or two from the big old warehouse that's for sale. Most of the time I am at home reading, doing homework, or watching television. But on weekends if I am not out with my friends I have nothing else to do. I think the big old warehouse would be a good place to renovate and turn it into a center for young people who have to go home to an empty house after school, latchkey kids, who need counseling, or just don't have nothing better to do on weekends, but sit around the house or go out and start trouble.

Sometimes I go home to an empty house and I'm scared or just down right bored. I wouldn't mind having a place to go where I can talk to other people my age or play with the little kids who are there.

The warehouse could even have counselors to help young people who have trouble in their homes, are on drugs, drink too much, or pregnant teenagers who have no one to share their feelings with.

I have seen some young people, even kids the age of six or seven stealing or starting fights or just hanging out late on school days and weekends because their parents are never home to take care of them. Maybe if they had a place to go; A place where they could do activities or have a chance to show the talent that they have things would be a little different.

I hope you think about everything I've said carefully before you make your decision. If you have any questions please feel free to call me at 465–8429 anytime after 4:00 p.m.

Sincerely yours,

LANGUAGE AND
CULTURE

A FUNDAMENTAL RULE for

using a language is knowledge of that language's cultural codes. As Fanon put it, to speak is to assume a culture. It is not enough just to know the syntax of a language, to know how to pronounce its sounds, to know its many words. You need also to know the rules of speaking the language in the social and cultural contexts that are an inextricable dimension of any language. Or as one scholar put it, being competent in a language means you know who can say what to whom and under what conditions (Hymes, 1974). This linguistic principle was only an abstract concept to me until my introduction into the world of

INTRODUCTION TO PART THREE

professional conferences many years ago. At the time, I was still a young member of the "Great Unwashed" – or ghetto, as they say these days. The speaker at the conference session my college advisor had steered me to was a white male linguist. The topic: Black English. The audience was a racially-mixed crowd of nearly 300 people. In his talk, the speaker kept bemoaning the fact that research on Black English was being blocked by "middle-class niggers," an expression he used at least three times in his presentation. Although some people walked out after the third "middle-class niggers," I recall that no one challenged the speaker about his use of "nigger." While it is true that African Americans do use the term, pronouncing it as *nigga*, and further, while it is the case that, among Blacks, it has a variety of meanings, only one of them negative (see e.g., Major, 1994; Smitherman, 1994b) this linguist had violated one of the two basic rules governing the use of this term: (1) *nigga* cannot be used by white folk; and (2) Blacks should not use the term in the public arena, and particularly not in the presence of whites. Although this second rule has been relaxed considerably, with the advent of Hip Hop Culture and the emergence of what Spears

(1998) has labeled "uncensored mode" language in the public culture, the sociolinguistic rule about white folk not using *nigga* appears to be as strong today as it was a generation ago.

The essays in this section focus on cultural codes and socio-linguistic rules for speaking US Ebonics. The first essay is taken from my first book on Ebonics, *Talkin and Testifyin*. "How I Got Ovuh" explicates the cultural-linguistic connection between Africa and African America.

"'If I'm Lyin, I'm Flyin': The Game of Insult in Black Language" analyzes the African American Verbal Tradition "playin the Dozens," aka "snappin" and "your mother" jokes. This is a top-ical area that is potentially as sensitive as talk about "niggers" and is generally reserved for conversations involving cultural familiars. Unlike the use of *nigga*, though, snaps, particularly those of the sig-nifyin variety, can be used by white folk if they are down, or have achieved the status of an honorary Black. This essay on the insult game was first published as the introduction to *Double Snaps*, a 1995 collection of contemporary snaps from all over the country. The authors, Percelay, Dweck, and Ivey, call their production company "2 Bros. & A White Guy." The essay traces the cultural and histor-ical roots of snappin, demonstrates its use in African American liter-ature and music, and documents its use by Black women. This dissin game involves playin with and on the word, which according to Morrison, is "the thing black people love so much − the saying of words, holding them on the tongue, experimenting with them, play-ing with them. It's a love, a passion" (1981). "'If I'm Lyin, I'm Flyin'" sets forth the cultural rules for this form of linguistic play, providing answers to the sociolinguistic question of who can say what to whom under what conditions.

Like the Dozens and signifyin, proverb use is part of the linguistic−cultural fabric of the Black speech community and requires knowledge of cultural rules when you use this style of speaking. "'Makin a Way Outa No Way': The Proverb Tradition in the Black Experience" discusses the socio-cultural factors involved in the use of proverbs, defined as "figurative, epigrammatic statements that express widely accepted strategies for addressing recurring situ-ations." The essay is based on a collaborative study of proverbs in Detroit and Pittsburgh in the US and in Antigua in the Caribbean. We make no claim that the 1,000-plus proverbs we collected are African in origin. We do claim, though, that certain proverbs are favored by African Americans − e.g., "God don't like ugly" and "The blacker the berry, the sweeter the juice." Further, African Americans use proverbs as a rhetorical strategy, such as in indirect confrontation and in socializing children. Unlike snaps, proverb use in African America and elsewhere in the Diaspora appears to be on the decline. We thus concluded our study with a call for language researchers to make collections of this significant verbal art form in the Black Language tradition.

The fourth essay in this section continues the focus on socio-cultural rules in the African American speech community, this time from the vantage point of a Womanist: "a Black woman who is rooted in the African American community and committed to the survival and development of herself and the community" (Smitherman, 1994b); "Responsible. In charge. *Serious*" (Walker, 1983). "Testifyin, Sermonizin, and Signifyin: Anita Hill, Clarence Thomas, and the African American Verbal Tradition" critically analyzes the language used by Hill and Thomas during the Congressional hearing for Thomas's nomination to the US Supreme Court in 1991. The essay was published in a book I edited, entitled *African American Women Speak Out on Anita Hill–Clarence Thomas* (1995), a collection of essays by Black women scholars and writers on the Hill–Thomas controversy. This analysis of Hill's and Thomas's contrasting rhetorical styles was motivated by the unexpected low support of Hill among everyday Black women. The analysis indicates that within the framework of cultural codes in the African American community, Thomas trumped Hill because he capitalized on and ruthlessly exploited Black verbal traditions, such as signi-fyin. Even though he did not use features of Black Language grammar or pronunciation, he effectively sounded "Black" because he situated his speaking style within the socio-cultural conventions of African America. The essay calls for the construction of a twenty-first century Womanist language grounded in the linguistics of leadership in Black women who come out of the tradition of struggle.

Rap music too reflects the tradition of struggle in African America even though members of the middle class and older adults often villify Hip Hop artists for the bawdy rhymes and loud-talkin verses in their music. "'The Chain Remain the Same: Communicative Practices in the Hip Hop Nation'" analyzes the language of Rap as a discourse of resistance that is grounded within the linguistic–cultural fabric of African America. It sets forth ideas which had been a part of my thinking and teaching for several years before these ideas were finally transformed into a formal essay. In fact, this essay might not have been written at all had I not been invited to present a paper on Rap at the conference, "English in Africa," which was convened in Grahamstown, South Africa in September of 1995. The essay briefly overviews the history of Rap from its beginnings in the 1970s and tracks the use of various linguistic, semantic, and rhetorical forms in work produced by a wide variety of Hip Hop artists, including so-called "gangsta rappers." The essay argues that the language of rap is a sociolinguistic strategy to "disturb the peace," to arouse the dead citizens of the USG (United States Ghetto), to represent for the dispossessed. As Chuck D., of Public Enemy, said "Rap music is Black folks' CNN." "'The Chain Remain the Same'" concludes that Rap is not a new kid on the block. Rather its language and resistance rhetoric are well within and as old as the Black Oral Tradition itself.

BOTH IN THE old-time black Gospel song and in black street vernacular, "gittin ovuh" has to do with surviving. While the religious usage of the phrase speaks to spiritual survival in a sinister world of sin, its secular usage speaks to material survival in a white world of oppression. Since men and women live neither by bread nor spirit alone, both vitally necessary acts of gittin ovuh challenge the human spirit to "keep on pushin" toward "higher ground." In Black America, the oral tradition has served as a fundamental vehicle for gittin ovuh. That tradition preserves the Afro-American heritage and reflects the collective spirit of the race. Through song, story, folk sayings, and rich verbal interplay among everyday people, lessons and precepts about life and survival are handed down from generation to generation. Until contemporary times, Black America relied on word-of-mouth for its rituals

"HOW I GOT
OVUH":
AFRICAN WORLD
VIEW AND
AFRO-AMERICAN
ORAL TRADITION
[1977]

My soul look back and wonder
How I got over.

of cultural preservation. (For instance, it was not until the late nineteenth century that the Negro spirituals were written down, though they date well back to the beginnings of slavery.) But word-of-mouth is more than sufficient because the structural underpinnings of the oral tradition remain basically intact even as each new generation makes verbal adaptations within the tradition. Indeed the core strength of this tradition lies in its capacity to accommodate new situations and changing realities. If we are to understand the complexity and scope of black communication patterns, we must have a clear understanding of the oral tradition and the world view that undergirds that tradition.

   The Black communication system is actualized in different ways, dependent upon the sociocultural context — for instance, "street" versus "church" – but the basic underlying structures of this communication network are essentially similar because they are grounded in the traditional African world view. In brief, that view refers to underlying thought patterns, belief sets, values, ways of looking at the world and the community of men and women that are shared by all traditional Africans (that is, those that haven't been westernized).

The mainstream tradition of European scholarship on Africa has rested on a conceptual framework relative to the so-called "diversity" of Africa. To be sure, there are differences in the many tribes, languages, customs, spirits, and deities that exist throughout the African continent, but these seeming diversities are merely surface variations on the basic "deep structure" themes of life acknowledged by traditional Africans. Focusing on such surface differences as tribal customs or politically defined African boundaries has only served to obscure the existence of the deep structure that is shared by all traditional African people. Robert F. Thompson conducted field studies of African art in nine different African cultures and was able to identify common canons of form pervading them all. Similarly, Darryll Forde's studies of African social values in various tribal cultures brought him to remark that: "One is impressed, not only by the great diversity of ritual forms and expressions of beliefs, but also by substantial underlying similarities in religious outlook and moral injunction." And the West African scholar Fela Sowande, as well as the East African scholar John S. Mbiti, present nearly identical descriptions of the African view of the universe and man's place in the scheme of things. To be sure, students of African culture have yet to detail *all* of the salient features that transcend tribal differences and constitute what is here being called the "traditional African world view." But recent findings and field studies, especially those of African scholars themselves, point to sufficient patterns of commonality to suggest an interlocking cultural and philosophical network throughout Africa. We can thus assert that similar underlying thought patterns do exist amid the unending diversity of African people, and therefore it is appropriate to speak of traditional African thought as a single entity – albeit with complex and diverse manifestations.

What is the traditional African world view? First, there is a fundamental unity between the spiritual and the material aspects of existence. Though both the material and the spiritual are necessary for existence, the spiritual domain assumes priority.

The universe is hierarchical in nature, with God at the head of the hierarchy, followed by lesser deities, the "living dead" (ancestral spirits), people, animals, and plants. Though the universe is hierarchical, all modes of existence are necessary for the sustenance of its balance and rhythm. Harmony in nature and the universe is provided by the complementary, interdependent, synergic interaction between the spiritual and the material. Thus we have a paradigm for the way in which "opposites" function. That is, "opposites" constitute interdependent, interacting forces which are necessary for producing a given reality.

Similarly, communities of people are modeled after the interdependent rhythms of the universe. Individual participation is necessary for community survival. Balance in the community, as in the universe, consists of maintaining these interdependent relationships.

The universe moves in a rhythmical and cyclical fashion as opposed to linear progression. "Progression," as such, occurs only into the past world of the spirit. Thus the "future" is the past. In the community, then, one's sense of "time" is based on participation in and observation of nature's rhythms and community events. (In the African conception of "time," the key is not to be "on time," but "in time.") And since participatory experiences are key to one's sense of "time," the fundamental pedagogy in the school of life becomes experience, and age serves as a prime basis for hierarchical social arrangements.

Community roles are equally governed by the hierarchical unity of the spiritual and material aspects of the universe. Since the spiritual realm is the ultimate existence of humankind, those closest to the spiritual realm assume priority in social relationships. Thus, elders are of great importance, and the spiritually developed people serve as rulers and doctors.

Naturally, Black Americans, having had to contend with slavery and Euro-American ways, have not been able to practice or manifest the traditional African world view in its totality. But, as we shall see in closely examining the many facets of the oral tradition, the residue of the African world view persists, and serves to unify such seemingly disparate black groups as preachers and poets, bluesmen and Gospel-ettes, testifiers and toast-tellers, reverends and revolutionaries. Can I get a witness?

Both in slavery times and now, the black community places high value on the spoken word. That community supports a tradition that the anthropologists would call "preliterate." (Although the great Margaret Mead laid the classic bomb on the superiority complex of the Western world when she said that the "influence" of Western culture on non-Western peoples was to make the "preliterate illiterate." In fact, the black oral tradition links Black American culture with that of other oral "pre-literate" people — such as Native Americans — for whom the spoken word is supreme.) The persistence

of the African-based oral tradition is such that blacks tend to place
only limited value on the written word, whereas verbal skills
expressed orally rank in high esteem. This is not to say that Black
Americans never read anything or that the total black community
is functionally illiterate. The influence of White America and the
demands of modern, so-called civilized living have been too strong
for that. However, it is to say that from a black perspective, written
documents are limited in what they can teach about life and survival
in the world. Blacks are quick to ridicule "educated fools," people
who done gone to school and read all dem books and still don't
know nothin! They have "book learning" but no "mother wit,"
knowledge, but not wisdom. (Naturally, not *all* educated people
are considered "educated fools," but if the shoe fits . . .) Furthermore,
aside from athletes and entertainers, only those blacks who can
perform stunning feats of oral gymnastics become culture heroes
and leaders in the community. Such feats are the basic requirement
of the trade among preachers, politicians, disc jockeys, hustlers, and
lovers. Like the preacher who was exhorting his congregation to
take care of themselves and their bodies:

PREACHER:	How many of y'all wanna live to a old age?
CONGREGATION:	Hallelujah!
PREACHER:	Or is y'all ready to die and go to Heaven?
CONGREGATION:	[*uncomfortable; some self-conscious laughter*]
	Well, no Lord, not yet, suh!
PREACHER:	Y'all wanna stay here awhile?
CONGREGATION:	Praise the Lord!
PREACHER:	Well, y'all better quit all this drankin, smokin,
	and runnin 'round. Cause, see, for me, I got
	a home in Heaven, but I ain't homesick!

And check out this from a black disc jockey on a "soul" station. He
is urging his audience to listen to his station because it's the best, and
to call in to win the "top ten" album, therein making the winner
eligible for the grand prize: "Super CHB . . . making the music work
for you. When one quits, another hits . . . Looking for that seventh
caller . . . Caller number seven, call, cop, and qualify."

In any culture, of course, language is a tool for ordering the
chaos of human experience. We feel more comfortable when we
have names for events and things. To know that "the earth is round
and revolves around the sun" might not bring us any closer to
solving the riddle of the universe, but at least it helps in imposing
an orderly explanation upon a seemingly disorderly world. To use
words to give shape and coherence to human existence is a universal
human thing — a linguistic fact of life that transcends cultural bound-

aries. The crucial difference in American culture lies in the contrasting modes in which Black and White Americans have shaped that language – a written mode for whites, having come from a European, print-oriented culture; a spoken mode for blacks, having come from an African, orally-oriented background. As black psychiatrist Frantz Fanon describes it, to "talk like a book" is to "talk like a white man."

The oral tradition, then, is part of the cultural baggage the African brought to America. The pre-slavery background was one in which the concept of Nommo, the magic power of the Word, was believed necessary to actualize life and give man mastery over things. "All activities of men, and all the movements in nature, rest on the word, on the productive power of the word, which is water and heat and seed and Nommo, that is, life force itself ... The force, responsibility, and commitment of the word, and the awareness that the word alone alters the world ...." In traditional African culture, a newborn child is a mere thing until his father gives and speaks his name. No medicine, potion, or magic of any sort is considered effective without accompanying words. So strong is the African belief in the power and absolute necessity of Nommo that all craftsmanship must be accompanied by speech. And it is not uncommon for a verbal battle to precede or accompany warfare. In the African epic of Sundiata, a renowned king of ancient Mali, the exiled king must wage war to regain his throne, but, as the griot tells us, "those fighting must make a declaration of their grievances to begin with":

> "Stop, young man. Henceforth I am the king of Mali. If you want peace, return to where you came from," said Soumaoro.
>
> "I am coming back, Soumaoro, to recapture my kingdom. If you want peace you will make amends to my allies and return to Sosso where you are the king."
>
> "I am king of Mali by force of arms. My rights have been established by conquest."
>
> "Then I will take Mali from you by force of arms and chase you from my kingdom."
>
> "Know, then that I am the wild yam of the rocks; nothing will make me leave Mali."
>
> "Know, also that I have in my camp seven master smiths who will shatter the rocks. Then, yam, I will eat you."
>
> "I am the poisonous mushroom that makes the fearless vomit."
>
> "As for me, I am the ravenous cock, the poison does not matter to me."
>
> "Behave yourself, little boy, or you will burn your foot, for I am the red-hot cinder."

"But me, I am the rain that extinguishes the cinder; I am the bois-
terous torrent that will carry you off."

"I am the mighty silk-cotton tree that looks from on high on the
tops of other trees"

"And I, I am the strangling creeper that climbs to the top of the
forest giant."

"Enough of this argument. You shall not have Mali."

"Know that there is not room for two kings on the same skin,
Soumaoro; you will let me have your place."

"Very well, since you want war I will wage war against you, but I
would have you know that I have killed nine kings whose heads adorn
my room. What a pity, indeed, that your head should take its place beside
those of your fellow madcaps."

"Prepare yourself, Soumaoro, for it will be long before the calamity
that is going to crash down upon you and yours comes to an end."

Thus Sundiata and Soumaoro spoke together. After the war of
mouths, swords had to decide the issue.

The above exchange of word-arrows is not unlike that of two
bloods squaring off on any street corner or in any cottonfield in
the US:

"If you don't quit messin wif me, uhma jump down your throat, tap
dance on your liver, and make you wish you never been born."

"Yeah, you and how many armies? Nigger, don't you know uhm so
bad I can step on a wad of gum and tell you what flavor it is."

Even though blacks have embraced English as their native tongue,
still the African cultural set persists, that is, a predisposition to imbue
the English word with the same sense of value and commitment
– "propers," as we would say – accorded to Nommo in African
culture. Hence Afro-America's emphasis on orality and belief in the
power of the rap which has produced a style and idiom totally
unlike that of whites, while paradoxically employing White English
words. We're talking, then, about a tradition in the black experience in which verbal performance becomes both a way of
establishing "yo rep" as well as a teaching and socializing force.
This performance is exhibited in the narration of myths, folk stories,
and the semi-serious tradition of "lying" in general; in black sermons;
in the telling of jokes; in proverbs and folk sayings; in street corner,
barbershop, beauty shop, and other casual rap scenes; in "signifying," "capping," "testifying," "toasting," and other verbal arts.
Through these raps of various kinds, black folk are acculturated –
initiated – into the black value system. Not talking about speech
for the sake of speech, for black talk is never simple cocktail

chit-chat, but a functional dynamic that is simultaneously a mechanism for learning about life and the world and a vehicle for achieving group approval and recognition. Even in what appears to be only casual conversation, whoever speaks is highly conscious of the fact that his personality is on exhibit and his status at stake. Black raps ain bout talkin loud and sayin nothin, for the speaker must be up on the subject of his rap, and his oral contribution must be presented in a dazzling, entertaining manner. Black speakers are flamboyant, flashy, and exaggerative; black raps are stylized, dramatic, and spectacular; speakers and raps become symbols of how to git ovuh.

In his autobiography *Black Boy*, Richard Wright excellently depicts the dynamics of a street corner rap in a Southern town:

"You eat yet?" Uneasily trying to make conversation.

"Yeah, man. I done really fed my face." Casually.

"I had cabbage and potatoes." Confidently.

"I had buttermilk and black-eyed peas." Meekly informational.

"Hell, I ain't gonna stand near you, nigger." Pronouncement.

"How come?" Feigned Innocence.

"Cause you gonna smell up this air in a minute!" A shouted accusation.

Laughter runs through the crowd.

"Nigger, your mind's in a ditch." Amusingly moralistic.

"Ditch, nothing! Nigger, you going to break wind any minute now." Triumphant pronouncement creating suspense.

"Yeah, when them black-eyed peas tell that buttermilk to move over, that buttermilk ain't gonna wanna move and there's gonna be war in your guts and your stomach's gonna swell up and bust!" Climax.

The crowd laughs loud and long.

"Man, them white folks oughta catch you and send you to the zoo and keep you for the next war!" Throwing the subject into a wider field.

"Then when that fighting starts, they oughta feed you on buttermilk and black-eyed peas and let you break wind!" The subject is accepted and extended.

"You'd win the war with a new kind of poison gas!" A shouted climax.

There is high laughter that simmers down slowly.

"Maybe poison gas is something good to have." The subject of white folks is associationally swept into the orbit of talk.

"Man, you reckon these white folks is ever gonna change?" Timid, questioning hope.

"Hell, no! They just born that way." Rejecting hope for fear that it could never come true.

"Shucks, man. I'm going north when I get grown." Rebelling against futile hope and embracing flight.

"A colored man's all right up north." Justifying flight.

"They say a white man hit a colored man up north and that colored man hit that white man, knocked him cold, and nobody did a damn thing!" Urgent wish to believe in flight.

"Man for man up there." Begging to believe in justice.

Silence.

"Listen, you reckon them buildings up north is as tall as they say they is?" Leaping by association to something concrete and trying to make belief real.

"They say they gotta building in New York forty stories high!" A thing too incredible for belief.

"Man, I'd be scareda them buildings!" Ready to abandon the now suppressed idea of flight.

"You know, they say that them buildings sway and rock in the wind." Stating a miracle.

"Naw, nigger!" Utter astonishment and rejection.

"Yeah, they say they do." Insisting upon the miracle.

"You reckon that could be?" Questioning hope.

"Hell, naw! If a building swayed and rocked in the wind, hell, it'd fall! Any fool knows that! Don't let people maka fool outta you, telling you them things." Moving body agitatedly, stomping feet impatiently, and scurrying back to safe reality.

Silence. Somebody would pick up a stone and toss it across a field.

"Man, what makes white folks so mean?" Returning to grapple with the old problem.

"Whenever I see one I spit!" Emotional rejection of whites.

"Man, ain't they ugly?" Increased emotional rejection.

"Man, you ever get right close to a white man, close enough to smell 'im?" Anticipation of statement.

"They say we stink. But my ma says white folks smell like dead folks." Wishing the enemy was dead.

"Niggers smell from sweat. But white folks smell *all* the time." The enemy is an animal to be killed on sight.

And the talk would weave, roll, surge, spurt, veer, swell, having no specific aim or direction, touching vast areas of life, expressing the tentative impulses of childhood. Money, God, race, sex, color, war, planes, machines, trains, swimming, boxing, anything . . . The culture of one black household was thus transmitted to another black household, and folk tradition was handed from group to group. Our attitudes were made, defined, set, or corrected; our ideas were discovered, discarded, enlarged, torn apart, and accepted.

While some raps convey social and cultural information, others are used for conquering foes and women. Through signification, the Dozens,[1] and boastful talk, a dude can be properly put to rest with words. (Recall the verbal duel in the Sundiata epic.) Hubert "Rap" Brown, the controversial black leader of the 1960s, describes this cultural phenomenon in his autobiography, *Die Nigger Die!*:

> what you try to do is totally destroy somebody else with words. It's that whole competition thing again, fighting each other. There'd be sometimes 40 or 50 dudes standing around and the winner was determined by the way they responded to what was said. If you fell all over each other laughing, then you knew you'd scored ... The real aim of the Dozens was to get a dude so mad that he'd cry or get mad enough to fight ... Signifying is more humane. Instead of coming down on somebody's mother, you come down on them ... A session would start maybe by a brother saying, "Man, before you mess with me you'd rather run rabbits, eat shit and bark at the moon." Then, if he was talking to me, I'd tell him:
>
> Man, you must don't know who I am.
> I'm sweet peeter jeeter the womb beater
> The baby maker the cradle shaker
> The deerslayer the buckbinder the women finder
> Known from the Gold Coast to the rocky shores of Maine
> Rap is my name and love is my game.

Since it is a socially approved verbal strategy for black rappers to talk about how bad they is, such bragging is taken at face value. While the speakers may or may not act out the implications of their words, the point is that the listeners do not necessarily *expect* any action to follow. As a matter of fact, skillful rappers can often avoid having to prove themselves through deeds if their rap is strong enough. The Black Idiom expression "selling woof [wolf] tickets" (also just plain "woofin") refers to any kind of strong language which is purely idle boasting. However, this bad talk is nearly always taken for the real thing by an outsider from another culture. Such cultural–linguistic misperception can lead to tragic consequences. Witness, for instance, the physical attacks and social repression suffered by black spokesmen of the 1960s, such as the Black Panthers. "Death to the racist exploiters!" "Off the pigs!" "Defend our communities by any means necessary!" – the white folks thought the bloods was not playin and launched an all-out military campaign. These aggressive moves resulted partly from White America's sense of fear that the radical rhetoric (much of which was really defensive, rather than offensive) constituted more than idle threats. The whites were not hip to braggadocio and woof tickets; at any rate, they wasn't buyin it.

While boastful raps are used to devastate enemies, love raps help in gittin ovuh with women. Both, of course, require speakers with intellectual adroitness and a way with words. Since it is believed that the spoken word has power, it is only logical to employ it with what many regard as men's most formidable obstacle – women. Many black rappers specialize in the verbal art of romantic rappin. Like Hubert "Rap" Brown said, love is his game. Examples of such "game," dating from the nineteenth century are provided in the folklore collection of Hampton University. Here is one such example which appeared in an 1895 edition of the *Southern Workman*, a journal published by Hampton: "My dear kin' miss, has you any objections to me drawing my cher to yer side, and revolvin' de wheel of my conversation around de axle of your understandin'?" A contemporary example is provided in the novel *Snakes* by Al Young, in which Young depicts a heavy love rapper in his main character, Shakes (short for Shakespeare). Exemplifying the rich ability of black speechmakers, Shakes gives propers to another great rapper who taught him that "you can get away with anything if you talk up on it right."

> I just wanna knock out chicks and show these other dudes they ain't hittin on doodleysquat when it come to talkin trash. I got it down, jim! You hip to Cyrano de Bergerac? . . . Talk about a joker could talk some trash! Cyrano got everybody told! Didn't nobody be messin with Cyrano, ugly as he was. Some silly stud get to cappin on Cyrano's nose and he don't flinch an inch. He get right up in the stud's face and vaporize him with several choice pro-nouncements, then he go and waste the cat in a suhword fight. Meantime, there's this little local lame that's tryna make it with Cyrano's cousin Roxanne, so old Cyrano and the lame get back up behind the bushes one night while the chick up there on the balcony. Cyrano whisperin all in the lame's ear what he spose to be sayin, but the lame messin up the lines so bad until Cyrano just sweep him on off to one side and stand up and make the speech his own self. He commence to messin up the broad's mind so bad she ready to out and out say I do. See, she don't know it's her own cousin that's been layin down that incredible rap. And now, to show you what kinda man Cyrano was, after that lady is on the verge of succumbing to the amorous design that his words had traced in the air of that night, so to speak, then he just step off to one side and let her old lame boyfriend move on into the picture and cop, like he the one been doin all that old freakish talk out there under the moonlight.

Contrary to popular stereotype, black men have never really regarded black women as sex objects, pure and simple, for the love rap, based on the African view of the reconciliation of opposites, is a synthesis of emotional and intellectual appeal and has as its ultimate objective the conquest not simply of the woman's body, but her mind as well. As one blood said, "Baby, I don't just want your behind, I want your mind." Romantic raps not only contain sweet and complementary "nothings" that lovers like to hear, but they must demonstrate the rapper's power and ability at persuasive verbal logic. An excellent example of a unique rap is provided by Woodie King in "The Game," a description of his early life in the streets. In an effort to git ovuh with Edith, a very foxy but "religious broad," Sweet Mac introduces the Bible into the game – surely an unprecedented technique in this tradition:

> for the last couple of weeks I been quoting the Good Book and all that stuff to her; telling her I am now saved myself, you dig ... I says to her, "Edith, baby, we can't go on like this. I dig you *but* ... baby I'm one hundred percent man. And baby, from looking at you, you are one hundred percent woman (the broad went for this evaluation) ... So ... if that is the case, something or someone is trying to keep us – two pure American religious people of the same order – apart." At this point, I drop a quote or two from the Good Book on her; *"Thou shall not covet thy neighbor's wife;* and baby since you're not anybody's wife, I pleaded, *do unto others as you would have them do unto you* ..." Next, I whispered to her secretly, doing the ear bit with the tongue, "Baby only something like that no-good Satan would want to stop something as mellow as laying naked in the Foggy Night with MJQ or Ravel on the hi-fi, me there playing with you, only Satan," I says. "He trying to put game on us, momma." The broad is looking dazed like she done seen the handwriting on the wall.

The existence of love rappin in the oral tradition allows a strange black man to approach a strange black woman without fear of strong reprisal. Black women are accustomed to – and many even expect – this kind of verbal aggressiveness from black men. Black culture thus provides a socially approved verbal mechanism with which the man can initiate conversation aimed at deepening the acquaintance. Rappin also accounts for what whites often label as "aggressive," "brash," "presumptive," or "disrespectful" behavior by black men toward black women. "Hey pretty momma, where you goin, wit yo baaaad self? I know you a movie star or somebody important, but could I just have a minute of yo time?" If she's interested, he gets more than a minute, if not, she just smiles and keeps on steppin.

Though this approach was previously reserved for males, with the advent of feminist assertion black women are beginning to develop the art of romantic rappin. However, it is a strictly contemporary, slowly developing trend, and verbal aggressiveness from women is still not approved in any but the most sophisticated social sets.

Figure 11.1   "That book ain't gonna teach you no French Bootsie. You got to live it. Now s'posin' you just had a fine feed at some chick's pad. You bows and says, 'Bon soir mademoisselle, et cetera.' Now that means 'Good night, Irene. Thanks for the fine scoff. The chitterlings was simply divine and I'll dig you by and by!'"

Source: "Bootsie" cartoon, by Ollie Harrington.

Black sermons also form an important part of the oral tradition. By now the sermonizing style of traditional black clergy is perhaps rather widely known, especially given the preacher imitations done by popular black comedians Flip Wilson and Richard Pryor. What has not been too well publicized is the devastating raps black preachers run down before and after their sermons. Since the traditional black church service is an emotion-packed blend of sacred and secular concerns, informality is the order of the day. It is not a lax, anything-goes kinds of informality, though, for there are traditional rituals to be performed, and codes of proper social conduct must be observed. For instance, if the Spirit moves you, it's acceptable to get up and testify even though that's not on the church program. On the other hand, when the preacher is "taking his text,"[2] a hushed silence falls over the whole congregation, and it is most out of order to get up, move around in your seat, talk, or do anything until he finishes this brief ritual in the traditional structure of the sermon.

Since the traditional black church is a social as well as a religious unit, the preacher's job as leader of his flock is to make churchgoers feel at home and to deal with the problems and realities confronting his people as they cope with the demands and stresses of daily living. Thus preachers are given wide latitude as to the topics they can discuss and the methods of presentation. Indeed, the congregation virtually demands digressive commentary and episodic rappin as a prelude to the big event. I mean, if you a preacher in a traditional black church you just don't be gittin up and goin right into yo sermon like they does in them other churches. The best preachers use this time wisely, as in the case of the big city "Reb" who was called on the carpet for healing and selling blessings over the radio:

PREACHER:	I thank God for this radio station.
CONGREGATION:	My Lord! Yes, Lord!
PREACHER:	Y'all know you got some radio directors with two years of edu-ma-cation.
CONGREGATION:	Look out, now! You on the case! Tell it! Tell it! Two years!
PREACHER:	And they have decided that they know what you want to hear. Who ever heard of a radio station licensed by the Federal Communications System that's gon tell *you* that you cain't heal?!!
CONGREGATION:	Right on, brother!
PREACHER:	Gon tell you that you cain't read a Scripture.

CONGREGATION:	Well, well!
PREACHER:	You don't tell them white folks that.
CONGREGATION:	Halleluhah!
PREACHER:	So don't tell me that 'cause I don't wonna hear it!
CONGREGATION:	No, Lord!
PREACHER:	If Jesus hada healed all the rich folks, he wouldn'ta had no problems!
CONGREGATION:	Amen! Speak on it!

The inclusion of church raps here in practically the same breath as street raps is to demonstrate the sacred–secular continuum in the oral tradition and to dramatize the importance of the black church in the culture and verbal style of black people. Very broadly speaking, and for purposes of illustration only, we can think of black language as having both a sacred and a secular style. The sacred style is rural and Southern. It is grounded in the black church tradition and black religious experience. It is revealed in the spirituals, the Moan, the Chant, the Gospel songs; it is testifyin, talkin in tongue, and bearin witness to the power of God and prayer. It tends to be more emotional and highly charged than the secular style. Though urban and Northern, the secular style also has its roots in the rural South. It is manifested in forms like the Dozens, the Toast, the blues, and folk tales, all of which were transformed to accommodate the urban experience. Within the secular style is the street culture style, the style commonly associated with, but not exclusive to, barbershops, pool halls, and street corners in black communities. More cool, more emotionally restrained than the sacred style, newer and younger in time, the secular style only fully evolved as a distinct style with the massive wave of black migration to the cities.

Sacred style is an important force in black culture because the traditional black church is the oldest and perhaps still the most powerful and influential black institution. To speak of the "traditional" black church is to speak of the holy-rolling, bench-walking, spirit-getting, tongue-speaking, vision-receiving, intuitive-directing, Amen-saying, sing-song preaching, holy-dancing, and God-sending church. Put another way, this church may be defined as that in which the content and religious substance has been borrowed from Western Judaeo-Christian tradition, but the communication of that content – the process – has remained essentially African. The specific convergence of Judaeo-Christian content and African process is found in Protestant denominations, such as Baptist, Methodist, Holiness, and Sanctified, where the worship patterns are characterized by spontaneous preacher–congregation calls and responses, hollers and shouts, intensely emotional singing, spirit possession, and extemporaneous testimonials to the power of the Holy Spirit.

The traditional black church is peopled by working-class blacks – domestics, factory workers, janitors, unskilled laborers. While today there is an ever-increasing number of high school graduates and college-educated members, most "pillars of the church" have less than a high-school education. The preacher of such a church may or may not be university-educated, but he must be able to "talk that talk" (preach in Black English style and lingo). It is within the traditional black church that traditional black folk (blacks who haven't been assimilated into the elusive American mainstream) create much of their reality, which includes the preservation and passing on of Africanized idioms, proverbs, customs, and attitudes. During slavery, the church was the one place Ole Massa allowed the slaves to congregate unsupervised and do pretty nearly as they pleased. Not surprisingly, a number of slave rebellions and revolutionary leaders (such as preacher Nat Turner) were spawned in the church. In addition to serving as a buffer and source of release against white oppression, the traditional black church functions as an important social unit where the rich and needy are helped, community news is exchanged, and black men gain opportunities (as deacons, trustees, officers) to play leadership roles. Speaking to the importance of the church, C. Eric Lincoln, the noted black historian, put it this way:

> The black man's pilgrimage in America was made less onerous because of his religion. His religion was the organizing principle around which his life was structured. His church was his school, his forum, his political arena, his social club, his art gallery, his conservatory of music. It was lyceum and gymnasium as well as sanctum sanctorum. His religion was his fellowship with man, his audience with God. It was the peculiar sustaining force which gave him the strength to endure when endurance gave no promise, and the courage to be creative in the face of his own dehumanization.

Viewing it from this perspective, we can see how the traditional black church became paramount in the history of Black America. But more than that, the embracing of a white God was a natural, cultural response based on the African way of life. Recall that in traditional African society it is believed that there is a unity between the spiritual and material aspects of existence. People are composed of both spiritual and material selves, but the prime force behind the movements of man and the universe is spiritual. This conception of a "spiritual universe" means that man's ultimate destiny is to move on to the "higher ground" of the spiritual world. Concomitant with the African's emphasis on spirituality, "religion"

Figure 11.2   "Smite them down to the third, yea, even unto the fourth generation. Even as King David smote down the mighty Philistines . . . An' watch that left jab!"

Source: "Bootsie" cartoon, by Ollie Harrington.

(in the sense in which Westerners use the term) becomes a pervasive dominating force in the society. Throughout Africa, there is no dichotomy between sacred and secular life, and there are no "irreligious people" in traditional African society, for to be "without religion amounts to a self-excommunication from the entire life of society . . . African people do not know how to exist without religion." As "common as daily bread, religion is not a sometime affair. It is a daily, minute involvement of the total person in a community and its concerns. Indeed, the spirit will not come forth with power apart from the community emptying itself (and thus the priest), so that the power can reign without interference ... The heart of traditional African religions is the emotional experience of being filled with the power of the spiritual." In the traditional black church, and in Black American culture generally, this aspect of the traditional African world view strongly continues in the emphasis on spirituality ("soul") rather than materiality. Black Americans believe that soul, feeling, emotion, and spirit serve as guides to understanding life and their fellows. All people are moved by spirit-forces, and there is no attempt to deny or intellectualize away that fact.

However, while blacks realize that people cannot live by bread alone, they believe that God helps those who help themselves. As the church folk say, "don't move the mountain, Lord, just give me strength to climb." Thus the traditional black church's other-worldly orientation is balanced by coping strategies for *this* world. And, like the traditional African God, the Black American God is viewed not only as Someone Who dwells on High but as One Who also inhabits this mundane earthly world of ours. As such, He too balances His other-worldly concerns with those of this world. Black American men and women, like traditional African men and women, are daily "living witnesses" to God's Supreme Power; thus they look up to God while simultaneously being on regular speaking terms with Him. As comedian Richard Pryor says, in talking about how a black preacher would function as an "exorcist": "Now, I knows you's busy, Lord – I done check yo schedule – but there's a person here who is PO-sessed."

Given the unity of the spiritual and the material, the sacred and the profane, in traditional African culture, it is not surprising to find the "circle unbroken" in Black America. None of this is to say that *all* black people go to and support the church. On the contrary, the stomp-down shonuff churchgoers are in the minority in the community. What we are stressing here is the heavy preser-vation of Africanisms in the church which have had an impact on Black American culture at large. For instance, when a soulful black singer or musician of secular music is really gitting down, members of the audience unconsciously respond by "shouting," (also referred to as "gittin happy"), that is, they show signs of being moved by the musical spirit – hollering, clapping hands, stomping feet, frenzied dancing, and other kinds of emotional responses. In other words, here is a secular audience gitting the Spirit! That very African tradition – belief in and expression of spirit possession – was retained in the traditional black church. ("If you got religion, show some sign.") Here we are in contemporary times finding this behavior being exhibited by blacks who don't even set foot inside the church door!

Thus, while the secular style might be considered the primary domain of the street, and the sacred that of the church, no sharp dichotomy exists, but a kind of sacred–secular circular continuum. As we have said, the black preacher's rap and traditional black church service tend to be highly informal and both abound in secularisms. For example, it is considered entirely appropriate for a preacher to get up in the pulpit and, say, show off what he's wearing: "Y'all didn notice the new suit I got on today, did y'all? Ain the Lord good to us?" Similarly, there is very often a sacred quality surrounding the verbal rituals of the secular style, with all gathered about the rapper, listening attentively, looking idolizingly and lingering on his or her every word, mystically engrossed in the rap. This is the effect achieved, for instance, by a black-culture poet such as Haki Madhubuti (Don Lee) or Imamu Baraka (LeRoi Jones) verbally performing ("reading") before a black audience. The most striking example of this merging of sacred and secular styles is in the area of black music, where lyrics, musical scores, and singers themselves easily float in and out of both worlds. Black blues and soul artists who came out of the church include the Staple Singers, Sam Cooke, Lou Rawls, Dionne Warwick, Dinah Washington, Nina Simone, Sly Stone – the list goes on and on. One of the deepest of this group is Aretha Franklin, who started singing and playing piano in her father's church at a very young age, went on to make record hits in the secular world, and then "returned" to the church to record the hit album, *Amazing Grace*, with the Reverend James Cleveland. (White America might have just "discovered" Gospel singers and Gospel rock, but they been there all the time in the traditional black church.) Another fantastic move was made by James Brown when he appropriated the preacher's concluding ritual for his secular performances. "Soul Brother Number One" has a classic number that climaxes each performance: he goes off-stage and returns wearing a black cape, reminiscent of the preacher's robe, then he proceeds to do his soulful thing until he gits the Spirit; he keeps on "shoutin" until he has to be pulled away from the mike, fanned, his perspiration toweled down, and his spirit brought back under "normal" control. Can I get a witness?

The language and style that comprise the sacred–secular oral tradition can be characterized in a number of ways. Here, we might speak in terms of the rhetorical qualities of smaller, individual units of expression. The qualities are: exaggerated language (unusual words, High Talk); mimicry; proverbial statement and aphoristic phrasing; punning and plays on words; spontaneity and improvisation; image-making and metaphor; braggadocio; indirection (circumlocution, suggestiveness); and tonal semantics. A black rap can have one, all, or any combination of these. Rappers must be skillful in reading the vibrations of their audience and situation, for the precise wording depends on what is said to whom under what conditions. We shall briefly illustrate each.

Exaggerated language

Rappers sprinkle their talk with uncommon words and rarely used expressions. Recall Shakes's lady "succumbing to the amorous design his words had traced in the air of the night." Martin Luther King, Jr., once referred to a matter as being "incandescently clear." A lesser-known preacher said emphatically in his sermon: "When Jesus walked the face of the earth, you know it upset the high ES-U-LAUNCE [echelon]." Sometimes the whole syntax of a sentence may be expressed in an elevated, formal manner, as in this invitation from a working-class black male: "My dear, would you care to dine with me tonight on some delectable red beans and rice?"

Mimicry

A deliberate imitation of the speech and mannerisms of someone else may be used for authenticity, ridicule, or rhetorical effect. For instance, whenever rappers quote somebody, they attempt to quote in the tone of voice, gestures, and particular idiom and language characteristic of that person. A black female complains to a friend about her man, for instance: "Like he come tellin me this old mess bout [speaker shifts to restatin and imitatin] 'Well, baby, if you just give me a chance, Ima have it together pretty soon.' That's his word, you know, always talkin bout having something 'together.'" Occasionally, the mimicking takes the form of a title or line from a song: "Told you she wasn't none of yo friend; [singing] 'smiling faces' . . ."

Proverbial statement

The rapper sprinkles his or her talk with familiar black proverbs and drives home the points with short, succinct statements which have the sound of wisdom and power. While proverbs have been around for ages, we are here referring to the black rapper's tendency to encapsulate and in a sense "freeze" experience through his or her own aphoristic phrasing. "It ain no big thang" originated in this manner; it was followed up by the aphoristic repartee: "But it's growing." Two well-known examples of proverbial-sounding statements often used by churchgoers are: "I been born again" and "My name is written on High."

Many old black proverbs become titles or lines in hit songs – for instance, Aretha Franklin's "Still Water Runs Deep" and Undisputed Truth's "Smiling Faces Sometimes Tell Lies." Many proverbs are quoted by mothers to their children and serve as child-rearing devices to teach rapidly and in no uncertain terms about life and living. "A hard head make a soft behind," "If you make yo bed hard, you gon have to lie in it," and "God don't like ugly" are three such frequently used proverbs. Proverbs and proverbial expressions are significant in the oral tradition because they hark back to an African cultural–linguistic pattern that was retained and adapted to the conditions of the New World. Among the Ibo people of West Africa, according to the African writer Chinua Achebe, "the art of conversation is regarded very highly, and proverbs are the palm-oil with which words are eaten."

Punning

While many verbal wits employ this rhetorical strategy, punning in the black heavily depends on the threads of the black experience common to all, and knowledge of black speech. For example, it is commonly believed that black people are adept with knives and razors as weapons. Thus James Brown's "I don't know Karate but I know Karazor." Another such example depends on one's know-ledge of how Black English is pronounced. It goes as follows:

> Knock, knock.
> Who's there?
> Joe.
> Joe who?
> Joe Momma.

This is a good example of playing the Dozens by punning on the similarity in sound between *yo* (not *your*) and *Joe*.

Spontaneity

Though black raps have an overall formulaic structure, the specifics remain to be filled in. The rapper is free to improvise by taking advantage of anything that comes into the situation – the listener's response, the entry of other persons to the group, spur-of-the-moment ideas that occur to the rapper. For example, the preacher will say, "Y'all don wont to hear dat, so I'm gon leave it lone," but if the congregation shouts, "Naw, tell it, Reb! Tell it!", he will. Rarely does the rapper have a completely finished speech, even in more structured "formal" minds of speech-making, such as sermons or political speeches. (Many a would-be romantic rapper has been known to blow his thang with a canned rap.) By taking advantage of process, movement, and creativity of the moment, one's rap seems always fresh and immediately personalized for any given situation. For instance, before Malcolm X's prison background became widespread knowledge, he mentioned to an audience the fact that he had once been in prison. He read the vibrations of the audience, sensing their surprise, and quickly reacted. Noting that all black people in this country were, in a sense, imprisoned, he capped: "That's what America means: prison."

Image-making

An important criterion of black talk is this use of images, metaphors, and other kinds of imaginative language The metaphorical constructs are what give black raps a poetic quality. Ideas, trivial or small though they may be, must be expressed in creative ways. Preachers especially must be good at image-making. The Reverend Jesse Jackson refers to the plight of black people as analogous to being on the expressway with all the entrances and exits closed off. Another Baptist preacher compared Christ's work to a "mission: impossible." The figures of speech created in black linguistic imagery tend to be earthy, gutsy, and rooted in plain everyday reality. One blood's distaste for wig-wearing females was expressed as: "They look like nine miles of bad road with a detour at the end."

Braggadocio

The rapper boasts a good deal, as we have seen in earlier examples. The bragging is of various kinds and dimensions. Instead of saying something limp like "If you so bad, gon and start something," one potential fighter boldly rapped: "If you feel froggy, leap!" Of course the badness of heroes must be celebrated, as for instance Stag-O-Lee, who was so bad "flies wouldn't fly around him in the summertime, and even white folks was scared of him." Whether referring to physical badness, fighting ability, lovemanship, coolness (that is, "grace under pressure"), the aim is to convey the image of an omnipotent fearless being, capable of doing the undoable. Consider two contrasting love raps using braggadocio. Smokey Robinson confidently croons:

> I'll take the stars and count them
>   and move the mountains
> And if that won't do
> I'll try something new.

But the Temptations, with all their badness, have run into some hard times:

> I can change a river into a burning sand
> I can make a ship sail on dry land
> All these things I'm able to do
> But I can't get next to you.

Indirection

The rapper makes his or her points by the power of suggestion and innuendo. It is left to the listener to decipher and explicate the totality of meaning. Much signifyin works through indirection. For instance, Malcolm X once began a speech in this way: "Mr. Moderator, Brother Lomax, brothers and sisters, friends and enemies: I just can't believe everyone in here is a friend and I don't want to leave anybody out." Not only is Malcolm neatly putting down his enemies in the audience without a direct frontal attack, he is also sending a hidden message (to those hip enough to dig it). Since it is an all-black audience, Malcolm is slyly alluding to the all-too-familiar historical and contemporary pattern of blacks being betrayed by other blacks; traitors in their midst who ran and told the white folks everything they knew. (A number of slave uprisings were foiled because of these "black Judases," and there is a saying that surely dates back to the slave experience: when a blood does something, however small or innocuous, maybe something not even having to do with white folks, he or she will typically say, "Now, run and tell that!")

Indirection gives longer black raps their convoluted style, that is, the rapper will start with a point, then proceed to meander all around it; he may return, circular fashion, to the point, but he typically does not proceed in a straight, linear, point-by-point progression. Unless you are good at circumlocution, it is difficult to win an argument with a rapper skilled in this device. For one thing, such rappers will refuse to confront head-on any contradictory points raised. When dealing with such rappers, it is best to remember that they depend on psychological and experiential logic, rather than some abstract system of logic that maybe exists nowhere but in somebody's head. As an example, Jesse B. Simple is trying to prove he is part Indian, but his friend says he is just plain "colored," and besides, "Jesse is not even an Indian name." Simple counters this with the fact that he had a Hiawatha in his family "but she died," whereupon he is promptly contradicted and threatens to be caught in his lie: "*She?* Hiawatha was no *she.*" Not at all undaunted by this correction of facts, Simple reasons that the sex of Hiawatha neither proves nor disproves that he has Indian blood. His experience has taught him that a lot of black people are part Indian. At any rate, he has to win the argument, so he refuses to even deal with the implications of the rebuttal, and in a smooth psych-out move, he promptly proceeds to change the subject: "She was a *she* in our family. And she had long coal-black hair just like a Creole. You know, I started to marry a Creole one time when I was coach-boy on the L & N down to New Orleans. Them Louisiana girls are bee-oou-te-ful! Man, I mean!"

Such indirection and circumlocutory rhetoric are also a part of African discourse strategy, and Afro-Americans have simply transformed this art to accommodate the English language. As an example of this technique in West Africa, Chinua Achebe in his first novel, *Things Fall Apart*, depicts the example of Unoka from the Ibo village of what is now Biafra. Supposedly, Unoka, father of the main character, Okonkwo, is a failure by village social standards; people laugh at him, and they "swore never to lend him any more money because he never paid back." However, "Unoka was such a man that he always succeeded in borrowing more, and piling up his debts." Surely part of his success must be attributable to the fact that Unoka can skillfully employ circumlocutory reasoning in his discourse, as Okoye found out when he came to collect the two hundred cowries that Unoka had been owing him for more than two years.

> As soon as Unoka understood what his friend was driving at, he burst out laughing. He laughed loud and long and his voice rang out clear as the *ogene*, and tears stood in his eyes. His visitor was amazed, and sat speechless. At the end, Unoka was able to give an answer between fresh outbursts of mirth.
>
> "Look at that wall," he said, pointing at the far wall of his hut, which was rubbed with red earth so that it shone. "Look at those lines of chalk"; and Okoye saw groups of short perpendicular lines drawn in chalk. There were five groups, and the smallest group had ten lines. Unoka had a sense of the dramatic and so he allowed a pause, in which he took a pinch of snuff and sneezed noisily, and then he continued: "Each group there represents a debt to someone, and each stroke is one hundred cowries. You see, I owe that man a thousand cowries. But he has not come to wake me up in the morning for it. I shall pay you, but not today. Our elders say that the sun will shine on those who stand before it shines on those who kneel under them. I shall pay my big debts first." And he took another pinch of snuff, as if that was paying the big debts first. Okoye rolled his goatskin and departed.

Tonal semantics

Verbal power can be achieved through the use of words and phrases carefully chosen for sound effects. This can be either a line or a pervasive structure in a total rap. In employing tonal semantics, the rapper gets meaning and rhetorical mileage by triggering a familiar sound chord in the listener's ear. The words may or may not make sense; what is crucial is the rapper's ability to make the words *sound* good. They will use rhyme, voice rhythm, repetition of key sounds and letters. Fighter–poet Muhammad Ali was working right in this tradition with his taunting rhymes predicting his opponents' defeats: "They all must fall/in the round I call" and "If he mess wif me, I'll drop him in three." Most Toast-tellers rely on tonal semantics, their verbal ingenuity taxed to the limit in trying to sustain the melodic structure. "I'm Peter Wheatstraw, the Devil's son-in-law," or "I'm sweet peeter jeeter, the womb beater." Obviously, preachers rely on tonal semantics. For example, my father, Reverend Napoleon, once expressed the following theme in a sermon: "I am nobody talking to Somebody Who can help anybody." Other deep-down church folks use tonal semantics too; for instance, they will use the Moan to trigger a responsive chord, establishing a kind of psycho-cognitive reality of one who knows the Lord: "Hmmmmm-mmmmmmmmmmmmmm," or "HHHHHHHHHHHHHHHHH-mmmmmmmmmmm."

12

I BET YOU a fat man against the hole in a doughnut that Hip Hoppers think they invented "yo momma" jokes. Well, yall better ask somebody cause the game has been around in the Black Oral Tradition for generations, even long before Sista Zora included this little "yo mamma" rhyme in her 1937 novel. "Oral Tradition" – which is also a part of the cultural experience of other groups such as Native Americans – refers to verbal games, stories, proverbs, jokes, and other cultural productions that have been passed on from one generation to the next by word of mouth. In Black America, this tradition preserves and celebrates African culture, which was adapted to a new way of life in America. Because Africans in America play with and on the Word, good talkers become heroes and she-roes. Bloods who can talk and testify, preach and prophesy, lie and signify, get much props. Enter Double Snaps and the aesthetics of the dis.

Literally speaking, when you "dis" someone, you discount, discredit,

"IF I'M LYIN, I'M FLYIN": THE GAME OF INSULT IN BLACK LANGUAGE [1995]

Yo' mama don't wear no draws
Ah seen her when she took 'em off
She soaked 'em in alcohol
She sold 'em tuh de Santy Claus
He told her 'twas against de law
To wear dem dirty draws.

(Zora Neale Hurston, *Their Eyes
Were Watching God* (1937)[1]

disrespect that person – a dis is an insult. In the Black Oral Tradition, however, a dis also constitutes a verbal game, played with ritualized insults. The disses are purely ceremonial, which creates a safety zone. Like it's not personal, it's business – in this case, the business of playing on and with the Word.

There are two kinds of disses. One type is leveled at a person's mother (and sometimes at other relatives). Traditionally, this was referred to as "the dozens" (or "playin the dozens"). The other kind of dissin is aimed at a person or a thing, either just for fun, or to criticize that person or thing. This was referred to as "signifyin." Today, the two types of dissin are being conflated under a more general form of play, which we may refer to as "snaps," an emerging term for the game. (Other older terms for this ritualized insult tradition are "joanin," "cappin," "soundin," and "droppin lugs.")

Back in the day, virtually everybody in the Black community would, from time to time, engage in signifyin. But if you tried to go to "yo momma," some folk would tell you quick, "I laugh and kid, but I don't play" (meaning, "I don't play the dozens"). Perhaps, as 1960s political activist Hubert ("Rap") Brown wrote: "Signifying is more humane. Instead of coming down on somebody's mother, you come down on them" (1969, p. 27). That, of course, was another era, when women were put on pedestals and mothers were considered sacred. Today, the role of women has undergone a fundamental change, which helps to explain why the traditional distinction between "signifyin" and "the dozens" is blurring. However, let us here sing no sad songs for the demise of that old-timey image of women; it was false and oppressive. As a woman and as a mother, I'm wit the change. So in the game of snappin, if you play, either you or yo momma got to pay.

Generally, the dozens involves insults of mothers, but on occasion, players will bring in fathers, grandmothers, and other kinfolk. Sista Zora once referred to the dozens as "low-rating the ancestors of your opponent" (1942, p. 96). Richard Wright's 1963 novel, *Lawd Today*, portrays one of the funniest dozens contests I've ever read or heard. Al, Jake, and two of their partners are playin the dozens during a card game. Al reaches back five generations to Jake's "greatgreatgreat*great* grandma . . . a Zulu queen in Africa. She was setting at the table and she said to the waiter: 'Say waiter, be sure and fetch me some of them missionary chitterlings . . .'" (1963, p. 81). But, like Langston Hughes's folk character Jess B. Simple said, "Most Black folk don't play the Dozens that far back."

The game was and is played by all ages and by males and females. One-upmanship is the goal of this oral contest, best played in a group of appreciative onlookers, who are secondary participants in the game. They provide a kind of running commentary, repeating a really clever dis or interjecting responses like "Did yall hear that?," "Oh, shit!," "Oooooweee!," etc. The audience, with its laughter, high fives, and other responses, pushes the verbal duel to greater and greater heights of oratorical fantasy.

So, whassup with this game? Ain it kinda weird to be talkin bout "yo momma" this and "his momma" that — for fun?

For a people trying to survive under an oppressive racist yoke, the dozens provided a way, to borrow from Ralph Ellison, to "change the joke."[2] The game functioned as an outlet for what countless blues people and Jess B. Simple[3] folk called "laughing to keep from crying." It was a form of release for the suppressed rage and frustrations that were the result of being a Black man or woman trapped in White America. Despite economic discrimination and racist assaults against your personhood, you could ill afford to be hot; the dozens taught you how to chill. As well, the game taught discipline and self-control; it was a lesson in how to survive by verbal wit and cunning rhetoric, rather than physical violence. Ultimately, though, somebody got to lose. What then? Well, the dozens possesses the kind of humor that makes you laugh so hard you cry. A loser is thus provided with a face-saving way out — blending right on in with the loud laughter of the group. Today, the dozens, with its infusion into other cultures, still serves as a release from the pressures of daily existence, a safe, nonviolent method of venting hostility and suppressed rage within acceptable confines. Surely a healthier alternative than the rat-tat-tat-tat of glocks, domestic abuse, and other kinds of violence ranging throughout *all* communities today.

The origin of the dozens, both the term and the game itself, remains debatable. (Readers interested in the intricacies of these various theories should consult Harris (1974); Smitherman ([1977] 1986); Dollard (1939); Abrahams (1964); Herskovits (1949); Dalby (1972); Holloway and Vass (1993); Kidd (1906); Mayer (1951); Simmons (1963); Elton (1950); Schechter (1970).[4] Here I shall briefly discuss the most plausible theory, which relocates the game to the several cultures of Africa from which Black Americans came. For example in a Bantu group in East Africa, described in a 1951 account, joking insults, such as "Eat your mother's anus," were observed among friends, and the Efik in Nigeria used ritualized insults such as "child of mixed sperm" (that is, you have more than one father, in other words, yo momma a ho). This theory about the dozens, which was advanced by Melville Herskovits and others, is consistent with what we know about the history of African people in the so-called "New World." Since culture is not only artefacts, but also the way people behave and think, it is logical that Africans in enslavement would tap into remembered cultural practices and verbal rituals from home and adapt them to life in a strange land. From Giddayup, the insult game would have been played in the slave communities, eventually taking on the English name, "the dozens."

The dozens existed literally in the *Oral* Tradition until the first-known written documentation in 1891. In a folk song collected in Texas, there are these lines:

> Talk about one thing, talk about another;
> But ef you talk about me, I'm gwain to talk about your mother.
>
> (Thomas, 1926)

Clearly, the dozens was widespread in early-twentieth-century Black culture. For example, John Dollard's 1930s research among young Black males in the rural and urban South reports snaps like: "Your ma behind is like a rumble seat. It hang from her back down to her feet," and "Nigger, if I was as ugly as you I would kill myself."

The dozens shows up in popular songs recorded by early bluesmen and -women. In 1929, Speckled Red (Rufus Perryman) made the first recording, which he called "The Dirty Dozen."[5] It became a big hit and was followed by virtually identical recordings by Tampa Red, Leroy Carr, Ben Curry, and other blues artists. World-renowned Leadbelly (Huddie Ledbetter), in his 1935 recording "Kansas City Papa," incorporated a few lines of the dozens. In the song, the game is played by two women who are "jiving one another."[6] Finally, female blues singer Memphis Minnie (Minnie McCoy) showed that women had skills in her 1930 recording "New Dirty Dozen," in which she rocked the house with such lines as:

> I know all about yo pappy and yo mammy,
> Your big fat sister and your little brother Sammy,
> Your aunt and your uncle and your ma's and pa's,
> They all got drunk and showed they Santy Claus.
> Now they all drunken mistreaters, robbers and cheaters
> Slip you in the Dozens, yo poppa is yo cousin
> Yo momma do the Lawdy, Lawd.[7]

Like other games, the dozens has its rules and stock conventions. The simplest form is the verbal retort: "Yo momma," or "Ask yo momma," casually invoked in passing conversation. Check out this recent exchange between two thirty-something Sistas:

> LINDA: Girl, what up with that head? [*referring to her friend's hairstyle*]
> BETTY: Ask yo momma.

Betty's rejoinder can be shrugged off or taken as slipping into the dozens. Linda takes the latter course of action.

> LINDA: Oh, so you going there, huh? Well,
>   I did ask my momma, and she said,
>   "Can't you see that Betty look
>   like her momma spit her out?"

Once again, it's on.

Another stock formula, both in the "yo momma" variety and in disses on the person, is the pattern "Yo momma is so *X* that *Y*," or "You are so *X* that *Y*.[8] For example:

> Your mother is so old, she went to the Virgin Mary's baby shower.
>
> (Percelay et al., 1995)

> Your mother's teeth are so big, she bit into a sandwich and clipped her toenails.
>
> (Percelay et al., 1995)

> Yo momma so slow, it take her an hour to cook Minute Rice, two days to watch *60 Minutes*, and a year to watch *48 Hours*.[9]

The dozens has some fairly sophisticated rules. A fundamental one is that players should be known to each other. Or if not familiar associates, they should at least share membership in and knowledge of the Black cultural context. On this latter point, however, John Baugh contends that the dozens should be restricted to familiar participants because "there is no reliable way to determine the reactions of unfamiliars" (1983, p. 26).

Within the hood, perhaps it would be wise to heed Baugh's advice. Traditionally, males and females only played in same-sex, intimate settings, without outsiders present (or if there were outsiders, the kind who had sense enough not to impose themselves into the game and to follow the cues of the insiders). However, outside the hood, as the game crosses over today, this rule is bending, allowing for public play in front of outsiders and allowing for play by people who may not be intimately known to one another but who are true to the game. Dynamic examples can be heard on television programs like *Def Comedy Jam*, *Martin*, *Living Single*, and *Fresh Prince*, and in films like *White Men Can't Jump*.

To be good in the game, your snaps must meet several criteria. First, they must be exaggerated, the wilder, the better, like: "Your mother's mouth is so big, when she inhales, her sneakers get untied" (Percelay *et al.*, 1995). Second, they must employ creative figures of speech, like: "I spoke to your mother today and she said the dentist refuses to give her braces because yellow and silver don't match" (Percelay *et al.*, 1995). Third, the timing of the snap is critical; it must be delivered immediately and spontaneously. This art form is about what Rap artists call "freestyling"; it does not allow for lengthy deliberation.

Back in the day, those who aimed for the highest level of mastery of the game insisted on a fourth criterion: rhyming. If you could construct insults that were creatively exaggerated and were expressed in metaphorical language, on time, and with rhyme, you were in the top ten.

Despite the emotionally charged subject matter, snappin works as a game because it is located within the realm of play. Thus the rule that is most crucial to the game is that the snap must not be literally true. For instance, despite all the sexual references in the dozens, nobody has actually gone to bed with anybody's mother. However, if you take snappin out of the realm of play, you enter the real world, where ain nobody playin. Occasionally, though, players will go there, especially when they run out of clever snaps.

As for Black women snappin, the Sistas are on it like a honet, especially when there are no outsiders around. Recently, I asked three professional African American women if they knew how to play the dozens. The women were my middle-aged contemporaries, but I am not part of their intimate circle, and so, as I had anticipated, there was instant denial. I broke the ice by coming out with the opening lines of something called "yo momma's signifyin monkey," which I had heard while hanging out back in the fast days of my youth:

> Down in the jungle where the coconut grows
> Lived yo old-ass momma who was a stomp-down ho.

They laughed, and although one of them continued to deny knowledge of the dozens, after a couple of minutes, all three got all the way up on it.

ARLENE: No, un-unh, I don't think I know any of that stuff.

RENEE: I remember something like, uh, I don't play the dozens cause the dozens is bad –

BARBARA: But, Arlene, I can tell you how many dicks yo' mama had.

ARLENE: Well, I hate to talk about yo momma, Barbara, cause she's a good old soul –

RENEE: Aw, naw, heifer, thought you didn't know any of that stuff.

ARLENE: She got a two-ton pussy and a rubber ass hole.

BARBARA: Hey, wait a minute; that ain't right.

We then got off into a debate about authenticity, Barbara remembering that the phrasing was a "*ten*-ton pussy," and Renee arguing that it was "bad-ass hole." Arlene ended up recounting how, as a teenager, she and her girls would, in effect, call somebody's momma a ho with this snap: "All yo momma's children are step."[10]

In her autobiography, *Gemini* depicting her childhood in the South, poet Nikki Giovanni, active in the 1960s Black Arts Movement, relates a story about her sister, Gary, doin the "yo momma" thang. Nikki and Gary were confronted by Peggy and her gang on the streets of Knoxville, Tennessee.

> "Hey, old stuck-up. What you gonna do when your sister's tired of fighting for you?" "I'll beat you up myself. That's what." ... "You and what army, 'ho'?" "Me and yo' mama's army," Gary answered with precision and dignity. "You talking 'bout my mama?" "I would but the whole town is so I can't add nothing." ... "You take it back, Gary." Deadly quiet. "Yo' mama's so ugly she went to the zoo and the gorilla paid to see her." "You take that back!" "Yo' mama's such a 'ho' she went to visit a farm and they dug a whole field before they knew it was her."
>
> (1971, p. 17)

Then there's Presidential inaugural poet Maya Angelou, who is so bad that she once played the *thirteens* in a pair of poems in which she dropped snaps on Blacks and whites to tell each group about their untogetha actions (1971, pp. 46–7).

The Sistas are deep off into the signifyin dis as well as "yo momma" snaps. The signifyin is generally delivered with a definite purpose in mind, as was noted by Claudia Mitchell-Kernan in her classic 1960s study of signifyin. Not that Sistas don't have fun with the Word, but the dissin game becomes a vehicle for social commentary. Like the Sista retirees I heard talking about being members of the "packer's club," a snap referring to men who had had so many women in their youth that now, in their mature years, all they could do during sex was "pack chitlins," i.e., they could not maintain a firm erection (Smitherman, 1994, p. 176). And especially like my girl, Janie, in Zora Neale Hurston's *Their Eyes Were Watching God*. Janie and her husband, Jody, are snappin in front of the group that always hangs out in their store to lie[11] and signify:

[JODY]   A woman stay round uh store till she get old as Methusalem and still can't cut a little thing like a plug of tobacco! Don't stand dere rollin yo pop eyes at me wid yo rump hanging nearly to yo knees!

[JANIE]   Stop mixin up mah doings wid mah looks, Jody. When you git through tellin me how tuh cut uh plug uh tobacco, then you kin tell me whether mah behind is on straight or not.

[JODY]   You must be out yo head ... talkin any such language as dat.

[JANIE]   You de one started talkin under people's clothes. Not me.

[JODY]   Whut's de matter wid you, nohow? You ain't no young girl to be getting all insulted bout yo looks. You ain't no young courtin' gal. You'se uh ole woman, nearly forty.

[JANIE]   Yeah, ah'm nearly forty and you'se already fifty. ... Talkin bout *me* lookin old! When you pull down yo britches, you look lak de change uh life.

(1937, pp. 74–5)

Like I said, the Sistas be all over signifyin. Excellent examples in the 1990s are the women's "war council" in Spike Lee's film *Jungle Fever* and the birthday celebration in Terry McMillan's novel *Waiting to Exhale*.

Today's snaps seem less reliant on the standard formulas and stock phrases that characterized old-school snaps. You don't hear too much of the "I hate to talk bout yo momma/She's a good old soul" rhyming style of the dozens. Still it's obvious that 1990s snaps are grounded in the African American Oral Tradition. As a linguist with an unabashed love and respect for the power of language, I can't wait to see how future generations will stamp their imprint upon the game. Like, don't you think that it would be fascinating to hear the snaps of, say, a hundred years from now? I'll be there to write about it. If I'm lyin, I'm flyin.

13

ALMOST EVERYONE KNOWS some of them but no one has adequately defined them. They offer conventional wisdom but sometimes they give contradictory advice. They are attributed to wise men such as Aesop, Confucius, and Solomon, but many people report that they heard their mothers and grandmothers use them most often. There are appropriate ones for almost every situation, but different ones can be used in the same situation, and the same one can be used in many different situations. They have been defined as the wisdom of many, the wit of one (Mieder and Dundes, 1981, p. 61).

Defining the proverb is an exasperating problem for scholars. While addressing this task, Beatrice Silverman-Weinreech (1981, p. 69) reported that

"MAKIN A WAY OUTA NO WAY": THE PROVERB TRADITION IN THE BLACK EXPERIENCE[1] [1987]

> Archer Taylor, America's foremost paremiologist, perhaps wisely refused to define a proverb: "An incommunicable quality tells us this sentence is proverbial and that one is not." In his monumental work on proverbs, Friedrich Seiler gives every possible example of functional criteria and stylistic devices but he ends by floundering in the sea of definienda and cannot arrive at an internally consistent definition to cover every proverb.

After discussing limitations of existing functional and structural definitions of proverbs, scholars either adopt or modify an existing definition, or stipulate yet another for purposes of their studies.

Within the framework of sociolinguistic theory, proverbs can be categorized as speech acts (Hymes, 1974, p. 53) in that they are shaped by specific sociocultural factors within a given speech community. Proverb users must know when, why, to whom, and for what purpose a proverb should be used. The sociocultural context governing proverb use encompasses the structural patterns of the speech community – its traditions, historical development, norms of interaction, and other patterns. Taken as a whole, the community's corpus of proverbs provides a mechanism for storing and disseminating the speech community's attitudes, beliefs, values, philosophical assumptions, virtues and vices, and, in general, much of its worldview. We shall here use the term *proverb* to refer to figurative, epigrammatic statements that express widely accepted strategies for addressing recurring situations. For example, "Don't put off until tomorrow what you can do today," suggests that life is uncertain and hence being thrifty is a virtue. Since reality is full of illusions, we should "not judge a book by its cover." We shall also include statements usually prefaced by "They say," "There is an old saying," or "Old people say." (In fact, even when such a prefatory comment is deleted, sufficient context makes for its recoverability within a grammar of deletion rules in linguistic theory. Possibly, this is the linguistic form in which proverbs are stored in the speaker's cognitive repertoire.)

The misinformed locate proverbs in the category of "fakelore" possessed by people lacking formal education, and even some folklore scholars ignore these "curious little sayings." However, just as "it is the still water that drowns the man," these seemingly simple proverbs yield considerable complexity by providing insight into group consciousness and confirming the notion that "by the words of a man's mouth, you can know his mind."

As scholars concerned with communication and development in the global African world, our position is that proverbs constitute an essential dimension of communication in Africa and the African Diaspora that reinforces cultural authenticity while simultaneously facilitating literacy, critical thinking, and technological development. Daniel (1972) indicated five significant areas of study relative to the proverb tradition:

1   Proverbs are an index of cultural continuity and interaction – they provide a mirror to the world of African and Diasporic people, they continue to exist in Black popular culture (e.g., Smitherman, [1977] 1986), and bear directly on the issue of African survivals in the New World.
2   Proverbs are significant in the socialization process – how do Black parents utilize proverbs to guide the thought and action of their children in a hostile environment, in contradistinction to other child-rearing practices?
3   Proverbs are central to mental development and abstract thinking and reasoning – training in proverbs can supplement formal education, particularly in the area of critical thinking.

4   Proverbs are significant rhetorical devices in arguments, debates, verbal dueling, and other interaction contexts where persuasion and manipulation of the rhetorical situation are paramount.

5   Proverbs are indices of cultural assimilation – just as Creole linguists have posited a *basilect* as the most culturally rooted language form in a speech community (e.g., Alleyne, 1980), we are positing *basi-proverb* as a corollary; further, the extent to which proverb knowledge and use decline may well indicate the extent to which "things fall apart" (Achebe, 1959).

THE AFRICAN EXPERIENCE

Africa appears to be saturated with proverbs. Other than one or two geographic areas, proverbs "seem universal and in some African languages occur in rich profusion" (Finnegan, 1976, p. 389). A Yoruba proverb states that "The proverb is the workhorse of conversation." Proverbs are said to be the Anang's "most frequently employed ... forms of verbal art, and are used in all manner of situation" (Messenger, 1959, p. 64). A study of West African proverb use revealed that proverbs are used to:

1   educate children
2   argue legal matters
3   embellish oratory
4   give ordinary advice
5   comment obliquely to avoid hostility
6   shame one into compliance
7   indicate irony and sarcasm
8   instruct initiates in secret societies
9   serve as oral and written literary devices
10   represent a people's philosophy
11   suggest widely held truths
12   accomplish indirect suggestions

(Finnegan, 1976)

C. A. Akrofi [n.d.] observed that "proverbs play a very important part in the everyday language of Twi-speaking people." Akrofi indicated:

> Twi proverbs are a reflection of the philosophy of Akan – of their outlook on life, their religious beliefs, their ideas on the Creator and creation, and on life, of death, and of life after death. Through the proverbs we also see mirrored Akan customs concerning men, women and children, and traditional ideas of the Akan concerning moral behavior and ethical standards [p. v].

J. B. Danquah (1968) relied heavily on proverbs to document the Akan concept of God. He maintained that without the 3,680 proverbs collected by J. G. Christaller (1873), his work could not have been conceived or written. In addition to serving as indices of Fante (an Akan group) religious beliefs, James Boyd Christensen (1973, pp. 509–24) discussed the role of proverbs in conducting Fante judicial proceedings delineating norms governing clan behavior (Because the tortoise has no clan, he has already made his casket), revealing notions about elders, child rearing (Short palm tree, stop complaining, for the tall palm started as you), entertaining, and, in general, reflecting ideal behavior and values (A wife is like a blanket, for even though it scratches you, you are cold without it).

J. T. Milimo (1972) entitled his proverb collection *Bantu Wisdom* "not only because it is in the proverbs that our people stored up all their wisdom and experience of the centuries, but especially because it was this wisdom of our forebears which led them to find simple but adequate means of teaching about life." Milimo noted that Bantu proverbs are full of imagery "deeply rooted in life as people know it." Similarly, George Merrick (1969) reported that his collection of Hausa proverbs could serve as guides to Hausa grammar, history, everyday manners and customs, virtues most admired, and vices most despised. Proverbs are so plentiful and significant in some African societies that Issac O. Delano (1966, p. 9) concluded: "In Yoruba society no one can be considered educated or qualified to take part in communal discussions unless he is able to quote the proverbs relevant to each situation." The outcome of African legal rituals, for example, might well be won by the person who is most skilled in proverb use. Consider the following instance:

> During a case in which a chronic thief was accused of robbery, the plaintiff aroused considerable antagonism toward the defendant early in the trial by employing the following proverb: "If a dog plucks palm fruits from a cluster, he does not fear a porcupine." A cluster from the oil palm tree contains numerous sharp needles that make handling it extremely hazardous, therefore, a dog known to pick palm fruits certainly would be unafraid to touch a porcupine.
>
> (Messenger, 1959, pp. 68–9)

Thus, it was argued that the accused was the logical suspect since he was a known thief. The accused later gained some sympathy with the statement. "A single partridge flying through the bush leaves no patch." The use of this proverb indicated that he was alone, without sympathizers, and that his past should be overlooked.

Ruth Finnegan's discussion of African oratory indicated that the legal context is one of the most common situations for displaying rhetorical skills. Of special note here is her observation that "in the case of the Anang Ibidio their famous eloquence arises largely from their skillful use of proverbial maxims, particularly in court" (1976, pp. 445–6). E. Ojo Arewa and Alan Dundes (1964, p. 70) also noted that "the impersonal power of proverbs is perhaps most apparent in the well-known African judicial processes in which the participants argue with proverbs intended to serve as past precedents for their present actions."

In addition to the formal court arena where conflict is involved, proverbs play a prominent role in resolving daily conflicts. Joyce A. Okezie's (1978, p. 4) analysis of proverb use in Igbo society demonstrated "proverbs are necessary verbal tools which can be used to achieve the goal of reducing conflict." She indicated that proverbs possess the following three functional properties that make them appropriate for handling conflict situations:

1 depersonalized nature, which protects the speaker and often the addressee from the message conveyed by the proverb;
2 authority that adds power and force to the message;
3 prestige, which by association elevates the speaker and allows role players to display their skill in language and the ways of culture.

In its sensory emphasis, African culture is primarily oral and aural rather than visual. Recognizing the importance of incorporating this oral tradition in order to have a culturally authentic African literature, Solomon O. Iyasere (1975, p. 107) stated: "The modern African writer is to his indigenous oral tradition as a snail is to its shell. Even in a foreign habitat, a snail never leaves its shell behind." That proverbs occupy a prominent position among the oral traditions on which African writers draw is evidenced in the writings of J. P. Clark, Wole Soyinka, Gabriel Okara, Chinua Achebe, Christina Aidoo, Christopher Okigbo, and Amos Tutuola.

While it might be an impossible task to *establish the pre-eminence of one African oral literary form*, proverbs certainly qualify as the most frequently employed form. The brevity of the proverb enabled it to be used when a myth, legend, or tale would simply take up too much time. Brevity, formulaic structures, and figurative language also contribute to widespread memory and use. Figurative language goes with the African emphasis on eloquence. The proverbs' form and content also are conducive with a tradition-bound culture.

Although there is a variety of peoples and cultures in Africa, certain cultural phenomena appear to be common among traditional African people. Proverbs provide excellent insights into the commonalities. For example, there is the well-documented notion of the traditional African sense of an essentially spirit-dominated universe, for example, "Whatever is is in the first place spirit" (Abraham, 1962, p. 50). Similarly, there is considerable evidence attesting to the widely-held belief of a universe formed by one contiguous order ranging from spirits to humans to nonliving entities. Wisdom is highly valued in this worldview, and elders are the repositories of communal wisdom. "The words of one's elders are greater than an amulet" (Abraham, 1962, p. 67).

Inherent harmony in the universe is a concept shared by many African people. There is a constant balancing of forces, and, thus, "When the moon is not full, the stars shine more brightly" (Leslau and Leslau, 1962, p. 13). Humans strive to maintain harmony found in the universe by avoiding and discretely resolving conflicts. Conflict resolution often requires indirect persuasion coupled with authority. Proverbs are excellent indirect, authoritative mechanisms for resolving conflicts and maintaining harmony. Indeed, a Yoruba proverb states that, "A wise man who knows proverbs, reconciles difficulties" (Leslau and Leslau, 1962, p. 6).

In the absence of a dominant written language, proverbs became the "daughters of experience." Learned early in life, as well as throughout, proverbs provided the deep structural basis for wisdom. Just as a child's early learning of the rudiments of the child's linguistic system enables him or her to produce an unlimited number of "new" sentences, proverbial learning provides wisdom that can be applied to an endless number of "new" situations. Kofi Asare Opoku (1975, p. 8) summed up the significance of proverbs in African societies:

> Proverbs have many uses in African societies; they may express an eternal truth; they may be a warning against foolish acts or be a guide to good conduct ... African proverbs express the wisdom of the African people and are a key to the understanding of African ways of life in the past and in the present.

THE CARIBBEAN CONNECTION

Throughout the Caribbean, African descendants continue to demonstrate propensity for the use of proverbs. There, to a far greater extent than in Black America, African survivals manifest themselves in a Caribbean Creole culture, the resulting combination of African retentions with European cultural elements. Because African descendants and indigenous Caribbean peoples remained the dominant (if not the sole) population on the islands throughout time, the pressure to *de-Creolize* (i.e., *de-Africanize*) has not been as severe as in the case of Black Americans. Thus the "Caribbean connection" is a rich and easily available source of present-day Africanisms – among which proverbs are virtually a fact of everyday life.

Of course, the proverbs used in the Caribbean are an amalgamation of European, African, and the islands' indigenous cultures; yet the fact remains that in African and African Diasporic cultures, the affinity for the proverbial genre is stronger than in other cultural groups. Jeanty and Brown (1976), for example, provided a collection of 999 proverbs frequently used by the Haitian people. This non-exhaustive listing was offered as a means for giving insights into Haitian thinking, living, expressing, and understanding things around them.

In addition to her listing of 972 Jamaican proverbs, Martha Warren Beckwith ([1925] 1970) reported on Frank Cundall's and Harry Franck's collections of 737 and 468 Jamaican proverbs, respectively. Beckwith (1925, p. 5) furnished an excellent summary of proverbial use as an index of African cultural continuity in Jamaica.

> African wit and philosophy are more justly summed up in the proverb or aphorism than in any other form of folk art, and the proverbial sayings collected from Negro settlements in the Americas or the West Indies give a truer picture of the mental life of the Negro than even story or song reveals. In them he expresses his justification of the vicissitudes of life ... Proverbs enter constantly into the life of the folk; borrowed sayings undergo a process of remolding under the influence of native conditions, being interpreted to meet the emergencies of native life, and new sayings patterned upon the old. There is no other art so thoroughly assimilated to the life of the people of Jamaica today as this of the aphorism and none employed so constantly in everyday experience.

As late as 1976, a Jamaican native son, Leonard E. Barrett (1976, pp. 36–7), using Captain Rattray's collection *Ashanti Proverbs*, provided twenty examples of Ashanti proverbs with Jamaican equivalents. Several illustrations are listed below.

Ashanti	Jamaican
1 When you have quite crossed the river, you say that the crocodile has a lump on its snout.	1 No cuss alligator long mouth till you cross ribber.
2 The hen's foot does not kill her chicken.	2 Hen neber mash him chicken too hard.
3 A sheep does not give birth to a goat.	3 Sheep and goat no add one.

Ashanti	Jamaican
4 It is the water which stands calm and silent that drowns.	4 Noisy ribber no drown nobody.
5 When one does not know how to dance he says, "The drum is not sounding sweetly."	5 When man can't dance him say music no good.

In a recent effort to document Caribbean continuity with Africa and Afro-America, Jeremiah has undertaken a study of proverb use in Antiguan life. One of the islands of the Eastern Caribbean, Antigua was dominated by various European powers from the arrival of Columbus in 1493. In 1981, the island was granted full independent status from Britain.

In present-day Antigua, the majority of the islanders are of African descent. The remainder of the population consists of affluent Portuguese, Syrian, Arabian, and other Middle-Eastern nationals who migrated to the island in the middle of the nineteenth century and who dominate much of the commercial and retail outlets on the island. A color class system such as that mentioned by Smith (1965) exists with a few whites at the head. Recently, however, there has been some degree of social mobility, chiefly among those Antiguans who have been fortunate to have achieved a college/ university education at the University of the West Indies, or at various institutions of higher education in Britain, Canada, and the United States. There are other Antiguans who have been able to make significant economic gains as a result of hard work and financial support from relatives overseas. In spite of these gains, however, the majority of Antiguans are at the lower socioeconomic strata.

Proverbs in Antiguan life mirror the values of the community and the standards that individuals are supposed to maintain. Among such values are moral rectitude, altruism, respect, and humility. Some allowance is also made for human frailty because people are subject to making mistakes. There is nothing wrong if a politician, "feeds his horse where it is tied." What is considered wrong is the amount of "feeding" that takes place. Thus one should act responsibly in office and not abuse his or her power.

Antiguan proverbs are used chiefly by adults and give us an inside view of socialization in the home. Parents instill in their children such ideals as respect for elders, adherence to moral and religious values, and a sense of presenting oneself "properly" in everyday life. At an early age, one is admonished to "have manners," for manners and behavior "will carry youth throughout the world." Two well-known proverbs used with Antiguan children are: "The same stick that hits the wild goat will come back and beat the tame one also" (one should be able to give, as well as receive, criticism); "Who no hear will feel" (those who are disobedient will pay a penalty).

As with proverb use in Africa and Afro-America, the example of Antigua suggests that Caribbean proverbs serve as channels for indirect confrontation. The speaker may or may not have an audience, but he or she masks his or her statements in sacred or secular proverbs – "De arms of flesh will fail you" (The arms of flesh will fail you); "A house divided cannot stand;" "Wata more dan flowa" (Water is more than flour). In their confrontational use, Antiguan proverbs evidence a high frequency of occurrence in political contexts. Antiguans, like other Caribbean peoples, take a very serious view of the political process, and, unlike the situation in Black America, they control it. For example, the proverbs below were used in political meetings and discussions by males and females who were young and older adults.

Proverb	Context and purpose
1 She nar hang she hat too high again	Political conflict; to highlight the failure of a housing project to come to fruition
2 Dog better than you if it have a bone	Failed political promise; directed at the same housing project in a more derogatory manner
3 Cockroach have no orders in fowl house	Political scrutiny regarding performance of other party; to berate the Minister of Agriculture for his professional incompetence
4 You can't have two man crab in a hole	Political conflict; to berate members of opposing political party for failed promises
5 Soon ripe, soon rotten	During election campaign; to demonstrate that intellectual and political acumen come only with experience

Perhaps Barrett (1976, p. 38) best summarized African proverbial continuity in the Caribbean when he wrote: "As it is in Africa, so it is in Jamaica: the proverbs are not merely told as stories, but are a living part of the folk tradition and the vehicles of conversation."

PROVERBS IN THE AFRICAN DIASPORA: CURRENT RESEARCH

Research and data collection in the Diaspora continue against the backdrop of the long-standing controversy over the existence of Africanisms in the culture and life of Black people in the United States and the Caribbean. Focusing on the use, not origin of proverbs, we claim no African origin for any of the proverbs in our data. However, we do claim that the use of proverbs as a rhetorical tradition, infusing every aspect of African Diasporic life, reflects the continuity of the African consciousness among "New World" Blacks.

Our research objectives are the following:

1 to collect texts, that is, proverbs themselves, representing an extensive corpus of examples, with as many different proverbs and as many different versions of each proverb as possible;
2 to obtain detailed explanations of meanings of each different proverb, including contextual descriptions (events, settings for use, norms governing use, and so on);
3 to update existing collections of Black proverbs;
4 to publish a dictionary of Afro-American proverb use, with cassette tapes of interviews.

Of course, these are ambitious research goals formulated without benefit of any external funding and by researchers who are also teachers and administrators at their home institutions. But that is the essence of the Black Experience: to make a way out of no way.

As speech acts firmly rooted in the cultural context of the speech community, proverbs are context specific, occurring only as communicative responses to real-life, everyday events and experiences; hence the difficulty of using structured interviews and just "coming at me cold," as one of our proverb users put it. Another informant, reportedly a raconteur well-versed in proverbs, said: "Oh yeah, ah know thousands of them things, but you have to catch me at a party after have had a few drinks" (Salaam, 1976). Methodologically speaking, we are clearly confronted with Labov's "observer's paradox" (to observe the way people use language when they are not being observed – Labov, 1972). Parties, family reunions, funerals, church services, daily conversations – all would be excellent places to collect proverbs. While this kind of naturalistic observation would provide much rich data, it poses limitations in terms of its yield of systematic, quantifiable data; additionally, it could be an exceedingly lengthy procedure – factors that have to be considered in light of the aforementioned research goals.

Our solution has been to employ a variety of methods – including naturalistic observation – because we are more concerned with chronicling the authenticity of Black life than with the purity of research paradigms. Data have been collected in two different sites: Pittsburgh and Detroit. Additionally, data collections have begun in Antigua, as briefly discussed in the previous section, and we anticipate reporting full results from our "Caribbean connection" in the very near future. Although the locations may be said to be sites of convenience, each contains highly representative Black communities: Pittsburgh and Detroit are the home of large, urban, highly industrialized Black communities with Southern-based, rural, agrarian roots, and Antigua is the home of African descendants, who have maintained a Creole culture dating back to slavery under various European powers.

PITTSBURGH

After a small experimental pilot study, Daniel found greatest success by combining self-report with base study. Recognizing the Traditional Black Church as a unique speech community within the Black community, he concentrated on a single sampling frame, the membership of Sixth Mount Zion Baptist Church. With the cooperation and blessing of Pastor Elmer Williams, Daniel distributed to all church attendees, one Sunday after church, a form requesting name, address, and a list of all sayings known to the informant. In most instances, the forms were simply collected. In some instances, however, older women of the church, who knew "lots of those old things," were interviewed in depth by Daniel. Most of them had recorded several proverbs on their forms when Daniel arrived for the interview. Since the proverb tradition resides within the cultural deep structure and thus is not readily accessible to context-free consciousness, the interview engaged the women in conversation, generally about the proverbs on their lists. This stimulated them to think of more and more proverbs, even beyond the interview, and several subsequently called Daniel on the telephone with yet another proverb or two they had thought of on a given day. Daniel's research yielded a corpus of over 200 proverbs.

The Pittsburgh data were subjected to a content analysis and the sayings organized according to central themes that represent clusters of sayings. The result is a monograph, *The Wisdom of Sixth Mount Zion from The Members of Sixth Mount Zion and Those Who Begot Them*, published by Daniel in 1979. Daniel's schema evolved the following categories:

1   Virtues and Vices – for example, "Your backyard should look as pretty as your front yard";
2   Human Nature – for example, "One bad apple can spoil the whole bunch";
3   Sacred and Secular Commandments – for example, "Don't bite off more than you can chew";
4   Child Development – for example, "If you give a child an inch, he will take a mile";
5   The Nature of Reality – for example, "Beauty is only skin deep, but love is to the bone." (More extensive examples appear in Appendix A).

Daniel concludes that his collection represents the "wisdom" of Sixth; these sayings that are "like honeycomb; sweet to the soul, and health to the bones" constitute Black beliefs that reflect "fundamental perceptions of reality . . . essential value orientations and . . . most basic rules for living." The Pittsburgh proverb collection

> reflects many Black folks' intellectual convictions and intuitions about (1) things thought to be eternal, for example, "To err is human," (2) fundamental value sensibilities, for example, "It is not how long you have lived but how well you have lived," (3) reliable prescriptions for living, for example, "Never trouble Trouble till Trouble troubles you," and (4) the submerged truths found in nature, for example, "Still water runs deep".
> (Daniel, 1979, p. ii)

Although the Detroit data have not yet been subjected to Daniel's schema, the categories appear to be highly useful and functional for classification purposes and particularly appear to fit the proverbs collected in Detroit. In fact, many of the same proverbs, in the same form, reappear in the Detroit data, for example, "What goes around comes around"; "Still water runs deep." This point, however, awaits further analysis.

DETROIT

As acknowledged by Daniel, one limitation of his work with the Sixth speech community was the lack of contextual information and systematic sociolinguistic data (Daniel, 1979, p. vii). The Detroit research, a larger pilot study (N = 80) conducted under the supervision of Smitherman, sought to address these limitations. The survey method, rather than case study, was employed, with a team of trained interviewers, rather than a single data gatherer. Focus was on instrumentation and refinement of elicitation procedures so as to yield quantifiable demographic and frequency variables and contextual data for proverb use. An additional focus in Detroit was testing of the de-Creolization hypothesis through comparison of older and younger Blacks' linguistic representations of the same proverb. (*De-Creolization* refers to the de-*Africanizing* of Black Language by collapsing its deep and surface linguistic structures in the direction of the standard European language.)

The Detroit sample was constructed from community survey data utilized by the Center for Black Studies, Wayne State University, Detroit, in its surveys of Detroit households; these are based on stratified probability samples, chosen to yield appropriate proportions based on population characteristics of Black residents of the city. Interviewers were trained and participated in mock interviews to refine their interviewing skills. Some interviews were tape recorded; others handwritten by interviewers. Many of the informants, especially older people, seemed uncomfortable and clammed up in the face of "modern technology," and thus taping was not always possible. Further, many also seemed uneasy about interviewers writing while they were talking, as if this constituted impoliteness. Additionally, the formality and rigidity of the questionnaire presented some initial problems, again particularly with older informants. Several modifications were made so as to develop an interview style that was not obtrusive and alien to the oral tradition, and the interviewers were oriented to be sensitive and not appear as "educated fools." Such measures slowed down the pace of the interview, and in some instances, interviews lasted as long as four hours.

While the Detroit research resulted in a fairly effective instrument, the problem of instrumentation is far from solved. The Detroit team encountered some of the more common problems involved in survey research in Black communities, such as resistance to revealing income information or level of education. Then there was the tendency to invoke the well-known Black call–response pattern, requiring interviewers to "participate" in the interview, thus opening the way for possible sources of interviewer "bias."

Another problem, which resulted from the particular sociolinguistic focus in Detroit, involved efforts to uncover speech interaction norms through direct self-report. Since such social norms are generally internalized early in life, conscious awareness is not readily accessible. For example, we posed a question in the form, "Whom would you not use this proverb to and why?" in order to elicit information governing Hymes's well-known "who can say what to whom and under what conditions" (1974). In one trial-run interview, a wise, signifying elder gave the proverb "Pretty is as pretty does," and his answer to the question about use was "Well,

I sure wouldn't say it to anybody that was ugly," the response accompanied by a what–a–dumb–question–you–educated–fools–ask look. (After the confusion was cleared up, this old sage went on to give us over a dozen proverbs.) The lesson from the Detroit experience is that interviewers must be carefully trained, skilled, highly verbal, and competent in Black communication norms themselves, excellent listeners, and most of all, patient.

Despite the obstacles delineated above, Smitherman's Detroit research yielded a corpus of over 800 proverbs and significant information on a number of demographic and sociolinguistic variables.

The focus of analysis was on:

1   the most frequently occurring proverbs;
2   the de–Creolization hypothesis;
3   contextual interpretation; and
4   correlations between demographic variables and knowledge of proverbs.

While aspects of the analysis are ongoing, sufficient data have been tabulated to indicate some important results at this time.

In terms of the most popular proverbs, the following seem to be particularly favored by users:

1   What goes around comes around – the most frequently given proverb of all;
2   A bird in the hand is worth two in the bush;
3   You reap what you sow;
4   What goes up must come down;
5   What happens in the dark must come to light. (See Appendix A for more extensive listing of proverbs.)

Possibly these are popular proverbs among Black folk because they speak to what Daniel (1979, p. 9) calls "the proverbial metaphysics which inform us that certain things are inevitable."

With regard to de–Creolization (i.e., leveling out of phonological and morphosyntactic features of Black English in the direction of white Euro-American English), the Detroit data indicate a tendency in this direction. For example, the proverb "action speaks louder than words" was rendered by an older Black following the zero *s-morpheme* rule whereas a younger Black in the sample employed the *s-morpheme* in his version. However, de-Creolization is more than its objective realization in linguistic forms. It is both a state of mind and of cultural consciousness. Some younger Blacks in Detroit expressed skepticism about the validity and efficacy of proverbs. One stated that these old sayings "were only used by old Black people to keep young Blacks in line"; another said that sayings like "an apple a day will keep the doctor away" have no applicability to life today and were developed during hard times to justify the poverty and oppression of Black people (i.e., doctors are scarce, especially for Blacks, so just eat an apple everyday).

Analysis of the contexts of proverb use seems to indicate that most informants first heard a proverb used as a child, and its purpose was what N'Namdi (1978) calls "corrective guidance," in which Black adults use indirect verbal devices in the socialization of children. One of the most interesting commentaries on context was the explanation of "the blacker the berry, the sweeter the juice," in which the informant related it to child socialization and color consciousness in her native Louisiana community. Dark complexioned adults used this proverb with dark-skinned children to "boost their self esteem." (See Appendix B for more extensive examples.)

The most extensive and complete analysis has been done on the relationship between demographic variables and proverb use. The Detroit sample provided a fairly representative group to test our hypothesis concerning age, sex, religion, socioeconomic status, parental factors, and other variables significant in characterizing proverb users. We have posited that proverb knowledge and use are greater among older, Traditional Black Church-going, working-class females, who either were born in the South themselves or whose parents were born in the South.

Our 80 Detroit informants ranged in age from 17 to 95. The four age groups (17–35; 36–50; 50–65; over 65) were fairly represented, with the smallest number being 36–50 (17.5 percent of sample). Informants were almost evenly divided between males and females, with slightly more females (54 percent). In terms of occupation, 63.7 percent were laborers (some retired or unemployed), and one-fourth were professionals. Well over half were Traditional Black Church members (Baptist, Pentecostal, Church of God in Christ, and so on), but 22.5 percent were Presbyterian, Episcopalian, and other non-fundamentalist sects, and 6.3 percent were Catholic. Some 93.7 percent acknowledged a religious affiliation, but only 61.2 percent were active. Slightly less than half (47.5 percent) were born in the South, and 53.5 percent outside the South.

Computerization of the data and statistical analysis yielded results that indicate the following conclusions. First, there were no informants who did not know some proverbs, including the very young (17–20) age group and those who were middle-class professionals. Second, while the Amen Corner of Sixth provided rich data in Pittsburgh, this group was not significant in terms of the number of proverbs provided in Detroit. That is, older church women may indeed be more frequent users of proverbs, but they do not necessarily know more proverbs. Third, in terms of age, sex, occupation, education, religion, level of religious activity, place of birth, and parental factors (i.e., place of birth and religion of mother and father), analysis of variance produced a significant main effect only for age. Younger Blacks (17–35 age group) knew significantly fewer proverbs than older Blacks (50–65 age group), with a mean of 8.6 for the former compared to a mean of 24.2 for the latter. This was the only demographic variable that reached statistical significance. Fundamentalists did not contribute significantly more proverbs than non-fundamentalists, women did not know more than men, and those who were less active in their religion did not contribute significantly fewer proverbs than the more active, and so on. In short, these results pose an interesting counterpoint to our long-held view concerning proverb users.

Finally, two significant implications of the Detroit study emerge: (1) with reference to methodology, the Detroit research demonstrates the possibility of the quantitative paradigm to corroborate naturalistic observation and resolve the "observer's paradox" for researchers attempting to chronicle the complexity and richness of Black communication in the Diaspora; (2) with reference to the level of interpretation, proverbs possibly can provide us with an empirical index of racial consciousness. That is, if Blackness is a "state of mind," as has been argued, and if it is true, as our social analysis suggests, that Blacks use proverbs much more frequently than whites, then proverb knowledge and use may be concrete manifestations of that state of consciousness.

IMPLICATIONS

Proverbs constitute a very significant African verbal art. The African disposition toward the use of proverbs is still alive among African ancestors in the Western world. Because of their importance to African people, and because they are oral devices that tend to decline in use as African people assimilate into Western culture and acquire formal education, proverb collections need to be made throughout the African Diaspora. Of course, these collections should contain full ethnographic data such as the texts, text meanings, context for use, the primary sources, and the primary receivers. Such collections can be used to facilitate the following efforts:

1   Serve as indices of basic attitudes, values, beliefs, and, in general, worldviews.
2   Serve as indices of cultural interaction, for example, British and African in Jamaica, Arabic and Hausa in Nigeria, and Black Americans and the British, Germans, and French Americans.

3   Document cultural change such as changes in one's knowledge and use of proverbs.
4   Conduct comparative studies of proverb use and function.
5   Develop culturally authentic materials for facilitating formal education, for example, the use of proverbs to develop reading activities.

Our research leads us to conclude that proverbs are significant in the continuing development and survival of African descendants. It is imperative that research efforts continue to document this legacy that has enabled African people to "make a way outa no way."

APPENDIX A: SAMPLE PROVERBS FROM PITTSBURGH AND DETROIT

VIRTUES AND VICES

1   Your backyard should look as pretty as your front yard.
2   Two wrongs don't make a right.
3   It's a poor dog that won't wag its own tail.
4   Your word is your bond.
5   The early bird catches the worm.
6   A fool and his money are soon parted.
7   An ounce of prevention is worth a pound of cure.
8   Waste not, want not.
9   A whistling woman and a crowing hen never will come to no good end.
10   There is nothing worse than an educated fool.

HUMAN NATURE

1   One bad apple can spoil the whole bunch.
2   The blind can't lead the blind.
3   An empty wagon makes the most noise.
4   Two heads are better than one.
5   He that pays the piper calls the tune.
6   You can't teach an old dog new tricks.
7   One monkey don't stop no show.
8   An apple doesn't fall too far from the tree.
9   You can lead a horse to water but you can't make him drink.
10   Birds of a feather flock together.

SACRED AND SECULAR COMMANDMENTS

1   Don't bite the hand that feeds you.
2   Don't count your chickens before they hatch.
3   Don't burn down bridges you have to cross.
4   Don't let your right hand know what your left hand is doing.
5   Don't cast your pearls before swine.
6   Don't judge a book by its cover.
7   Never trouble Trouble till Trouble troubles you.
8   Think twice and speak once.
9   Don't make a mountain out of a mole hill.
10   Don't lie with the dead.

CHILD DEVELOPMENT

1   If you give a child an inch, he will take a mile.
2   Spare the rod, spoil the child.
3   A hard head makes a soft behind.
4   The blacker the berry, the sweeter the juice.
5   As the twig is bent, so shall the tree grow.
6   A burned child dreads the fire.
7   A little child can tell you something big.
8   Children should be seen and not heard.
9   Leave half of what you know in your head.
10   Don't let anyone outpick you in your own field.

THE NATURE OF REALITY

1   What goes around comes around
2   You can't judge a book by its cover.
3   What happens in the dark must come to the light.
4   You can't have your cake and eat it too.
5   If you play with a puppy, he will lick your face.
6   If you dig a ditch for your brother, dig two.
7   All that glitters ain't gold.
8   Beauty is only skin deep, but love is to the bone.
9   Smiling faces sometimes lie.
10   If you lay down with dogs, you'll get up with fleas.

APPENDIX B

Each person in the Detroit interviews was asked to select three proverbs from among the list he or she generated and discuss the meaning of each. The following are excerpts from this section of the interviews.

"WHAT GOES AROUND COMES AROUND"

Selected by Black male, 27 years old, born in Detroit, working as a mortgage appraiser. He states: "Whatever you do to someone will always come back to you ... I have heard this used mostly when playing basketball. The winning team will boast of its great ability to play, and the losing team will say this to them. Then the next game, my team, which was the winning team, will lose real bad." He has heard this and other proverbs used by his mother, who was born in Alabama.

(002)

"A ROLLING STONE GATHERS NO MOSS"

Selected by Black male, over 65 years old, born in Louisiana, retired from Chrysler. He states: "If you keep moving from one place to another, you cannot accumulate anything." He heard this proverb told to "a young fellow who didn't stay on the job more than four or five months." He also heard this proverb used by his parents, both of whom were also born in Louisiana.

(024)

"THE BLACKER THE BERRY THE SWEETER THE JUICE"

Selected by Black female, 74 years old, born in Louisiana, now a housewife. She states: "There was class among Black folks based on color. Lighter skinned people were considered better, and lighter skinned Blacks got the first and best jobs. Old folks said it to boast the self-esteem of darker Black children, especially girls. They were saying 'hold your head up.'" She has heard older, darker people use this proverb.

(076)

"DON'T COUNT YOUR CHICKENS BEFORE THEY HATCH"

Selected by Black female, 19 years old, born in Detroit, a student. She states: "You shouldn't count on things before they happen ...

Like my girl friend was expecting a call from a young man, and I interjected the aforementioned proverb." She has heard her mother, grandmother and older sister use this proverb most often. Her mother was born in Detroit.

(041)

"AN EMPTY WAGON MAKES THE MOST NOISE"

Selected by Black female, age 38, born in Detroit, working as a teacher in the public schools. she states: "If one is always talking and ranting and raving, he cannot receive, he is always giving off, but not taking in. Therefore, he is empty." This proverb was used often by her mother, who was born in Georgia, in 1897. She states: "I was always talkative and had to have my say; so my mother would tell me this because I wouldn't listen." She has also heard the proverb expressed as "A fool speaks loud, and a wise man only listens."

(012)

"A WHISTLING WOMAN AND A CROWING HEN NEVER WILL COME TO NO GOOD END"

Selected by Black male, age 36–50, born in Detroit, working as a social worker for the Michigan Department of Social Services. He states: "Whistling was looked on as a sign of bad morals for a woman. This proverb speaks to the ethics of the Black community. It is a display of bad morals for which one will come to a bad end and reap what you sow." His mother was a frequent user of proverbs; she was born in Marianna, Arkansas. Another version of this proverb that he has heard is "Boys must whistle and girls must sing."

(013)

"DON'T PUT OFF TOMORROW WHAT YOU CAN DO TODAY"

Selected by Black female, age 50–65, born in Des Moines, Iowa, working as a housewife. She states: "It was the way of life with older Blacks who felt that you should give a full day's work to whatever you're trying to achieve." She feels this proverb should be used with anyone who was not doing his or her daily duties, and this was the way it was said to her by her father, who was born in Monroe County, Missouri.

(003)

14

SPEAKING THE TRUTH TO THE PEOPLE

TESTIFYIN, SERMONIZIN, AND SIGNIFYIN

ANITA HILL, CLARENCE THOMAS, AND THE AFRICAN AMERICAN VERBAL TRADITION [1995]

SEVERAL EXPLANATIONS HAVE been advanced to account for the Anita Hill–Clarence Thomas phenomenon, both in terms of the conduct of the Thomas hearings themselves and in terms of public reaction to the hearings and the controversy. Such theories have ranged from the argument that US senators lack sensitivity to and understanding of the dynamics of sexual harassment (they just don't get it); to the issue of Hill's and Thomas's credibility; to a recognition of the continuing cataclysmic significance of race over gender (it's better to be a sexist than a racist); to the ludicrous notion advanced by Orlando Patterson (1991) that Thomas was simply engaging in a "down-home style of courting" toward Hill. Attention has focused on the issue of sexual exploitation, the historical facts surrounding the Hill–Thomas relationship, and legal and social arguments about how to operationalize the construct of sexual harassment. For the African American community, however, the Hill–Thomas phenomenon raises issues far beyond the immediate problematic of sexual harassment in the workplace. This essay seeks to advance our understanding of these broader implications from the vantage point of the African American Verbal Tradition.

The rhetorical situation created by the Hill–Thomas conflict represents an excellent case study for revisiting the linguistics of the "Talented Tenth" (see Woodson, 1925; Smith, 1969; Smitherman and Daniel: see Smitherman, 1979a). As articulated by W. E. B. Du Bois ([1961] 1903), the notion of a Black talented tenth refers to the strategy for creating a leadership class by targeting societal resources to the development of the upper 10 percent of the community. This group of African Americans would then struggle for the uplift and betterment of the remaining 90 percent. Although their leadership has often gone unheralded, both as activists and as public spokespersons among the Talented Tenth, African American women have played a significant historical role in the Black struggle. At the dawning of the twenty-first century, with victory still on the distant horizon, African American women face a rhetorical dilemma in our continuing struggle to be free. As even greater numbers of African American women enter positions of influence and leadership, there is a critical need to reclaim a rhetorically effective voice that can, as Margaret Walker Alexander said long ago, "speak the truth to the people." The truth has to be spoken in a language that the people understand — with both their heads and their hearts. As the Greek story goes, when Demosthenes spoke, the people applauded, but when Pericles spoke, they marched. The people's response is a function of the speaker's adaptation of her language to the people. This is so because language is not mere words; nor can mere words, as they occur in conversation, dialogue, and speeches, be dismissed as just semantics. Rather, language plays a dominant — if not the dominant — role in the social construction of reality. Let us review the role of language in society generally and in African American society in particular.

Berger and Luckmann (1966) contend that language constitutes the most important content and instrument of socialization. Extending their paradigm, I posit that reality is not merely socially but also sociolinguistically constructed (Smitherman, 1989a). Social experience and even experience of physical, objective phenomena are filtered, apprehended, codified, and conveyed via some linguistic shape. This linguistic form exists in a dialectical relationship with cognition and social behavior. While Von Humboldt ([1810] 1963) and Humboldtian linguists and most Whorfians ([1941] 1956) perhaps overstate the case for language as the determiner of thought, consciousness, and behavior, language does play a dominant role in the formation of ideology and consciousness and in race, gender, and class relations — and in the sociolinguistic case study under examination here.

Language operates on the subtle, subliminal level, thus rendering it all the more effective in the sociolinguistic construction of reality. Manipulation of the sociolinguistic construction of reality by this country's power elites results in serious acts of linguistic trickeration, or what Lutz (1987) and other scholars refer to as "doublespeak." Bush and his military leaders made the Persian Gulf War palatable to US citizens with such terms as "security review" to refer to the censorship of news reports and "collateral damage" to refer to civilians killed or wounded by "smart bombs" that were "servicing the target" (Committee on Public Doublespeak 1992).

Yet verbal operations on social reality can lead to progressive constructions. J. T. and Sam, two African American assembly-line workers at Detroit's old Jefferson Avenue Chrysler automobile plant extend the semantic space surrounding the word "nigger," going beyond a racial epithet to encompass the historical oppression of African slaves and the exploitation of any worker. They are talking about the large number of Vietnamese – "boat people," as many Americans derisively refer to them – who had sought refuge in the United States:

> J. T.:   The Vietnam who didn't git off the boat, they was gon be the new niggas – for the Whiteys and us.
>
> SAM: Well, I wish they hadda come on out there to work, cause I'm tired of being the nigga.
>
> (Smitherman, 1976)

It isn't only in the semantic realm but also in syntax, discourse structures, speech acts, and verbal registers of communication that we can witness the subtle impact of language in constructing reality. Syntax can code a worldview. Power elites, aided by the media, make objects into subjects and use the passive voice, allowing those who commit an act to go unnamed. Making bad linguistic matters worse, everyday people often adopt these pernicious uses of language as their linguistic role models. For example, one of my students wrote, "The invasion of Grenada was officially approved," thereby permitting the agent, President Reagan, to escape unnoticed.

Consider the following interaction between a receptionist and one of her bosses in the outer office of a Black corporate setting:

> RECEPTIONIST: Good morning, Mr. Jones.
>
> MR JONES: What's happenin', baby?
>
> (Smitherman, unpublished manuscript)

The receptionist, a Black woman, has used for her greeting the verbal register expected of a receptionist in a formal business setting. Her boss, a Black man, not only responds in Black English Vernacular (BEV) but also uses a BEV informal, socially intimate style, rather than a formal BEV greeting pattern. To be sure, in this country, the sociolinguistic rules allow the superior in a communication interaction to dictate the verbal styles and registers used in that interaction. So perhaps Mr. Jones, as the boss, is asserting his right to redefine this formal situation and recast it into an informal, more comfortable linguistic zone. Perhaps he wants to do so in the interest of cutting through the coldness and impersonality of the corporate world (in this instance, the Black corporate world). All of which he might have done by using the receptionist's first name, for instance, coupled with a more conversational form of the Language of Wider Communication – "Hello, [or Hi], how you doin' today, Barbara?" However, Mr. Jones code-switches to BEV. This asymmetrical ("down-home"?) greeting pattern is viewed by the receptionist as a sign of disrespect. In fact, however subliminal, Mr. Jones's greeting serves as an act of subordination, in essence, sociolinguistically putting the receptionist in her place, in terms of both class and gender. As she put it, "It's like he was saying, 'Since you are only a receptionist and a woman, I can talk to you any kind of way.'" (This interaction took place while I was waiting to see another of the corporate bosses, who had hired me as a consultant because the business was experiencing communication problems between staff and management!)

While African and European Americans share similar language norms and functions, there is an added dimension to the sociolinguistic condition of African Americans: the linguistic–cultural clash between the African American Verbal Tradition and that of European Americans. I am not simply referring to that frequently oversimplified issue about whether Black-English-speaking students should be taught "standard English." (For the record, I don't know of anybody – linguist or otherwise – who says they should *not*; the issue is how, when, and for what purposes such students should be taught "*the* standard.") I am talking about something more fundamental than the grammar of BEV – such as "She be looking good" – or the Black English pronunciation of "thing" as "thang." The African American Verbal Tradition clashes with the European American tradition because there are different – and, yes, contradictory – cultural assumptions about what constitutes appropriate discourse, rhetorical strategies, and styles of speaking. While the African American linguistic style has been described as passionate, emotional, and "hot" and the European as objective, detached, and "cold," we are seriously oversimplifying if we assert that one tradition is superior. What is not an oversimplification, however, is that African and European Americans have different attitudes about and responses to a speaker depending on whether she uses one style or the other.

The foregoing discussion is the vantage point from which this essay compares the linguistic styles of Anita Hill and Clarence Thomas in phase two of the Thomas confirmation hearings. AVT refers to the African American Verbal Tradition; LWC will refer to the Language of Wider Communication, that is, a language that facilitates communication beyond one's own speech community, i.e., in this country, European American "standard English." My thesis is that Hill used LWC, whereas Thomas used AVT, and that these contrasting styles had differential impact on African Americans.

While the language of the Chrysler workers and Mr. Jones, quoted above, illustrates obvious examples of BEV within the AVT, the rhetorical strategies and discourse modes of the AVT are more subtle. And they are powerful persuasive devices that can be used by a Supreme Court justice without the stigma generally attached to Black "slang" or BEV grammatical patterns. We shall examine four dimensions of the AVT that Thomas employed: signification, personalization, tonal semantics, and sermonic tone.

SIGNIFICATION

Signification, or signifyin, is the verbal art of ceremonial combativeness in which one person puts down, talks about, "signifies on" someone or on something someone has said. Also referred to as "joanin'," "cappin'," "soundin'," and currently "dissin'," this rhetorical modality is characterized by indirection, humor, exploitation of the unexpected, and quick verbal repartee. Sometimes done for just plain fun, signifyin is also a sociolinguistic corrective employed to drive home a serious message without preaching or lecturing. For example, Malcolm X once began a speech this way: "Mr Moderator, Brother Lomax, brothers and sisters, friends and enemies: I just can't believe everyone in here is a friend, and I don't want to leave anybody out." Without a direct frontal attack, Malcolm neatly put down his known enemies as well as those traitors in the all-Black audience – the "smiling faces" who sometimes "lie" (Smitherman 1986).

As various scholars have noted (e.g., Hurston 1935; Mitchell-Kernan 1972; Gates 1988b), Signification has a long, honorable history in the Black Experience and is strongly rooted in the African American Verbal Tradition. Black preachers are and must be adept signifiers. For example, one big-city preacher in a broadcast church service used extended signifyin to dis his sacred and secular competition in the "blessing business," the business of dispensing advice, prayers, fortune-telling, symbolic artifacts, or other types of "mojo" that will help people achieve their desired goals. Such pretenders, so this preacher contended, are unqualified, either because they aren't successful themselves or because their "magic" demands too great an investment, such as traveling long distances or large financial donations. Simultaneously, the preacher is promoting and marketing his own power – his "thang" (also requiring a donation).

PREACHER: I say this thang I got, this thang, yeah this thang, it ain' like what the other folks telling you 'bout.
CONGREGATION: Yeah! Yeah! Tell about it! Say so! You on the case!

PREACHER:	This thang will make a way outta no way, and, listen to me church, you ain't got to go no long way to git it, not *my* thang.
CONGREGATION:	Yessuh! I hear you!
PREACHER:	You ain' got to catch no bus, you ain' got to fly no airplane, go no long ways, just come on over here and git this thang and help yo'self.
CONGREGATION:	Say the word! Talk about it!
PREACHER:	You see, like I was sayin', talk is cheap, plenty peoples go 'round sayin' what they gon' do for you and they ain' got nothin theyself.
CONGREGATION:	Look out now! Well, come on out wit it! Un-huh, un-huh!
PREACHER:	I say, what I look like askin' you to pray for me and you ain' got a pot nor a window!
CONGREGATION:	Watch yo'self, Doc! You gon' tell it in a minute! Go 'head, go 'head!
PREACHER:	Y'all know what uhm talkin' 'bout that's a word my grandmomma used to say. Come on over here to 14873 Puritan and git my thang!

(Smitherman 1986, p. 125)

Locating his rhetorical posture squarely in this tradition, Thomas's speaking style throughout the second phase of his hearings was rife with the verbal aggressiveness, indirection, and repartee of signification. From Giddayup, he comes on with an attitude, big-time, signifyin about the chain of events that have led to the reopening of the confirmation hearings:

> I have experienced the exhilaration of new heights from the moment I was called to Kennebunkport by the President to have lunch and he nominated me. That was the high point. At that time, I was told eye-to-eye that, 'Clarence, you made it this far on merit. The rest is going to be politics.' And it surely has been.

He concludes his opening statement by putting the Senate Judiciary Committee on defensive notice that racism is the name of this game, and he ain gon play in it, through this Signification: "I am a victim of this process. . . . I will not provide the rope for my own lynching."

Two of Thomas's best signifyin jabs occurred in the exchange between him and Senator Howell Heflin in his second appearance after Hill had testified. After Thomas boldly announced that he hadn't listened to Hill's testimony (which obviously is dumbfounding to Heflin), he and Heflin go at it, with Thomas's signifyin carrying the day:

> HEFLIN: We're trying to get to the bottom of this, and if she is lying, then I think you can help us prove that she was lying.
>
> THOMAS: Senator, I am incapable of proving the negative. It did not occur.
>
> HEFLIN: Well, if it did not occur, I think you are in a position, certainly, your ability to testify to in effect to try to eliminate it from people's minds.
>
> THOMAS: Senator, I didn't create it in people's minds.

The clear implication here is that Hill, the Senate Judiciary Committee, the news media, the person who leaked the FBI files, whoever, is responsible for planting this "scurrilous" charge against him in the public mind. So why should he be called on to eliminate it?

In the matter of the leaking of Hill's charges, Thomas gets in another good bit of Signification:

> THOMAS: This matter ... was leaked last weekend to the media ... leaked to national newspapers [creating] a national forum ... allegations that should have been resolved in a confidential way.
>
> HEFLIN: Well, I certainly appreciate your attitude toward leaks. I happen to serve on the Senate Ethics Committee, and it's been a sieve.
>
> THOMAS: Well, but it didn't leak on me.

In other words, don't even try it – don't deflect the power of my claim by suggesting that leaking is a general governmental concern; this one is personal, and it's killing me.

PERSONALIZATION

The oratorical style of the AVT eschews the detachment and (presumed) "objectivity" of Eurocentric discourse. Personalization demands concreteness and specificity, not abstraction and generalization. In fact, there is distrust and suspicion of someone who is too clinical and distances himself or herself from phenomena and events that are under consideration. Do they care? Are they sincere? Well, if "they got religion, they oughtta show some sign." Some Afrocentric psychologists call this demand for personal involvement a "field-dependent" cognitive style (e.g., Wilson 1971; Pasteur and Toldson 1982). The style draws the audience into the arena of conflict; in so doing, the speaker seeks to establish a psychic bond. The theoretical abstract issue is thus brought right down front. Like, what if it was you, homey, how would you feel? Or in Thomas's words: "And how many members of this committee would like to have the same scurrilous, uncorroborated allegations made about him, and ... then be drawn and dragged before a national forum of this nature ... ?"

Again and again, Thomas posed this same question in different forms. The ultimate personalization occurs when he likens his employees to family and implies that the committee should visualize their own reactions if a family member should turn on them. This exchange takes place with Thomas and Senator Leahy:

LEAHY: Spoke of them really basically almost as family, the people that have worked for you ... correct?

THOMAS: Yes ... Anita Hill came to me through one of my dearest, dearest friends ... They are family. My clerks are my family.

LEAHY: Well, then, having done all this for Professor Hill and knowing now ... and hearing her statement under oath, explicit as it was, the statements that you've categorically denied, to use your term, why would she do this?

THOMAS: I don't know why family members turn on each other. I don't know why a son or a daughter or brother or sister would write some book that destroys a family.

(Like, you Senators know about that, don't you, like Reagan's daughter writing that book of hers?) Thomas, continuing to go straight for the jugular, signifyin even as he personalizes.

TONAL SEMANTICS

Not only is AVT personalized, it reflects impassioned language use and is characterized by a high-spirited style of delivery. The speech rhythms reflect emotional intensity. The voice itself, the choice of words, and the pattern of communication is high-energy, passionate, "soulful." Holt (1972) and Kochman (1981) refer to this as "expressive" style; I call it "tonal semantics" (Smitherman 1986). Kochman contends that this is a significant source of black–white communication difference and conflict:

The black mode ... is high-keyed: animated, interpersonal, and confrontational. The white mode ... is relatively low-keyed: dispassionate, impersonal, and non-challenging. The first is characteristic of involvement; it is heated, loud, and generates affect. The second is characteristic of detachment and is cool, quiet, and without affect.

(1981, p. 18)

Through emotion-laden words and the rhythmic repetition characteristic of the AVT, Thomas employed his dynamic verbal energy to superb rhetorical effect. The hearings were a "travesty," the charges "scurrilous," full of "sleaze," "trash," and "dirt" from the "sewer" of life. He is "stunned," "hurt," "confused," "abused,"

in "pain" and "anguish." He is being "pilloried" by this "debilitating," "Kafkaesque" "horror," beginning with "Charges . . . leveled
against me from the shadows . . . drug abuse, anti-Semitism, wife
beating. . . and now this." Ever since this occurred, Thomas's "days
have grown darker," and he, his family, and his friends have endured
"enormous pain and great harm." In fact, he asserts, "I have never
in my life felt such hurt, such pain, such agony." Finally, he pulls
out all the stops: "Yesterday I called my mother. She was confined
to her bed, unable to work and unable to stop crying."

In the tonal semantics dimension of AVT, there is rhythmic,
evocative repetition. This characteristic feature reinforces the high-
spirited, emotional, expressive intensity of the Black speaking style.
Thomas's rhetoric is shot through with this feature. An extended
harangue by his boy, Senator Hatch, sets out the "totally offensive"
Long Dong Silver pornographic story that Hill said Thomas discussed
with her. Hatch laments the activation of the stereotype about the
size of Black men's penises conveyed by the "Long Dong" metaphor,
all of which has been used against Thomas. In obvious sympathy with
Thomas, Hatch asks him, "What do you think about that?" Thomas
replies: "I wasn't harmed by the Klan. I wasn't harmed by the Knights
of Camellia. I wasn't harmed by the Aryan race. I wasn't harmed by
a racist group. I was harmed by this process."

He continues:

> If someone wanted to block me from the Supreme Court of the United
> States because of my views on the Constitution, that's fine. If someone
> wanted to block me because they felt I wasn't qualified, that's fine. If
> someone wanted to block me because they don't like the composition of
> the Court, that's fine. But . . . I would have preferred an assassin's bullet
> to this kind of living hell.

Successive repetitions of key statements and/or phrases, ending
with the punch of counterstatement – a classic rhetorical device in
AVT. Thomas worked it effectively throughout the hearings. Hatch
asks him if he ever thought he'd have to "face scurrilous accusations
like those which you have refuted?" Thomas's tonal semantics answer:

> I expected it to be bad. I expected to be a sitting duck for the interest
> groups. I expected them to attempt to kill me. And yes, I even expected
> personal attempts on my life . . . I did not expect this circus. I did not
> expect this charge against my name. I expected people to do anything,
> but not this.

SERMONIC TONE

As scholars have demonstrated (e.g., DuBois, [1903] 1961; Woodson, 1921; Mitchell, 1970; Lincoln, 1990), the Traditional Black Church has had a profound impact and influence on the African American Experience. For example, virtually all Black (male) leaders have come out of the Church – either the Christian or the Muslim, for instance, such as Reverend Jesse Jackson and Minister Louis Farrakhan. Being not simply a religious unit but the center of social life, the Church has influenced the development of AVT. Ordinary statements take on the tone of pronouncements and are given the force of the moral high ground; they are proclaimed with the profundity and moral sobriety of divinely inspired truth. This gives Black speech its elevated, "fancy talk" quality. Thomas speaks of the "destruction of my integrity" and says that he "would not want to – except being required to here – dignify those allegations with a response." And "God has gotten me through the days since September 25, and he is my judge." (Not you Senators!)

Indeed, with the "help of others and with the help of God," Thomas has been able "to defy poverty, avoid prison, overcome segregation, bigotry, racism, and obtain one of the finest educations available in this country." Yet he has not been able "to overcome this process." Nonetheless, he reminds us that within the Judeo-Christian community of the saved, one can be sustained, as he has been, by "prayers said for my family and me by people I know and people I will never meet, prayers that were heard." (Jesus on the mainline and connected!)

ANITA HILL AND LWC

In contrast to Thomas's use of AVT, Anita Hill employed LWC. This style is low-keyed, clinical, dispassionate, unemotional. Despite the psychic wounds inflicted on her by Thomas, Hill exhibits no signs of anger, but methodically details his advances.

> His conversations were very vivid. He spoke about acts that he had seen in pornographic films involving such matters as women having sex with animals and films showing group sex or rape scenes. He talked about pornographic materials depicting individuals with large penises or large breasts involved in various sex acts. On several occasions, Thomas told me graphically of his own sexual prowess.

In contrast to Thomas's "scurrilous" allegations, she speaks of "unpleasant matters." Whereas her verbal accusations have visited "agony," "anguish," and "pain" upon him, his sexual verbalisms have only made her "extremely uncomfortable."

Hill remains stoically principled and refuses to personalize her assessment of Thomas, despite his sexual intimidation. She is undaunted by Senator Specter's attempts to rattle her when, for instance, he wonders why, if Thomas were such a bad fellow, did she give a high assessment of him?

> SPECTER: There is a report in the *Kansas City Star* ... quoting you ... 'the Clarence Thomas of that period ... would have made a better judge on the Supreme Court, because he was more open-minded.' Now, how is it that you would have said that ... considering all of the things you have said that he told you about at the Department of Education and also at EEOC?
>
> HILL: That opinion, Senator, was based strictly on his experience, his ability to reason; it was not based on personal information. ... I was trying to give as objective an opinion as possible ... as a university professor ... you have some obligation to try to make objective statements ... based on his record as a public figure ... not relying on my own private understanding and knowledge.

Nor does Hill have angry words of denunciation for the conduct and nature of the hearing, as does Thomas. Yet she had struggled to maintain her privacy and would not have come forth if someone hadn't leaked the information she had given in confidence to the FBI. Further, it is clear that *she* is the one on trial, not him; it is she who has been put on the defensive and discounted. Thus, she had every reason to feel as violated by the questioning as Thomas felt. Yet she maintains her objective, unemotional, depersonalized rhetorical stance. Her dialogue with Senator Deconcini is illustrative.

> DECONCINI: Do you think, now having told your side and responded to these questions, that your reputation from your standpoint could ever be fully restored?
>
> HILL: Not in the minds of many. Never. It will not be.
>
> DECONCINI: ... Is the committee more culpable for causing you to have to come forward? Is the press more culpable? Or is it all just a big bunch of stuff that we've got to deal with, and everybody's culpable?
>
> HILL: I think it's just the reality, Senator, of this situation, the nature of this complaint. And I cannot point my finger at any one entity, and say that you are responsible for this.

Finally, rather than signifyin, testifyin, or sermonizin, Hill remains cool and detached, even in the face of blatant attacks on her integrity and audacious attempts to impugn her character. Specter is most vicious and vociferous in this regard.

> SPECTER: Well, when you say you wanted to maintain a cordial profes-
> sional relationship, why would you do that, given the comments
> which you represent Judge Thomas made to you ... Was it
> simply a matter that you wanted to derive whatever advantage
> you could from a cordial professional relationship?
>
> HILL: It was a matter that I did not want to invoke any kind of retal-
> iation against me professionally. It wasn't that I was trying to
> get any benefit from it.

THE RHETORICAL CONTEST

The only tool Hill and Thomas had available to them was their
language. Their rhetorical presentations had to substitute for standard legal evidence and judicial forms of proof.

Thomas did not simply revert to *race* in the construction of his
proof. He also reverted to the race's *rhetorical paradigm*. His recourse
to AVT accomplished two purposes: (1) It humanized him and
created the mythology that he was like Sly Stone and Arrested
Development's "everyday people." (2) Targeted at the weak side,
his rhetorical stance was a verbal offense that put his enemies on
the sociolinguistic defensive.

By using the age-old ethnolinguistics of the Black Tradition,
Thomas became a person, rather than an abstraction, to African
Americans. Even those who didn't like him, or his politics, grudg-
ingly identified with his pain and his "down-home" personhood.
When he describes the impact of all this on him, he brings the
emotional suffering home with familiar concreteness:

> The last two and a half weeks have been a living hell. I think I've died
> one thousand deaths. What it means is living on one hour a night's sleep.
> It means losing fifteen pounds in two weeks. It means being unable to
> eat, unable to drink, unable to think about anything but this and wondering
> why, how. It means wanting to give up.

When Hatch asked him, "How do you feel right now, Judge,
after what you have been through?" he came off just like your
next-door neighbor:

> I'll go on. I'll go back to my life of talking to my neighbors, and cutting
> my grass, and getting a Big Mac at McDonald's, and driving my car, seeing
> my   kid   play   football   ...   If   I'm   not   confirmed,   so
> be it – [I will] continue my job as a court of appeals judge, and hope-
> fully live a long life, enjoy my neighbors and my friends, my son, cut my
> grass, go to McDonald's, drive my car, and just be a good citizen, and a
> good judge, and a good father, and a good husband.

The second critical function Thomas's AVT rhetoric served was to sound a sociolinguistic clarion call to the Senate Judiciary Committee. The African American Verbal Tradition is perceived to be aggressive, threatening, intimidating. When Hatch posed the possibility of Thomas withdrawing from the process, he said, "I'd rather die than withdraw. If they're gon kill me, they're gon kill me . . . I never cry 'uncle,' and I'm not going to cry 'uncle' today." (Like, kill me you Marilyn Farmers!)

It wasn't just the racial content, then, that Thomas introduced on Capitol Hill. He did not talk about ropes and high-tech lynchings in the restrained LWC style. It was the Black Expressive Style that sent them all running for cover. It constructed the reality of a strong, angry African American man (a "crazy nigga") who might explode at any minute. AVT upped the ante. As Kochman says, "Whites are constrained not only by the higher level of energy and spiritual intensity that Blacks generate. They are worried that Blacks cannot sustain such intense levels of interaction without losing self-control" (1981, p. 31).

Hill, by contrast, remained something of an abstraction, an unknown. Although many African Americans tried to empathize with her powerlessness, she didn't provide any graphic specificity about her hurt and feelings. For instance, when she told of being hospitalized for stress during the sexual harassment period, she didn't try to make us *feel* her pain the way Thomas did (he says he had lost weight, was only sleeping one hour each night, had died one thousand deaths, etc.). Whether his pain was real or feigned is ultimately irrelevant; he made it real. Hill, though, didn't concretize her suffering. How did her stress manifest itself? Did she lose or gain weight? Did her hair fall out? Such personalization and use of emotional strategies, however, violate LWC conventions.

The two contestants also contrast in terms of their rhetorical exploitation of family and family traditions. While Thomas constantly invoked his elders (his sharecropping grandfather's legacy, mother wit, etc.), Hill never incorporated any talk about her family or the lessons and legends of her Blood. In fact, even though she brought her family members with her, they remained just there, in the background like stage props.

TOWARD TWENTY-FIRST-CENTURY WOMANIST LANGUAGE

A few days after the Thomas hearings ended, I sat among a group of African American women, some of them from the hood, at a hair-braiding shop. The hair-braiding thing is an all-day affair. My well over eight hours at the shop was my first introduction to the possibility that many African American women did not support Hill. So what if the Black men I talked to, heard and read about, supported Thomas and favored his nomination? "You know how a lot of the Brothas be, all nationalistic sometime, just when you need them to be critical," I reminded myself. And never mind those Black women demonstrating for Thomas on the day of the confirmation vote. "That's just an anomaly; besides, maybe he even paid them," I comforted myself. Surely most African American women understood and supported Hill's position, many having been subjected to such intimidation themselves. Certainly Black women recognized that Thomas's confirmation and the sure-to-be-regressive Supreme Court opinions his vote would solidify would be devastating, not only to the progress of women but to our children and the entire Black community. Surely this is how African American women are looking at this thing, I told myself.

That day at the hair-braiding shop let me know quick, fast, and in a hurry that I had another think coming. These Black women expressed strong negative reactions to Hill: "phony," "saddity" (stuck-up), "I don't trust her," they said, as they discredited her and her story. Even the couple of women who believed her said they could see why those Black women who testified for "Clarence" didn't like "Anita," that they found her kind of "strange," not like anybody *they* knew who had grown up in a poor family of thirteen children on a farm. I was to hear a similar refrain in a number of places − in my Traditional Black Church that Sunday; at a housewarming party I attended in the hood of another city; in the sauna at a city-owned community center in yet another city. I discovered that the opinions of everyday women, those who weren't the "Ds" − i.e. Ph.D., M.D., J.D. − that I talked to in my personal travels around the country coincided with national poll data as well as with a pilot study done in Boston.

How do we account for these reactions − the strong Black support for Thomas, which actually *increased* after Hill's allegations, and the concomitant discounting of Hill herself? I want to suggest that language played a fundamental role in this construction of reality in African America. Suspicion and skepticism are common Black reactions to Black users of LWC rhetorical style. These perceptions exist simultaneous with the belief that one needs to master LWC in order to "get ahead." I call it "linguistic push−pull"; DuBois called it "double consciousness." The farther removed one is from mainstream "success," the greater the degree of cynicism about this ethnolinguistic, cultural ambivalence. Jesse Jackson knows about this; so did Malcolm X and Martin Luther King; so does

Louis Farrakhan. The oratory of each is LWC in its grammar but AVT in its rhetorical style.

Thomas capitalized on and ruthlessly exploited the African American Verbal Tradition for all it was worth. He seized the rhetorical advantage, swaying Black opinion by use of the touch-stones of the Oral Tradition and sociolinguistically constructing an image of himself as culturally Black and at one with the Folk. Hill, on the other hand, utilized the European American rhetorical tradi-tion in which she had been trained and which she had mastered. Deploying the dispassion, logic, and verbal forms of support of this tradition, she met white male adversity head on. (Of course, Senator Heflin referred to her as a "meek woman," but I'm sure he simply meant "meek" for a *Black* woman.) She did it all with eloquence, grace, and style. But it was a *European* American, not an *African* American, style.

Now, let us be clear because much is at stake here. In no way should the analysis presented and the conclusion arrived at be construed to be a condemnation of Hill. And it certainly *ain't* no celebration of Thomas. Rather, the crucial lesson to be extrapo-lated from this sociolinguistic case study is this: African American women must fashion a language, building on and rooted in the African American Experience, that speaks to the *head* and the *heart* of African America if we are to provide the necessary leadership, not only for Blacks, but for the nation, in the twenty-first century. In cautioning us to be wary of "uncritical acceptance of Hill," bell hooks advises: "While it is crucial that women come to voice in a patriarchal society that socializes us to repress and contain, it is also crucial what we say, how we say it, and what our politics are" (1992, p. 21). We are here concerned with the how. Is the African American Verbal Tradition the purview of Black men only? What are the discourse options available to Black women? Who is the Black woman, and how *do* a Black woman sound? Hard, complex questions, requiring collective work to arrive at answers. Here, however, is a way we might begin to chart the journey.

While there is an emerging Womanist paradigm, and while African American women are fast at work recovering Black women's history, still Toni Morrison's classic 1971 statement characterizes the current situation:

> For years in this country there was no one for black men to vent their rage on except black women. And for years black women accepted that rage – even regarded that acceptance as their unpleasant duty. But in doing so, they frequently kicked back, and they seem never to have become the "true slave" that white women see in their own history. True, the black woman did the housework, the drudgery; true, she reared the

children, often alone, but she did all of that while occupying a place on the job market, a place her mate could not get or which his pride would not let him accept. And she had nothing to fall back on: not maleness, not whiteness, not ladyhood, not anything. And out of the profound desolation of her reality she may very well have invented herself.

(p. 63)

As African American women, we need to ask ourselves: What is the nature and linguistic character of this invented personna? Must everything be cut whole from new cloth today, with no connecting threads to the past? What are the African American woman's traditions that can be part of the formula for the necessary rhetorical invention?

Given the construction of race, gender, and sexuality that Hill symbolized, coupled with the fact that *she* was the one on trial, she was in an untenable, no-win situation. The only way to win in this kind of battle is to jump outside the established logic and make winning irrelevant. Redefine the rhetorical moment as a forum for instruction. The issue of sexual harassment in the workplace is not merely a middle-class white women's issue. It is an even more crucial issue for women in the underclass, and for those in the working and un-working classes in the United States, all of whom are disproportionately women of Color. These women are highly vulnerable because they have fewer options than the female "Ds." As for Thomas, he is not bad news just because he might have been a sex harasser. His is a retrogressive position that threatens the rights of *all* working and un-working people. He is opposed to equity policies and affirmative action for people of Color. He is opposed to abortion. He supports the conservative agenda whole hog. Thus, here was a prime opportunity to "speak the truth to the people," before, during, and after the hearing.

For the African American woman in leadership and struggle today, construction of this twenty-first-century Womanist language requires that we revisit the linguistics of leadership located in Black women's traditions and rhetorical archetypes – linguistic role models like Zora Neale Hurston's signifyin Janie, Fannie Lou Hamer, Barbara Jordan, Ella Baker, and others who come out of the Black tradition of struggle. The most renowned speaker in this tradition is the great Sojourner Truth. In 1852, she made her famous "And Ain't I A Woman?" speech at a Women's Rights Convention in Akron, Ohio. She tells the white men gathered there a thing or three about women's equality, including the right to vote. As Arthur Huff Fauset describes the situation in his book, *Sojourner Truth*, she is thinking:

> Who were these people anyway that they imagined they could make laws just to suit themselves — ministers, thugs, and barbarians? They with their laws about Negroes, laws about women, laws about property and about everything under the sun ... There was only one Lawgiver. He could make these picayune creatures fly, law or no law. He was on *her* side; assuredly He was *not* on their side.
>
> (Fauset quoted in Davis and Redding, 1971, p. 79)

Much has been made of the dramatic gesture of Sojourner Truth baring her breast in this famous speech to demonstrate that in spite of being forced to enact many male roles, she was indeed a woman. Yet more critically, this dramatic rhetorical gesture and the entire discourse itself are straight out of the African American Verbal Tradition, with Tonal Semantics, Personalization, Sermonic Tone, and, most of all, exhibiting the greatest Signification in the history of the tradition.

> Den dat little man in black dar [pointing to a minister], he say women can't have as much rights as man, cause Christ warn't a woman. Whar did your Christ come from? WHAR DID YOUR CHRIST COME FROM? From God and a woman! Man had nothing to do with Him!

Yes, African American women do indeed signify. We also play the dozens and "talk shit," but save that for another day. The point is that the AVT does not belong to the Brothas alone. African American women must appropriate the African American Verbal Tradition for the advancement of our children, our communities, and our people. We must build on the Womanist tradition of talk in the legacy of Sojourner Truth, Ida B. Wells, Frances E. W. Harper, and the many thousands gone. It is the only way to make sure we ain talkin in ways peculiar to our people's minds.

15

"THE CHAIN REMAIN THE SAME"[1]

COMMUNICATIVE PRACTICES IN THE HIP HOP NATION

[1997]

It is true that the nature of society is to create, among its citizens, an illusion of safety; but it is also absolutely true that the safety is always necessarily an illusion. Artists are here to disturb the peace.

Baldwin (1992)

THE TERM *HIP HOP* refers to urban youth culture in America. Hip Hop is manifested in such cultural productions as graffiti art, break dancing, styles of dress (e.g., baggy pants, sneakers, Malcolm X caps, appropriately worn backward), love of b-ball (basketball), and so forth. Although the Hip Hop Nation is predominantly Black, Latinos comprise a significant minority within this nation. Three different New York artists have been credited with coining the term Hip Hop (which dates back to the 1970s): Busy Bee Starski, DJ Hollywood, and DJ Afrika Bambaataa (founder of the Zulu Nation in New York). It is uncertain which of the three is *the* originator of the term, but according to Kool DJ Herc (24 January 1994, personal communication), the acknowledged father of Hip Hop, "only these three could argue it." Fernando (1994) indicates that the term was given broad popular exposure by "Rapper's Delight," the first commercially successful rap song, which was released by the Sugar Hill Gang in 1979.[2] The song featured the lyrics: "With a hip hop, the hipit, the hipidipit, hip, hip, hopit, you don't stop" (p. 13).

Rap music and rappers — such as Treach of Naughty by Nature, Ice Cube (aka Cube), formerly of NWA (Niggas Wit Attitude), P. E. (Public Enemy), Ice-T, Queen Latifah, Snoop Doggy Dogg, Dr. Dre, Yo-Yo, Kam, 2 Pac — and others are the artistic representative of the Hip Hop Nation. Through their bold and talented productions, they are fulfilling the mission of the artist: "disturb the peace." Of course, the United States Ghetto (USG) is a hotbed of unrest, dispossession, and powerlessness; so, for African Americans living on the margins, for this "underclass," there is no "peace." What is being disturbed is the peace of middle-class White and Black America.

Interestingly enough, the term *rap* was originally used in the African American speech community to refer to romantic, sexualized interaction, usually originated by a man for purposes of winning the affection and sexual favors of a woman (see, e.g., Kochman, 1972). By the late 1960s, when the term crossed over into mainstream public language, it had lost its sexual innuendo and came to mean *any* kind of strong, aggressive, highly fluent, powerful talk. One finds both uses of the term in today's Black speech community, and of course, rappers represent both meanings in their artistic productions.

Rap music is rooted in the Black Oral Tradition of tonal semantics, narrativizing, signification/signifyin, the Dozens/playin the Dozens, Africanized syntax, and other communicative practices. The Oral Tradition itself is rooted in the surviving African tradition of "Nommo" and the power of the word in human life (see, e.g., Dance, 1978; Dundes, 1973; Gwaltney, 1980). The rapper is a postmodern African griot, the verbally gifted storyteller and cultural historian in traditional African society. As African America's "griot," the rapper must be lyrically/linguistically fluent; he or she is expected to testify, to speak the truth, to come wit it in no uncertain terms. Further, in the early formation of Rap music, the rapper was expected to speak with a quickness.

> The rate of speech in Rap must be constant in order to correlate it with the beat of the music ... A Rap song averages one hundred forty-four beats per minute ... each beat of the music can be correlated to a stressed syllable. If the number of unstressed syllables is equal to the number of stressed syllables in a Rap song, the rapper utters a minimum of two hundred and fifty eight syllables per minute.
>
> (Yasim, 1995, p. 38)

A blend of reality and fiction, Rap music is a contemporary response to conditions of joblessness, poverty, and disempowerment (Smitherman, 1994b), which continue to be the norm for the Black *un*working class. A cultural critic, describing himself as from the "front lines of the White Struggle," provides this description of rap music: "[It is a rebellion against] white America's economic and psychological terrorism against Black people" (Upski, 1993). Morgan (unpublished manuscript) expresses it this way: "Petulant, raw, and screaming with vibrant and violent images . . . [Rap music] represents people who are angry that the power apparatus tried to bury it alive."

Given its mission — "disturb the peace" — much of Rap music has a moral edge. As Poor Righteous Teachers (a Five Percent Nation rap group)[4] says, "The gods are ruling up in hip-hop" (quoted in Ahearn, 1991). This music has become a — or, perhaps *the* — principal medium for Black youth to "express their views of the world" and to seek to "create a sense of order" (Allen, 1996) out of the turbulence and chaos of their, and our, lives. Despite the 1990s' emergence of guns, violence, misogyny, and overused taboo language in rap music, the founding mission of Rap remains that clearly reflected in Rapper Grandmaster Flash and the Furious Five's 1982 hit song, "The Message." Here they decry, for all the world to hear, the deplorable conditions of the hood:

Broken glass everywhere,
People pissin on the stair,
You know they just don't care.
I can't take the smell, I can't take the noise ...
Don't push me cause I'm close to the edge,
I'm trying not to lose my head.
It's like a jungle sometimes
It makes me wonder
How I keep from going under.
(used by permission, Sugarhill Publishing Company)

For contemporary Blacks, then, as Naughty by Nature raps, the chain remain the same as in enslavement.

[*Introduction*]: I think it's about time you explained to everybody the real reason you wear this chain
around your neck ...
[*Treach*]: Too many of my people got time
It shows as crime unfolds
... their goals locked in a facility where time is froze
God knows the heart hurts
To see no sky, just dirt
They give a man a cell quick before they give a man work ...
Bars and cement instead of help for our people
Jails ain nothin but the slave-day sequel
Tryin to flee the trap of this nation
Seein penitentiary's the plan to plant the new plantation ...
Who's locked up, who's shot up, who's strung out, who's
bleedin — keep readin
I need to explain: the chain remain the same
("Chains Remain," Naughty by Nature, 1995)
used by permission, © 1995 WB Music Corp.
[ASCAP] & Naughty Music [ASCAP]

There is currently afoot a concerted campaign against Rap music despite its political and moral messages and its celebration of the Black Oral Tradition. On 5 June 1993, African American minister Reverend Calvin Butts held a "rap in" in Harlem, New York, to which he had invited participants to bring offensive tapes and CDs to be run over with a steamroller. (The steamroller effort was foiled by members and supporters of the Hip Hop Nation who blocked the steamroller. Reverend Butts and supporters thus took the pile of CDs and tapes to the Manhattan office of Sony and dumped them there.) In 1994, Dr C. Delores Tucker, head of the National Political Congress of Black Women, was successful in getting the US Congress to hold hearings against Rap music. She joined forces with a white male conservative, former Secretary of Education William Bennett, to mount an all-out campaign against rap music. By late September 1995, Tucker and Bennett had succeeded in forcing Time Warner to sell off their interest in Interscope, the recording company for the most prominent of the "gangsta" rappers.

Admittedly, Rap has its violence, its raw language, and its misogynistic lyrics. However, it is an art form that accurately reports "the nuances, pathology and most importantly, resilience of America's best kept secret ... the black ghetto" (Dawsey, 1994). Hip Hop/Rap culture is a resistance culture. Thus, Rap music is not only a Black expressive cultural phenomenon; it is, at the same time, a resisting discourse, a set of communicative practices that constitute a text of resistance against White America's racism and its Euro-centric cultural dominance.

AFRICAN AMERICAN LANGUAGE, US EBONICS, AND HIP HOP

It is critical to keep in mind that the racialized rhetoric of rap music and the Hip Hop Nation is embodied in the communicative practices of the larger Black speech community. The language of Hip Hop is African American Language (hereafter AAL). It has been studied extensively during the past three decades (see, e.g., Baugh, 1983; Costello and Wallace, 1990; Dandy, 1991; Dillard, 1972; Fasold and Shuy, 1970; Garofalo, 1992; Ice-T, 1994; Jones, 1994; Kochman, 1972, 1981; Labov, 1972; Major, 1970, 1994; Nelson and Gonzales, 1991; Rickford, 1992; Rickford and Rickford, 1976; Scott, 1986; Smitherman, [1977] 1986, 1994; Stewart, 1967; Wolfram, 1970).

AAL is a product of free African slave labor, having evolved from a 17th-century pidgin English that was a lingua franca in the linguistically diverse enslavement communities throughout Britain's

North American colonies that became the United States of America. The pidgin blended European American English (hereafter EAL) with patterns from West African languages (see, e.g., Asante, 1990; Turner, 1949). The result of this blend was a communication system that functioned as both a resistance language and a linguistic bond of cultural and racial solidarity for those born under the lash.

Although the lexicon of AAL can readily be identified as EAL, it is the nuanced meanings, the linguistic rules, the rhetorical and semantic strategies, the ways in which the EAL words are strung together to form a set of discursive practices that distinguish AAL from EAL. Statements such as "The Brotha be lookin good" may be considered illustrative of implied racial resistance – that is, in the continued use of these kinds of verbal forms despite White America's linguistic disapproval – other forms of AAL suggest a more explicit rhetoric of resistance. In Lonne Elder's late 1960s' play, *Ceremonies in Dark Old Men*, there is a debate between the central protagonists in which one Brotha, articulating a key theme in the drama, says to another, "Don't nobody pay no attention to no nigga that ain't crazy!" Because EAL stigmatizes the use of double negatives, AAL goes one better and uses multiple negation (a characteristic feature of AAL grammar). Because "nigger" is a racialized epithet in EAL, AAL embraces its usage, encoding a variety of unique Black meanings. And "crazy niggas" are the rebellious ones, who resist racial supremacist domination and draw attention to their cause because they act in ways contrary to the inscribed role for Africans in America.

As we move toward the twenty-first century, it is clear that African America continues to constitute itself as a distinct speech community, with its own linguistic rules and sociolinguistic norms of interaction.

COMMUNICATIVE PRACTICES AND LINGUISTIC PATTERNS IN RAP AND HIP HOP

GRAMMATICAL AND PHONOLOGICAL FORMS

One of the most distinctive and widely cited grammatical features of AAL is the use of *aspectual be* to indicate iterativity; that is, actions or attributes that are continuous, intermittent, or ongoing, as in "The Brotha be looking good" statement cited above. Also referred to in the AAL research literature as "habitual be," this feature is pervasive in the Hip Hop Nation. In his big seller, "Big Poppa," the late Notorious B.I.G. used this form extensively. And from the Geto Boys:

He be in for a squabble no doubt/So I swung and hit
the nigger in his mouth/He was goin down, we fig'ged,
but this wasn't no ordinary nigga/He stood about six
or seven feet/Now thass the nigga I be seein in my sleep.

("My Mind is Playing Tricks on Me,"
Geto Boys, 1992; lyrics reprinted with permission
© N-The Water Publishing Inc.)

Another copula pattern common in AAL is *zero copula*. This form occurs in environments where the meaning is noniterative or static. The sense of the utterance characterizes the present moment only, as in "This bus on time today, but most times, it be late"; or the utterance has the force of an all-time truth, as in "This my brother." Some examples from Hip Hop can be found in Ice-T's (1988) "I'm Your Pusher" and in Queen Latifah's "Ladies First": "Yeah, there gon be some changes over here" (Latifah with Monie Love, 1989) used by permission, T-Boy Music L.L.C., © Warner-Tamerlane Publishing Corp. [BMI], Now & Then Music [BMI], Queen Latifah Music [BMI], & Forty Five King Music [ASCAP].

The past participle *been*, when stressed, is used to denote the remote past. It appears in written form in the following excerpt from an interview in *The Source* (a widely read Hip Hop magazine):

SOURCE:	Tell me about the beef you had with Three Times Dope.
RAPPER STEADY B: AKA MC BOOB:	That's a old story ... Come to find out the tables turned and they was right ...
SOURCE:	Y'all worked that out? Are you down with E-S and them now?
COOL C:	We *been* worked that out.

In AAL, future tense is often indicated with *go*, a nasalized vowel sound close to, but not identical with, EAL's "gone," and *not* the same as colloquial EAL's "gonna." Artistic pioneers of rap, Public Enemy (known as "P. E.") – consistently political – give us: "Black is back, all in, we gon win" ("Bring the Noise," 1988; used by permission, courtesy Bring the Noiz, Inc.). (See also the Queen Latifah Monie Love line above.)

AAL speakers use *they* for the third singular plural possessive. In Hip Hop, we hear:

All the girls had they turkish link/If it broke, they
made errings to it, like they meant to do it.

("Back in the Day," Ahmad, 1994,
used by permission, Interscope Records)

And from Nation of Islam Rapper Kam:

> You know, we all looking out for Number One
> That's why Brothas sell dope and girls get they nails done.
>> ("Trust Nobody," 1995, by DJ Battlecat and Kam,
>> used by permission, © Famous Music Corporation,
>> Vent Noir Music Publishing, and I Slam Music)

The post-vocalic -r sound of EAL does not exist in many West African languages nor in AAL. This so-called "r-lessness" is widespread among AAL speakers. And, of course, in Hip Hop, as for example in Snoop Doggy Dogg's 1993 top seller, "Gin and Juice." And from the Geto Boys:

> Hey, yeah, man, I got Willie D. on the other end
> Say fellas, I been kickin a few lyrics in the back
> of my mind . . . I'm tied [tired] of muthafuckas disrespec-
> tin us because we're Black-own and won't sell out.
>> ("Do It Like A G.O.," Geto Boys, 1992) lyrics reprinted
>> with permission © N-The Water Publishing, Inc.)

Among AAL speakers, /Ang/ and /ank/ are used in words such as *think*, *sing*, and *drink*. This is how we get the popular expression, "It's a Black Thang" [not "thing"]. From *The Source*, we read: "Sangin' sistahs Brownstone feelin' it in Oaktown . . ." (photo caption, July 1995). Given that the rapper has to meet the artistic demand for rhyme, use of this systematic AAL pronunciation rule can generate a unique rhythmic line, as in the following:

> Hittin all the spots but I'm comin up blank
> I'm headed to the liquor stowe [store] to
> git myself some drank.
>> ("Big Pimpin'," Tha Dogg Pound, 1994)
>> used by permission, © 1994 WB Music Corp.
>> [ASCAP] & Suge Publishing [ASCAP]; also on the
>> motion picture soundtrack, *Above the Rim*)

Notwithstanding the grammatical integrity of AAL, by now well established in the scholarly literature, the syntax of rap music is often attacked for its departures from "standard English." Because many rap artists are college educated, and most are adept at code switching, they obviously could employ "standard English" in their rap lyrics. However, in their quest to "disturb the peace," they deliberately and consciously employ the "antilanguage" of the Black speech community, thus sociolinguistically constructing themselves as members of the dispossessed. Even when the message in the music does not overtly speak to racial resistance, the use of the Black speech community's syntax covertly reinforces Black America's 400-year rejection of Euro-American cultural, racial – and linguistic – domination.

RHETORICAL AND SEMANTIC STRATEGIES/DISCOURSE MODES

Given that the rapper recalls the griot of old, rap lyrics are often woven into a narrative. Indeed, although there are ritualized forms of storytelling in AAL – such as the Toasts (see, e.g., Jackson, 1974) – *Narrativizing* is a characteristic feature of general Black discursive practices. Everyday conversational talk may be rendered as a "story." Narrativizing is a Black rhetorical strategy to explain a point, to persuade holders of opposing views to one's own point of view, and to create word-pictures about general, abstract observations about life, love, and survival. Rapper Ice Cube rules [reigns supreme] in his artistic deployment of this Black communicative practice to explain racialized oppression, for instance, how it happens that such huge numbers of African American men are in prison:

> [*Voice*]:   In any country, prison is where society sends its failures, but in this country, society *itself* is failing.
>
> [*Ice Cube*]:   How you like me now? I'm in the mix, it's 1986, and I got the fix . . ./Dropped out the 12th cause my welfare's shorter than a midget on his knees . . ./Fucked up in the pen, now it's '94, back in L.A. and I'm fallin in the door/Everybody know I got to start from scratch . . ./No skills to pay the bills/Talkin bout education to battle inflation/No college degree, just a dumb-ass G . . ./I got a baby on the way/Damn, it's a mess/Have you ever been convicted of a felony? – Yes!/Took some advice from my Uncle Fester, all dressed up in polyester/"Welcome to McDonald's. May I please help you?"/Shit, what can I do?
>
> ("What Can I Do?" Ice Cube, 1993) used by permission [Street Knowledge Music (ASCAP)]

Braggadocio is richly interwoven into the everyday AAL conversational context, and it is ritualized in the toasts, long-standing narrative epics from the oral tradition. "Shine," "Stag-o-Lee," "Dolemite," "the Signifyin Monkey," and other well-known toasts are rendered with clever rhymes, puns, and culturally toned experiences and references from a fresh and new perspective. The toast-teller projects himself (or herself, but usually himself) as a powerful, all-knowing, omnipotent hero, able to overcome all odds.

In this way, her personifies the self-empowerment dreams of his Black audience and symbolizes for them triumph and accomplishment against the odds. In the Hip Hop/Rap generation, the braggadocio theme is generally about the rapper's lovemaking or verbal skills. While Notorious B.I.G. boasts about his rapping prowess in male–female relationships (see, e.g., his "Big Poppa") gifted producer Dr. Dre brags about his ability to "flow" [verbal skills]:

> Well, uhm beepin and uhm creepin and uhm freakin . . ./Now it's time for me to make my impression felt/So sit back, relax, and strap on yo seat belt/You never been on a ride like this befo/With a producer who can rap and can throw the maestro/At the same time wit the dope rhymes that I kick/You know and I know I throw some ol funky shit/To add to my collection, this selection symbolizes/Take a toke, but don't choke/If you do, you'll have no clue of what me and my homey Snoop Dogg came to do.
>
> ("Nuthin' but a 'G' Thang," Dr. Dre, 1992)
> used by permission, Interscope Records

The art of verbal insult is displayed in AAL's communicative ritual, *the Dozens/playin the Dozens* (traditional terms) or *snappin* (newly emerging term; see, e.g., Smitherman, 1995a). It has analogues among some ethnic groups in West Africa, such as the Efik in Nigeria (see, e.g., Dalby, 1972; Simmons, 1963). This linguistic-cultural practice involves what Black woman writer Zora Neale Hurston (1942) referred to as "low-rating the ancestors of your opponent." Although any relative may be the target of a *snap*, the mother is generally the preferred subject. Given its ritual nature, there are stock linguistic conventions for launching the verbal insult, the most common being "yo momma." And there are some critical rules. For one thing, the insult must be funny and original (or a new twist on an old line). And, most important, it must not be literally true because, then, it is no longer a game.

> Yall remember way back then . . ./I think I was about
> ten/One of those happy little niggas . . ./Always tryin
> to rag . . ./Sayin, "Yo momma black," "His momma this,"
> "His momma that."
>
> ("Back in the Day," Ahmad, 1994)

> Yo momma so fat, she fell over, her leg broke off,
> and some gravy poured out.
> I saw yo momma kickin a can down the street
> I asked her what she was doin, and she said movin.
>
> (*White Men Can't Jump*, 1992 film)

Your mother is so old, she went to the Virgin
Mary's baby shower.
Your sister is so nasty, I called her on the
phone and got an ear infection.

(by Percelay, Dweck, and Ivey, *Double Snaps*, 1995)
collected from Hip Hoppers, older musicians,
and others from across the USA)

Signification/signifyin is a type of verbal insult that is leveled at a person, rather than at his or her mother or relatives. Whereas the Dozens is fairly blunt and pointed, signifyin is subtle, indirect, and circumlocutory (see e.g., Asante, 1972; Lee, 1993; Mitchell-Kernan, 1969; Morgan, 1989; Smitherman, 1995d; Watkins, 1994). Although it may be employed for just plain fun, it is often used to make a point, to issue a corrective, or to critique through indirection and humor. In rap and hip-hop, as in contemporary African American literature, women rule when it comes to signifyin. Female rappers use this age-old rhetorical strategy to launch critical offensives against the sexual objectification of women practiced by some male rappers.

In "Fly Girl," the ever-inventive Queen Latifah strikes back at what many women consider a disrespectful form of address: *Yo, baby!* Other female rappers respond to rap's sexism by coming hard themselves. Smooth provides such an example in her 1993 hit, "Ya Been Played":

Ya been played and I think you know it
You too large to even try to show it ...
I used you as a steppingstone
Then when I was through, I sent yo sorry butt home ...
You know that ya been played, git out my face

(used by permission, © 1993 Zomba Enterprises, Inc.
[ASCAP], Teaspoon Music [BMI])

In their 1993 hit, "Shoop," Salt N Pepa not only create an entire rap (and music video) full of sexual hyperbole and the sexual objectification of a Black male, they also weave in a bit of signifyin on rapper Big Daddy Kane. In his "Very Special" jam, Big Daddy Kane celebrates the sexual beauty of a woman and gives tribute to her father: "For giving me something this beautiful, have mercy, I want to kiss yo father." So in "Shoop," Salt N Pepa credit the mother for the sexual beauty of the male they rap about.

Like Prince said, you're a sexy mother ...
Makes me wanna do tricks on him
Lick him like a loly pop should be licked ...

Don't know how you do the voodoo that you do
So well, it's a spell, hell
Makes me wanna shoop shoop shoop
You're packed and you're stacked
Especially in the back
Brother wanna thank your mother for a butt like that . . .
You're a shot gun bang! What's up with that thang!
I wanna, know, how does it hang . . .

(used by permission, © 1993 Bed of Nails Music, Inc., Tyran Music,
UniChappell Inc., Next Plateau Music, IZA Music Corp., and Sons of
K'Oss Music, Inc.)

Revisiting the Black musical tradition is what rap's sampling is all about. Some critics of rap music have argued that the use of lyrics and melodies from older work in the Black musical tradition demonstrates that rap is not innovative, that it merely imitates rather than creates. Yet, what rappers are doing when they sample is revisiting and revising earlier musical work. As a rhetorical strategy, sampling is a kind of structural signifyin, similar to what Henry Louis Gates (1988b) and others have shown that contemporary Black writers, such as Toni Morrison, Alice Walker, and others are doing: They are indirectly commenting on the work of earlier Black writers within the narrative structure of their own literary productions. The sampling of rappers thus represents a conscious preoccupation with artistic continuity and connection to Black cultural roots. In this sense, the Hip Hop Nation is grounding itself squarely and unabashedly in the Black musical-cultural tradition, even as they extend that tradition and put their own imprint on the game. In fact, there are clear aesthetic distinctions between this kind of sampling, which triggers the cultural memory associated with a given musical work, and sampling, which simply *duplicates* that work. An example of the latter is "Bop Gun," from Ice Cube's *Lethal Injection* album, which merely replays George Clinton's 1970s' hit, "One Nation Under a Groove," with no modification, throughout the entire song. (However, this purely imitative sampling is rare for Cube, who is one of the most verbally clever and innovative rap artists.)

As with other discursive practices, sampling reflects the way in which rap music capitalizes on Black cultural expression as a scaffold for resistance rhetoric. P. E.'s "By the Time I Get to Arizona" was released in 1991, when Arizona was the only state that did not honor the national holiday for Dr. Martin Luther King, Jr. With appropriate irony, P. E. samples what was a popular talk-singing love jam, "By The Time I Get to Phoenix," recorded by musical giant Isaac Hayes in 1969. The rhetorical effect is a text of racial protest that became a popular 1990s' rallying cry against racism, Arizona-style.

> Why want a holiday? Fuck it, cause I wanna/So what if I
>   celebrate it
> standin' on a corner/I ain't drinkin no 40
> I be thinkin time with a nine/Until we get some land
> Call me the trigger man . . ./They can't understand why he
> the man/I'm singin bout a king/They don't like it When I
> decide to mike It . . ./I'm on the one mission To get a
> politician/To honor or he's a goner/By the time I get to
>   Arizona.
>
> (used by permission, courtesy Bring the Noiz, Inc.)

The late 2 Pac [Tupac Shakur], whose mother was a member of the 1960s'–1970s' revolutionary group, the Black Panthers, pays tribute to his mother in "Dear Mama." The song recalls "Sadie," recorded in the 1970s by the Spinners, a male ballad/Rhythm N Blues group. In "Sadie," they celebrate the devotion and love so unselfishly displayed by the mother of one of the Spinners. Similarly, in 1995, 2 Pac raps:

> When I was young, me and my momma had beefs
> Seventeen years old, kicked out on the streets . . .
> Back at the time I never thought I'd see a face
> Ain a woman alive that could take my momma's place . . .
> I reminisce on the stress I caused/It was hell huggin
> on my momma from my jail cell . . ./One day, runnin from
> the po-lice, momma catch me, put a whuppin to my
> backside . . ./Even as a crack fiend, momma, you always
> was a Black Queen, momma/I finally understand for a
> woman it ain easy tryin to raise a man/You always was
> committed/A poor single mother on welfare – tell me how
> you did it/There's no way I can pay you back, but my
> plan is to show you that I understand/You are appreciated
> [Chorus]: Lady, don't you know we love you, sweet lady/
> Place no one above you, sweet lady.
>
> (used by permission, Interscope Records)

One of the least understood communicative practices in AAL is the manipulation of EAL's semantic structure. Often inappropriately dismissed as "Black slang," this rhetorical maneuvering amounts to linguistic appropriation, what late linguist Grace Holt (1972) called "semantic inversion." Today Hip Hoppers call it *flippin the script.* It is a process whereby AAL speakers take words and concepts from the EAL lexicon and either reverse their meanings or impose entirely different meanings. In the Hip Hop world, New York and Los Angeles, gigantic sites of Black oppression, become "Zoo York" and "Los Scandalous." Semantic inversion/flippin the script was an act of linguistic empowerment as Africans in America took an alien tongue and made it theirs; simultaneously, they created a communication system that became linguistically unintelligible to the oppressor, even though it was his language.

Given this origin as an antilanguage, when an AAL term crosses over and gains linguistic currency in the EAL world, AAL speakers generate a new term to take its place. Of course, many words in the script do not cross over. For example, historically, *Miss Ann* did not refer to *any* woman named "Ann" but, derogatorily, to the white mistress of the slave plantation. Today, the term still refers to the white woman, and by extension, to any Black woman, who acts uppity, or "white." Historically, *the Man* was not *any* man but, again, derogatorily, the white man. In the 1960s and 1970s, the term came to be applied not only to the white man but also to the policeman. Among Hip-Hoppers, this script has been flipped again, as *the Man* has come to mean a person with great power, knowledge, skill, and so forth. (This sense of the term is in the process of crossing over.)

Semantic inversion: in the Hip Hop lexicon, to be *down* is to be "up for something," that is, enthusiastic and supportive, like Ice Cube who is "down for whatever," and like Brandy who croons to her would-be man: "I wanna be down with you." Kam plays with semantic inversion when he raps "People make the world go round/They ask me, What's up?/I tell 'em what's going down" ("Trust Nobody," 1995, by DJ Battlecat and Kam, used by permission, © 1994 by Famous Music Corporation, Vent Noir Music Publishing, and I-Slam Music).

D-Knowledge [i.e., THEE Knowledge], a "spoken word artist," flips the script to create a text contrasting Hip Hop/AAL meanings with those from the EAL cultural context. The resulting subtext symbolizes linguistic resistance to the dominant culture's lexicon:

> Like when a brotha's talkin' 'bout a beautiful sistah
> An' he says that this sistah is phat
> But not "fat" like overweight or obese
> 'Cuz this sistah's fresh
> An' not fresh like she's got attitude or fresh like
> she's inexperienced
> 'Cuz this girl's tight
> But not tight like uptight or stiff

'Cuz this girl's dope
An' not dope like the stuff some of us smoke
'Cuz this girl's fine
But not fine like "just awright" or fine like "that'll do" . . .
'Cuz this honey's the shit
An' not and not like the real, stanky shit
'Cuz this honey's fly
But not like the buzz, buzz flyin' fly that hangs around
the shit . . .

("All That And A Bag of Words," D-Knowledge/
Derrick I. M. Gilbert, [9/28/93; recorded, 1995],
words by D-Knowledge, music by Mark Shelby,
© D-Knowledge Music/Chrysalis Songs/Mark Shelby
Music. All Rights Reserved. Used by permission)

The inversion/script flippin that has taken place with "nigger" is often misunderstood by European Americans and castigated by some African Americans. When used by AAL speakers, "nigger" has a different pronunciation, because of AAL's postvocalic -r rule, and in today's Hip Hop world, a different spelling: nigga, and for the plural, niggaz. In AAL, the term has a variety of positive meanings. Your best friend, your homey, is your nigga; so, 2 Pac dedicated a rap to his "homiez," titled "Strictly for My Niggaz." Black women use nigga to refer to their boyfriends and lovers; so, female rapper Yo Yo celebrates the fact that she has a "down-ass nigga on my team" in "the Bonnie and Clyde Theme" duet she recorded with Ice Cube. Further, even the negative meaning of "nigger" has a different nuance from the racial epithet of White Americans in that the genetic/racial/bloodline association does not apply. Rather, in AAL, negative "nigger" refers to negative social behavior, and thus, anybody − including white folk! − who is "acting out" may be called "nigger."

Encoded within the rhetoric of racial resistance, nigga is used to demarcate (Black) culturally rooted from (white) culturally assimilated African Americans. Niggaz are those Bloods (Blacks) who are down for Blackness and identify with the trials as well as the triumphs of the Black experience in the USG. NWA provides: "EFIL4ZAGGIN" [NIGGAZ 4 LIFE represented backward], title of their 1991] album, a reaffirmation of cultural pride and life in the hood.

In yet another flippin of the nigga script, rap group Arrested Development plays on the negative meaning of nigga, that is, the negative meaning in AAL, to illustrate the difference between Black, Nigga, and African. In their 1992 hit, "People Everyday," they use

"Black" as a generic racial term to refer to anybody of African descent. "Nigga" refers to the negative antisocial behavior of a Black person who lacks a sense of kinship and brotherhood. "African" is the positive "Black" person, who doesn't "act out," and who practices love, brotherhood, and respect for other Blacks.

> I was pleased, my day was going great, and my soul
> was at ease/Until a group of Brothas started buggin
> out, drinking the 40 oz., going the nigga route, dis-
> respecting my Black Queen, holdin their crotches and
> bein obscene/At first I ignored 'em cause, see, I
> know the type/They got drunk, they got guns, and they
> want to fight/And they see a young couple havin a time
> that's good, their egos want to test a Brotha's man-
> hood/I stayed calm and prayed the niggas please leave
> me be/But they squeezed a part of my date's anatomy . . .
> I told the niggas please let us pass/I said, please,
> cause I don't like killin Africans/But he wouldn't stop
> And . . . I was mad by then/It took three or four cops to
> pull me off of him/That's the story, yall, of a Black
> man actin like a nigga get stomped by an African . . . The moral of the
> story is that you better look very hard at
> who you steppin to/You might get killed or shot at, and
> it's not worth it. Africans supposed to be lovin one
> another.
>
> (used by permission, Speech/Arrested Development)

CONCLUSION

The communicative practices of the Hip Hop Nation are firmly rooted in the African American speech community. Hip Hop's rappers are both in and of this community, sounding the clarion call, arousing the dead citizens of America [those lacking in consciousness], showcasing the culture of the USG and representing the case of America's still dispossessed slave descendants. Chuck D., of Public Enemy, summed it up this way: "Rap music is Black folks' CNN" (quoted in Chambers and Morgan, 1992, p. 83).

Rapping about their pain and the violence they live with has rescued several rappers from "thug life" and given them legitimate, productive careers – such as Ice Cube and Ice-T, both former California gang members, and Notorious B.I.G., former drug dealer. In fact, it is no secret that the culture of hip-hop has created a multi-billion-dollar industry. What *is* a secret, however, is that the big paper [lots of money] in this multi-billion-dollar industry goes to big business. For instance, out of every album, CD, or tape sold, the artist gets only 5.7 percent, the songwriter, only 3 percent, but the recording company get 43.4 percent, and the record store, 31.7 percent (*Vibe*, 1995).

In the absence of a national movement to provide a cohesive political framework, such as that which emerged during the 1960s–1979s, the Hip Hop Nation grapples with contradictions it lacks the political experience to resolve. Moreover, there is little help from their elders, as few of these African Americans, those who have "made it," are offering guidance to rappers. Legendary singer and entertainment artist Stevie Wonder (1995) addressed this void when he was asked to comment on rap music:

> I learn from rap ... Listen hard, and you'll hear the pain. Without feeling the pain yourself, you'll never understand. And what we don't understand, we can't change, can't heal. I hate it when the very folks who should be listening to rap are attacking it so hard they miss the point. The point is that children and the neighborhoods – the whole country – is drowning in violence.

The Hip Hop Nation employs African American communicative traditions and discursive practices to convey the Black struggle for survival in the face of America's abandonment of the descendants of enslaved Africans. The rap music of the Hip-Hop Nation simultaneously reflects the cultural evolution of the Black Oral Tradition and the construction of a contemporary resistance rhetoric. Of course, one might be moved to reflect on Maya Angelou's words: "My people had used music to soothe slavery's torment or to propitiate God, or to describe the sweetness of love and the distress of lovelessness, but I knew no race could sing and dance its way to freedom" (1981, p. 22). Nonetheless, the rap artists of Hip Hop appear to have heeded poet Margaret Walker's admonition to "speak the truth to the people," and they are doing it in a language that the people know and understand. As a Womanist activist from back in the day, I applaud the Hip Hop Nation for seeking to disturb the peace lest the chain remain the same.

Part four

LANGUAGE POLICY,
POLITICS,
AND POWER

A LANGUAGE POLICY is a law, rules, or precepts designed to bring about language change. Such a policy is encoded in mechanisms of language planning undertaken by governments, schools, and other institutional bodies. Some scholars collapse language policy and language planning into a single entity: language planning–policy. Whatever the label, the overriding objective is conscious and deliberate change in the language and language behavior of groups of speakers. Language policies are bound up with questions of political and economic power; they are not value free, nor are they immune to ideology. In Tollefson's work on the "ideology of language policy" (1991, p. 9), he casts the purpose of his book in language suggestive of an admonition to language planners and policy-makers:

> This book investigates the reasons for the failure of millions to speak the language varieties they need to survive and prosper in the modern world. It concludes that inadequate language competence is not due to poor texts and materials, learners' low motivation, inadequate learning theories and teaching methodologies, or the other explanations that are commonly proposed. Instead, language competence remains a barrier to employment, education, and economic well being due to political forces of our own making ... A central mechanism by which this process occurs is language policy.
>
> (1991, p. 7)

In looking at language planning–policy in the educational system and in the larger society, the essays in this section call the question of the effect of language policies on the linguistically

marginalized. In our modern world, the effect of past language policies has been to sustain existing power relationships. For example,
the spread of English, which is on its way to becoming the global
lingua franca of the twenty-first century, did not occur in a linguistic
vacuum, isolated from the conquest and colonialism of Britain
and the US. Phillipson, in fact, rejects the concept of the "spread"
of English, arguing instead, that it is a case of the "imperialism" of
English:

> English linguistic imperialism is . . . the dominance of English . . . asserted
> and maintained by the establishment and continuous reconstitution of
> structural and cultural inequalities between English and other languages
> . . . English linguistic imperialism is one example of *linguicism*, which is . . .
> "ideologies, structures, and practices . . . used to legitimate, effectuate,
> and reproduce an unequal division of power and resources (both material
> and immaterial) between groups which are defined on the basis of
> language . . ."
>
> (Phillipson, 1992, p. 47; see also Phillipson and
> Skutnabb-Kangas, 1986)

The English-Only Movement in the US is illustrative of the
social and political forces outlined in the theories of Tollefson and
Phillipson. The first essay in this section, "African Americans and
English Only," analyzes these forces from the vantage point of the
African American community, which has, for generations, borne
the brunt of "linguistic imperialism." Adapted from a paper presented
at Troutman's conference on Language Pluralism in 1991, the essay
discusses the results of my national survey of Blacks in five major
cities and raises methodological questions about mainstream opinion
polls such as the Gallup. One of the objectives of the survey was
to assess African Americans' awareness of and concern about the
movement to amend the US Constitution to make English the official language. In the course of that project, I discovered that some
African American leaders had taken a stand against English Only,
and that right in my backyard, two Black politicians (one a member
of the Michigan House, the other a member of the Michigan Senate)
had sponsored anti-English-Only bills. The survey results demonstrated that voters can be fooled by the seemingly innocuous wording
of an English Only proposition, which on the surface, sounds like
a reasonable idea. So there is need for community education on
this issue. However, the survey also demonstrated that when
presented with information about the concrete social changes that
an English Only law would bring into being, African Americans
view such legislation with a jaundiced eye. Apparently, English

Only is a painful reminder of apartheid legislation (separate and unequal) in the history of African America. Perhaps also, on some subliminal level, African Americans realize that if they come for the Spanish language in the morning, they'll be coming for Black Language that night cause clearly, the "Official English" they bees talkin bout ain my girl, BEV (Black English Vernacular).

"The 'Mis-Education of the Negro' – And You Too" locates the English Only language policy within the context of the education, or rather, "mis-education," of Black and White Americans. This essay argues that neither group is taught the real history and factual data about the linguistic and cultural diversity of the US – and the world. The essay takes its title from Woodson's study of Black education after emancipation and extends his concept to include the linguistic and historical mis-education of all groups in the US. It was written for Daniels's anthology, *Not Only English: Affirming America's Multilingual Heritage*, published by the National Council of Teachers of English in 1990. The essay concludes with proposals for action by language arts educators and calls on them to join forces to prevent continued mis-education of this country's youth.

As "Language and Democracy in the USA and the RSA" shows, linguistic imperialism is a factor not only in terms of English, but also in the life history of African languages. This essay reflects my continuing interest in and research on South African language policy, a project I launched in 1995 during my sabbatical research leave, a major portion of which I spent in South Africa. Colonial language planning–policies relegated African languages to the status of "dialects" and forced different ethnolinguistic groups into the same categories in order to make the bureaucracy of domination and control more efficient. In South Africa, these new categories became the basis for dividing the Black population into separate ethnolinguistic "homelands," one of the apartheid policies that made it possible for a small white minority to divide-and-rule the African majority for nearly half a century. The parallels with African Americans and language issues in the US are striking. The essay compares these two Black groups in terms of past and present "Black language politics" and the quest for power. It concludes with a critique of the policy provision for eleven official languages enshrined in the new South African Constitution.

The last essay in this section is a review of *Multilingual Education for South Africa*, edited by Heugh, Siegruhn, and Pluddemann. The book grows out of South Africa's new Constitutional language policy, which designates official status for nine South African languages, plus English and Afrikaans. The policy seeks to redress the historical denigration of the indigenous languages by elevating them to co-equal status with English and Afrikaans, which were the only official languages under apartheid. It is a bold effort to use language as a tool of social transformation. In this effort, educational language policy becomes crucial because schools are the dominant institution in the preparation of the next generation, a fact recognized by the editors of this collection of eighteen articles about language in education in South Africa. The country's educational language policy calls for a minimum of two of the eleven official languages to be used in the schools, and strongly encourages a third language.

Tumelontle Thiba and I were keenly attuned to the profound uncertainty and unsettling complexity of language planning–policy in South Africa when we were asked to review this book by Heugh *et al.* Thiba is a South African who has been studying for her Ph.D. with me for the past two years. She is fluent in seven languages, including English and Afrikaans, and was an anti-apartheid activist. Before coming here to study, she was a trainer of teachers in multilingual rural and township schools near her historically disadvantaged institution (to use South Africa's official terminology), the University of North–West. Given Thiba's background and my several years of personal and intellectual interest in and commitment to South Africa, reviewing the Heugh *et al.* book was not just an intellectual exercise. Every phrase, every sentence was subjected to close scrutiny and often became the source of intense debate between us about issues of language policy, politics, and power. The abstract theories of language planning–policy scholars were put to the test of real-world experience. (As a consequence, it took us about five times as long as it usually does to write a short book review for an academic journal.) A serious problem we both had with the book was that all the articles in the anthology were in English. We contend that in light of South Africa's eleven official languages policy, and the two/three languages of education policy, for this book to be entirely in English was linguistic capitulation. We reasoned that at least *one* article in one of the Black languages should have been included. (To their credit, the editors acknowledge this shortcoming.) Nonetheless, we had to concede that as the first book to address language policy issues in education in the new South Africa, it was a valuable text that we could recommend.

16

INTRODUCTION

THE MOVEMENT TO amend the
US Constitution and/or pass local laws
declaring English the official language
of the United States began in 1981
when the late Senator S. I. Hayakawa
introduced the English Language
Amendment for such a Constitutional
change. The effort proved unsuccessful, however. Thus in 1983,
Hayakawa founded "US English," an
organization committed to the establishment, through legislative action
(locally for now but ultimately Federally), of English as the sole official
language of the US. As of this date,
over thirty state legislatures have
considered or are considering such
legislation, and seventeen states have
passed "English-Only" laws, all but
four of these since 1984 (Roy, 1991,
p. 520).

On its face, what has come to be
known as the "English-Only Movement" seems to be innocuous and a
natural course of events. That is, since
the US is an English-speaking country,

AFRICAN AMERICANS AND "ENGLISH ONLY"[1] [1992]

Official language smitheried to sanction
ignorance and preserve privilege is a
suit of armor, polished to shocking
glitter, a husk from which the knight
departed long ago. Yet there it is;
dumb, predatory, sentimental. Exciting
reverence in schoolchildren, providing
shelter for despots, summoning false
memories of stability, harmony among
the public.

(Toni Morrison, 1993 Nobel
Prize Lecture and speech of
acceptance, 1994)

it seems only logical that legislation be designed to insure that
English is utilized in all social domains. However, there are problematic language policy implications of such legislation on a macro-
institutional level, as evidenced in US English's efforts to repeal
"laws mandating multilingual ballots and voting materials" and to
restrict "government funding for bilingual education" (Wright, 1983,
p. B9). Further, the implementation of such language legislation
and its operationalization on the micro-level have resulted in the
following adverse situations:

1   The Mayor of Monterey Park, California, refuses to accept a
     gift from the government of Taiwan of 10,000 Chinese-language
     books to the Public Library. Although the City has thousands
     of Chinese speakers, the Mayor refuses the gift because English
     is the approved legal language.
2   The Parole Board in Arizona cancels a parole hearing for a
     non-English-speaking prisoner, fearing that Arizona's English-
     Only law prohibits the translation necessary to make the
     proceedings understandable to him.
3   A restaurant worker in Denver, Colorado is asked by a patron
     from South America to translate an item on the menu. The
     worker complies and is fired by the manager who cites
     Colorado's recently-enacted English Language Amendment.
     (Califa, 1991, 7; see also Balliro and Nash, 1990, for additional
     examples of the effects of English-Only legislation.)

From the perspective of what has been called the "browning of
America," English Language Amendment proposals call attention to
the relationship between the changing demographics of the Nation
and the current English-Only Movement. People of Color are beginning to dominate the population – and the voting booths in such
states as California, Arizona, and Florida. Then there is the matter of
the increased immigration of Asians and Hispanics into the country
in recent years whose numbers are further increasing the Nation's
population of Color. These population shifts and the mounting cases
of abuse of linguistic minorities have raised serious questions about
the underlying motives of English-Only legislation. Many scholars
and political activists have concluded that the Movement is a back-
lash against People of Color masquerading as linguistic patriotism
(see, e.g., the articles in Daniels, 1990). Several human rights organizations and professional societies – e.g., the National Council of
Churches, the National Council for Black Studies, the Conference
on College Composition and Communication, the American Civil
Liberties Union – have reacted by passing resolutions against English
Only and by working actively in opposition to such legislative
and language policy initiatives. And the English Plus Information
Clearinghouse (EPIC) was launched in Washington, DC to dis-
seminate information about multilingualism, language policy and
planning, and English-Only activities, and to function as an umbrella
organization for English-Only opposition groups.

In the midst of the Nation-wide response to the attempted
suppression of outsider languages, some political activists and scholars
(e.g., Zentella, 1988) have called attention to the struggles for human

rights by America's largest linguistic minority – Blacks – and have raised the question of the African American position on English-Only legislation. Since there exists no systematic analysis and research on this topic to date, this article takes up the challenge of exploring the English Language Amendment controversy from the Black Perspective.

AFRICAN AMERICANS, SOCIAL CHANGE, AND "DOUBLE-CONSCIOUSNESS"

The African American stance on the English-Only issue is critical, both because of the impact of Black voters generally and because of the historical struggle of African Americans for justice and equity. The Black vote is often pivotal in election campaigns. Given proposed English language legislation in several states with sizable African American populations, such as Michigan, African Americans have the potential to determine the election outcome on this issue. And if the US Constitutional Amendment provision should even-tuate in a national referendum, the Black vote is sure to be decisive.

More importantly, inherent in the African American position on English Only is the possibility of a catalytic social change agent. Social theoretician and revolutionist James Boggs (1982) declares that African Americans have the longest, continuous history of prin-cipled struggle of any US ethnic or outsider group. Because of this unceasing history of struggle, it has come to be expected that Blacks will assume a progressive posture on most social issues.

Former Harvard law Professor Derrick Bell contends that despite the 1960s quest for racial justice, "like Jeremiah, the harvest is past, the summer is ended, and we are not saved" (1987, epigraph). According to Bell, advancements in securing Black rights have ended up primarily benefiting the dominant society – even European American males. In the Federal race discrimination case involving Kaiser Aluminum, the court-ordered training and certification program to upgrade Kaiser's African American males resulted in numerous European American males getting certified as craft workers right along with the Black males. The Voting Rights Bill of 1965, spearheaded by African American protest, led to the subsequent legal mandate for election ballots to be printed in local community languages, such as Spanish. The Civil Rights Act of 1964, designed to stop discrimination against Blacks primarily, with women being added as an afterthought, or as some social analysts argue, as a strategy to get the bill defeated, has been used most effectively by white women. For example, they have filed the most lawsuits against institutions of higher education and won about 30 percent of them while African Americans have yet to prevail using this legislation. (Even Black women, according to Paula Giddings (1984) have made more gains as a result of gender-based policies than racial policies.) Several public school systems, such as the Louisville–Jefferson County School District, undergoing court-ordered desegregation, implemented special programs that resulted in higher standardized test scores and educational achievement levels for both their African and European American students.

The late Supreme Court Justice Thurgood Marshall summed up the wider societal significance of the Black struggle for justice and equality thus:

> Negroes ... were enslaved by law, emancipated by law, disenfranchised and segregated by law, and finally, they have begun to win equality by law. Along the way, new Constitutional principles have emerged to meet the challenges of a changing society. The men who gathered in Philadelphia in 1787 could not have envisioned these changes ... but the credit belongs to those who refused to acquiesce in outdated notions of "liberty," "justice," and "equality" and who strived to better them.
>
> (1987, p. 2)

Given this centuries-old struggle for justice and equity and its positive consequences for the total society, the question for multi-lingual policy and planning advocates is: does the "principled" history of Blacks inform their consciousness about legislative attempts to establish English as the sole official language of the US? It is not a foregone conclusion that African Americans will position themselves on the side of linguistic minorities and against the political tendencies of the dominant majority. That is, they are African, but they are also *American*, thus predisposed to embracing both the progressive and the retrogressive norms, values, and actions of the dominant American society. In the nineteenth century, Blacks joined in the "Indian campaigns" against North American Indians and in later years cheered for the European American cowboys against the Indians in US films. In the twentieth century, Blacks have, on occasion, embraced the anti-Hispanic and anti-Asian biases of the dominant culture. W. E. B. DuBois termed this cultural and political ambivalence "double-consciousness," asserting that

> the Negro is a sort of seventh son, born with a veil, and gifted with second-sight in this American world – a world which yields him no true self-consciousness, but only lets him see himself through the revelation of the other world. It is a peculiar sensation, this double-consciousness, this

sense of always looking at one's self through the eyes of others ... One
ever feels his twoness — an American, a Negro; two souls, two thoughts,
two unreconciled strivings; two warring ideals in one dark body.

([1903] 1961)

Relating this psychological ambivalence to language, I analyze
the "linguistic push–pull" of African Americans and detail "the
historical development of Black English in the push toward
Americanization ... counterbalanced by the pull of retaining its
Africanization" (1986, p. 11). In an effort to establish and maintain themselves as first-class citizens, African Americans, on the one
hand, subscribe to the linguistic ethnocentricism of the dominant
society; for example, they may decry those speakers with foreign-
accented English. On the other hand, their history of struggle has
depended for its success on cultural and linguistic solidarity situated
within a Black Experiential, that is, Afrocentric, framework. Black
leaders, for instance, have had to be linguistically competent in
Africanized English Vernacular styles. This "linguistic push–pull" is
a reflection of DuBoisian "double-consciousness."

THE "TALENTED TENTH" AND ENGLISH ONLY

The "Talented Tenth" was DuBois's conceptualization of a leadership strategy for the political empowerment of post-Emancipation
Blacks ([1903] 1961). It was his philosophy that educational,
economic, and community resources should be committed to the
development of talented Blacks — the upper 10 percent. Their role
was to return to the African American community and provide
uplift for the remaining 90 percent. The "Talented Tenth," which
has become a driving force in African American political philosophy, would constitute the Black group's politicians, educators,
intellectuals, medical and legal professionals, and others of the leadership class.

Black America's "Talented Tenth" of the 1990s appears poised
to oppose English-Only legislation. Several African Americans on
the national and local scenes have come out against these laws.
During both of Reverend Jesse Jackson's Presidential campaigns, in
keeping with the political principle of his Rainbow Coalition, he
took a strong stand against such legislation (Watkins, personal
communication; see also *Clemente and Watkins*, 1989). And nationally syndicated columnist Carl T. Rowan stated recently:

No. Why throw a gratuitous insult at millions of Hispanic citizens? We
levy no such law against Americans from other places who now make up

the so-called melting pot. We need no such law aimed at Hispanics. They will learn and use English when they find that that is one key to success in this society.

(1990, 6A)

On 21 October 1987, African American Representative, Joe Young, Jr., of Detroit, Michigan introduced House Resolution 376 calling for Michigan to "be maintained a multi-lingual state" and urging rejection of his European American colleagues' proposals to make English the official state language. Simultaneously, African American Senator Jackie Vaughn, also of Detroit, introduced an identical resolution, SR 310, into the Michigan Senate. Both ELA bills died in the House State Affairs Committee without a hearing. According to Representative Keith Muxlow, debate on his and Representative Claude Trim's bills never occurred because of Representative Young's resolution: "I feel he [Young] was unwilling to take up the debate because he's a minority and some feel this is an anti-minority issue. But that didn't stop us" (1990). Indeed, it did not. On 14 February 1989, Muxlow and Trim jointly sponsored House Bill 4166, the exact same ELA-type bill Trim had introduced in 1987. On 7 March 1989, Young reintroduced his multi-language resolution, in the form of House Concurrent Resolution 89, indicating that "it is essential to keep this bill before the people as long as the other restrictive side is out there applying pressure" (1990).

As for African American educators, illustrative is the response of the National Council for Black Studies (NCBS), an organization of African American Studies scholars who teach in Black Studies and in traditional departments at universities and community colleges. After research and analysis of the English Language Amendment issue by its Afrocentric Language Caucus, NCBS passed the resolution drafted by that Caucus on 3 April 1987. The resolution opposes the English-Only Movement and calls for a national language policy that would be multilingual in scope. The main text of that resolution is as follows:

GIVEN that the English-only movement has already succeeded in the state of California in the passage of Proposition 63;

GIVEN that the English-only movement can lead to the political and economic disenfranchisement of many American citizens;

GIVEN that the English-only movement can deprive American English of the rich influence and contributions of America's diverse languages and cultures;

GIVEN that the National Council for Black Studies is concerned about the impact of the English-only movement on Black students;

GIVEN that the National Council of Teachers of English, the Conference on College Composition and Communication, the Linguistic Society of America, and the Board of Trustees of the Center for Applied Linguistics have passed resolutions opposing English-only legislation;

Be it resolved that the National Council for Black Studies opposes the US English-only movement because it is contrary to our national heritage of ethnic diversity and linguistic tolerance. All immigrants recognize the importance of English as the language of wider communication in the United States. English is already the dominant world language, and ¾ of all world publications are produced in English. It is our contention that the multilingual history of the United States is a valuable resource to be nurtured. Thus, we call for the development of a national language policy to:

1   Reinforce the Need for and Teaching of the Language of Wider Communication.
2   Reinforce and Reaffirm the Legitimacy of Non-Mainstream Languages and Dialects and Promote Mother Tongue Instruction (including African American Language) as a Co-Equal Language of Instruction Along with the Language of Wider Communication.
3   Promote the Acquisition of One or More Foreign Languages, Preferably a Language Spoken by Persons in the Third World, Such as Spanish, Because of its Widespread Use in this Hemisphere, and/or a Major *Lingua Franca* of Africa.

Responses from the "Talented Tenth," while strong, as the foregoing examples demonstrate, have been sparse. For instance, traditional mainstream organizational leadership, such as that of the National Association for the Advancement of Colored People (NAACP), has not articulated a position on the issue. Yet the voice of the "talented 10 percent" is critical because of its impact and influence on the 90 percent.

A PUBLIC OPINION SURVEY OF BLACKS ON ENGLISH ONLY

SAMPLE AND METHOD

In an attempt to assess the status of the English–Only controversy among the everyday people in Black America, I included a question about this legislation in a language attitude instrument designed to elicit opinions about foreign language teaching in the public schools. This survey research project involved five cities with large African American populations and utilized telephone surveys and written self-report questionnaires. It was conducted from May–September 1989. The cities are Atlanta, Chicago, Cincinnati, Detroit, and Philadelphia. Response data from Atlanta and Detroit, which represent the scientifically selected samples, will be the main focus here (although a brief commentary may be in order about results from the other cities whose respondents were public school teachers, police officers, community workers, and graduate and undergraduate students).

Data in Atlanta and Detroit were collected through telephone surveys utilizing an instrument designed with the assistance of a social psychologist with expertise in survey research. Sample selection began with census data indicating areas that were 75 percent or more African American. These areas were then matched up with their respective ZIP codes, which were used to obtain a list of computer-generated random telephone numbers. A staff of interviewers conducted the surveys. All were African American, males and females, trained by the social psychologist and supervised by the investigator and a graduate research assistant.

If a respondent was not reached on first try, the number was recalled, during both morning and evening hours, for a maximum of six attempts, before the number was discarded and a new number from the list selected. Interviewers used response forms to indicate the time, date, and disposition of each call.

When a respondent was reached, there was a brief introduction by the interviewer, after which the respondent was queried as to whether he/she was an adult over eighteen and a resident of the city being surveyed. If the response was negative to both inquiries, information about the availability of anyone in the household who fit both criteria was obtained, and where necessary, there were call-backs.

Demographic data on respondents was obtained at the end of the interview, and as anticipated, the question about racial identity generated the most refusals. Although the list of telephone numbers reflected households in 75 percent (or more) Black census tracts, and although interviewers were adept at identifying African Americans (by their use of syntactical, phonological, and/or prosodic features of African American speech), no racial designations were assigned to any respondents by the research team. However, we also did not encounter any discrepancies between self-reported racial identity and interviewer assessment of race based on telephone numbers and speech cues.

The total sample for the entire two-city survey was 414. Since not all respondents answered all the English-Only set of questions, and since not all respondents supplied their race, total respondents for this section of the questionnaire ranged from 408 to 356.

At the end of a series of questions about foreign language instruction in the public schools, respondents were asked three questions about the English-Only controversy:

1   "Some people want to pass laws to make English the *official* language of the United States. Have you ever heard of this?" [yes/no]
2   "If these laws were passed, it would mean a lot of changes for many Americans. For example, courts, public medical and social services communications would be in English only. Are you in favor of such a law?" [yes/no]
3   "Why/Why not?"

RESULTS

First, let us consider the combined responses of African and European Americans in the survey. Less than half (41.4 percent) of the respondents had heard of English Language Amendment proposals. However, when asked if they would support such laws, over half (64.6 percent) said "No." (See Table 16.1.)

Next, consider responses from African Americans as a group, then in comparison to European Americans. Among Blacks in Detroit and Atlanta, 70.4 percent had not heard of English-Only laws. (In the convenience sample, i.e., in the other three cities, 61.5 percent of the Blacks had never heard of English Only, and yet this sample consisted of large numbers of public school teachers and university students.) Only 29.2 percent of Black Atlantans and Detroiters support English only laws. Thus slightly over 70 percent of these African Americans are opposed to English only. However, only 53.6 percent of European Americans in Detroit and Atlanta were opposed to such legislation. (See Table 16.2.) Stated differently, among those who said "no," there were twice as many African as European Americans (i.e., 43 percent vs. 21.2 percent). These Black Americans overwhelmingly cited as the reason for the opposition the negative impact that such a law might have on non-English speakers. (See Table 16.3.)

These results are at great variance with those of a January, 1991 Gallup Public Opinion Survey conducted for US English. In the Gallup Poll, 78 percent of registered voters favored English Only,

Table 16.1 Knowledge and support of English–Only laws
(All respondents)

	YES	NO
Heard of English–Only Laws	41.4%	58.6%
	N = 169	N = 239
	(*AA = 67/29.6%;	(*AA = 159/70.4%;
	**EA = 102/56%)	**EA = 80/44%)
Support for English–Only Laws	35.4%	64.6%
	N = 134	N = 245

* AA = African American
** EA = European American

Table 16.2 Support for English–Only by race

	African Americans	European Americans	P-Value
Yes	29.2%	46.4%	
	N = 63	N = 65	
No	70.8%	53.6%	0.001*
	N = 153	N = 75	

* Statistically significant

Table 16.3   Support/opposition to English–Only laws (African
Americans only)

Reasons for opposition

1 Unfair/Harmful to non–English speakers	47.3%
2 Many Americans speak other languages	34.4%
3 Takes away freedom of choice	6.1%
4 Other	12.2%
	100%
	N = 131

Reasons for support

1 Majority speak English	59.3%
2 English already the official language, so	
pass the law	16.7%
3 Too many foreigners in the US	9.3%
4 Other	14.8%
	100%
	N = 54

a figure significantly higher than response results from European or African Americans in our survey project. Further, the Gallup Poll indicates that "a majority from most demographic groups (except Hispanics) favor" English-Only laws (1991, p. 3). Presumably this statement includes African Americans among "most demographic groups" although Gallup does not give a response by race breakdown in reporting on this particular question.

Although the two-city survey reported here was more modest in scope than the Gallup Poll, I think it raises a critical challenge to the Gallup results for several reasons.

First, unlike both our convenience and our scientifically drawn samples, Gallup does not target large cities where the Black population is concentrated. Thus its US English survey includes only 69 Blacks in the 995 interviews Gallup conducted, compared to our responses from 216 African Americans.

Second, as is typical of surveys conducted by Gallup, the sampling frame is based on *registered voters*, and further, it targets those persons *likely to vote* in a forthcoming election. Gallup states: "Interviewing was conducted by telephone among registered voters who reported they were likely to vote in the election this fall" (1991, p. 1). Such a sampling frame excludes scores of Blacks who are members of what Baugh has termed the "Vernacular African American Culture" (1991, p. 133). This cultural group includes marginally employed African Americans and the vast number of Blacks in the underclass, which now constitutes about one-third of urban Black America (Brooks, 1990). Moreover, Gallup's sampling frame excludes scores of *young* Black adults, particularly males. Black voter apathy is strongest among all of the aforementioned groups; their ranks are comprised of thousands of the *unregistered*, the *young*, and the *not likely to vote* (unless given a good reason) African Americans. These citizens constitute a critical mass who will register and vote given the right motivation, as was demonstrated by Reverend Jesse Jackson when he successfully mobilized large numbers of disempowered and young African Americans in his Presidential campaigns. The latent power of Blacks in what Pasteur and Toldson (1982) have analyzed as the "root culture" resulted in Jackson's carrying the State of Michigan in the Democratic primary.

A third problematic the Gallup Poll calls attention to is the possible impact of the wording of the question on citizens' opinions – and ultimately their votes. The phrasing of the English-Only issue in the Gallup Poll seems to neutralize the consequences of these laws.

> I would like to ask you some questions related to the use of the English language in various activities. As you may know, while the majority of Americans speak English, there is no law making English the official language of the United States. There has been discussion of making English the official language, and we would like your opinion on a number of related issues. Designating English as the official language would mean official government business would only be conducted in English. For example, government forms would be in English and no other language, and proceedings of the legislature would be in English. However, making English the official language of government would not affect the use of other languages in everyday life.
>
> (1991, p. 2)

Next comes the question to respondents with no reference to the passage of *laws*, thus: "Would you favor or oppose making English the official language of government in the United States?" In our survey, in all five cities, we specifically and pointedly asked if the respondents favored the passage of *laws*. Preliminary interviews with African Americans had revealed that to the average person, the phrasing "official language" does not connote legislation. The form of the Gallup question is thus ambiguous and masks the fact that legislation is the issue here. Making it explicit that a *law* would be enacted might have had a different effect on African Americans, whose history shows only too clearly that once a law, however unfair and racially harmful, gets on the books, it is not only hard to repeal, it can be devastating to generations yet unborn.

ACTIVATING AND EDUCATING THE AFRICAN AMERICAN COMMUNITY

Our two-city survey results notwithstanding, it is clear that there is a pressing need to educate and activate African Americans on the English Language Amendment issue. Considering that there is pending legislation in several states with sizable African American populations that could turn the tide in an election, more needs to be done to educate the Black community and to activate the Black moral consciousness about language pluralism. Indeed, there is a need for massive voter education across the board. In a classroom experiment conducted in May 1990 by a faculty member at Delta College in Michigan, students (virtually all Anglo) in four English Composition classes were asked to vote on the following question: "Would you favor a constitutional amendment that would make English the official language in Michigan?" The vote was *49 yes,*

31 no. After the vote, students viewed a video, read articles, and wrote position papers to support their opinions. The vote was taken again: *34 yes, 46 no*.

CONCLUSION

The English–Only Movement represents a specific instance of language policy and planning in that it is a deliberate attempt to manipulate language change. This article has explored the African American stance on this controversy from the vantage point of Blacks as social change agents in US political life. The sampling of Black public opinion in our big-city surveys and the pronouncements of African American elites suggest that consistent with our history of principled struggle, African Americans will rally to the fore when minority rights, in this case, minority language rights, are threatened. I have suggested that Blacks are the Nation's moral conscience and that having been the victims of regressive legislation in the US's segregationist past, we tend to view with a jaundiced eye legislation, such as English–Only laws, that appears to be directed against particular racial or ethnic groups. Yet we are compelled to conclude that there is insufficient Black community knowledge and an inadequate number of widely articulated positions by African Americans opposing the English Language Amendment. It is time to sound the clarion call to multi-lingual advocates to mount an aggressive campaign of education and information dissemination in Black America.

APPENDIX I

Reps. Joe Young, Jr., Saunders, Harrison, Dobronski, Joe Young, Sr., Barns, Perry Bullard, Clack, Dutko, Hart, Hood, Hunter, Jacobetti, Jondahl, Kilpatrick, Murphy, Porreca, Sitz, Sofio, Terrell, Varga, Watkins and Weeks offered the following resolution:
House Resolution No. 376
    A resolution declaring Michigan to be a multi-language state.
    Whereas, With the future economic, social, and intellectual aspects of our society in mind, it is most appropriate that we take this opportunity to reflect upon the importance of maintaining a multi-language state. Michigan is a state that relies a great deal on trade with foreign countries as well as international exchanges through its businesses and industrial firms and its many schools, colleges, and universities. To limit communications by making English the official language would stifle these vital interactions; and

Whereas, The establishment of an official monolingual state would serve to encourage the false notion that only one language is needed to conduct business in a multilingual world. This would undoubtedly foster a chauvinistic mentality in which it would be assumed that others must conform to our system and our language if they wish to deal with us; and

Whereas, The importance of foreign language study, not only as a tool for communication, but also as a bridge in understanding other peoples and their cultures, would be minimized in a mono-lingual state. It must be emphasized, therefore, that the promotion of English as the official state language, such as is proposed by House Bill Nos. 4673 and 4681, would be detrimental to commercial, social, and intellectual activity in the state of Michigan. We in turn wish to maintain the multi-lingual nature of communication that currently exists in our state and promote a broad-minded approach toward dealing with the many diverse peoples across the globe; now, therefore, be it

Resolved by the House of Representatives, That Michigan be declared a multi-lingual state, and that proposals to make English the official state language be rejected; and be it further

Resolved, That a copy of this resolution be transmitted to representatives of the Michigan for English Plus Coalition.

APPENDIX II

Senator Vaughn offered the following resolution:
Senate Resolution No. 310.
A resolution to maintain Michigan as a multi-language state.

Whereas, With the future economic, social, and intellectual aspects of our society in mind, it is most appropriate that we take this opportunity to reflect upon the importance of maintaining a multi-language state. Michigan is a state that relies a great deal on trade with foreign countries as well as international exchanges through its businesses and industrial firms and its many schools, colleges, and universities. To limit communications by making English the official language would stifle these vital interactions; and

Whereas, The establishment of an exclusively monolingual state would serve to encourage the false notion that only one language is needed to conduct business in a multilingual world. This would undoubtedly foster a chauvinistic mentality in which it would be assumed that others must conform to our system and our language if they wish to deal with us; and

Whereas, The importance of foreign language study, not only as a tool for communication, but also as a bridge in understanding other peoples and their cultures, would be minimized in a monolingual state. It must be emphasized, therefore, that the promotion of English as the official state language would be detrimental to commercial, social, and intellectual activity in the state of Michigan. We in turn wish to maintain the multi-lingual nature of communication that currently exists in our state and promote a broad-minded approach toward dealing with the many diverse peoples across the globe; now therefore, be it

Resolved by the Senate, That Michigan be maintained a multi-lingual state, and that proposals to make English the official state language be rejected; and be it further

Resolved, That a copy of this resolution be transmitted to representatives of the Michigan for English Plus Coalition.

APPENDIX III: HOUSE BILL No. 4166

February 14, 1989, Introduced by Reps. Trim, Muxlow, Bartnik and Randall and referred to the Committee on Education.

A bill to adopt English as the official state language; and to prohibit the requirement of the use of a language other than English under certain circumstances.

THE PEOPLE OF THE STATE OF MICHIGAN ENACT:

Sec. 1. The English language is adopted as the official language of this state.

Sec. 2. Except as provided in section 3, a law, ordinance, rule, regulation, order, decree, program, or policy of this state or political subdivision of this state shall not require the use of a language other than English.

Sec. 3. A law, ordinance, rule, regulation, order, decree, program, or policy of this state or political subdivision of this state may require educational instruction in a language other than English for the purpose of making students who use a language other than English proficient in English.

17

THE "MIS-EDUCATION OF THE NEGRO" – AND YOU TOO [1990]

IN 1933, Dr Carter G. Woodson, a Harvard-trained historian, published his analysis of the education of Black people. Entitled *Mis-education of the Negro*, Woodson's critique was based on his forty years of experience in the education of "black, brown, yellow and white races in both hemispheres and in tropical and temperate regions . . . in all grades from kindergarten to the university" (p. xxix). The central thesis of this scholar–activist is that the educational curriculum does not reflect the true history, sociology, politics, economics – and language – of Americans: "The description of the various parts of the world was worked out according to the same plan. The parts inhabited by the Caucasian were treated in detail. Less attention was given to the yellow people, still less to the red, very little to the brown, and practically none to the black race" (p. 18). Consequently, there had been a "drifting from the truth" in the education of African Americans since Emancipation such that by 1933, the result was the "mis-education of the Negro." And beyond that, Woodson argued, the "educational system . . . is an antiquated process which does not hit the mark even in the case of the needs of the white man himself" (p. xxii). The educational deprivation of *all* Americans begins in youth and crystallizes in an adult society characterized by "deep-seated insecurities, intra-racial cleavages, and interracial antagonisms" (p. viii). Mis-educated adults are served up more mis-education in college, they return to the public schools to train and mis-educate youth, and this mind-set is thus perpetrated for generations. The year was 1933, but Woodson's message has an all-too-familiar ring sixty-six years later as we head toward the new millennium. The suppression and denigration of Ebonics and other non-mainstream languages and dialects, coupled with the movement to establish English as the only officially recognized language of the US, represent a tragic instance of the continuing mis-education of the people of the United States.

FROM JUMPSTREET

Wie geht's? Que tal? What up doe?

The true history of America is one that reflects large numbers of citizens who have continued to speak "English plus" (some other language) since the pre-Revolutionary War era. This has been the case even for African Americans. In spite of all attempts to strip the enslaved African population of its language and culture, it is clear that the first slaves spoke Pidgin English as well as their own West African languages. And in subsequent generations, a Plantation Creole existed alongside the White English spoken by some Africans in the enslavement community. Native Americans, who were here before Columbus "discovered" them, continued to maintain their own languages even as some of them learned the English of the white settlers who would decimate their ranks in years to come. During the Revolutionary War, proclamations of the Continental Congress were printed in German and French (Kloss, 1977, p. 26). In subsequent years, several state constitutions were printed in languages other than English. For instance, Colorado's constitution, which was adopted over a hundred years ago, was printed in English, Spanish, and French (Landers, 1989, p. 26). During World War I, the Federal Government advertised its liberty bonds in every language used in the United States (Kloss, 1977, p. 33). As we approach the dawning of the twenty-first century, nearly 32 million Americans report that a mother tongue other than English is spoken at home. By no means are these speakers all located in California, New York City, or the Southwest, nor is Spanish the only foreign language. In my home state, Michigan, for instance, there are at least 90,178 speakers of Polish.[1]

Not only is the United States diverse in terms of the many non-English language groups, there may be as many as the proverbial fifty-seven varieties of American English, depending on how you slice the pie. In New York city, there is a moving company known as "Schleppers," taking its name after the popular New York verb *schlep*, to carry or move (*American Tongues*, 1987). In Jackson, Mississippi, you *take sick*, but in Chicago, Illinois, you *get sick*. And the response to the Black English greeting, "What up doe?" in standard English is "I'm fine. How are you?"

The United States *is* a land of many voices; it *is* a nation of many cultures. Its diversity has been its strength. Despite one or two shameful moments when there were attempts to suppress this diversity, e.g., the incarceration of Japanese Americans during World War II, the pull of the United States has been its embrace and celebration of cultural and linguistic diversity. You know, the Statue of Liberty, out there in New York's harbor, bees sayin, "All yall come now." The success of the American democratic experiment is manifest in the many tongues and cultures of the United States and in the citizens who have proudly retained their native heritage while simultaneously adopting US culture. Most citizens will quickly and with pride tell you that they are Italian-American, German-American, Polish-American, etc.[2] The reality, then, is that there is a living heritage of linguistic–cultural diversity in the United States. Kloss eloquently sums up the true linguistic history of the US:

> One notion dear to Americans has been that the American society has wrought miracles in assimilating the numberless hordes of non-English immigrants ...The popular image of the United States as a nation united by one language and one culture has always been illusory ... Although the American melting pot has indeed fused millions of second and third generation immigrant families into unilingual English-speaking Americans, unmelted or partially melted millions have also survived ... [and maintained] their ethnic identity in their new and spacious land ... It is only fitting that it should be so. For the concepts of diversity and political pluralism are the very ones which permitted the creation of the United States.
>
> (1977, pp. vii-xiii)

BACK-SLIDIN

English is the native language of twelve nations and an official or semiofficial language in thirty-three more nations. It is the first language of 345 million people and the second language of another 400 million (MacKaye, 1988, p. 23).[3] As anyone who has traveled abroad knows, English speakers can expect to be understood in most major cities of the world. In 1977, Fishman *et al.* called this the "century of English." Burchfield asserted that the lingua franca status of English was such that "any literate educated person is in a very real sense deprived if he does not know English" (1985, p. 160). He suggests that this is a form of "linguistic deprivation."

At the same time that English has spread, however, the perception and image of the United States have deteriorated around the world. Because of its often reactionary policies in the Mideast and in Central and Latin America, its long years of support for apartheid

South Africa, its invasion of the tiny little island of Grenada, and similar abuses of its superpower status, the United States is viewed as exploitative, imperialistic, and supportive of oppressive governments. Further, US multinational corporations, who retreated from workers' wage demands at home and relocated industries abroad, come under fire for their gross exploitation of foreign laborers, who are paid a mere fraction of what US workers were paid by these same corporations.

The highest proportion of births in the US has continued to be among People of Color, and the vast majority of immigrants to the US are People of Color from "Third World" countries. However, despite the continued influx of monolingual immigrants, which would appear to delay the learning of English, research shows that, for example, many Hispanics are not only bilingual, but go on to become English monolinguals by the second generation and most by the third generation (Veltman, 1988, p. 47).

In this historical moment, in November of 1988, Colorado, the same state that had printed its constitution in three languages a little over a hundred years ago, passed an amendment to the State Constitution making English the official language of the State. A few years earlier, in 1983, the late S. I. Hayakawa teamed up with Dr. John Tanton to establish US English, a lobbying group for English Only legislation. In addition to his work with US English, Tanton is founder of the Federation for American Immigration Reform (whose acronym, ironically, is FAIR). This organization is devoted to curbing immigration into the United States although there has been no outcry against European immigration, only that of People of Color. Tanton, an opthamologist residing in Petoskey, Michigan — if me and him coexisting in the same state ain living proof of democratic pluralism, I don't know what is! — wrote a memo to a group called "WITAN" (Old English for "wise men") that makes racially offensive remarks about Hispanics:

> Will the present majority peaceably hand over its political power to a group that is simply more fertile? Is apartheid in California's future? As whites see their power and control over their lives declining, will they simply go quietly into the night? Or will there be an explosion? ... Perhaps this is the first instance in which those with their pants up are going to get caught by those with their pants down.
>
> (Hacker, 1989, pp. 3A, 6A)

In a Detroit bar some years ago, a Chinese man, Vincent Chen, was beaten to death by two white men, one of whom had recently been laid off from his job in a Detroit automobile plant. Thinking

Chen was Japanese, he yelled out, "There's one of those [expletive] who's taking all our jobs." The two of them beat Chen to death but were acquitted of murder charges.

BE WHAT YOU IS INSTEAD OF WHAT YOU AINT, CAUSE IF YOU AIN WHAT YOU IS, YOU ISN'T WHAT YOU AINT

It is clear that the US is troubled and seeking quick-fix solutions to its staggering and complex problems. The suppression of linguistic–cultural diversity passes itself off as a unity movement and cloaks itself in red–white–blue apple pie. We are told that a common language is the tie that binds. But US history belies that. The Nation has been linguistically and culturally diverse from Gidayup. The common thread of unity has been our shared values around and belief in the democratic ideal, that all men − and women, at least since 1920! − are created equal, and that all people, regardless of race, color, creed, sex, or national origin, have the right to life, liberty, and the pursuit of happiness.

To be sure, inequality still exists, for women, People of Color, the white un-working class, and others. Yes, for a lot of folk, the American Dream turned into a nightmare. And yes, as African American poet Haki Madhubuti says, the pot melted and we Blacks burned. But recognition of this inequality is what the movements of the 1960s and 1970s made the Nation face up to. Spearheaded by the Black Liberation Movement, other groups, who, like African Americans, had been "invisible," began to assert their claim to equality − Native Americans, women, Latinos, the disabled, gays, and others who had historically faced an unlevel playing field. It was that motion of history that produced teacher education programs in multiculturalism, the "Students' Right to Their Own Language," the eradication of speech tests for teacher certification, and the *King* ("Black English") case. I here bear witness to the reality that out of social struggle, there has been progress. Yeah, we done come a long way, baby, but we still ain come far enough.

In 1984, in the keynote presentation at Howard University's Black Communications Conference in Washington, D.C., I called for the adoption of a language policy for the African American community. I proposed a tripartite policy, a "perfect, inseparable trinity":

1   acquisition of the language of wider communication, so-called "standard American English" (however, "wider communica-

tion" more properly speaks to a language that goes beyond one's own community);

2 reinforcement of the legitimacy and maintenance of Black English and implementation of it as a language of coequal instruction; and

3 promotion of one or more Third World languages.

In 1986, as a featured speaker at the CCCC Convention, I presented my Black Language Policy again. In the audience was a Feminist scholar, Professor Elizabeth (Auleta) McTiernan, who challenged me not to limit something that sounded "good for white folk too." Of course, how could I have missed it? What is good for African Americans is usually good for the Nation. In 1987, the Language Policy Committee of CCCC (the membership of which includes McTiernan and me) took my more narrowly conceived Black Language Policy to the next evolutionary stage: a broadened, fully worked-out language policy for the entire nation (Language Policy Committee, 1987). The Language Policy Committee's work thus reaffirms the value of collective work and vision. (See "CCCC and the 'Students' Right to Their Own Language'", this volume, pp. 375–99, for an analysis of the CCCC National Language Policy.)

For fundamental change to take place that will put a stop to the mis-education of the Negro – and you too – it is necessary to venture into the political mine fields. The following strategies have been (or should be) undertaken by language arts educators:

1 Work with elected public officials for legislation declaring and providing resources to promote multilingualism and multi-culturalism. For example, the work of multilingual advocates resulted in New Mexico's legislature passing House Joint Memorial 16 in which it "reaffirms its advocacy of the teaching of other languages in the United States and its belief that the position of English is not threatened." The resolution goes on to declare that "proficiency . . . in more than one language is to the economic and cultural benefit of our state and the nation, whether that proficiency derives from second language study by English speakers or from home language maintenance plus English acquisition by speakers of other languages" (State of New Mexico Thirty-Ninth Legislature, 1989). As another example, Michigan passed a law in 1985 allowing high school credit in a foreign language to students who had attained proficiency in that language *outside* of school (State of Michigan 83rd Legislature, 1985). The National Governors' Association Task Force on International Education recommended not only that

foreign language study begin in the first grade and continue throughout schooling, but that foreign languages be taught during the summer, after school, and on weekends. Further, the Task Force recommended that school districts provide inservice teacher training in foreign language and international study (Advocates for Language Learning, 1989, p. 1). The US Department of Education has made a significant budget allocation to fund the establishment of national centers to promote foreign language study.

2   Organize campaigns for voters to voice their opposition to pending ELA legislation. In 1988, during the Congressional hearings on ELA, an extensive letter-writing campaign was promoted among churchgoers, community organizations, and other everyday people. The Conference on College Composition and Communication's (CCCC) Language Policy Committee, the English Plus Information Clearinghouse (EPIC), Michigan's English Plus Coalition, the American Civil Liberties Union, Californians United, and numerous other groups were involved in this concerted effort. The impact of the letter-writing campaign was evident in reactions from Congresspersons, such as Congressman John Conyers, in a letter to the CCCC Language Policy Committee, indicating his view that "restrictive 'English-only' legislation has had such bad effects as discouraging performance in schools, making entire communities feel segregated, and discouraging American students from the need to learn foreign languages" (Conyers, personal communication, 1988).

3   Professional organizations must widely publicize their opposition to English-only policies and their support of multilanguage policies and practices. While it is necessary to pass resolutions and work throughout the profession, this action alone is insufficient. The public and policymakers must be informed of organizational positions and efforts. For example, the leadership of CCCC has written several letters in this vein, both to state and national elected officials. Current CCCC efforts are in place to target the presidents of state boards of education throughout the country for letters and other forms of communication about this critical issue.

4   Promote progressive thinking about language issues through the media, both print and broadcast (e.g., letters to the editors, opinion editorials, appearance on radio and television news and talk shows). An example was Professor Ana Celia Zentella's television debate on the twenty "speech demons" that were

proposed as the language program for New York City's students. (See "Ebonics, *King*, and Oakland: Some Folk Don't Believe Fat Meat Is Greasy" this volume, pp. 150–62, for a list of these demons.)

The critical point is that the public, elected officials, and policy-makers greatly benefit from and indeed welcome the expertise and experience of professionals. We cannot afford to be silent, for our efforts can and do bear fruit. English educators, language and composition professionals, must continue to speak the truth to the people about what America *is*: a land of linguistic and cultural diversity. While this might not be what some folk *want* it to be, that's what it is. The United States has welded together peoples and races, with their many tongues and cultures – including even the 35 million African descendants of an enslaved population, including even the millions of descendants of Native American and Spanish intermixture – it has welded together a host of variegated peoples into one nation. This is the essence of America, and it stands as a singular achievement in the history of humankind. A multilanguage policy, such as the CCCC "National Language Policy," and the implementation of multilingual instructional programs throughout America's educational system are a significant beginning in the move to halt mis-education because it speaks to what we *is* instead of what we *ain't*.

Auf wiedersehen. Adios. Uhm outa here.

18

LANGUAGE AND DEMOCRACY IN THE USA AND THE RSA

I recall vividly my initial reaction to South Africa on my first visit there during my sabbatical research leave in 1995. How much like me my South African Brothers and Sisters look, act, and think. "Girl, check this out," I said to myself. I noted, for example, that Black South Africans come in "all colors of the rainbow," as we say about ourselves here in African America. (The single difference being that "Coloreds" would all be considered "Black" in the U.S. – on the one drop theory, i.e., one drop of African blood defines you as "Black" over here.) Then when I witnessed the "straight for English" and the "pressurizing for English" in education, even as I was struggling to master the click system of isiXhosa (an effort that an isiXhosa-speaking house servant gently upbraided me for – "Ah, you are paying good American dollars for *this*?") – it was then that I realized for better or for worse, I was right at home.

(*Memoirs of a Daughter in the Hood*, Smitherman, work in progress)

THE STRUGGLE FOR language rights in the United States of America (hereafter USA) and the Republic of South Africa (hereafter RSA) have a number of startling parallels. While there are, to be sure, distinct differences between the USA and the RSA, there are also formidable similarities in terms of political economy, issues of linguistic imperialism, and domination and subordination *vis-à-vis* the European settler population and African descendants. Using what he terms "comparative Black politics," Walters provides a brilliant analysis of the past and present condition of Black South Africans and Black Americans. He states:

> Despite the dissimilarities of culture, history, demography, legal structure and other important elements of state between the United States and South Africa, there does exist a basis for the comparative analysis of Black politics in the two countries. It rests upon the similar characteristics of the internal political dynamics ... between the white and Black community in each society.
>
> (1993, 246)

Presently, post-apartheid South Africa struggles to implement a Constitutional provision that would elevate the status of its African languages. Theirs is a policy of "English Plus." By contrast, the post-apartheid, post-Civil Rights USA struggles to amend its Constitution to declare English the sole official language. This would be a policy of "English Only." Since the USA currently has no *de jure* language policy at all, the movement to enshrine an "English Only" policy in the US Constitution presents a fundamental challenge to all of those on the linguistic margins, including speakers of Ebonics.

Following Walters, I take the perspective of what I term "Black language politics" to analyze the dynamic relationship between language and politics in the USA and the RSA. This comparison employs a class analysis and is situated in the profound similarities in historical, educational, and linguistic experiences that link these two Black groups. (In fact, RSA and USA Blacks are, in some senses, linked in a more profound way than Black Americans are linked to West Africans although West Africa is generally considered to be our ancestral homeland.)

INTERNAL COLONIALISM IN THE USA AND THE RSA

In the USA, internal colonialism begins with the conquest and near-extermination of the indigenous peoples (so-called "Indians" after Columbus's mistaken belief that he had "discovered" India when he landed in the Western hemisphere in the fifteenth century). British settlers encountered these native peoples when they established the colony of what would become the new nation-state of America in the early years of the seventeenth century. Beginning with the introduction of African slavery into the British colony of America in 1619, early white settlers came to recognize the value of the African as human capital, unlike the "savage" Indian who rebelled against the agrarian lifestyle of Colonial America's farms and cotton plantations. These white settlers, themselves colonial subjects of the British Crown until the American Revolution in the late eighteenth century, in turn subjugated and colonized the

Africans. For well over two centuries, this free African slave labor was expropriated to build a society, that, according to Minister Louis Farrakhan in his 1995 Million Man March speech, "was to be a nation by white people and for white people. Native Americans, Blacks, and all other non-white people were to be the burden bearers for the real citizens of this nation" (Farrakhan, 1996, p. 10).

In the RSA, the stage was set for internal colonialism with the conquest of South Africa by Holland and Britain, beginning with the establishment of the Cape Colony by Dutchman Jan van Riebeeck in 1652, followed by the British occupation of the Cape in 1795. Internal colonialism was solidified in 1910, with the consolidation of the white settler colonists, Boer and British, into the South African nation-state, essentially a "state of the white race" (Barnes, quoted in Jaffe, 1994). In this process, it was critical that all whites, including workers, be elevated to a level above all Africans in order to maintain white minority rule and simultaneously secure "capital in the masses of cheap black labor" (Magubane and Mandaza, 1988, p. 10). In the USA, similar white capitalist hegemony operated, despite whites being the overwhelming majority of the population. Racism and appeals to white racial superiority effectively divided the working class and facilitated the capitalist exploitation of both Black and white workers.

In the RSA, as in the USA, the internal colonialist formation is not the classic polarization between an oppressor nation and a dominated colonized subject people, as was the case elsewhere in Africa (and in India, Mexico, the Sudan, etc.). Rather, RSA and USA colonialism – also deemed a "system of racial capitalism" (Alexander, 1989, p. 20) – manifests itself as a fundamental contradiction between Europeans of all nations, socially constructed as a "superior" race, and Africans of all nations, socially constructed as an "inferior" race (see, e.g., Magubane and Mandaza, 1988; Jaffe, 1994; Walters, 1993). In order to make this internal colonialism work, the white ruling class in both countries created elaborate superstructural systems of law, education, politics, custom, and cultural belief-sets to support the economic exploitation and domination of Blacks by the USA and RSA capitalist economies. Apartheid, whether in the RSA or the USA, via *de jure* policies and *de facto* practices, involved not merely the social segregation of the races, but the segregation of "whites with superior material status and political rights from Blacks [with] inferior material status and political rights" (Walters, 1993, p. 199). In both countries, then, Black participation (or lack of such) in the labor force was critical and remains so today. Walters states:

in both countries, Blacks make up the largest proportion of the unskilled work force, and the economic projections for such labor are not bright because employers are adding technologically sophisticated capital equipment and trained employees ... it is a modern feature of the workings of the American and South African capitalist economies that Africans suffer high levels of unemployment ... In the United States, the undercount of the Black population and the much higher rate of short-term unemployment for Blacks mean that the real rate could also be as high as 30% of the potential Black work force ... In South Africa, the only factor which makes possible the growth of the Black labor participation rate is the easing of the job reservation system, making possible the hiring of semi-skilled Blacks in jobs formerly reserved for whites. Nevertheless, South African economists admit that the economy is currently unable to generate the requisite jobs needed to keep pace with the expanding African population.

(1993, p. 201)

The devastating material exploitation of Blacks was compounded by psychological subjugation. Not only were the colonized Black subjects relegated to an inherently "inferior" racial group, their culture and historical past were devalued. Fanon states:

Nothing has been left to chance ... the total result looked for by colonial domination was indeed to convince the natives that colonialism came to lighten their darkness ... if the settlers were to leave, they would at once fall back into barbarism, degradation, and bestiality.

(1963, 210–11)

The resulting crisis in identity among Blacks, both in the RSA and the USA, created a sense of dual consciousness at war with itself. As Fanon put it:

Because it is a systematic negation of the other person and a furious determination to deny the other person all attributes of humanity, colonialism forces the people it dominates to ask themselves the question constantly: "In reality, who am I?"

(1963, p. 250)

The answer to Fanon's question was captured nearly a century ago by DuBois, who coined the term "double consciousness" to refer to the ambivalent identity created in Black Americans. It is an ambivalence exacerbated in the lives of RSA and USA Black subjects forced to live daily in the midst of the colonizer. DuBois states:

The Negro is a sort of seventh son, born with a veil, and gifted with second-sight in this American world – a world which yields him no true self-consciousness, but only lets him see himself through the revelation of the other world. It is a peculiar sensation, this double-consciousness, this sense of always looking at one's self through the eyes of others ... One ever feels his two-ness ... two souls, two thoughts, two unreconciled strivings; two warring ideals in one dark body ...

([1903] 1961, pp. 16–17)

LINGUISTIC COLONIALISM IN THE RSA AND THE USA

SIMILARITIES

Given the nature of internal colonialism as it adversely affected Black participation in the political economy of both countries, it follows that the languages and cultural–communicative practices of both groups would also be adversely affected. The colonizer's languages (English and Afrikaans in RSA, English in USA) were accorded more prestige than the African languages in RSA and Ebonics in USA. Further, the use of the non-African tongue affected the sociolinguistic construction of reality of the colonized Black subjects. What Marx called the "language of real life" became distorted among Blacks, whose own languages were suppressed and devalued. Ngugi wa Thiong'o argues that:

> By imposing a foreign language and suppressing the native languages as spoken and written, the colonizer was already breaking the harmony previously existing between the African child and the three aspects of language as communication. Since the new language was a product reflecting the "real language of life" elsewhere, it could never, as spoken or written, properly reflect or imitate the real life of that community. This may, in part, explain why technology always appears to us as slightly external, *their* product and not *ours*. The word *missile*, for instance, used to hold an alien faraway sound until I recently learnt its equivalent in Gikuyu, *Ngurukuhi*. Learning, for a colonial child, became a cerebral activity and not an emotionally felt experience.

> (1984, in Turner and Alan, 1986, pp. 76–7)

While USA Blacks were stripped of their African languages (though not entirely – of which, more momentarily), RSA Blacks were allowed to retain theirs. However, British colonial language policy relegated these languages to low status by considering them "dialects," rather than languages, and by establishing a system of material rewards for Africans who spoke English. According to Alexander:

> For the colonised people ... [British colonial language policy] meant that English language and English cultural traits acquired an economic

and social value that was treasured above all else while their own languages
and many of their cultural traits were devalued and often despised ...
built into the consciousness of black people (and of many whites) [was a]
programme [that stressed that] all ... one had to do was to climb up the
socio-economic ladder which stood ready for every competent, abstinent
and disciplined person to mount. If one had these attributes and was able
to communicate in English, then – in the mythology of colour-blind individual rights – the sky was the limit!

(1989, p. 20)

Although the African languages were not eradicated in RSA,
in one of the great ironies of linguistic colonialism, the languages
became the source of a viciously effective divide-and-rule strategy
by South Africa's white minority elite. The establishment of
Bantustans and Verwoerd's post-1948 blueprint for apartheid dictated
that Africans who spoke different languages had to live in separate
quarters (Alexander, 1989, p. 21). Under the guise of promoting
linguistic dignity and freedom for each and every group, the
apartheid emphasis on African languages was, in reality, designed
to "break up the black people into a large number of conflicting
and competing so-called ethnic groups" (Alexander, 1989, p. 21).
The foundation for the division of RSA Blacks into ten ethnic
"homelands" had already been established by Christian missionaries
who "invented ethnicity" (Ranger, quoted in Alexander, 1989,
p. 22) by cutting up the African linguistic continuum and erecting
other boundaries in such a way as to "restructure the African world
... to make it more comprehensible to Europeans" (Alexander,
1989, p. 23).

In addition to rewarding a small Black elite proficient in English,
RSA's internal colonialism privileged whites through socio-
economic policies (e.g., job reservations) that led to the association
of Afrikaans and English with high status since these were the
languages spoken by whites. This linguistic colonialism was reinforced by the devaluing of the indigenous languages by RSA's Boer
and British ruling elite – and, unwittingly, by the promotion of
English over Afrikaans by RSA's Black intelligentsia. Alexander
notes that traditionally, Black intellectuals conceptualized RSA's
language conflict as being only between English and Afrikaans.
While this "fragile class of people" was promoting "what to them
represented 'liberty' as against enslavement," nonetheless, as
Alexander notes, the result was that no "serious thought [was given]
to the claims and rights of the African languages spoken in South
Africa, beyond the issue of the medium of instruction in primary
schools" (1989, p. 29).

STATUS OF EBONICS

In the USA, linguistic colonialism took a slightly different, but no less viciously effective path. Enslaved Africans arriving in the British colony of America brought their African languages with them (see e.g., Turner, 1949; Vass, 1979). In addition, given what we know about the Slave Trade, we can also assume that some brought with them an Africanized form of English acquired during their often-lengthy imprisonment in the slave fortresses ("castles") in West Africa and during the long Middle Passage across the Atlantic. Those who didn't know the Africanized English soon added it to their multilingual repertoire in order to be able to communicate with their fellow slaves as well as the European settlers (e.g., Dillard, 1972, 1977). Given the European colonizer's linguistic hegemony, neither the African languages, nor the Plantation Ebonics was valued by whites. In fact, the status of Africans during enslavement was characterized in great part by their competence in the variety of English spoken by Colonial whites. Advertisements for runaway slaves generally cited the slave's degree of competence in English as a badge of identification using descriptors such as "bad English," "tolerable English," or "good English." Some samples:

> Ran away ... a new Negro Fellow named Prince, he can't scarce speak a Word of English.

> Ran away from the Subscriber, living near Salisbury, North Carolina ... a negro fellow named JACK, African born ... about 30 years of age ... speaks bad English

> Run away ... a Negro Man named *Jo Cuffy*, about 20 Years of age ... speaks good *English*.
>
> (Smitherman, [1977] 1986, pp. 12–13)

In the system of USA internal colonialism, not only was the older form of Ebonics devalued, the same holds true for the contemporary variety. Because this language resembles English and does not reflect a preponderance of words from African languages; because it does not have a wholly different grammatical system from European American speech/"White English"; because it is spoken by racially oppressed descendants of slaves from an "inferior" race – for these reasons, Ebonics today, as in the past, is often labeled a broken, bastardized form of English, both by colonizers and by some members among the colonized.

To date, the US government has refused to recognize Ebonics as a separate and distinct language although the government has, for instance, recognized Hawaiian Pidgin English as a language. Essentially, the language–dialect question is a political issue, not a linguistic one, which is why linguist Weinreich admonished us that the difference between a language and a dialect is whoever's got the army and the navy. What is critical, and a fundamental issue the scholarly community can agree on, is that the language is systematic and rule-governed, that its speakers are not deficient or linguistic freaks, and that the schools need to recognize this reality in teaching African American children. Thus, the Linguistic Society of America – some 7,000 strong – united around the Oakland, California Ebonics resolution and issued a strong statement of support at its national convention in early January, 1997.

Notwithstanding the unity of linguists around the Ebonics issue, the status of Black Language and its speakers remains problematic among governmental and social policy makers, educators, and the lay public. Despite the massive body of research on USA Ebonics over the past two decades, attesting to its rule-governed dynamism and demonstrating that its speakers do not have cognitive–linguistic deficiencies as had been asserted in earlier times; despite the tremendous crossover of Ebonics into the media and mainstream public discourse; despite its creative use by writers such as Alice Walker, who won the Pulitzer Prize for her 1982 novel, *The Color Purple*, written almost entirely in Ebonics – despite these linguistic and social realities, Ebonics remains on the margins of mainstream society.

Within the Black community itself, the status of Black Language reflects the class and ideological contradictions of that community, contradictions that problematize the very concept of "community," contradictions that threaten the unity which has historically been vital to the survival of Africans in America. Black youth, Hip Hop artists and intellectuals, progressive Black scholars, community activists, many Traditional Black Church leaders, the working and *un*working classes accept and even celebrate Ebonics. Which is not to say that they decry the Language of Wider Communication/aka "Standard American English," but that they recognize the root connection between language, history, identity, and peoplehood.

On the other hand, older, middle-class, established Blacks – some of whom are also seen as leaders – reject Ebonics. Kwesi Mfume, President of the National Association for the Advancement of Colored People (NAACP) was quoted in the national press as calling the Oakland, California Ebonics resolution a "cruel joke" (Leland and Joseph, 1997, p. 78) and as asserting that folk in the hood need to shape up and speak "correctly" (Simmons, 1997, p. 5).

Reverend Jesse Jackson, Reverend Al Sharpton, and Maya Angelou also attacked the Oakland School Board resolution arguing that this language policy would "build barriers between the races" and "insult the Black community" (quoted in Boyd, 1996). On the national television program, "Meet the Press," Jackson went so far as to call the use of Ebonics as the medium of instruction "un-acceptable surrender border lining on disgrace." (He later expressed support for what Oakland was trying to do in educating its youth to acquire literacy in "Standard American English," but he seems still to have some lingering ambivalence, or at least linguistic caution, about the value of Ebonics.)

EBONICS AND THE USA ENGLISH-ONLY MOVEMENT

The American sociolinguistic condition is such that not only does American culture devalue Ebonics, Spanish, Native American languages, and even to some extent, other European languages, it also devalues varieties of white-working/lower-class English. While the English-Only Movement would hit Blacks, Latinos, and other People of Color hardest, it would also suppress all varieties of American English other than the economically dominant Anglo middle- and upper-class variety.

Figure 18.1 "Talk American" cartoon, by Don Wright

Source: *Detroit Free Press*, 6 November, 1995.

The roots of English Only can be traced back to Colonial America. For example, in the eighteenth century, large groups of Germans immigrated to America, settling in the Pennsylvania colony, where they established their own schools to promulgate their traditions and the German language. However, Benjamin Franklin, a major figure in the American Revolution and one of the drafters of the US Constitution, expressed concern that the Germans would soon outstrip the English in Pennsylvania and that "we ... will not ... be able to preserve our language, and even our government will become precarious" (Franklin, 1753, see Crawford, 1992, p. 19). As a counter move, Franklin, together with other leading Anglos, established English schools in the German-speaking areas under the auspices of the Society for the Propagation of Christian Knowledge, a plan which failed when the Germans discovered that it had to do with language, not religion (Crawford 1992, p. 17).

The contemporary English–Only Movement – also known as the "Official English Movement" – dates back to 1981 when late US Senator S. I. Hayakawa, a Republican from California and an American of Japanese ancestry, introduced the first English Language Amendment to the US Constitution. Resolution 72 had six short sections:

> Section 1. The English language shall be the official
> language of the United States.
> Section 2. Neither the United States nor any State shall
> make or enforce any law which requires the use of any
> language other than English.
> Section 3. This article shall apply to laws, ordinances,
> regulations, orders, programs, and policies.
> Section 4. No order or decree shall be issued by any
> court of the United States or of any State requiring that
> any proceedings, or matters to which this article applies,
> be in any language other than English.
> Section 5. This article shall not prohibit educational
> instruction in a language other than English as required as
> a transitional method of making students who use a language
> other than English proficient in English.
> Section 6. The Congress and the States shall have the power
> to enforce this article by appropriate legislation.
>
> (Crawford, 1992, 112)

Over the ensuing years, an additional fifteen English Language Amendments have been introduced into the US Congress although none have yet come to a vote. In the meantime, individual states have taken up Hayakawa's cause and passed such amendments at the state level. At present, 22 states and 40 cities have passed English–Only laws. In March of 1997, the US Supreme Court, with conservatives and moderates now comprising the majority of the Court, overturned a lower court ruling which had declared that the state of Arizona's English–Only law was unconstitutional. However, on a procedural technicality, the Supreme Court decided that the proper lower court had not acted on the case and sent it to the Arizona Supreme Court to make a decision. On 28 April 1998, a decade after the law had been passed with 50.5 percent of the vote, and with continuing legal challenges during most of that decade, the Arizona Supreme Court unanimously declared the Arizona English–Only Law unconstitutional. Advocates of multi-lingualism and diversity are only cautiously proclaiming this a victory for there are reports of Arizona English–Only advocates mounting another ballot initiative.

The English–Only Movement continues to be well financed. Crawford noted that one organization, US English, had spent upwards of $18 million since 1983 to promote English as the official language of USA (Crawford, 1992, p. 171). It has an annual budget in excess of $6 million, a membership of over 400,000, and a broad-based following.

The USA is often erroneously perceived to be a wholly English-speaking nation. Yet there are 35 million Blacks, at least 80–90 percent of whom understand and speak Ebonics some of the time. In addition to speakers of Ebonics, there are nearly 32 million other American citizens who speak a language other than English, as indicated in Table 18.1, constructed from the 1990 Census.

Threatening to and undoubtedly motivating English–Only advocates is the rapidly shifting demographics of USA. The population growth of People of Color is outstripping that of whites, and projections are that this will continue. (See Table 18.2.) In some areas of the USA already – e.g., major cities, such as Detroit, Atlanta, and Washington, DC, the Nation's Capitol – African Americans range from 80–85 percent of the population, and in some counties of the Western USA, Latinos constitute over 50 percent of the population. What has been called the "browning of America" is threatening to the dominant white elite.

As Gramsci taught: "Whenever the language question surfaces, in one way or another, it means that another series of problems is imposing itself . . ." (quoted in Nunberg, 1992, p. 480). The USA economic crisis, evidenced, for example, in an unresolved Federal

Table 18.1   US citizens speaking languages other than English

Language spoken at home, persons 5 years and over	
German	1,547,987
Yiddish	213,064
Other West Germanic language	232,461
Scandinavian	198,904
Greek	388,260
Indic	555,126
Italian	1,308,648
French or French Creole	1,930,404
Portuguese or Portuguese Creole	430,610
Spanish or Spanish Creole	17,345,064
Polish	723,483
Russian	241,798
South Slavic	170,449
Other Slavic language	270,863
Other Indo-European language	578,076
Arabic	355,150
Tagalog	843,251
Chinese	1,319,462
Hungarian	147,902
Japanese	427,657
Mon-Khmer	127,441
Korean	626,478
Native North American languages	331,758
Vietnamese	507,069
Other and unspecified languages	1,023,614
Total, speak language other than English	**31,844,979**
Total, speak only English	**198,600,798**
Total US population over 5 years old	**230,445,777**

Source: US CENSUS, 1990.

deficit crisis that caused Congress to shut the government down twice in the 1995–6 legislative year; citizens' anxiety about social deterioration; whites' fears about loss of power and status; accelerating unemployment exacerbated by increased technological capitalist (over) development; limited resources that will make it impossible for everyone to have a slice of the traditional American (materialist) pie – in such a climate, African Americans and other People of Color become ready scapegoats, especially when their language marks them as different. English Only can be used to

Table 18.2 US population – 1980, 1990, 2000 (projection)

Race	1980	1990	2000 Projection
African American	26,104,173	29,216,293	33,568,000
Spanish/Hispanic origin	14,608,673	22,354,059	31,366,000
White	180,256,366	188,128,296	197,061,000
American Indian, Eskimo, or Aleut	–	1,793,773	2,054,000
Asian or Pacific Islander	–	6,968,359	10,584,000
Other	5,576,593	249,093	1,000
Total	226,545,805	248,709,873	274,634,000

Source: US Census Bureau, 1996.

accomplish what America's internal colonialist apartheid once did: outlaw resources for Blacks (and other People of Color) to learn the language and literacy skills needed for them to participate in the USA political economy. They will thus be kept out of competition in the marketplace and "will always be a ready pool of laborers for the dead-end, risky, low-paying jobs that 'true' Americans do not want. At the same time they will be easily expendable in the marketplace" (Davis, 1990, p. 76).

In the classic divide-and-rule fashion employed by the masters of internal colonialism, the USA English-Only Movement threatens the developing political alliance of Blacks, Latinos, and other People of Color. For instance, if there is a repeal of the Voting Rights law which mandates the printing of multilingual election ballots, Blacks would still be able to cast their vote, since most know enough written English to decipher a ballot. However, Latinos who are not fluent in English would be unable to vote, thereby jeopardizing the fragile political unity between Blacks and Latinos and their potential to determine and/or influence election outcomes. Another possible threat to the unity of People of Color would be if a version of the 1996 "Language of Government" Act (essentially an English-Only bill) should pass the US Congress. The revised version of this bill now excludes Native American languages, thereby siphoning off opposition to English Only from Native Americans and the liberals who support their cause.

Yet another internal colonialist scenario would be a policy change in the requirements and a diminution in the funding for bilingual educational programs. Generally, these programs operate on a language maintenance, rather than language shift, model, seeking to make non-native English speakers bi and multilingual. English-Only legislation would call for a reduction in funding for such programs. Further, such legislation would mandate that all bilingual education programs be geared toward the eradication of the native language and the shifting of non-English speakers toward the monolingualism of English Only.

In the wake of *King* (the "Black English" case) which was filed in 1977 and set off a firestorm of national controversy for quite a few years after that, the Federal Government quickly issued an edict declaring that Black English was only a "dialect." The Secretary of Education reaffirmed this position a generation later, in early 1997, after the Oakland, California resolution, effectively negating the possibility of bilingual funding for the education of Ebonics speakers. Yet this continues to be a point of contention among educators working in urban Black districts with mounting language–literacy problems. If bilingual education funding is not expanded to accommodate this new demand, and further, if such funding is reduced as a result of English-Only legislation, then we would have a situation of African and Latino Americans competing for the crumbs from the colonial master's table. A not very different situation from the historical conflict and competition among RSA's internally colonized linguistic ("ethnic") groups under apartheid.

Finally, an English-Only policy would undoubtedly have an adverse impact on the development and maintenance of Ebonics which enjoyed a positive period of creative and dynamic development during the Black Pride–Black Power era (roughly 1966–80). The title of one educator's article sums up the language attitudes of the pre-Black Power era: "Negro Dialect, the Last Barrier to Integration" (Green, 1963). The Black Movement ushered in new attitudes among African Americans about their language. Black Power–Black Pride leaders, activists, intellectuals, and writers freely and defiantly employed Black Language and Black communicative practices, cognizant of the need for linguistic decolonization of Africans in America. They took a language that was in the throes of decreolizing and recreolized it. What I have called the Recreolization Movement was captured in the words of publisher, activist, and poet Haki Madhubuti:

> blackpoets [will] deal in ... black language or Afro-American language in contrast to standard english ... will talk of kingdoms of Africa, will speak in Zulu and Swahili, will talk in muthafuckas and "can you dig it."
>
> (1969, 56)

Although there was a hiatus in the Recreolization Movement with the election of President Reagan in 1980, toward the end of that decade, and especially in the decade of 1990s Hip Hop Culture and Rap Music, the language of Black youth and of the Black *un*-working class, has regenerated widespread use and creative development of Ebonics. An English-Only legislative policy would intensify the class and generational conflicts about language among African Americans, as well as hamper progressive educational efforts to use Ebonics as a medium of literacy acquisition for Blacks.

LANGUAGE AND DEMOCRACY IN THE RSA

Roman scholar, Pliny, the Elder, speaking about Africa, stated: "Ex Africa semper aliquid novi," there is always something new out of Africa — in this instance out of South Africa. At a time when there is a movement to amend the US Constitution to declare English the sole, official language, newly-democratic RSA has adopted a Constitution that mandates eleven official languages: the nine major Black languages (Sepedi, Sesotho, Setswana, siSwati, Tshivenda, Xitsonga, isiNdebele, isiXhosa, and isiZulu), and the two former official languages, English and Afrikaans. Speakers of these eleven languages comprise the overwhelming majority of the South African population. (See Table 18.3.)

The democratic need for such a language policy was perhaps foreshadowed by President Nelson Mandela, before he was "President" Mandela. In his autobiography, *Long Walk to Freedom*, he recounts a significant historical moment which symbolizes for him the sober recognition that "without language one cannot talk to people and understand them; one cannot share their hopes and aspirations, grasp their history, appreciate their poetry or savour their songs." Mandela writes:

> I recall on one occasion meeting the queen regent of Basutoland, or what is now Lesotho ... The queen took special notice of me and at one point addressed me directly, but spoke in Sesotho, a language in which I knew few words. Sesotho is the language of the Sotho people as well as the Tswana ... She looked at me with incredulity, and then said in English, 'What kind of lawyer and leader will you be who cannot speak the language of your own people?' I had no response. The question embarrassed and sobered me; it made me realize my parochialism and just how unprepared I was for the task of serving my people.
>
> (1994, pp. 96–7)

Table 18.3 Official languages of South Africa

Language	Percent	Number of speakers (in millions)
isiZulu	21.95	8.8
isiXhosa	17.03	6.8
Afrikaans	15.03	6.0
Sepedi	9.64	3.8
English	9.01	3.6
Setswana	8.59	3.4
Sesotho	6.73	2.7
Xitsonga	4.35	1.8
siSwati	2.57	1.0
Tshivenda	2.22	0.9
isiNdebele	1.55	0.6

Source: Sinfree Makoni, "Some of the Metaphors About Language," in *Language Planning Discourses in South Africa: Boundaries, Frontiers and Commodification*," *ELTIC Reporter*, vol. 19(1), 1995, p. 21.

In establishing the eleven official languages policy, South Africa's Constitution mandates that

> conditions shall be created for their development and for the promotion of their equal use and enjoyment ... A person shall have the right to use and to be addressed in his or her dealings with any public administration ... of government in any official South African language of his or her choice.

Further, the Constitution calls for provisions to promote multilingualism, for translation facilities, and for the "prevention of the use of any language for the purposes of exploitation, domination or division."

There are three significant points to note about language and democracy in RSA's language policy. First, the Constitution sets forth a policy not of *English Only*, but *English Plus*, that is, English plus ten other languages as the national official languages of the new democracy. Second, although Blacks constitute 75 percent of South Africa's population, the new Constitution protects the language rights of the English-speaking minority, the descendants of the British colonizers, as well as the rights of speakers of Afrikaans, the language developed by Dutch colonizers and associated with the architects of apartheid. Third, in implementing the national language policy in the schools, the language in education policy mandates that in *all* schools, white as well as Black, from primary school, the curriculum must offer two of the official languages as the language of learning and instruction, and at least one of these must be a home language among large numbers of the students in a given school. Further, all students are to be encouraged to add a third language as a subject. Thus the RSA is promoting **additive**, not **subtractive**, language policy. The Project for Alternative Education in South Africa (PRAESA), under the leadership of South Africa's leading linguist, Neville Alexander, summed up South Africa's multilingual education policy with this headline in its 1996 newsletter: "The Power of Babel."

I applaud South Africa's national language policy and see it as a major step forward in the decolonization of the minds of Black South Africans. Like many other US Blacks, I enthusiastically look forward to the unfolding of democracy in RSA. Nonetheless, it would be the height of irresponsibility to espouse uncritical and unquestioning acceptance of the policies of the new South Africa. In the spirit of political responsibility and Black camaraderie, I respectfully offer the following observations about efforts to promote language and democracy in South Africa.

First, let us be reminded that the eleven-languages policy represents a compromise on the part of the African National Congress (ANC), the majority (Black) party in the new government, to secure the National Party's (the minority white party) agreement to the Constitutional negotiations hammered out at Kempton Park in 1993. The policy elevated the nine major Black languages to national official status in recognition of the need for linguistic decolonization of South African Blacks. On the other hand, the policy left untouched the hegemonic status of English and Afrikaans. In the case of English, especially, this poses a particular problem for the elevation of the Black languages as South African Blacks seek English medium schools, "pressurize for English," promote "straight for English" patterns of education, and resist the curricular inclusion of languages other than English – including isiXhosa, the language of the President (see, e.g., Samuels, 1995). That the hegemony of English is problematic was forcefully brought home in 1996 when the ANC-dominated Joint Standing Defense Committee issued an order that only English (rather than Afrikaans – or isiZulu, isiXhosa, etc.) be used as the language of military command and instruction. President Mandela rebuked the Defense Committee and informed the South African Defense Force to ignore the order (reported in *The Christian Science Monitor*, 29 February 1996).

An alternative language policy would have been to establish the nine African languages at national level and English and Afrikaans as official provincial languages. Another option would have been a policy with two of the major African languages at national level, English as a link language at national level, and the other languages as official provincial languages. There are a number of possibilities, all of which were undoubtedly considered but rejected in the art of compromise that constitutes politics. One can only hope that this compromise does not come back to haunt the ANC.

Second, the language in education policy requires only *two* languages and leaves it to local schools to select those two languages. This leaves open the possibility of the two languages being English and Afrikaans. At present, only about 7.5 percent of those formerly classified as White, Colored, or Indian can speak a Black language (Human Sciences Research Council, quoted in Desai, 1994, p. 21). If these groups and the Black elite do not embrace the African languages, there is a distinct possibility that we will witness the reinscribing of the apartheid linguistics of the past.

Third, there is the persistent problem of ambivalent, if not outright negative, attitudes toward the African languages (see, e.g., Gough, 1996; Kamwangamalu, 1996) – even among members of the Black intelligentsia (e.g., Phaswana, 1994). If the status of these languages is to be elevated, their use must be aggressively promoted among both the Black majority and the white minority (as well as among former "Coloreds" and "Indians"). Serious thought needs to be devoted to creative ways to advance the African languages, above and beyond using them as media of teaching and learning. One idea might be massive public displays of these languages, in signs, on billboards, etc., and encouraging and rewarding their pervasive use throughout the mass media – radio and television programs, advertisements, etc.

In the first Parliamentary session of newly-Democratic South Africa, 87 percent of the speeches were given in English (Quirk, 1995). It is hoped this will not become a pattern. Rather, Black members of Parliament should take leadership in using the languages of their nurture in Parliamentary deliberations and discussions. University students might be encouraged to major in translation of these languages with language internships in Parliament.

With its eleven-languages policy, RSA has embarked on a bold new course in which it can and should take pride. But it has to be made real. Continued adherence to what Nigerian author Chinua Achebe once referred to as the "fatalistic logic of the unassailable position of English" could eventuate in South Africa going the way of

other post-colonial African countries, with the emergence of a Black
elite, highly fluent in English, and the continued downward oppression of the Black working and underclass, who lack English fluency.

CONCLUSION

Among both USA and RSA Blacks, the lingering legacy of internal
colonialism continues to characterize Black language politics and to
pose a barrier to the full flowering of linguistic democratization. In
the USA, the linguistic manifestation of this colonialism is the historical division of the African enslaved community into those who
speak "good" and "bad" English, the devaluing of African languages,
the denigration of past and present forms of USA Ebonics, and the
awarding of jobs and material benefits to speakers of European
American English. In the RSA, the linguistic manifestation is the
historical apartheid policy of using African languages to divide the
Black community into competing ethnic enclaves, the devaluing of
these languages and dismissal of them as dialects and gibberish, and
the awarding of jobs and material benefits to speakers of English
and Afrikaans.

Both in RSA and USA, linguistic colonialism and material
deprivation are still the order of the day for everyday people. As
a result of the Civil Rights–Black Power Movement of the 1960s–
1970s, the US Black community has at last produced a substantive,
critical mass of what DuBois foreshadowed as the "Talented Tenth,"
who would return to the Black community and use their skills,
education, and money to uplift the Black masses. During these same
years, however, the condition of the Black masses has worsened, a
fact which the Talented Tenth has thus far either ignored or dealt
with ineffectively. US Ebonics enjoys crossover status, and American
public culture, fueled by the energy and dynamism of African
American linguistic–cultural production, is a multi-billion-dollar
business, little of which has trickled down to the Black underclass.
It remains to be seen whether the African American community
will resolve its internal contradictions and unite (as it has effectively
done in the past) to push the dominant white elite toward linguistic
democratization and empowerment for those on the margins.

As for RSA Blacks, their country entered a new democratic
era in 1994, instituting a Constitution designed to elevate its African
languages. It remains to be seen whether the material conditions
and sociolinguistic status of the masses of Black South Africans will
be fundamentally altered. As of this writing, this is not yet the case
although it is important to remember that the new South Africa is

still young. Walters concluded the following about Blacks in the RSA and the USA:

> The United States accepted full legal status for Blacks and afforded a modest amount of racial integration and economic, political and social mobility. However, while there has been some absolute change in the status of Blacks, the dominant material conditions and the pattern of social stratification between them and whites has remained largely unchanged ... there is in each society [i.e., the RSA and the USA] an enduring pattern of race stratification based on the white dominance–Black subordinate model ... this pattern owes its maintenance to such factors as the persistence of institutionalized race prejudice and capitalism.
>
> (1993, pp. 210, 213)

The above, as the saying goes in the USA, is the bad news. The good news, and what provides hope for the future of Blacks in both countries, is the fact that Black South African languages and USA Ebonics are alive and well, with no prognosis of linguistic demise in sight. What DuBois called the "dogged strength" of Black consciousness has continued to resist the linguistic imperialism of internal colonialism. I conclude with the words of Ngugi wa Thiong'o – words which capture the dogged linguistic spirit of both US Ebonics speakers and speakers of Black South African languages:

> [African languages] would not simply go the way of Latin to become fossils for linguistic archaeology ... these national heritages of Africa were kept alive by the peasantry [who] saw no contradiction between speaking their own mother-tongues and belonging to a larger national or continental geography ... These people happily spoke Wolof, Hausa, Yoruba, Ibo ... Kiswahili ... Shona, Ndebele ... Zulu or Lingala without this fact tearing the multi-national states apart ... African languages refused to die.
>
> (1984, p. 23)

19

REVIEW OF *MULTILINGUAL EDUCATION FOR SOUTH AFRICA* BY HEUGH *ET AL.* [1998]

THIS COLLECTION OF eighteen articles (two of which are contributed by the editors) is an important first that initiates a much-needed debate on language in education in the South African context. Intended as a resource book for teachers, teacher–educators and language planners, the work is arranged in four sections that cover significant dimensions of multilingual education: (1) "Classroom Practice"; (2) "Major Issues"; (3) "Proposals and Models"; (4) "Aspects of Implementation". Each section is preceded by a very useful introductory overview and summary of the chapters. As a pleasant surprise, these turn out to be highly readable and accessible across disciplines. The contributors include university teachers and teacher–educators, an editor at a major publishing house, a USAID officer, members of NGOs involved in language matters, and the internationally-known linguist–educational activist, Neville Alexander.

In keeping with the book's dual goals of presenting "successful examples of teaching/learning in multilingual classrooms" and a "coherent framework for the debate on multilingual education . . . in South Africa", the editors have carefully and wisely selected material that presents the voices of practitioners and theorists. The success of multilingualism depends on the interaction of theory with practice, and as the editors quite rightly assert, teachers are all too often excluded from theorizing and decision-making about Language Planning Policy. (However, as far as we can determine, only a few of the contributors seem to have experience in primary or secondary school teaching; future editions of the book should try to enlarge this group.) In keeping with the book's promotion of multilingualism, we give the editors high praise for their selection of a cover design that reveals a mosaic of cultural artifacts representing various cultures in South Africa, with textual excerpts from different languages. Yet the work itself is written entirely in English, an ironic shortcoming which the editors, to their credit, acknowledge themselves. They attribute this linguistic capitulation to the "dominant status and role of English in politics . . . and publishing in South Africa" and call for a day "when the river carries many tongues in its mouth." Though fully sensitive to the dilemma facing the editors and contributors, still one cannot but think: If not now, when? Why not publish a book on multilingual education in post-Apartheid South Africa that includes at least *one* article in isiXhosa, or Setswana, or isiNdebele, or isiZulu, etc.?

For nearly fifty years, during which education was segregated along racial and linguistic lines, the use of either English or Afrikaans as the medium of instruction was a given. Now, enshrined in the Constitution of the new South Africa is a policy calling for eleven official languages. The contributors assembled by Heugh *et al.* effectively address ways of implementing the new dispensation in the schools. A consistent motif throughout the book is the questioning of English hegemony and the promotion of additive bilingualism as a solution to the issue of the language of teaching and learning in the schools. This is a commendable stance as there is research from other societies to corroborate the efficacy of such an approach. Another significant motif throughout the work is the necessity for preparing teachers to work in multilingual settings, an idea which implies radical change in current teacher education programs. Various concrete models for implementing multilingualism are presented, e.g., the use of learners' first language(s) for instruction in the lower grades and the gradual introduction of English at upper levels of primary education.

Multilingual Education for South Africa makes a significant contribution to issues of language policy globally as well as in the South African context. While the contributors call for promotion of indigenous languages, they do not do so naively, and are fully cognizant of the push for English only, at least in the school setting, that comes from some parents whose home language is not English (e.g. anecdotal data involving isiXhosa speakers). In light of such experiences, systematic study needs to be made of parental views on multilingual education. Exactly how widespread is the "straight-for-English" momentum? Does it characterize the majority of isiXhosa-speaking parents (or the majority in other indigenous speech communities)?

The contributors' illustrative language examples and experiences are drawn from either isiXhosa or isiZulu groups. (By the way, not to be picky, but some of the translations are inaccurate, both in terms of linguistic structure and pragmatics.) Although isiXhosa and isiZulu groups comprise the dominant numbers, language planners and educators should be on guard against neglecting, however unwittingly, the language experiences of the other seven indigenous groups enshrined in the Constitutional provision lest we find ourselves revisiting the divide-and-rule linguistics of a by-gone era. In this same regard, we strongly urge that in any subsequent revisions of this work, the editors monitor the representation of the nine indigenous languages, i.e., include the prefixes for these languages. Labeling and codification of the African languages resulted from the work of non-L1 speakers, who renamed the languages creating an Afrikaans and/or English version of the African languages. Just as there are no attempts to shorten Afrikaans to something like 'Frikaans,' there should be no anglicizing of the African languages, a practice not only contrary to the sociolinguistic norms of L1 speakers of these languages, but one which also smacks of the Apartheid linguicism of old.

Subsequent work should address critical areas not adequately dealt with in this collection, e.g., the precise scope and shape of teacher preparation programs for multilingual education; attitudinal data on learners' views; case studies of indigenous speakers in school settings where they are the majority; research on if/to what extent one can acquire second language competence when L2 is taught as a subject only (a need also recognized by Heugh *et al.*).

These matters aside, as the first work to address language policy issues in education in the new South Africa, this cutting-edge book is a valuable text and we recommend it highly.

Part five

COLUMNS

INTRODUCTION TO PART FIVE

THE SHORT JOURNALISTIC writings in this section are included both for the historical record and because of the many requests I've received for copies of this work, especially for the "Soul 'N Style" series written for the *English Journal* twenty-five years go. I wrote four columns in 1974, beginning in February of that year, one in 1975, and the last in 1976. Most of the ideas presented in "Soul 'N Style" ended up in various chapters of *Talkin and Testifyin*.

Steve Tchudi, the *English Journal* editor at the time, invited me to create a column for the *Journal* and gave me free rein to conceptualize the series. I was on a shonuff mission back in those years. I had three goals I wanted to accomplish.

First off, I felt it was absolutely crucial to present concepts and scientific information about language because most English professionals are steeped in literature and know little about language. That's the nature of the English curriculum in colleges and universities. Further, not only did the typical college English curriculum not include language courses for teachers, in those days it didn't include courses in African American literature or culture. Many English teachers were teaching Black students in urban school districts, but most didn't have a clue about Black linguistic–cultural reality, nor knowledge of the research on Black Language that was coming out of the Academy. I wanted "Soul 'N Style" to make a contribution to building this knowledge base for English professionals. My third goal was going to be the toughest – I knew it going in: to demonstrate what could be done with, on, in the language of Black America, the "dialect of my nurture," as the "Students' Right to Their Own Language" resolution had put it back in 1972.

When Tchudi asked my permission to submit the "Soul 'N Style" series for an awards competition, I didn't give it a second thought. I was sure that my unorthodox style of writing and the focus on Black Language and Culture would not be winning any of the white folks' awards. In 1975, "Soul 'N Style" received the award for Excellence in Educational Journalism from the Educational Press Association of America.

"Black English: So Good It's 'Bad'" came about when an *Essence* editor saw me (along with Janice Brenen, one of the parents in *King*) on the Phil Donahue show explaining the "Black English case." I was invited to write an essay for the "Speak!" column that regularly appears in that monthly magazine. My essay was published in the September, 1981 issue. (And I even got a small honorarium for it! For those who don't know it, writing for academic journals is strictly a labor of love.)

Essence is a Black women's magazine that came out of the Black Movement of the 1960s and 1970s, during which period African Americans established numerous magazines, newsletters, and small publishing houses. Most have fallen by the wayside. *Essence*, now over twenty-five years old, is one of the few survivors. I accepted the challenge because I knew it was a way to get the message about *King* to the thousands of folk who don't read the *Harvard Educational Review*. "Black English: So Good It's 'Bad'" presents a brief description of Black English and a synopsis of *King*, with a lil bit of Black Language flava here and there. Seems like I was writing on it for days; it's easier to peep through muddy water and spy dry land than to write short pieces with rigid space limitations.

"'Still I Rise': Education Against the Odds in Cuba" is a more recent piece of journalism, published in 1993, after a visit to Cuba (my first). It was published in a community newspaper, the *East Lansing Voice*. I was part of a delegation of unionists and researchers participating in a travel-seminar. We attended lectures and visited Cuban factories, hospitals, housing projects, trade/vocational schools, and other institutions. Little known is the fact that Cuba's population is 70 percent Black or Brown, and only 30 percent white.

The highlight for me was the opportunity to observe Cuban education first hand. Cuba is noted for its quantum leap from an agrarian, impoverished, illiterate peasantry, into the twentieth century after 1959 (the year of the Revolution). Today, Cuba's literacy rate is higher than that of the US: 96.1 percent there, 87 percent here. I sat in on English classes, both on the mainland and on the "Isle of Youth," where, at that time, 22,000 primary and secondary level students from African countries were being educated at the expense of the Cuban Government. Language is not an issue there. While Spanish is the national, official language, all school-children have to learn English, a policy that has been in place for many years despite the US campaign against Cuba. They recognize that English is spoken by millions of people outside the US. More importantly, they are secure in their own language and culture. Thus, these Spanish-speaking children readily learn English as a necessary tool for international communication. I left Cuba thinking that the people's watchword must be "Still I Rise."

20

FEBRUARY 1974

FIRST OFF, WE got to start with some basics. This gon be a column bout the language aspect of English teaching. Since Black Idiom is the "dialect of my nurture," and since I believe in the legitimacy of *all* dialects of American English, uhm gon run it down in the Black Thang. Course this ain gon be totally possible due to the limitations of print media, but uhm gon be steady tryin. Therefore, just in case certain idioms present a problem — though context should clarify 'em all — but just in case, uhm gon include some references at the end of this piece so that all the unhip will be up on the Black Idiom [see, this volume, References: Bailey, 1969; Kochman, 1972; Simmons, 1972; Dillard, 1972; Dundes, 1973; Fanon, 1967; and "White English in Blackface," pp. 57–66].

SOUL 'N STYLE [1974–6]

Another basic has to do with the title and the philosophy undergirding it. In *Black Scholar* (June 1970), anthropologist Johnetta Cole ran down some exploratory thoughts on the constituents of Black American Culture. First, she noted that all cultures of oppression share certain commonalities. Then she rapped on how Black Culture shares many aspects with mainstream white culture. Finally, as the third dimension of Black culture, the Sistuh contended that there are features unique to Black Americans, possible residuals of our African heritage and sensibility. Prime among these unique components were "*soul and style.*"

Now I've taken some liberties with Sistuh Johnetta's articulation of these concepts, but it ain nothin she'd disagree with. (I know the Sistuh and done rapped with her bout this.)

Soul is: a concerned perspective for the condition of man; a world view of a God-centered universe in which Goodness and Justice is gon prevail; what that old Mississippi, unfortunately racist dude, Faulkner, called the verities of the human heart – pride, compassion, endurance, and so on, y'all know Faulkner's rhetoric. (Which he was unable to live up to – his Anglo-American ethnocentrism kept gittin in the way, that's how come you see such ambivalence towards Blacks in his work and thought.) Style is: the articulation and active expression of this Concern; TCB-in for righteous causes; doin it to death to achieve a humanistic social order. If you got soul, yo style oughta reflect it.

Teachin with *soul 'n style* means recognizing that we don't impart knowledge in a vacuum. However subtly, we bees conveyin viewpoints toward our disciplines and attitudes toward society. We oughta make sure those viewpoints and attitudes is ethical, moral, and humane. If all this sound like preachin, it is – after all, my daddy is one, and maybe like he say, the world is standin in need of some preachin (and prayin) long bout now.

This ain no long way from *English teachin*, cause uhm gon run down now some points bout inhumane language attitudes. Y'all follow me now cause it gon get deep.

Though most of the recent hullabuloo on dialects done focused on Black speech, a social dimension interacts with the racial factor, throwing standard vs. nonstandard English into a wider realm that affects whites also. What linguist Donald Lloyd called the "national mania for correctness" stems from a long-standing tradition of elitism in American life and language matters. Though Americans preach individualism and class mobility, they practice conformity and class stasis. Further, those folk on the lower rung of the socio-economic ladder, in their upwardly mobile, catch-up-with-the-Joneses efforts, become unwitting accomplices in their own linguistic and cultural demise.

Reflecting this class anxiety (neurosis?), schoolroom grammars are grounded in the "doctrine of correctness" which emerged during the eighteenth century and was coincident with the rise of the so-called primitive middle classes and the decline of the mythical refined Aristocracy (those same "high class" folk, mind you, whose greed both led to wars over land and property and initiated the slave trade). In determining educational policy for the middle class, the power elite decided that the kids should be instructed in their vernacular, the Anglo-Saxon tongue, since their "lowly" origins indicated that they could not possibly master Latin, which had been the lingo of instruction for the Elite.

Now in those days, English was considered quite disorderly

and godawfully discordant with Latin rules. Moreover, the fresh-from-the-bottom middle-class speakers of English wanted neither themselves nor they kids to reflect any kinship with those they left behind. Therefore early English grammarians sought to regularize and "purify" English speech by superimposing upon it the "prestigious" Latinate grammatical model. Like the good Bishop Robert Lowth, who conceptualized his grammar in terms of giving what he called "order and permanence to the unruly, barbarous tongue of the Anglo-Saxons" (*Short Introduction to English Grammar*, 1763).

The killin part bout the whole mess, though, is there ain no correspondence between the two languages! For instance, dig on the fact that in Latin, you really *can't* end sentences with pre-positions cause Latin prepositions are attached to the verb, prefix-style, but in English, prepositions are movable. Hence Latin *devoro* for English swallow *down* – i.e. in the sense of *put up with*. (Y'all know my man Winston Churchill's thang on this don't you: "This is the kind of nonsense up with which I will not put." Git it, Winston!)

Americans fought a war to sever they colonial ties, but these British-based language attitudes came right on cross the water. Lowth's American counterparts are dudes like Lindley Murray and Gold Brown.

In the twentieth century, the individual, Latinate-based norms were replaced by social group and ethnicity-based norms. Structuralist grammarians studied English in action and revealed that "socially acceptable" and highly educated types were making all sorts of departures from Latinate rules, like saying "*It is me.*" Consequently the definition of "standard" English shifted to "the type of English most used by the socially acceptable of most of our communities" (Fries, 1940). Instead of freeing speakers and writers from petty and elitist linguistic amenities, the imme-diate educational application of structuralist research was towards linguistic and social conformity for the children whose parents had immigrated to this country in massive numbers around the turn of the century. "No broken English in this class, Antonio," and so on like that.

Dig where uhm comin from: this new "standard" didn't make thangs no better for common folk, nor for so-called "divergent" speakers. It wasn't never no meltin pot. As Don Lee has said, it melted, and we Blacks burned. In the process so did a lot of other beautiful "divergent" languages and cultures. Cause the immigrants' kids became ashamed of they mommas and daddies, who had sweated and toiled to bring they families to this country and then turned around and sweated some more to send they kids to school only to find those kids embarrassed about them and they speech.

Now teachers in general, but English teachers in particular, got to take some of this weight, cause they bees steady intimidatin kids bout they "incorrect English." Yet this superimposition of a polite usage norm has *nothin* to do with linguistic versatility, variety of expression, and the "power of the rap," but *everythin* to do with the goal of cultural and linguistic eradication by making what one seventeenth-century grammarian called the "depraved language of common people" and by extension, the common people themselves, conform to the dominant (white, middle-class) ethic of the new Aristocracy.

Hey, why don't y'all cool it, cause that sho ain humane.

MARCH 1974

> "A riot is the language of the unheard."
>
> (Martin Luther King)

The 1960s and racial upheaval. The 1970s and . . .

American educational institutions is continuing they role as passive reflectors of a racist, inhumane society. In part, the contemporary madness bees manifest in the "language deprivation" teaching strategies for the "disadvantaged" Black American. *Suddenly* after more than three centuries on this continent, the educational and societal consensus is that Blacks have a "language problem." But wasn't nobody complainin bout Black speech in 1619 when the first cargo of Africans was brought here on the Good Ship Jesus – yeah, that's right. Nor in 1719, 1819, 1919 – really, it wasn't till bout the 1950s when it became evident that Afros was really beginning to make some economic headway in America that everybody and they momma started talkin bout we didn talk right.

In the current controversy surrounding the Black Idiom (as well as other so-called "minority" dialects) linguists/educators/ English teachers/and just plain folk bees comin from one of three bags: (1) eradicationist; (2) bi-dialectalist; (3) legitimizer. These positions have undergirding them not simply linguistic issues but important socio-political concerns. (I mean, where is yo head?) While Ima rap specifically bout the Black Thang, with minor modifications, what Ima say can apply to most "divergent" dialects. (Now I ain gon cite no specific folk since this piece ain bout name-calling. But once upon a time, I did this. See my "The Black Idiom in White Institutions," *Negro American Literature Forum*, Fall 1971.)

ERADICATIONIST

Now this is a old position and don't too many people hold it no more since it ain considered cool (if you Black) or liberal (if you white) to be one. Essentially, they say get rid of the dialect; it's illogical, sloppy, and underdeveloped. It retards reading ability and the acquisition of language skills and thus is dysfunctional in school. It is the language of Uncle Tom and thus is dysfunctional in the socio-economic world. Ergo, the only way to facilitate the up-from-the-ghetto rise of Black folk is to obliterate what one educator deemed "this last barrier to integration." (Couldn't resist that one!)

BI-DIALECTALIST

Not so, say these holders of the most popularly prevailing position. Linguistic analysis demonstrates that the dialect is perfectly systematic and capable of generating cognitive concepts. Blacks acquire language at the same rate and with the same degree of fluency as whites. Because Blacks learn they language patterns in a Black environment, they manifest they linguistic competence in Black English whereas whites do it in white English. And if reading teachers is hip to the phonological system of Black speech, then there ain no reading problem.

However, there do be that social/real(?) world out there. And Blacks will need to acquire the "prestige" usage system in order to facilitate they socio-economic mobility. At the same time bi-dialectalists recognize that Blacks need they powerful and efficient dialect to function/survive in they own communities. So the solution is for Blacks to be bi-dialectal.

LEGITIMIZER

Now enterin the lists is a small but highly vocal group who bees contendin that while the former group is linguistically inaccurate and outright racist, the latter is politically naive and pedagogically wrongheaded. After all, if the dialect is not a problem, but socio-linguistic attitudes are, then why not work to change those attitudes? While we may be talking bout Blacks enterin the mainstream, we can change the course of that stream. Not CAN but IS – since Black language (as well as other Black cultural patterns) is rapidly being adopted by whites. Not CAN but GOT TO – since cultural plurality don't mean remake Black folk in white face. Anyway, if racism persist, all the language education in the world won't help you.

It is simply hypocritical to tell kids that they lingo is cool in the home environment, but not in school and mainstream America. (That's how come Black folk bees so schizophrenic seemin, all time havin to front and mask, go through linguistic and other kind of changes round whites.) Kids say don't run that game on me bout it's good enough for the ghetto but not the suburbs. Like everybody know the suburbs represent money and success, so who want anythang associated with the opposite? Eventually then, Black bi-dialectalists become mono-dialectalists cut off from those they left behind. Moreover, the way this country is presently constituted, it ain enough jobs for NOBODY, don't care how well they can manipulate *s'es* and *ed's* in they speech. Thus bi-dialectalism is not based on a sophisticated analysis of American power relations.

We legitimizers query: Why waste valuable school time on polite usage drills when, in a sense, Black kids is already bi-dialectal? Due to mass media, and after a few years in school, they understand white English and can produce reasonable facsimiles. Witness a group of Black kids "playing white." (Remember that scene from *Native Son?*) Listen to them, and you will hear the most amazing (amazing to the unhip that is) mimicking of white folks' language you ever heard. Or get on the bus and check out a group of domestics on the way home talkin bout and linguistically imitatin Miss Ann. I mean, they bees doin a pretty good (i.e., accurate) job of it.

Bi-dialectal classroom approaches and drills are all the more pointless when we note the lack of deep-structure difference between these two closely related dialects of American English. Bi-dialectalists note this too, and some done admirably demonstrated it through linguistic analysis. Yet, ironically, they persist in devising and teaching materials stressing these superfluous features of English usage. (I told y'all in the beginning this was all bout madness, didn I?) For instance, the kid who wonders what's the difference between what I wrote – "he do" – and your correction – "he does" – is really posing a linguistically legitimate question since there ain no deep structure – underlyin semantic differentiation – between the two. As a matter of fact, most features of Black English usage, which teachers bees so uptight bout, is simply surface features of English, differing in "flavoring but not in substance." Thus *Ain nobody doin nothin* is merely another surface representation of *Nobody is doing anything; I seen him = I saw him; They lost they books* is deep structurally the same as *They lost their books*. And so on.

Speaking to the legitimacy of minority dialects in the English classroom do not mean abdication of responsible language teaching. It do not mean lettin kids get away with irresponsible disorganized uses of language and communication. Righteous teachers taking care of business in the English classroom must see to it that kids learn to compose coherent, documented, specific, logical – in short, rhetorically powerful oral and/or written communications. There's good rappers and there's bad rappers, and anythang do not go in the Black community, just as anything does not go in the white community. Uhm talkin bout redefinin what *do* go. And it mean more than zeroin in on usage, on such trivia as movin students from *they house* to *their house*. This is an abdication of responsibility, for that's only a lateral move, and like my man Curtis Mayfield sing, we got to keep movin on up – UP, not sideways.

In movin up, however, we must be careful to sustain our moral–ethical vision of the Universe and if, necessary, choose goodness over grammar. As Jess B. Semple says:

> If I get the sense right ... the grammar can take care of itself. There are plenty of Jim Crowers who speak grammar, but do evil. I have not had enough schooling to put words together right – but I know some white folks who have went to school forty years and do not DO right. I figure it is better to do right than to write right, is it not?[1]

APRIL 1974

> "It bees dat way sometime."
>
> (Nina Simone and Ed Bullins)

What is it! What is it?

It is the voice of Black America: the language of the old folks down South; the lingo of the young, urban hipster; the dialect of educated, professional Blacks; the idiom of the preacher; the rhetoric of Black Power; the speech of the Black working class. The varying social groups in Blacktown share common linguistic registers whose constant reference point is the Black experience. This has not been well understood, let along discussed in any reasoned way. Mainly 'cause most definitions of Black Idiom done been did by outsiders, who ain' up on the history and culture of the people; who is prone to divisive moves like confining the dialect to one particular socio-economic class or age group; and who's fixated on discrete, "objective" linguistic Black Idiom units like *dis heah, they house, three book, he pass by him yesterday*, etc. No attempt is made to codify the commonalities which cut 'cross generational, regional, socio-educational, and even sexual lines. Yet there do be levers of common linguistic experience that all Blacks have come into contact with, recognize, and use in varying degrees, and which are foreign to whites (unless they've associated with Blacks on an intimate social basis and therein learned to interpret these registers). Many Blacks speak Negro who do not use linguistic features like "It bees dat way sometime." (Hey, cause, like despite dem language programs for the Black disadvantaged, nigguhs is more than invariant *be's!*) Even somethin so simple as *un-huh* said in a certain Black way is psycho-semantically meaningful (it generally is used to register a note of sarcastic disbelief or contradiction about what somebody has just said). Because of the common experience and history of oppression in which the Black idiom flourished, Black English, in this larger sense uhm tryin to convey here, is not simply the language of the ghetto but the language of Black America.

Yeah, I know, like you know Dr. So and So who is Black, and he don't sound like dem wearisome (Black pronunciation: *were-some*) kids you teach second hour. But that's cause you got to know what to listen for. See, what you hear from professional Blacks when in socially sensitive situations (how bout that?) is the usage patterns of so-called standard English (i.e. *he does* rather than *he do*), plus a lexicon (vocabulary) commensurate with they education. (But then of course you don't expect school kids of any hue to have a word hoard like that of educated adults.) Okay, but listen to those telling phonemic registers, which very, very few Blacks have erad-icated, listen for certain intonation patterns, a particular quality of resonance, and other features of phonology (sound) that go deeper than *dat* for *that*. Like regardless of they station in life, it's few Blacks that don't have the Black sound, which is what gives away Black telephone operators and enables most people to distinguish the race of even Southerners by sound alone (Black folks, espe-cially, is good at makin this distinction). Uhm talkin then bout a Black standard English which is different from a white standard English. Furthermore, uhm talkin bout these same Black standard speakers when they ain in "socially sensitive" situations and is speakin to other Blacks, professional or not, doan make no difference. They bees intuitively incorporatin Black linguistic *registers*, like: a familiar Black gesture such as eye-rolling, to indicate disapproval; a well-known Black Idiom like *down home* to refer to the South; reliance on the dynamics of larger Black communication patterns, such as *call–response*, to convey the message; even on occasion, conscious employment of a usage thang like "*God don't never change*" or *he do* for rhetorical effect (cognitively, it emphasizes the thought by affectively sayin "I been there too").

The psycho-cultural processes which nurtured the Black Idiom go back to slavery time and the necessity for a system of commu-nicating which could go undeciphered by Ole Massa. It wasn't possible to use the African tongue cause that was forbidden, and anyway the slavers had made that difficult by mixing together Africans with all different kinda tribal dialects. What evolved then was a lingo that would have one meaning for the white slave master, another for African slaves. Ain talking just bout words neither, but a whole (linguistic) rappin style shot through with ambiguity, irony, paradox, and bound to the immediate linguistic context as well as to the context of Black enslavement in White America.

What uhm runnin on you is bout a cognitive linguistic style whose semantics bees grounded not only in words but in the socio-psychological space between the words. In sum: a Black-based communications system derived from the oppressor's tongue – the words is Euro-American, the meanings, nuances and tone African-American.

Dig on this: a Black Language model encompassing the broad range of Black Idiom speakers, tieing together seemingly disparate linguistic emphases into a coherent unified whole. A model which, for purposes of analysis only, categorizes Black English as both language and style, which speaks to style as the lowest common denominator of Black talk, which even finds as part of that style the use of Black English linguistic expressions to sound a familiar racial chord. Like *Style* is where it's at.

I have developed a taxonomy which codifies these features of style, shared by all segments of the Black community. (This will be described in my forthcoming *The Black Idiom: Soul and Style*.) Here Ima have to rap bout them briefly and broadly. Style consists of: (1) Black Non-verbal Cues; (2) Black Lexicon; (3) Black Modes of Discourse.

NON-VERBAL CUES

This is Black body language – gestures, facial expression, body posture, etc. I mentioned eye-rolling above. Check out the female gesture of hands on hips to indicate, depending on context, indignation, boasting, or disgust. The most well-known feature here is probably giving skin (palm-slapping), a greeting of soul identification; a hand substantiation of some action that just went down; a reaffirmation of what somebody said. A natural, then, for non-verbal linguistic strategy to be extended into the Black Power Movement, producing the hand shake and the symbolic raised, clenched fist.

BLACK LEXICON

Common English words with a Black semantic slant and double or even quadruple level meanings for Blacks. *I got a bad cold* means just that whereas *I got a bad dress* means a *good* i.e., *beautiful* dress.

Some so-called "slang," yes, but more than that. Recall what I said above about how it all goes back to slavery-time and the development of this "code" among the slaves. Terms then, growing out of the Black Experience, like *high-yellow* for very light–complexioned Blacks; *ofay* from the Pig Latin for "foe" (enemy) to refer to whites; *do* or *process* to refer to artificially straightened hair of Black men; *nigger* referrin both pejoratively and lovingly and approvingly to Black folk.

BLACK MODES OF DISCOURSE

Verbal strategies, rhetorical flourishes, stylistic orderings – Black communication patterns writ large to move audiences and convey meaning. Too deep and complex to run down all of these here. Try one: *Call–response* – a dynamic interplay between speaker and audience. As Black communication is a two-way street, shot through with action and interaction, the listener is expected to respond verbally or non-verbally, giving approval, even directing the route of the speaker's rap. The best immediate ritualistic example is the church. The preacher issues the initial call: *My theme for today is Waiting on the Lord.* His congregation responds with: *Take your time! Amen! Fix it up, now!* etc. The same communication pattern goes down in non-ritualistic, secular, just plain ordinary Black conversations too. The speaker says (i.e., "calls"): *Hey, the other day, I was* . . . The listener(s) responds: *Un-huh . . . yeah . . . I hear you;* he gives skin, slaps the wall or back of a chair, laughs, shouts, etc. Thus as listener, yo participation/interaction is necessary to co-sign what is being run on you.

Call–response, which is a basic pattern in both Black speaking style and Black musical style, often can make for an interesting case of cross-cultural communication interference. In a Black–White conversation, the White person obviously does not engage in this process since it ain part of his culture. Judging then, from the White person's passivity or maybe an occasional low-voiced "mmmmmhhhmm," the Black person gets the feeling that the White isn't listening to him. On the other hand, when the White is speaking, the Black typically responds according to the Black call–response pattern. Thus the White person gets the feeling that the Black person isn't listening to him because he "keeps interrupting." Similarly, note that in the classroom, rich verbal response from Black kids – rather than the often-demanded quiet passivity – should inflate and excite a teacher, cause it mean they diggin on what you sayin.

Hey! Realize I ain even done nothin here but scratch the surface, but it bees dat way sometime.

MAY 1974

"Keep the faith, baby."

(The late Adam Clayton Powell)

If y'all been following this column monthly, by now you's bound to be wonderin: where do we go from here? Let me suggest some "places."

First and most important is the reading problem in Black schools which crops up in all areas. Kids fail social studies and science classes cause they can't read the text; in math, they can't understand the story problems; they love gym and drivers' training, but they have trouble with the health ed manuals and the written tests for drivers; girls in sewing classes can't read the pattern instructions and so on – every school subject as well as survival in the larger society depends on ability to read. Research has shown that, ironically, the longer Black kids stay in school, the further behind they get – e.g., if they reading level is two years behind at grade five, it'll be about four years behind at grade ten.

Now, don't get shook, I ain gon say (as some Blacks have indeed advocated) that Black kids oughta drop out of school alto-gether – I knows better, cause ain *nothin* on the streets but trouble. Nor am I gon say, as some whites have, that schools don't count – educational remediation programs failed, after all, cause schools spent all that cash doing more of the same thangs they done wrong in the past; the instructional forms were different but the under-lying ideology was the same. For example, due to hang-ups about Black English, some school systems invested much time, effort and money in language change programs and in dialect readers, some even going so far as making kids plod through two versions of the same story, one in so-called "home" dialect, the other in "school" dialect. Yet the only dialect "interference" in communication and in the learning-to-read process is the teacher's inability (or unwill-ingness?) to accept the Black kid's dialect.

Dig on the fact that before about 1950, most Black folks going through the educational system learned reading and communica-tion skills, despite speaking the Black tongue. This same dialect has only in the last twenty years or so "interfered" with the learning process, due on the one hand to white fear of the rapid socio-economic advancement of Blacks during the forties and fifties [see above, "Soul 'n Style," March 1974], and on the other, to the Blackenization of American cities. As urban areas and subsequently their schools became Blacker, whites fled to the suburbs. Though the teachers continued to work in city schools, they no longer lived in the environment. Thus these teachers as well as the generation after them became vastly alienated from Black Language and culture. In addition to the white teachers who don't know what's goin down with Black Language, there are Black teachers who, being recent arrivals from the lower class themselves, reject the dialect as a stigmatized reminder of where they came from. (There may be some Blacks who are truly ignorant of the forms of the Idiom, but there sho ain many. For more on Black ambivalence toward Black language, see Fanon, 1967.)

Enter: a Black kid reading the sentence, "*The boy needs more money*," as "*De boy need mow money*." All he has done is deleted the final *r* in *more*, the *s* in the third person verb, and substituted *d* for initial *th* in *the*. Teachers hip to the system of Black pronunciation patterns know that obviously such a kid does not have either a perceptual/vision problem or a coding/decoding linguistic one – he has simply "translated" the sentence on the printed page into good Black English. Doing this often produces homophonic pairs like: then/den (initial *th* pronounced as *d*); more/mow, four/foe, during/doing, Paris/pass, sore/so (due to intervocalic and final *r* not being pronounced); sing/sang, ring/rang (vowel i + consonant cluster *ng* = æ + ng). If this seems odd, recall that there are homophones in white middle-class dialect, like here/hear; their/they're/there. It's simply that Black English speakers have some additional and/or different sets of homophones. With this kind of knowledge and acceptance of Black English in mind, language arts teachers can push on toward increasing the Black kid's cognitive command of reading materials – and do so with the regular basal reading material, which represents, after all, the functional dialect of newspapers, street signs, application forms, and most of what they'll have to read outside of school. (For research in this reading–dialect area which supports what I'm runnin down here, see the works of Labov, Goodman, and the articles in *Teaching Black Children to Read*).

On the secondary level, English teachers should put aside the diagramming exercises (yeah, I done recently seen teachers *still* doing this!), postpone the transformational grammar lessons and more profitably sail full speed ahead on a real need: functional literacy. Get out the reading kits, set up reading labs, design remedial reading programs and if necessary, concentrate *all* classroom time on this excruciating problem. (You can still even teach literature this way:

just make each lesson in literature a reading lesson also.) Especially on this level, students should be learning to comprehend the structure and language of what I call *social negotiation forms* – marks of this highly bureaucratic society we live in, such as forms for health insurance, job applications, voter registration, social security, driver's license, college entrance, medicare, etc.

Another "place" to go to is the media. We live in a multi-media world where most of our important and even complex information and ideas are acquired and transmitted through audio-oral-visual processes. Help students critically examine various media, noting how visual arrangement, selection of material, style of presentation, and the like all help to color our perceptions of reality and convey hidden messages. (For example, until recently, Black ad models were all high-yellows with straight hair). Students should be encouraged to evaluate and develop standards of excellence for television programs and films. A quick glance at the recent (t)rash of Black exploitation films makes this an absolute necessity, and as for seeing Black dudes like Shaft on the tube, if they ain gon be no more ethical and responsible than whites, then we've only substituted Black trash for white.

While our society is such that basic literacy is still vital, professional writers and English majors aside, don't nobody else be needin to write. Thus, since students (both Black and white) will do far more speaking than writing in life after school – this applies even to college graduates – the English classroom's conventional written tasks should give way to speech activities. Specific assignments might involve simulation routines, such as job interview situations, panel discussions, debates, improvisational drama, and so on. Needless to say, listening skills should be stressed as an important counterpart to speaking. Assessment of student products and follow-through teaching still applies because contrary to what is often said, anythang do not go in speech just as anything does not go in writing. Whether we're talking about Blacks or whites, even the most casual speech events have their norms and stylistic criteria – which – do it need sayin? – ain got nothin to do with dialect but with thangs like strategy of presentation.

If writing *is* taught, it should be used as a vehicle for teaching thought – logic, organization, critical thinking and analysis. This approach to writing sees language as a way of organizing experience, and it emphasizes written composition as a process of discovery – often writing is a way of finding out what you think about a subject.

With this approach the question is: does the paper communicate the writer's message? (indeed, does it even have a message – some of the papers written in even the most "whitest" English bees sometimes *pointless!*); is the paper well-organized, logical?; are there facts and supporting details for the writer's ideas?; did he take his audience into account in selecting a suitable topic and in presenting the pertinent facts about the topic? Thus traditional notions of mechanical correctness become irrelevant, but the English teacher's job becomes harder since red penciling Black English forms is really a faster and easier method of grading papers.

Whenever possible, work in some lessons on language and culture and social and regional dialects. Since English is the one school subject that everybody takes, and since people's language attitudes are fostered in the schools, you, the English teacher, can do a great deal to eradicate the nonsense about, and push for the acceptance of, dialects in both white and Black students. Dig it: today's students will become the employment managers, businessmen, and social managers of tomorrow. Since "divergent dialects" have been used as a tool of oppression, refusing to accept the biases of the world "out there," and effectuating language attitude change is a route to the achievement of cultural pluralism and the American ideal. If schools are to be the leaders that they should be, rather than the followers that they have been, the task of bringing the American dream to fruition has to begin with the individual teacher in his individual setting. And it ain too far-fetched to talk bout the English/language arts teacher as an agent of social change, cause like I said, everybody and they momma pass through school, even if they don't stay too long. If English teachers would work to change attitudes about dialects, both in and, wherever possible, outside of school, it would be a major step in the direction of a humane social universe. What "Soul 'n Style" been urging you, the English teacher, to do amounts to an individual social and political act, which like charity, begins at home.

Y'all keep the faith.

SEPTEMBER 1975

> "Don't nobody pay no attention to no nigger that ain't crazy!"
> (Ceremonies in Dark Old Men by Lonne Elder III)

Following the style of the Black preacher's sermon, uhma begin by "taking a text." The work of Dr. Carter G. Woodson gon serve as my "Scriptural" reference. In 1916 Dr. Woodson founded the Association for the Study of Afro-American Life and History. An esteemed historian, author, social critic and giant intellectual among men, Dr. Woodson authored numerous books and articles on the Afro-American Experience. One of these was a baaaaaaad little book of criticism about the education the Negro needed but had not gotten in America. Published in 1933, the book was appropriately titled, *The Mis-education of the Negro*. I choose for my theme here, then, "Black English and the mis-education of the Negro – again."

Befo gittin deep off into it, though, let me lay one thang out up front so everybody will know where uhm comin from. My perspective on Black speech is not simply that of a Ph.D. researcher-academician, though I've done my share of that, beginning in Detroit when I worked (for a minute) on the Detroit Dialect Project and did (for a long minute!) the research for my dissertation. I also collected a good deal of data in Boston and Cambridge when I was on the Harvard faculty. However, mostly I done come into my knowledge and perspective on Black English, having been baptized by fire, beginning with constant corrections of my ghetto dialect from public school teachers and culminating in a speech therapy course forced upon me by university officials. (Now, I ain unique in this respect cause tons of other Black folk been down the same road and still today beaucoup Black kids bees going through these same ol changes.) My father traversed the long distance from our shot-gun sharecropper's shack in Brownsville, Tennessee, to the promised lands of Chicago and Detroit only to have his kids confronted with social and educational institutions that leveled constant onslaughts at our speech, our folkways, and our Traditional Black Church culture. To sum it up, my life, as James Baldwin would say, was "the usual bleak story." (But don't sing no sad songs for me cause a change is gon come!)

To get back on the case of "Black English and the mis-education of the Negro – again," we talkin bout how in the 1960s, we was bombarded with a plethora of studies and remediation systems pushing language-learning techniques for the Black "disadvantaged," guides for teaching "standard" English as a second language, and various other up-from-the-ghetto programs. One or two of these gave lip service acceptance to Black dialect; a few contrasted it with White English; some *said* they was teaching language as a tool for manipulating conceptual ideas: *all* were concerned with socio-linguistic etiquette and the correctness norms determined by the white middle class; and *none* concentrated on developing the power and uniqueness of Black verbal ability. Indeed most had as their goal either the total eradication of Black speech altogether, or the bi-dialectalization of Blacks (but not, of course, whites). In any case, these uplift efforts, in addition to being linguistically questionable, blatantly obfuscated the real issues which have to do with culture, politics, and economic power.

Now two interrelated thangs account for this contemporary mis-education of the Negro. First, it is just another example of the inadequacy of the American educational system writ large and Black. As Dr. Woodson said back in 1933, "The educational system as it has developed both in Europe and America is an antiquated process which does not hit the mark even in the case of the needs of the white man himself." Second, this contemporary mis-education of Blacks is an example of Black people crying for bread and white America sayin, "let 'em eat cake." Language teaching that seeks to put white middle-class English in Blackface ain did nothin to inculcate the Black perspective necessary to address the crises in the Black community. Again I consult Dr. Woodson:

> In this effort to imitate, however, these educated Negroes are sincere. They hope to make the Negro conform quickly to the standard of the whites and thus remove the pretext for the barriers between the races. They do not realize, however, that even if the Negroes do successfully imitate the white, nothing new has thereby been accomplished. You simply have a larger number of persons doing what others have been doing.

Lord knows we don't need to add more folk (Black or white, for that matter) to the economically exploitative Doublespeak Club or the inhumane, "Standard"-English-Speaking Racist Club. Rather we bees needin skilled Blacks who can rap and communicate with power and persuasion, with or without *s'es* and *ed's* – doan matter – and who will use that Nommo power for community, national and world improvement. Further, we gots to have mo serious study of the African linguistic history of Black speech as well as conceptual analysis of the communicative registers and linguistic modalities of contemporary Black English. Now here's a place where everybody can git some. Cause we all can benefit from knowledge of language systems and culture. Like, if you was to reproduce the opening statement by sayin: "Don't nobody pay any attention to no nigger that ain't crazy," that would be incorrect Black English cause the rule is that in negation structures, *every* possible negatable item must be marked with a negative. Or, like, when we query, "What's happenin?", we liable to get a response tellin bout somethin that happen last week or even somethin that gon happen. See, in the Traditional African World View, time is cyclical, and verb structure is not concerned with tense, but with modality or aspect. So "What's happenin?" could mean what happen in the past, what's happenin now, as well as what's gon happen in the future. Or, like, you got to get down into the symbolic system of the lingo if you's any way to understand the tonal semantics of the "Reben Jesse" when he be sayin, "Africa would if Africa could. America could if America would. But Africa cain't, and America ain't." Check it out.

Like I said, we bees needin serious scholarly study of Black communication patterns, their origins and impact on present-day Black life and culture. Early in the game, we should be developing students with this kind of healthy perspective and sense of social responsibility, who can go on and do this much-needed work using they knowledge as a basis for living in a transnational, multicultural world. But certainly in the 1960s, and even now into the 1970s, such was/is not the case. Black students was not encouraged to study they own language system, just as they predecessors in the schools of the past were taught to ignore it. (Yet, ironic, isn't it, that as we move towards the bicentennial, we is hard pressed to locate examples of America's diverse cultural–linguistic heritage except in the living color of Blacks, Browns, and Reds.) As Dr. Woodson said in 1933:

> In the study of language in school pupils were made to scoff at the Negro dialect as some peculiar possession of the Negro which they should despise rather than directed to study the background of this language as a broken-down [i.e., linguistically polluted by English] African tongue – in short to understand their own linguistic history, which is certainly more important for them than the study of French Phonetics or Historical Spanish Grammar.

Instead of such serious study, Black students were/are being forced into rote memorization of paradigmmatic forms like "John walks," "My mother walks," "My brother walks," and so on. This elitist and racist concentration on ruling-class forms of speech has generated a pedagogy which is the basis of the mis-education of the Negro – again.

> "Talk white? Hush, not tonight.
> My abode's restricted code,
> say 'ain't' without complaint."
> SCHOOL, disagree with you,
> a second code's the mode.
> A rude attitude?
> I reflect Black dialect,
> "F'get you."
> LANGUAGE: deprived, Afro-derived!
> Who's right? Don't start a fight!
> Free language style's on trial.
> It's late, cooperate.
> Why reject Black dialect?

Talk white don't seem quite right
though may another day.
"Aw, go on."
Sounds of free society
await a better state!
Meet eyes, don't criticize,
respect Black dialect!
"It ain't the same social frame!
Shared contexts are prereqs."
What'd you say? Shush, someday.
"F'get you!" "Aw, go on!"[2]

FEBRUARY 1976

If a student has the right to his own language, then what do I teach him? Queries like this are often run on me when I bees gittin down tough on the legitimacy of Black communication. Underlying the question is a sense of uncertainty and confusion about the role of the English teacher who is right now going through some shonuff changes. But then, so is everybody involved in the educational enterprise as schools and teachers are being forced to take the leadership to meet the demands of our contemporary multi-cultural, transnational world. Because I believe with the late Martin Luther King that we must learn to live together or we shall all die together, we teachers should boldly and bravely accept the challenge.

In the English/language arts area, the challenge comes down to accepting the students' native language/dialect while simultaneously heightening their consciousness of the communications process and enhancing their capabilities therein. To cope with this brave new world of ours, students need knowledge of and performance competence in the use of language and meta-language as fundamental dynamics in social interaction. Now, didn't nobody say this was gon be easy to teach, but methinks English teachers is baaaaad enough to do it! And if some of y'all need some mo edumacation in this area, just pressure yo school system to provide a staff development program. (After all, they did it for the "new math.")

More specifically, where all this is comin from is a redefinition of language arts teaching to focus on language as a dynamic, communications system used in everyday discourse, rather than as a frozen set of rules confined to the pages of a grammar text. The users of this system must be tuned in to all the vibrations of a particular speaking environment – the age, sex, race of the people involved; the degree of familiarity between them; the physical

DOONESBURY   by Garry Trudeau

Figure 20.1 "Doonesbury" cartoon, by Garry Trudeau

Source: Copyright G.D. Trudeau. Distributed by Universal Press Syndicate.

location where the rappin takes place, etc. – all such factors determine who says what to who(m) under what conditions. This way
of approaching language means that you will have to cross disciplines;
that knowing subjects and verbs ain enough – you gots to be able
to deal some psychology, some sociology, some cultural anthropology, etc. – and understand how these areas of human behavior
and knowledge impact on the words, expressions and structures
chosen by a given speaker.

Like, all the subject–verb agreement in the world didn't help
the "colleged" secretary who addressed her bosses by their first
names (as they addressed her – after all, she had a college degree
too, or so she reasoned. Personally, I don't go for these status/rank
distinctions in forms of address, but they do be there.) Now this
was a white-on-white situation, and there was communication interference. Dig on how complex the communication process becomes
when it's black-on-white. A white gym teacher recently complimented a Black basketball player with the following: "Attaboy, go
get 'em!" *BOY* . . . the unforgivable form of address for a Black
male; the message of praise never got through. See, due to white
America's historical emasculation efforts directed against Black
manhood, "boy" is an offensive term to Black men – even to the

young Black dudes. Check it out, they always address one another as "man" – uhm talkin bout even the lil biddy cats four and five years old!

Still another twist to this matter of forms of address is provided by the Black executive who had some problems adjusting to the use of first names on various levels of management in his firm. Now, characteristically, Blacks will cop a 'tude quick when white strangers be callin them by they first name, especially if it's in a formal or business setting. See, historically, whites done use this as a sign of disrespect and thus as a verbal mechanism for putting Blacks in they "place." However, in the white business world, being addressed by your first name signifies that you in the inner (power) circle; it's like an immediate acknowledgement that you is in the club. So in this more liberal (?) world of the 1970s, which finds Blacks in high-level positions in a number of white institutions, my man, the showcase Black exec, had to discard many of his old perceptions about language and learn some new rules. At the same time, he had to teach his white peers a lesson in the semantics of race relations, for many of them had often made such verbal blunders in their interaction with Blacks.

Another area of possible Black–white communication conflict is in labels for racial identification. While many whites would probably cop a 'tude at being called "whitey," Blacks now use the term as a neutral way of referring to a white person. Unlike "honky" or "peckerwood," "whitey" (or its less often heard predecessor, "ofay") has become neither positive or negative – but just another way of saying "white person." Similarly, check out the term "nigger," often used by many Black folk. Coming from a "whitey," it is always a racial epithet – a way of calling a Black person outa they name. But among Blacks, the term has *at least* four different meanings, plus a different pronunciation – *nigguh*:

1   Personal affection or endearment, as in "He my main nigguh," and "You my nigguh if you don't get no bigger, and if you get bigger, you gon be my bigger nigguh."
2   Culturally Black, identifying with and sharing the values and experiences of Black people. At a Black rally, when the Sistuh shouted out "Nigguhs is beautiful, baby," she was referring to shonuff nigguhs, as contrasted to Oreos. Since the spread of Black Consciousness, there is a move to replace this use of nigguh with Black or Afro-American.
3   Disapprobation, a way of expressing disapproval of a person's actions. In this sense, even white folk, when they is acting bogue is called nigguhs.

4   Identification for Black folks – period. In this sense, the word
     has neutral value. "All the nigguhs in the Motor City got rides"
     means simply and *not* pejoratively, that all persons of African
     descent that live in the city of Detroit have automobiles.

   One other example before I split!
   At the heart of the African-based Oral Tradition, which has
survived in Afro-America for centuries, lies the belief that the spoken
word can give man mastery over natural events and men. Like
arrows, the proper word can devastate yo enemies (as well as conquer
women's hearts), or so the Bloods believe. In the African epic of
Sundiata, we find the following "war of mouths" between the
reigning king and the exiled warrior-king, Sundiata:

> I am the poisonous mushroom that makes the fearless vomit.
> As for me, I am the ravenous cock, the poison does not matter to me.
> Behave yourself, little boy, or you will burn your foot for I am the red-
>   hot cinder.
> But me, I am the rain that extinguishes the cinder; I am the boisterous
>   torrent that will carry you off.

The above rap is not unlike the following from two Afro-American
dudes:

> If you don't quit messin wif me, uhma jump down yo throat, tap dance
>   on yo liver and make you wish you never been born.
> Yeah, you and how many armies? Nigguh, don't you know uhm so bad I
>   can step on a wad of gum and tell you what flavor
>   it is.

   Now since in Black communication, it is cool for a dude to
talk about how bad he is, such bragging is taken at face value. The
speakers may or may not act out the implications of their words,
but the listeners do not necessarily *expect* any action to follow. Thus
baaaad Black rappers often avoid having to prove themselves
through deeds. "Sellin woof [wolf] tickets" (sometimes just plain
"woofin") refers to the kind of strong language which is purely
idle boasting. However, to whites, this bad talk is nearly always
taken for the real thing. Such communication interference can lead
to tragic consequences, as for instance, the physical attacks and social
repression suffered by Black spokesmen of the 1960s, such as the
Black Panthers. "Death to the racist exploiters!" "Off the pigs!"
The white folks thought the Bloods was not playin and launched
an all-out military campaign against them. The whites was not hip
to braggadocio and woof tickets.
   What I been layin on y'all relates to the fact that there are

fundamental linguistic–cultural differences between Blacks and whites, and these differences impact on and often adversely affect the communications process. Teachers as well as students, Blacks as well as whites, need to be hipped to these differences, and in the process learn some general concepts and principles about language and human communication throughout the world.

21

FROM THE VERY jump (also git-go, begin), we need to establish just what Black English is – and is *not*. Now, I want yall to follow me close cause it's gon get a little deep.

First off, relinquish the myth – contrary to all scientific and observable fact – that Black English is merely bad grammar and the speech of "street folk" or "ignut nigguhs." In fact, the language is spoken at various times by some 90 percent of the Black community – regardless of socioeconomic

BLACK ENGLISH: SO GOOD IT'S "BAD" [1981]

status – including poets and professors, entertainers and elites, reverends and revolutionaries. For instance, Detroit's dynamic, colorful mayor, Coleman Young, complains loudly and publicly about the "*po*-lice union" trying to "put the city in a trick bag." The late Dr. Martin Luther King once preached, "Lord, we ain't what we ought to be, and we ain't what we want to be, we ain't what we gon be, but thank God, we ain't what we was."

In what Black linguist Dr Grace Holt [1972] calls our "semantics of inversion," Black people have retained a feature of Mandingo, Ibo, Yoruba, Wolof and other African languages in which something can be so good that it's "terrible." As a people, we have a connected culture and experience that comes out in our shared language. The difference between Black "leaders" or the Black "middle class" and the Black "underclass" is that leaders and the middle class can shift to white English when the situation calls for it. Thus, this group commands two languages, while the "underclass" is fluent in only one. It has been necessary for survival and Black community solidarity for all of us to "talk that talk."

This "talking and testifying," as I call it, is a combination of the cultures and languages of Africa and America. For instance, the Black English pronunciation of "mo" instead of "more" reflects those African languages of our ancestors that do not have an *r* sound. These and other surviving Africanisms – such as the absence of the *th* sound – help us to reconstruct how Black English developed in the American slave community. Several typical speech tests used in the schools require the child to distinguish between sounds like *Ruth* and *roof*. But Black English speakers pronounce both as "ruf." Our slave ancestors took the English words and used them according to the rules of grammar and structure that existed in their native African languages. This language mixture enabled them to communicate with their slave masters. At the same time, double meanings and linguistic "slickerations" made it possible for them to communicate with one another without the Man's knowing what they were talking about.

"That teacher, he too mean. He be hollin at us and stuff."

"Browny, he real little, he six, and he smart cause he know how to read."

These words were spoken by two of fifteen Black elementary school students from Ann Arbor, Michigan's Green Road Housing Project. In the 1977 *Martin Luther King Junior Schoolchildren* v. *Ann Arbor School District Board* case, parents sued their school district because it wasn't taking care of educational business. In their own way, the children speak to the two main issues in the *King* case. One factor is that of teachers who "be hollin" instead of teaching. They do not accept the speech and cultural differences the children bring to school, and that, in turn, leads to poor education.

The other critical issue is the school's failure to produce kids who, like Browny, can read. Now, the language, in and of itself, does not prevent Black children from getting educated. It is what teachers, principals, schools, standardized tests and speech tests do *to*, *with* and *against* the language of some Black children that is a barrier to their education. Rather than accept the Black child's language as legitimate, schools use it to label the child "slow," "mentally retarded" or "learning disabled." The children then are put into remedial and speech pathology classes for their Black "impediments." Even those children who remain in regular classrooms may be written off as "uneducable."

My own experience is a case in point. As a young college student, I was almost prevented from obtaining a Michigan teaching certificate because of my Black English. Fortunately, though, my church and my family had given me a strong sense of pride and belief in my intellectual capabilities. I not only got my teaching certificate; I went on to get a Ph.D. from one of the top graduate schools in the country, and I ain't never looked back!

As a result of the *King* case, Black parents now have written into United States law a ruling that not only says our language is legitimate but also demands that school districts educate Black children. If your children have been classified as "slow," make sure that their language and cultural style have not been the basis for this labeling. Demand that they be evaluated by a psychologist and speech professional who is knowledgeable about Black language and culture and can distinguish between Black children who are truly retarded and those who simply speak and think differently from the white, middle-class standard. If necessary, take the school district to court!

Black English has changed over the past 400 years, but it still isn't the same as white English. As long as we have two separate societies in contact and conflict, we're going to have two separate languages. It just bees dat way.

22

"STILL I RISE": EDUCATION AGAINST THE ODDS IN CUBA [1993]

I HAVE WANTED to visit Cuba since the 1970s when I first met Dr. Johnetta Cole, now "Sista President" of historically Black Spelman College, then a national committee member of the Venceremos ("We shall win") Brigade, a volunteer group of Americans who travel to Cuba to work in the fields with the Cuban people. Cole spoke of the progress this small island nation had made in eradicating institutional racism, which had been a successful strategy of the exploitative Batista regime. Indeed, it was Cole's pro-Cuba stance that figured in President Clinton's post-election decision not to consider her for Secretary of Education, though she had been a strong and influential get-out-the-vote supporter and was a member of his transition team. First JohnettaCole, then Lani Guinier – what's up with this dissin of African American women who dare to think for themselves? But that's grist for another mill.

As a disillusioned Black woman who had been active in struggles around racism on college campuses, I was impressed by Cole's report of the fundamental change in race relations in Cuba. But I was also an educator who had cut her pedagogical teeth on inner-city students like M. C. Lyte's "ruffnecks." So what I found really astounding was Cole's commentary on educational progress in this "Third World" country, with its 30 percent white and 70 percent Black or Brown population.

There are several legal ways to visit Cuba, one of which is to go with a delegation of unionists and researchers. And so this year, I finally went to Cuba. I participated in a travel-seminar sponsored by the Detroit-based US Cuba Labor Exchange. We visited a pediatric and a psychiatric hospital, a glass and a cigar factory. On my own, I toured a ceramics and a citrus-fruit factory. We attended Cuban

Federation of Union meetings and lectures. We toured housing projects and construction sites where everyday people were hard at work
building – I mean this literally – their own homes with land and
resources supplied by the Cuban Government. Each tour concluded
with seminar sessions with the workers and managers at the site.

We observed Cuba's advancements in medicine at the
International Conference of the World Health Organization, which
was held in Havana, where our delegation was based. Along with
delegations from over 100 other countries, we were guests at a
reception, hosted by "Fidel" (as the Cuban people refer to him)
and the Cuban Federation of Unions, to celebrate May Day. Most
importantly, my twenty-year-old appetite for first-hand observation
of Cuban education was finally satisfied. Our delegation, which was
comprised of unionists from all over the US, toured a School of
Tourism, a school for the physically challenged, and several pre-
schools (which in Cuba include kindergarten). On my own, I visited
additional educational sites, sat in on a seventh-grade class in English,
talked with teachers, interviewed administrators, and partied with
the English Language Supervisor for the Province of Havana.

Before 1959, only 23.6 percent of the Cuban population could
read and write. Today in 1993, Cuba boasts a literacy rate of 96.1
percent. Not only is this rate far higher than that of other Caribbean
nations (Brazil's rate is 23 percent, El Salvador's 38 percent), it is
even higher than the literacy rate of the US, which is 87 percent.
This high degree of literacy was achieved through National Literacy
Campaigns that began shortly after 1959, the year of what the
Cuban people refer to as "The Revolution," a recurring phrase in
their daily conversations. This country of 10 million people knew
that their nation had to make a quantum leap in order to come
into the twentieth century. Students, some as young as twelve or
thirteen, would go into the countryside, live and work in the fields
with farm families, and teach them the "three r's" at night.

Dental and medical care and education, including college, is
completely free for every Cuban citizen. All students, on both
primary (Grades 1–6) and secondary (Grades 7–9) level, study and
work. A typical school day begins at 7:30 a.m. and ends at 11.30
a.m. After lunch, the student spends four hours working in the
fields. This also goes for pre-university, "college prep" in US lingo.
Pre-university education, equivalent to grades 10–12 in this country,
takes place in residential schools, generally located in the countryside, where the students grow their own food and do all the cooking
and cleaning. I visited one such school, the Lenin School of Math
and Science, and was delighted to learn that the student body was
70 percent female!

Figure 22.1   The author during her visit to Cuba in 1993

Basic education, which is compulsory, extends from kinder-garten through Grade Nine. After that, students are examined to determine placement in technical, trade, or pre-university school. Unlike the US, however, a college prep student ain't all that. All students must do manual labor and after graduation, give back in the form of two years of national service. Furthermore, Cubans with a college education and a "D" (M.D., Ph.D., J.D., etc.) are not economically privileged. This is a society where each citizen is a worker in a collective (whether doctor, lawyer, professor, brick-layer, janitor, or waitperson), and every worker makes pretty much the same money as every other worker. This society's vision is about education for enhancing the quality of life, not for materi-alist consumption. In Cuba, there are no Joneses to keep up with.

Cuba's educational philosophy is reflected in Jose Marti's slogan, which I heard often from teachers: "An informed people is a free people." Teaching and teachers are highly valued. For instance, to enhance their instructional performance, teachers systematically observe and critique the teaching of their colleagues several times throughout the school year. The Minister of Education also observes and critiques each teacher several times a year. Teachers who need it are given special help to improve their instructional strategies. Since the Cuban Constitution guarantees every citizen a job, emphasis is on development. Nobody worries about getting or losing their teaching certificate.

Cuba's commitment to education has extended to African countries for over two decades. On my own, I took the twenty-minute plane ride from Havana to the "Isle of Youth," formerly the "Isle of Pine," one of Cuba's 1,600 islands. Before "The Revolution," a huge Alcatraz-style prison complex housed hundreds of captives, criminal and political, among them, the young revolutionary, Fidel Castro. Now the largest of the prison buildings is a museum (which the personnel graciously took me through although I happened to be there on the day they're closed). And the island is home to 22,000 students, on primary and secondary school level, from Angola, Mozambique, Namibia, Tanzania, Kenya, and Ghana, who are being educated at the expense of the Cuban Government.

Per capita, Cuba has the highest number of doctors, nurses, teachers, scientists, and engineers in Latin America. This has been achieved without fancy new school buildings, glossy hardcover, multi-colored textbooks, multi-media educational aids, or other kinds of post-modern pedagogy. The schools are the old mansions of the former ruling class, unrenovated, in need of a paint job, and looking pretty much as they must have looked in Batista's day. The beat-up looking blackboards are a throwback to those I remember in my early years in a one-room school in the rural, outhouse South. The textbooks are worn and old-style, paperback types. All students wear ordinary, rather drab-looking uniforms, color-coded to distinguish primary from secondary level. Other than the small classes for the physically challenged, class size ranges from 25–35 students, pretty much the same as K–12 classrooms in the US. The students are well disciplined, and they stand when they recite, but outside on the playground, they are as loud and raucous as any American kid.

Truth be told, education anywhere is a matter of societal commitment, not books and buildings. And it goes on in Cuba, despite thirty years of US aggression against this tiny nation, and despite the recent acceleration of this aggression embodied in the Cuban Democracy Act of 1992, which effectively punishes any country that trades with Cuba by cutting off US aid to and/or trade relations with that country, combined with the Torricelli Resolution of 1993, which seeks to have the United Nations institute a mandatory international embargo against Cuba. One struggles to understand this aggression, especially given the fact that the US is now in bed with its former Communist enemy, the Soviet Union. For its part, Russia has cut off all aid to Cuba in exchange for a massive infusion of economic aid from the US. The Cubans refer to this as a "double embargo," as they struggle to cope with the scarcity of basic necessities like milk, toilet paper, and soap.

Education against the odds: in 1993 I witnessed it for myself. I saw little children in hearing-impaired classrooms struggling to learn despite the double embargo which makes batteries for their hearing aids a scarce, often unobtainable commodity. I jogged my daily four miles amidst eighth graders on bicycles, many of whom had ridden twice that far because of the shortage of fuel and buses. I talked at length with a Ghanaian teacher of English on the Isle of Youth, who spoke with pride about how his young students just take things in their stride and continue with lessons despite frequent brown-outs from energy shortages, the consequence of US efforts to bring this proud country of Black and Brown peoples to its knees. And I was reminded of Maya Angelou's poem:

> You may write me down in history
> With your bitter, twisted lies,
> You may trod me in the very dirt
> But still, like dust, I'll rise.[1]

Part six

THE STRUGGLE
CONTINUES

23

It HAS NOW been well over a generation since Kwame Ture issued his clarion call for "Black Power"[2] and thus charted a new course for the Civil Rights Movement in the US. But his cry, horrendous and frightening as it seemed to be to some in 1966, was not without precedent in the annals of the African American Struggle. For just twelve years earlier, Richard Wright had entitled his book on the emerging independence movements in Africa, *Black Power*. And surely Rosa Parks' historic refusal to give up her seat to a white man and move to the back of the bus, on 1 December 1955, paved the way for Kwame Ture's "Black Power" – a bold call for new directions and strategies. These actions and events from the Black Experience symbolize the motive forces that led to the unleashing of Brown Power, Woman Power, Poor People's Power, Gay Power, and other human energy sources that fundamentally altered American power relations in our time.

CCCC AND THE "STUDENTS' RIGHT TO THEIR OWN LANGUAGE"[1]

As marching, fist-raising, loud-talking, and other forms of resistance marred the landscape of "America, the beautiful," the power elites huddled to design reforms to acculturate the oppressed into the dominant ideology. The Unhip among researchers, scholars, and intellectuals assembled the database upon which these reforms were built, arguing, for instance, that even though the linguistic–cultural differences of those oppressed by race, class, and/or gender were *cognitively* equal to those of the mainstream, they were *socially* unequal. Early on, a few scholars tried to pull folks' coats to the trickeration of the power brokers. They argued that it was purely academic to demonstrate, in Emersonian, arm-chair philosophizing style, the legitimacy of the oppressed's language and culture without concomitantly struggling for institutional legitimacy in the educational and public domains. If the patriarchally-constituted social and economic structure would not accept non-mainstream speech varieties, then the argument for *difference* would simply become *deficiency* all over again.

Against this backdrop, enlightened academics envisioned their task as one of struggle for such legitimacy. They began working within their professional societies and organizations to bring about recognition and legitimacy of the culture, history, and language of those on the margins. And it was not only within a group such as the Conference on College Composition and Communication (CCCC) that this struggle was waged, but all across the alphabetic spectrum – the APA (American Psychological Association); the ASA (American Sociological Association); the MLA (Modern Language Association); the SCA (Speech Communication Association); the ABA (American Bar Association); the ASHA (American Speech and Hearing Association); and on and on across disciplines and throughout the educational system on all levels. Though the struggles were spearheaded by Blacks, it quickly became a rainbow coalition as Hispanics, women, Native Americans, and other marginalized groups sought redress for their ages-old grievances against an exploitative system.

It was in this historical moment that the Conference on College Composition and Communication (aka "4Cs") took up the cause of student language rights, particularly the rights of those students from disadvantaged communities and communities of Color. CCCC is an organization of college-level English teachers, with a membership some 9,000 strong, only a very small percentage of whom are People of Color. When I heard about its campaign for student language rights, I decided to join forces with this essentially white organization. The "Students' Right to Their Own Language" policy resolution was short, but powerful. It had the effect of a bomb being dropped right in the midst of the English profession:

> We affirm the students' right to their own patterns and varieties of language – the dialects of their nurture or whatever dialects in which they find their own identity and style. Language scholars long ago denied that the myth of a standard American dialect has any validity. The claim that any one dialect is unacceptable amounts to an attempt of one social group to exert its dominance over another. Such a claim leads to false advice for speakers and writers, and immoral advice for humans. A nation proud of its diverse heritage and its cultural and racial variety will preserve its

heritage of dialects. We affirm strongly that teachers must have the experiences and training that will enable them to respect diversity and uphold the right of students to their own language.

(Passed by the Executive Committee of the Conference
on College Composition and Communication in 1972
and by the membership in April, 1974.
First published in the organization's journal, *College
Composition and Communication,* Fall, 1974.)

CCCC became famous (or infamous, depending on your vantage point) for its "Students' Right" language policy resolution. However, virtually since its inception fifty years ago, this organization has served as the site of dialogs about language rights issues, particularly as these issues impact on students. Poring over nearly fifty years of back issues of *College Composition and Communication* (*CCC*), I was struck by the fact that the organization has consistently provided a forum for scholars as well as activists to raise up the issue of language rights. The historical record of CCCC mirrors the contradictions of language policy, politics, and power that exist in the larger society.

DONALD J. LLOYD[3] AND THE "NEW LINGUISTICS"

The [article] is an expression at the very least of a frivolous obscurantism, or at the most of a vigorously cultivated ignorance ... The failure to know [the factual studies of language] and what they mean ... is responsible for the fact that the educational heart of darkness ... is the English course ... Emphasis on "correctness" – at the expense ... of a fluid, knowledgeable command of our mother tongue – is responsible for the incompetence of our students in handling their language, for their embarrassment about their own rich ... dialects, for their anxiety when they are called upon to speak or write ... and for their feeling that the study of English is the study of trivialities which have no importance or meaning outside the English class.

... In our day, to make statements about English and about language which do not square with linguistics is professionally reprehensible. Yet it is an indulgence arrogantly and wilfully permitted themselves by many English teachers, not decently hidden in class, but in open publication in the journals of our field and in the concoction of the dreariest collection of ignorantly dogmatic textbooks that dominates any discipline in the schools.

It was February 1951. Lloyd was replying to "The Freshman is King; or, Who Teaches Who?" which had been published in the

December 1950 issue of *CCC* by Kenneth L. Knickerbocker. In his scathing critique, with its signifyin title, "Darkness is King," Lloyd took Knickerbocker to task for coming to conclusions about the actual use of nineteen "controversial" expressions (e.g., Who did you meet?) based on an opinion survey by a lay person that had been published in *Harper's Magazine*. Lloyd argued that the "disputed expressions" had all been studied and "found to be in good use in this country," and he stated unequivocally that "the language of a person who uses none of these expressions is not superior to the language of one who uses some of them, or indeed, to that of one who uses all of them." Not content with just knocking Knickerbocker upside the head, Lloyd also slammed the journal and the organization: "[The] appearance [of this article] in the bulletin of the CCCC is a little shocking," and "The assertion or implication that the language of a person who uses none of these expressions is superior on that account is a professional error which no English teacher should commit in print, and no editor should permit him to make."

From the Jump, then, CCCC functioned as a forum for debates about student language rights. To a great extent, this is attributable to the parallel development of Composition Studies and Linguistics in the 1950s and 1960s as both fields sought to reinvent themselves and stake intellectual claim to distinct identities among the established disciplines of the Academy. Indeed, in those early years, linguistics was breaking away from anthropology and philosophy and formulating new grammars truly reflective of how English works (e.g., Structural, Transformational), grammars which were replacing the misfit Latinate-based models of old. At the time, there was a good deal of excitement about the "New Linguistics," which held great promise for resolving a host of social and pedagogical problems, including analysis and understanding of the "language of the ghetto" (as it was sometimes called in those days). Thus the most frequently cited authors in *CCC* articles from 1950–64, a period that Phillips *et al.* consider the first phase of CCCC's development, were linguists – e.g., Charles C. Fries (13 cites); Paul Roberts (10 cites); Kenneth Pike (11 cites); Noam Chomsky (7 cites); Donald Lloyd (8 cites) (Phillips *et al.*, 1993, p. 452). These articles generally focused on the relevance, for Composition Studies, of the theories and research coming out of Linguistics, and within this general focus, the concern was for the teaching of literacy to those students who used nonstandard forms and *did not* "carry on the affairs of the English-speaking people." In this early period, those students were typically not students of Color, but rural and/or working-class whites. Lloyd spoke up for these white regional and social class dialects quite poignantly:

> You discover ... that dialects you have grown up to despise are rooted in respectable antiquity and still reflect the vicissitudes of pioneer life. If you respect American traditions, you find these traditions best embodied in the language of the illiterate back-country farm families, whether they still stand on their own land or congeal in uneasy clots in our industrial cities. You come therefore to describe with respect. You give information; you do not devise new decalogues.
>
> (1953, p. 41)

Beginning with the proposition that "an English composition course around linguistics would "take the English language as a social instrument expressing, conditioning, and conditioned by the society that uses it" (1953, p. 40), Lloyd even goes so far as to say that linguistics "is a promised land for the English teacher" (1953, p. 43). However, Long expressed disdain for this linguistics-as-the-promised-land-business. In his "Grammarians Still Have Funerals," he lambasts linguist Roberts for the declaration, in Roberts' chapter, "A Grammarian's Funeral," that "a person would just as soon call himself a con man or an alchemist as a grammarian." Long rebuts:

> I have called myself a grammarian for many years ... Until Roberts' work came along, it would not have occurred me to compare grammarians — or even New Linguists, in spite of the extravagant claims many of them make for their work — with con men and alchemists ... the grammar Lloyd and Warfel and Roberts give at great length — at greater length than seems desirable for Freshman English — is about as vulnerable as the school grammar these men scorn ... It is unlikely that the New Linguists have really achieved immortality.
>
> (1958, pp. 211–16)

Linguist Sledd, however, seems to have put the lie to Long's assertion. His work dates back at least to 1956, the year that marks his first appearance in *CCC*. Often referred to as "the conscience of the field" (e.g., Olson, 1997), Sledd, a Southern white linguist, has been a regular on CCCC and National Council of Teachers of English (NCTE) conference programs over the decades. During this time he has consistently challenged English teachers on behalf of linguistically marginalized and economically disenfranchised voices. Now Professor Emeritus, Sledd continues to "stir up trouble" (as he puts it) on behalf of linguistic minorities. Although his 1956 article doesn't deal directly with language rights issues – a theme that Sledd would, in the coming decades, write about eloquently and powerfully (see e.g., his "Bi-Dialectalism: The Linguistics of White Supremacy," 1969) – his article is important in this historical account because Sledd demonstrates that teachers hold mis-assumptions about language in general. These language myths get extended and compounded with racial myths in the case of the language of Black America.

While throughout the 1950s and 1960s linguists and other CCCC scholars advocated the legitimacy and adequacy of all language variations, consistently they called for English teachers to toe the line in terms of teaching the social inadequacy of nonstandard forms. "If a new doctor or minister says "you was," confidence in him is lowered. Educated people should talk like educated people, no matter who is listening or what the occasion may be" (Ives, 1954, p. 154). Allen advocates that the instructor should "help students to substitute one set of language practices for another set" (1952, p. 11). Essentially, these scholars were promoting a philosophy of linguistic eradication or subtractive bilingualism, exactly the position that Kelly would lambast the entire CCCC organization for in her 1968 "Murder of the Dream" speech.

Lloyd too acknowledged that instructors would find that they had to make a "change" in their students, but the "change" should be in the direction of an additive bilingualism:

> If we find anything that we have to change – and we do – we know that we are touching something that goes deep into [a given student's] past and spreads wide in his personal life. We will seek not to dislodge one habit in favor of another but to provide alternative choices for freer social mobility. We seek to enrich, not to correct ... By respecting their traditions and the people from whom they come, we teach them to respect and to hold tight what they have as they reach for more.
>
> (1953, p. 42)

Over the years, Lloyd refined his pedagogy for using "New Linguistics" concepts (e.g., pattern practice drills, contrastive analysis) to teach alternative language habits while simultaneously promoting retention of the Mother Tongue. In a class all by himself in those years, Lloyd reflects the thinking that would lead to the "Students' Right" resolution two decades later.

Concern about the dialect of rural and working-class whites demonstrates the social class bias used to distinguish "standard" from "nonstandard" speech and clearly reveals that the speech of the lower class is dissed irrespective of race. This perception of white nonstandard speech is significant in the issue of Ebonics because Ebonics is perceived as lower-class speech. One explanation for this perception is the fact that the language is spoken more often among everyday people than among educated professionals. Then too, it is the ordinary folk who have maintained Ebonics over time and who continue to enrich it with linguistic innovations. Further, you rarely hear middle-class Blacks using Ebonics outside intimate Black community contexts since they have access to another language – the Language of Wider Communication – to use in the workplace and in non-Black settings. Hence, the mis-perception of Ebonics as "lower class" or "ghetto." The complexities of class and status that characterize linguistic and educational issues involving white "illiterate back-country farm families" and "uneasy clots in our industrial cities" are compounded by Blackness in the case of Ebonics. In the struggle for Black Language rights, then, you are doing battle on two fronts: class and race.

"MURDER OF THE AMERICAN DREAM"

One major result of the social movements of the 1960s and 1970s was the creation of educational policies to redress the academic exclusion of and past injustices inflicted upon Blacks, Browns, women, and other historically marginalized groups. Programs and policies such as Upward Bound, open enrollment, EOPs (Educational Opportunity Programs), preferential/affirmative action admissions, and the development of special academic courses (e.g., "basic" writing) brought a new and different brand of student into the college English classroom. Unlike the returning military veterans and other working-class white students of the 1950s and early 1960s, this new student spoke a language which not only reflected a different class, but also a different race, culture, and historical experience.

The symbolic turning point was 1968. The assassination of Dr. Martin Luther King, Jr. during the CCCC Annual Convention in Minneapolis brought the organization "shockingly to an awareness of one of its major responsibilities: to communicate" (Irmscher, 1968). In his memorial to King in the May 1968 issue of *CCC*, the editor, William Irmscher, goes on to indicate that the organization now had a "new demand" placed upon it. Although he does not put it in these terms, for the first time, race/Color as a central component of linguistic difference became an in-yo-face issue that the organization could no longer ignore. Not that race/Color was a new issue that had somehow just fallen from the sky. Rather, the organization had heretofore simply proceeded as if racial differences did not exist and as if race did not need to be taken into account in the life of 4Cs. In a sense, Irmscher's half-page homage to King symbolizes the loss of innocence, a loss reflected not only in this organization in 1968, but in American society at large.

Kelly's speech, "Murder of the American Dream," was delivered at the Annual Meeting in Minneapolis after the news of King's assassination and reprinted in the May 1968 issue of *CCC*. In this brief, but powerful work, this most eloquent Sista reproaches CCCC for the lack of Black representation in the program, rebukes the organization for the exclusion of Black intellectual and literary products in anthologies, and takes it to task for the way it deals with Black Language. Kelly states:

> Here we meet to discuss the dialects of Black students and how we can upgrade or, if we're really successful, just plain *replace* them. Why aren't there Blacks here who will talk about the emergence of an image among Blacks which does not permit them to even bother with the question of whether or not the white man understands their dialect? . . . Why aren't there Blacks . . . [dealing] with the richness and values of the language of the Black ghetto? . . . such ideas have been dealt with and their complexities examined. Why weren't these papers presented here?
>
> (1968, p. 107)

Subsequently, and as a direct response to her "Murder of the Dream" speech, Kelly was invited to co-edit an issue of *CCC,* which appeared later that year, in December 1968. That issue includes articles by four African American scholars, a first for *CCC.*

The late Sarah Webster Fabio poses the questions, "What is Black?" (also the title of her article) and "What is Black language?" Indicating that these questions were frequently being asked during that time, she defines Black Language as

> direct, creative, intelligent communication between black people based on a shared reality, awareness, understanding which generates interaction; it is a rhetoric which places premium on imagistic renderings and concretizations of abstractions, poetic usages of language, idiosyncrasies – those individualized stylistic nuances . . . which . . . hit "home" and evoke truth . . .
>
> (1968, p. 286)

James Banks's "Profile of the Black American" deals with a range of cultural issues, one of which is language. His brief comments on language and composition assert the legitimacy of Black students' language and downplays the need to master "standard English":

> When evaluating their compositions, the teacher must realize that these students emanate from a different culture . . . which possesses a language with a different structure and grammar, but nevertheless a valid structure and grammar. Thus the teacher must concentrate on the quality of ideas in the composition rather than on the student's use or misuse of standard American English grammar. Our mission is to teach these students how to think, to describe their environment, and to encourage their

creativity ... Grammar is incidental; the student will later pick up standard English grammar if he sees a need for it and if we have succeeded in developing his reflective and problem-solving skills.

(1968, p. 296)

In the same issue, Leonard Greenbaum's "Prejudice and Purpose in Compensatory Programs" predicts an Orwellian nightmare for those seeking to suppress African American speech and other non-mainstream languages.

Dialect has positive aspects ... that are not part of standardized English ... The desire to eliminate dialect is an egocentric solution proposed out of power and out of traditional modes of education that have always shunned the experimental in favor of the pragmatic. This was how the "system" dealt with immigrants at the turn of the century and just prior to and during World War II, and it is how, similarly, some propose it should deal with rural or inner-city dialects in the 1960s. This desire, no doubt, will win out. I can predict what lies in our future – a uniform society, most likely in uniform ... we are hastening to our meeting with Orwell.

(1968, p. 305)

It is interesting that several of the articles in this special issue touch on the question of language even when that is not a particular article's central focus. The late Elisabeth McPherson's brilliant, thoughtful piece, "Hats Off – or On – to the Junior College," employs, as a point of departure, a controversy about male students wearing their hats inside a community college building.

There was more involved than a possibly out-of-date, middle-class custom. There was a racial issue, too; it was only the Negro students for whom the hats, very narrow-brimmed and often very expensive, were a badge and a symbol.

In the course of her discussion, she touches on the matter of language as a mark of identity and culture, citing the work of linguist Benjamin Whorf and invokes the hat metaphor to address the question of dialects:

The question of usage ... is very much like the question of hats. Which is the more important status symbol for the student: leaving his hat on and keeping his own identity? Taking it off and learning to be an imitation WASP? This is a decision only the student can make ...
    If changing his dialect is not the student's own idea ... we have no right to insist on it simply because we prefer the sound of our own. If we are a college, and not just defenders of the status quo, we've more important business than worrying about dialect changes.

(1968, p. 322)

Three years after the publication of this essay, McPherson would become a crucial member of the "Students' Right to their Own Language" Committee. Nearly two decades later, in 1987, she accepted appointment to the Language Policy Committee, on which she continued to serve despite a lingering and debilitating illness.

"STUDENTS' RIGHT TO THEIR OWN LANGUAGE"

This language policy resolution followed logically on the heels of 4Cs dramatic 1968 Annual Meeting and the subsequent 1968 special issue of *CCC*. These English professionals, like other segments of American society, were affected by the social movements and political realities outside of Academe. The "Students' Right" resolution represented a critical mechanism for CCCC to address its internal contradictions as the resistance of the Black Liberation Movement called the Question of justice in all areas of American life – including language and education. Some language scholars had begun to question bidialectalism as a goal for the linguistically marginalized, arguing that the bidialectalism philosophy was only being promoted for those on the margins. Further, since linguistic research had demonstrated the linguistic adequacy of "nonstandard" dialects, why wouldn't the "system" accept them? To reject them was tantamount to making them *deficient*.

The charge to scholar-activists was to campaign for the wider social legitimacy of all languages and dialects, and to struggle, wherever one had a shot at being effective, to bring about mainstream recognition and acceptance of the culture, history and language of those on the margins. It was this line of thinking that moved me to get involved in CCCC and the "Students' Right" struggle. It also moved my peers in other fields to become involved in their respective professional organizations. Most of us had been baptized in the fire of social protest and street activism. No romantic idealists, we knew the roadblocks and limitations involved in trying to effectuate change within the System. But we also knew that without "vision, the people perish." Besides, as I commented to a fellow scholar and kindred spirit (a psychologist, who was one of the founders of the Association of Black Psychologists), what else was we gon do while we was waitin for the Revolution to come?

In this socio-historical climate, in the fall of 1971, C's officers appointed a small committee to draft a policy resolution on students' dialects. I was a member of that committee – the "Students' Right" committee[4] – and by the time of the 1972 vote, I was also a member of the CCCC Executive Committee. In March, 1972, the Executive Committee was presented with the "Students' Right," position statement, a terse, highly controversial, and, according to some, an explosive paragraph. The Executive Committee passed the resolution at its November, 1972 meeting, promptly enlarged the Committee, and charged it with developing a background document to elaborate on the meaning and implications of the "Students' Right" language policy. The Executive Committee realized that this resolution would generate controversy and that many language arts professionals, including those teaching college English, held a variety of myths and misconceptions about languages and dialects. Our job on the "Students' Right" committee was to amass the latest scholarship and research on language diversity and on language matters relevant to the teaching of composition. The monograph we produced would be distributed to the membership in preparation for a vote. At the Annual Meeting in Anaheim, California in April of 1974, the "Students' Right to Their Own Language" passed by a wide margin and subsequently became organizational policy. That fall, the resolution and supporting background document were published as a special issue of *CCC*.

As an organization, 4Cs was responding to a developing crisis in college classrooms, a crisis caused by the cultural–linguistic mismatch between higher education and the non-traditional (i.e., by virtue of color and class) students who were making their imprint upon the academic landscape for the first time in history. The movement in the streets was forcing US society to level the playing field, and to make it possible for students from the margins to enter colleges and universities. Most of these students, however bright, did not have command of the grammar and conventions of Academic Discourse, nor of everyday "Standard American English." Yet they often had other communicative strengths – creative ideas, logical and persuasive reasoning powers, innovative ways of talking about the ordinary and mundane. How was this contradiction to be resolved? What professional advice could CCCC provide to frustrated instructors charged with teaching English to this new and different student clientele? What could be done to help these students succeed in the English classroom? And in the long view, how could the English classroom, as part of the higher education of these students, prepare them for life beyond Academe? The Introduction to the "Students' Right" background document indicates that 4Cs was sharply and painfully cognizant of these issues

> Through their representatives on Boards of Education and Boards of Regents, businessmen, politicians, parents, and the students themselves insist that the values taught by the schools must reflect the prejudices held by the public. The English profession, then, faces a dilemma: until

> public attitudes can be changed — and it is worth remembering that the
> past teaching in English classes has been largely responsible for those atti-
> tudes — shall we place our emphasis on what the vocal elements of the
> public think it wants or on what the actual available linguistic evidence
> indicates we should emphasize?
>
> (CCC, 1974, p. 1)

In the "Students' Right" resolution and in the subsequent background document, we sought to accomplish three broad goals: (1)
to heighten consciousness of language attitudes; (2) to promote the
value of linguistic diversity; and (3) to convey facts and information about language and language variation that would enable
instructors to teach their non-traditional students — and ultimately
all students — more effectively. In pursuit of these goals, the
Introduction of the background document posed several issues for
English teachers to consider:

> We need to discover whether our attitudes toward "educated English"
> are based on some inherent superiority of the dialect itself or on the
> social prestige of those who use it. We need to ask ourselves whether
> our rejection of students who do not adopt the dialect most familiar to
> us is based on any real merit in our dialect or whether we are actually
> rejecting the students themselves, rejecting them because of their racial,
> social, and cultural origins.
>   . . . Our major emphasis has been on uniformity, in both speech and
> writing; would we accomplish more, both educationally and ethically, if we
> shifted that emphasis to precise, effective, and appropriate communication
> in diverse ways, whatever the dialect?

To convey facts and information about the latest research on
language and language diversity, the background document was
structured in the form of fifteen discussion sections, each beginning
with a question implicit in the resolution. All of the fifteen questions
were similar in content, if not form, to areas of concern about which
members of the profession were agonizing as they sought to understand what it means, in practice, to advocate, in theory, that students
have a right to their own language. The questions were:

1   What do we mean by dialect?
2   Why and how do dialects differ?
3   How do we acquire our dialects?
4   Why do some dialects have more prestige than others?
5   How can concepts from modern linguistics help clarify the question
     of dialects?
6   Does dialect affect the ability to read?
7   Does dialect affect the ability to write?

8   Does dialect limit the ability to think?

9   What is the background for teaching one "grammar"?

10   What do we do about handbooks?

11   How can students be offered dialect options?

12   What do we do about standardized tests?

13   What are the implications of this resolution for students' work in courses other than English?

14   How does dialect affect employability?

15   What sort of knowledge about language do English teachers need?

Finally, the background document concluded with an annotated bibliography of 129 entries keyed to the answers to the fifteen questions.

Of course Black Americans weren't the only "submerged minorities" forcing the question, "Should the schools try to uphold language variety, or to modify it, or to eradicate it?" Yet a good deal of the examples, illustrations, bibliographic references, etc. focused on Black speech. This is logical given not only the large numbers of African Americans among the oppressed, but also given that Blacks were the first to force the moral and Constitutional questions of equality in this country. Further, among marginal groups in the US, Blacks are pioneers in social protest and have waged the longest, politically principled struggle against domination. It is an ironic footnote in American life that whenever Blacks have struggled and won social gains for themselves, they have made possible gains for other groups – even for some white folk! The nineteenth-century emancipation of African slaves in this country paved the way for the first Women's Movement, and Black champions for the abolition of slavery – Frederick Douglass and Sojourner Truth, for example – fought vigorously for women's rights. Thus, *Black* students' right to *their* own language made possible the claim of *all* students' right to their own language.

BEHIND THE SCENES

Both supporters and detractors have assumed that the "Students' Right" Committee was comprised of like-minded individuals. Although all of us were committed to addressing the language crisis facing the new wave of students in English classrooms, and to helping resolve this crisis, there was a wide range of personal styles and great diversity in political ideologies among us. On one level, we might have been considered "progressives," but we clearly had our own internal contradictions. And so in the production of the resolution and the supporting monograph, our long hours of scholarly work were accompanied virtually every step of the way by intense political and ideological struggle.

One of our early debates occurred over the use of "his," i.e., "students' right to his own language," which was the wording of the original resolution. While a couple of the women in the group put forth strong objections to the masculinist tone, one of the men thought the whole argument was silly and a waste of time because the generic "he" had been used for centuries, and everybody knew it included women too. He then began to quote several historical examples, going way back to the Bible. One of the women inter-rupted this filibuster-like strategy and suggested that we should call it "students' right to her own language" since "her" was just as generic as "he." Then we tried "his or her," but someone objected to this on grounds of verbosity. We even tried using "people," but someone remarked that we were dealing with "students," not "people." Whereupon a lengthy debate ensued over whether or not the labels "people" and "students" could be used interchange-ably. At the time, my Womanist consciousness was just developing, and so I was not very vocal in this hours-long debate, for which I was soundly blessed out by one of the women when we took a bathroom break, who wanted to know what kind of linguist was I that was "afraid" to challenge male hegemony? The debate was finally resolved when Elisabeth McPherson, genius that my girl was, proposed that we cast the wording in third person plural. We had all been so locked into our linguistic prisons that we hadn't even thought of this quite simple solution to the problem. While this issue seems old hat now as we head for the twenty-first century, lest we forget, concerns about sexism in language did not always exist – even among many women.

Nor were we of identical persuasion on the issue of America's linguistic ills and the solutions to them. Hey, some members were even opposed to the use of four-letter words among us, not just the big, bad ones, but even the little ones like "damn" and "hell." (I report with pride that I was the first to introduce "cussing" into Committee discourse, to the relief of one of the males on the Committee.) The debates that were going on in the society at large, in the language profession, and in this organization about how to address America's social and sociolinguistic problems went on among us, filtered through the prism of language. Why should linguistic minorities have to learn two languages and majority members of society get by on one? That's linguistic domination. Why not accept a student paper with nonstandard features of language if the message was clear and the argument well supported? That's what the "right" to their own language means. No, giving two grades, one for content, one for grammar, is a cop-out, you are still saying there is something "wrong" with the writer. Let's make the medium the message and write this monograph in a combination of Black English. Spanglish and "Standard American English." And so it went.

It has been said that politics is the art of compromise. And compromise we did. After the lengthy debates and verbal duels, we finally produced a document that we all felt we could live with. Credit for blending the multiple writing styles into a readable document goes to the talented editorial hand of Richard ("Jix") Lloyd-Jones and the skillful diplomacy of the late Melvin Butler, linguist and Committee Chair, whose tragic, untimely death prevented him from witnessing the fruits of his labor.

REACTIONS TO "STUDENTS' RIGHT"

There was fall-out throughout the entire educational spectrum, on all levels, from kindergarten to graduate school. Stringent, vociferous objections were put forth. There were calls for the resolution to be rescinded and the background document recalled. Some blasted 4Cs for abdicating its responsibility and pandering to "wide-eyed" liberals in the field. Others accused the organization of a "sinister plot" to doom speakers of "divergent" dialects to failure in higher education by telling them that their stigmatized language was acceptable. A few simply said that 4Cs had done lost they cotton-pickin minds.

On the other hand, there were many who embraced the spirit of the resolution. They thanked CCCC for the supporting document, which many found extremely helpful, even as they acknowledged its flaws. Some complimented the organization for its "moral and professional courage." Others stepped to the challenge of developing language and literacy assignments to "tap the potential" of marginalized students. A few simply asked 4 Cs why it took yall so long.

Ideas about student-centered approaches to instruction and about sensitivity to students' language/dialects have by now become fairly commonplace not only in the discourse community of Composition Studies, but also in the language teaching profession generally. Which is not to say that everyone subscribes to these ideas today, just that talk about them is no longer perceived as "weird." However, in the context of the 1970s, to promulgate ideas about students' right to *anything* was a bold, new style of pedagogy. Such ideas elicited strong reactions from English professionals (irrespective of whether they supported the "Students' Right" resolution or not). Freeman (1975) examined Constitutional Amendments and court cases that provide legal justification for students' right to their own language. Citing such cases as *Wisconsin v. Yoder* and *Griggs v. Duke Power*, he argued that language rights can be seen as protected by custom and that there is a legal basis for hiring instructors who are skilled in the dialect or language of the students they will instruct. Clark (1975) critiqued the background document for what he deemed hypocrisy in its recommendation that teachers inform students preparing for certain occupations about the necessity of Edited American English. He asserted that this advice undermined the resolution's claim about all dialects being equally valuable, implicitly valorized standard English, and was a cop-out on the part of 4Cs. Taking the issue to the philosophical level, Smith (1976) contended that language is a social act, and that the resolution was a contradiction in terms, as "no one has a right to his own language."

The organization held its ground, it did not revoke the resolution, nor did it recall the background document. (In fact, that 25-year-old document is still in print and can be obtained by special order from *CCC*.)

The "Students' Right to Their Own Language" was a policy formulated to address the contradictions developed in the midst of a major paradigm shift in education, itself the result of a major paradigm shift in the social order. Educators across the Nation and on all educational levels from kindergarten through graduate school were encountering the new brand of students and experiencing common classroom crises. The "Students' Right" language policy opened up a national dialog about language diversity and professional responsibility. As Lloyd-Jones, a long-time CCCC leader and member of the "Students' Right" Committee said:

> The statement had an intellectual base in sociolinguistics, but its energy came from support of social diversity. It forced a reconsideration of "correctness." It implied a model of language as "transactional" rather than as artifact. Behind the anger of the political oratory was acceptance of a thesis about the nature of language.

> (1992, p. 490)

In due course, other professional organizations adopted policies reflecting the new research and scholarship on language diversity. But lest we forget, the Conference on College Composition and Communication was the pioneer.

CCCC DURING THE "SECOND RECONSTRUCTION"

Although many English professionals greeted the "Students' Right" policy with high enthusiasm, still a great degree of lingering confusion existed – "Well, then, if I don't correct the grammatical errors, what do I *do*?" as one very well-meaning instructor queried. The "Students' Right" background document was welcomed because it was informative in terms of theory; however, it did not go far enough in praxis. CCCC leadership acknowledged the need for something more in the form of explicit teaching materials, sample lesson plans, and a more practically-oriented pedagogy. Thus, in 1976, the Executive Committee appointed the "Selection and Editorial Committee for Activities Supporting Students' Right to Their Own Language," on which three of the original "Students' Right" Committee members – McPherson, Lloyd-Jones, and I – served. This new "Students' Right" Committee was charged with assembling, for publication, practical classroom assignments, activities, lectures, and teaching units that would show and tell how to apply the philosophy of the "Students' Right" resolution to the day-to-day experience of teaching and learning. This Committee spent nearly *four* years compiling and editing teaching materials, solicited from practitioners at all levels of language arts education, only to be informed that 4Cs had "reluctantly decided" not to publish the collection. What had happened within this organization since the passage of the "Students' Right" resolution reflected the changed national climate of the 1980s.

Owing to the socio-political, educational and economic decline in Black and other historically disenfranchised communities during the 1980s, some political theorists, such as Walters (e.g., 1993), have dubbed the years, 1980–92, the "Second Reconstruction." The "first" Reconstruction had been launched in the late 1870s, with the Federal Government's abandonment of ex-slaves to Southern governments, which promptly rolled back the freedmen's political gains, ushered in US-style apartheid and began an era of lynchings and brutal assaults against Blacks which would not be redressed until the Black Freedom Struggle of the 1960s. After the promise and *some* fulfillment of the social movements of the 1960s and 1970s, the US moved to a more conservative climate on the social, political, and educational fronts, a move, according to Walters, that was solidifed in 1980 by the election of President Ronald Reagan and the subsequent Reagan–Bush years (1980–92) in the White House. By 1980, the mood of 4Cs, like the mood of America, seemed to have shifted from change and promise to stagnation and dreams deferred.

It was within the climate of the Second Reconstruction that Thomas J. Farrell's 1983 bombshell, "IQ and Standard English," appeared in *CCC*. Like some of his contemporaries in other fields, Farrell re-raised the old linguistic–cognitive deficiency theory about Blacks. Even though he asserted that the "mean IQ difference" between "black ghetto children" and speakers of "standard English" has "nothing to do with genetics or race, *per se*," still he contended that:

> The non-standard forms of the verb "to be" in . . . Black English may affect the thinking of the users . . . Black ghetto children do not use the standard forms of the verb "to be" . . . Many of those same black ghetto children have difficulty learning to read, and they do not score highly on measures of abstract thinking . . . I am hypothesizing that learning the full standard deployment of the verb "to be" is integral to developing Level II thinking because the deployment of that verb played a part in the development of abstract thinking in ancient Greece.
>
> (1983, pp. 477, 479)

The publication of Farrell's article in 1983 recalls Lloyd's 1951 reaction to the publication of Knickerbocker's essay: "[Its] appearance in the bulletin of the CCCC is a little shocking . . . The assertion or implication that the language of a person [who uses certain linguistic patterns] is superior on that account is a professional error which no English teacher should commit in print, and no editor should permit him to make." The Farrell article is a crucial installment in the history of the language rights struggle. First, it is a reminder that old arguments, which are assumed to be dead and long since buried, can resurface in new and potentially more dangerous forms, distorting current research for supporting evidence. Second, despite my Lloydian reaction to this article's appearance in *CCC*, and notwithstanding my disillusionment about 4Cs rejection of the follow-up volume to the "Students' Right" publication, by 1983 there had emerged a critical mass of language and literacy practitioners who could and did provide solid rebuttals, relying on the tremendous body of research on Ebonics that had been conducted since the 1960s. For example, Karen Greenberg argued in her brilliant response (the lead essay in a lengthy collection of "counterstatements") that "be" verb constructions are simply applied according to different but identifiable rules of Black English. She blasts Farrell's terminology (e.g., "paratactic" and "hypotactic") as "pseudo-scientific," adding only the "gloss of respectability" (1984, p. 458).

"NATIONAL LANGUAGE POLICY"

In the 1998 celebration of African American History Month, there was a commercial for Mickey D's [gloss: Ebonics for McDonald's] which featured a white father and his young son browsing through a gallery with paintings of African American heroes and she-roes. The father points to the work of Jacob Lawrence, and tells his kid "That's Jacob Lawrence, a famous painter." Next, they come upon a painting of Harriet Tubman, and the father says, "That's Harriet Tubman, a leader in the Underground Railroad." The kid exclaims, "Wow, that's cool" as the voice-over comes on saying, "It's not just Black History, it's *American* history." [emphasis Mickey D's]

The recognition that the story of Africans in America is the story of all Americans, that indeed, the history of other marginalized groups is also *American* history, marks the beginning of this nation's journey toward a mature social consciousness. Although the US is comprised of diverse racial and ethnic groups, the common goal is to make this democratic experiment a success. In this quest, and in objective historical reality, the experience of one group is inextricably bound up with the experience of other groups. As King often said during his lifetime, we are one nation, and we must all learn how to live together, or we shall all die together.

Much like the theme of the Mickey D's commercial, and the legacy of King, the CCCC "National Language Policy," passed in 1988, is a linguistic imperative for *all* groups, not just Blacks, Browns, the poor, and others on the margins. This policy does not seek to replace the "Students' Right" resolution, which was the right move for that historical period, filling a deep pedagogical void. Rather, the "National Language Policy" symbolizes the next logical, evolutionary stage after the "Students' Right" campaign.

In the Fall of 1986, California passed its English Language Amendment to the State Constitution, making it the first state in contemporary times to establish, by law, a policy of "English Only," that is, English as the only officially recognized language of the State. A number of organizations and caucuses opposed California's measure and the growing formation of an English Only Movement. Within 4Cs, the opposition came during the 1987 convention from the Progressive Composition Caucus (PCC); now reconstituted under a different name. The Caucus described itself as a group of "composition instructors who view writing as a potentially liberating activity and teach from a socialist–feminist perspective. Our curriculum often emphasizes non-canonical literature and exposes sexist, racist, homophobic and corporate manipulation of language" (Caucus newsletter, April 1987). Although PCC wanted 4Cs to take a stand against English Only, there was sharp tension between PCC and the CCCC Executive Committee and leadership over the issue of conducting the Convention in a hotel involved in a labor action by hotel workers. Uncertain whether or not they could trust 4Cs to do the right thing, PCC decided that their sense-of-the-house motion should not only call for concerted opposition against English Only but should also include the name of someone they trusted to carry out the mandated opposition. The day before the Annual Meeting, PCC asked me if I would accept the charge and if I would allow my name to be included in their resolution. As I listened to their arguments, all I could think about was the dissin and doggin I had endured during the "Students' Right" years, and I kept saying "no way."

At the CCCC Annual Meeting in 1987, the Progressive Composition Caucus submitted the following sense-of-the-house motion:

> *Preamble*: As the leading professional organization dealing with language and literacy, the CCCC should be in the forefront of the effort to decide issues of language policy.
>
> Resolved: That the CCCC support the NCTE resolution opposing English-only legislation by appointing a well funded task force, chaired by Geneva Smitherman, to articulate the issues and formulate and implement strategies to educate the public, educational policy-makers, and legislatures; further, that this issue receive major emphasis in the 1988 Conference theme, "Language, Self, and Society."

The motion passed. The task force that was appointed was called the "Language Policy Committee" (LPC).[5] Its charge was to develop a proactive response to the English Only Movement for consideration by the CCCC Executive Committee, to compile information on English Only, and to network with other professional organizations and groups mounting English Only opposition campaigns.

4Cs kept its part of the bargain. The organization provided funding, full support and resources for the LPC to carry out its charge. At the Annual Meeting in March, 1988, the following language policy resolution passed unanimously:

Background

> The National Language Policy is a response to efforts to make English the "official" language of the United States. This policy recognizes the historical reality that, even though English has become the language of wider communication, we are a multilingual society. All people in a democratic society have the right to education, to employment, to social services, and to equal protection under the law. No one should be denied these

or any civil rights because of linguistic differences. This policy would enable everyone to participate in the life of this multicultural nation by ensuring continued respect both for English, our common language, and for the many other languages that contribute to our rich cultural heritage.

CCCC National Language Policy

Be it resolved that CCCC members promote the National Language Policy adopted at the Executive Committee meeting on 16 March 1988. This policy has three inseparable parts:

1   To provide resources to enable native and non-native speakers to achieve oral and literate competence in English, the language of wider communication.

2   To support programs that assert the legitimacy of native languages and dialects and ensure that proficiency in one's mother tongue will not be lost.

3   To foster the teaching of languages other than English so that native speakers of English can rediscover the language of their heritage or learn a second language.

(Conference on College Composition and
Communication, 1988, brochure)

The adoption and implementation of this policy across the land would mean that on *all* levels of education, every student would be required to develop competence in at least three languages. One of these would be, of course, the Language of Wider Communication, which everyone would learn. The second would be the student's Mother Tongue – e.g., Spanish, Polish, Ebonics, Italian, Arabic, Appalachian English. The legitimacy of the home language would be reinforced, and students' ability to function in that language would be part of their expanded linguistic repertoire by the end of twelve years of schooling. Third, every student would have command of at least one totally foreign language. That language would vary, depending on the options and social conditions in local communities and schools. In sum, the CCCC "National Language Policy" stresses the need not just for marginalized Americans but *all* Americans to be bi/multilingual in order to be prepared for citizenship in the twenty-first century global, multilingual/multicultural world.

CONCLUSION

If it is true, as Gere and Smith (1979) have asserted, that changing language attitudes is tantamount to changing a world view, then there may not be a lot that a language policy from a professional organization can do about the myths and misconceptions about language that continue to plague the struggle for language rights. These myths are prevalent not only among the public but even among those in the professions. One cannot erase long-held attitudes and deeply-entrenched biases and stereotypes with the stroke of a pen – you know, go henceforth and sin linguistically no more. On the other hand, those who (whether consciously or unconsciously) display what linguist Phillipson calls "linguicism" (1992) are products of the school (and the college, though in fewer numbers) because everybody goes through school. The classroom, then, is a major player in shaping language attitudes, and the classroom that is particularly crucial for the formation of ideas about language is that of the K–12 level. And here is where 4Cs, as a post-secondary organization, has very limited influence.

In 1971, after the formation of what was to become the "Students' Right" committee, 4Cs leadership and members began lobbying within the National Council of Teachers of English (NCTE) to endorse the "Students' Right" language policy. However, this did not come to pass. Instead, at the 1974 NCTE Convention, the membership passed a weak version of a language rights resolution. It was simply called NCTE Resolution number 74.2, which carefully bypassed the label "Students' Right." While Resolution 74.2 "accept[s] the linguistic premise that all these dialects are equally efficient as systems of communication," it goes on to "affirm" that students need to learn the "conventions of what has been called written edited American English." This was a posture that 4Cs deliberately and consciously sought to avoid in its policy resolution because usage, spelling, punctuation, and other "conventions" of "written edited American English" were (are?) typically the *only* aspects of the writing process that teachers focus on. Thus, the "Students' Right" background document had asserted that

> dialect ... plays little if any part in determining whether a child will ultimately acquire the ability to write EAE ... Since the issue is not the capacity of the dialect itself, the teacher can concentrate on building up the students' confidence in their ability to write ... If we can convince our students that spelling, punctuation, and usage are less important than content, we have removed a major obstacle in their developing the ability to write.
>
> (1974, p. 8)

Many people in the field (and, I would wager, most of those outside the field) erroneously credit the NCTE with the "Students' Right" resolution. I have repeatedly heard this from numerous people over the years since 4Cs passed its resolution in 1974. In the *Journal of English Linguistics'* special 1998 issue on Ebonics, linguist

Walt Wolfram bemoans the persistence of negative language attitudes despite the efforts of professional organizations:

> Furthermore, the adoption of strong position statements on dialect diversity
> by professional organizations such as the National Council of Teachers of
> English (namely, the statement on Students' Right to Their Own Language)
> (Butler 1974, 2) . . . barely made a dent on entrenched attitudes and prac-
> tices with respect to language differences.
>
> (1998, p. 109).

In order for a "dent" to be made in these attitudes and practices,
the "Students' Right" language policy needed to be embraced by
K-12 teachers. Adoption by NCTE would have gone a long way
towards building the K-12 support necessary to make such a "dent"
because NCTE (with its some 100,000 members and public policy
connections) is a major player in the K-12 language arts arena. The
struggle waged by 4Cs leaders and members to get NCTE support
for the resolution was acrimonious and fierce, in-yo-face kind of
fights. (To date, some of them folk still don't speak to each other!)
And so it is a bitter irony that NCTE is credited with passage of
this progressive language policy. In retrospect, NCTE's rejection
might have been anticipated because its language rights history is a
mixed one. For instance back in 1917, NCTE led a national promotion of "Better Speech Week," with a language correctness pledge
to be recited by students on a regular basis. (See "Ebonics, *King*,
and Oakland: Some Folk Don't Believe Fat Meat is Greasy," this
volume, pp. 150–62, for the pledge.)

It is crucial to have organizational positions as weapons which
language rights warriors can wield against the opponents of linguistic
democratization. "Students' Right" and the "National Language
Policy" provide the necessary intellectual basis and rhetorical framework for waging language debates and arguments. Further, since
intellectuals provide the ideological rationale for public policy, it
was and is important for organizations like 4Cs to go on record as
supporting language rights. Organizational pronouncements about
language can and do have influence and impact. Case in point.
There was a time, up until around the mid-1970s, that speech tests
were required to qualify for entry into university teacher education
programs. People like me flunked these linguistically, culturally, and
gender-biased tests and got forced into speech therapy. These tests
have now been eradicated. This is a direct result of the intellectual
and the activist wings of the social movements of the 1960s and
1970s, manifested in the Academy in research that came out of
sociolinguistics and in professional organizational positions like
"Students' Right to Their Own Language."

It has been said that those who do not learn from the past are doomed to repeat it. A genuine recognition of African American students' culture and language is crucial if the literacy crisis in urban school districts, such as Oakland, California, is to be addressed. I say "genuine" because, in spite of the controversy surrounding the "Student's Right to Their Own Language," the bicultural, bilingual model has *never* really been tried. Lip-service is about all most teachers have given this model, even at the height of the Civil Rights and Black Liberation Movements. The game plan has always been linguistic and cultural absorption of the Other into the dominant culture, indoctrination of the outsiders into the existing System, to remake those on the margins in the image of the patriarch, to reshape the outsiders into talking, acting, thinking, and (to the extent possible) looking like the insiders. Multilingual scholars and activists frame the issue as one of language *shift* vs. language *maintenance* (e.g., Fishman 1989, 1991). That is, the philosophy of using the native language as a vehicle to teach and eventually *shift* native speakers away from their home language vs. a social and pedagogical model that teaches the target language while providing support for *maintaining* the home language.

The spirit of resistance in the "Students' Right to Their Own Language," as well as in the CCCC "National Language Policy," is an important symbol of change. Of course the battle is not over; there is still work to be done in the vineyard.

In the December 1997 issue of *CCC,* Ball and Lardner revisit *King* (the "Black English case"; see "'What Go Round Come Round': *King* in Perspective," this volume, pp. 132–49, for an analysis of the case). Beginning with the teachers in *King* in terms of their knowledge (or lack of such) of language principles, Ball and Lardner analyze the constructs underlying current "teacher knowledge." They contend that teacher "lore" often substitutes for scientific knowledge about languages and dialects and that "[teachers are] willfully ignorant . . . and "think they should be free . . . to ignore . . . modern linguistic scholarship" (p. 476). This essay recalls Lloyd's battle for linguistic enlightenment forty-eight years ago, and in the context of this historical narrative says that the struggle for language rights continues.

In the same 1997 issue of *CCC,* Coleman demonstrates the ineffectiveness of traditional grammar approaches which result in "iatrogenic" effects (a borrowing from medicine, meaning that the so-called corrective creates new problems). His work, applicable to Black Language speakers, as well as to ESL students (English as a Second Language), draws upon linguistic knowledge to pinpoint specific speech practices and to suggest ways of teaching literacy that are informed by knowledge of those practices. Like Ball and Lardner's article, Coleman's essay also recalls Lloyd and the (now-old) "New Linguistics." However, Coleman's work says that although the struggle for language rights continues, we can win.

NOTES

INTRODUCTION: FROM GHETTO LADY TO CRITICAL LINGUIST

1   The sharecropping system, which was instituted among newly-freed slaves after the Civil War, provided a share of a farm's crop in exchange for a Black family's labor to produce the crop. The family was allowed a portion – e.g., a third – of the crop (usually cotton) and provided with a house, sometimes food, and other necessities, all of which were deducted from the family's share of the crop at the end of the year. John Hope Franklin notes that the "cost of maintenance was so great that at the end of the year the freedman was indebted to his employer for most of what he made, and sometimes it was more than he made" (1967, p. 311). As one ex-slave put it: "Dem sharecroppuhs is jes like slaves" (Gaspar and Hine, 1996, p. 29).

2   The concept of the "Talented Tenth" was put forth by W. E. B. DuBois in his ideological formulation for Black liberation (1903; 1968). It was his view that the upper 10 percent of the Black population – the intelligentsia, professionals, business people, etc. – should take leadership and responsibility for the other 90 percent – the masses – and be in the forefront of the Black Struggle. Otherwise, Blacks would have white leadership forced upon them. In this connection, DuBois also urged the higher education of this group who would be expected to return to the community and contribute their talents to the advancement of the entire race. Some Black political theorists have questioned the validity of this ideology given the context of Blacks in a quasi-colonial existence under American capitalism.

I   INTRODUCTION TO EBONICS

1   "African Holocaust" is a term used by Black writers, Rappers, activists, and others to refer to the enslavement of African people in the US and throughout the Diaspora. The term captures the experience of the wholesale disruption of African communities in the European slave trade, during which it is estimated that as many as one hundred million Africans were forcibly removed from their native lands, not all of whom reached the "New World." Millions perished as a result of torture, disease and the horrendous Middle Passage across the Atlantic Ocean. A number of contemporary Black historians and other scholars have argued that the consequences of the African Holocaust and its impact on present-day Black communities have yet to be fully assessed.

2   Other African American Verbal Traditions are:
        1   Call–Response;
        2   Tonal Semantics;
        3   Narrativizing;
        4   The Dozens/Snappin;
        5   Proverb Use.

2 FROM AFRICAN TO AFRICAN AMERICAN

Research for this article was made possible by a Research Stimulation Grant from Wayne State University. My thanks to Vice President Garrett Heberlein at Wayne State. I also wish to acknowledge the assistance of Thomas Kochman, Laverne Summerlin, and Ronald Stephens for assistance with data collection; Alida Quick for assistance with research design, instrumentation, and statistical analysis; and Joshua Bagakas, statistician. Any shortcomings are entirely my own.

1   Countee Cullen (1903–1946) was a Harlem Renaissance poet whose "Heritage" is considered "perhaps the finest statement of the then-popular [1920s] alien-and-exile theme in Black writing" (Davis and Redding, 1971, p. 323). Italics appear in the original poem.

2   The program was aired on 16 January 1989. Panelists were poet Sonia Sanchez, Temple University; political scientist James Turner, Cornell University; and the author.

3   I employ the term *European American* to refer to the "white" population in the United States. Just as *Black*, an adjective, a color term only, is an inappropriate sociolinguistic construction for Africans in America, so too is the label *white* inappropriate for Europeans in America. Further, shifting from *white* to *European American* resolves the seeming contradiction of capitalizing Black while lower-casing *white*, a practice I have used in the past and have defended on the following grounds. First, Black as a racial designation replaced *Negro*, and *Negro* was capitalized (at least since 1930), whereas *white* was not. Second, for people of African descent in America, Black functions to designate race *and* ethnicity because the slave trade and US enslavement practices made it impossible for "Blacks" to trace their ethnic origins in Africa. This has not been the case for Europeans in the US, who typically have labelled themselves German, Italian, English, Irish, Polish, etc., according to their European ethnicity. In fact, it was not until the rise of *Black* that European Americans raised questions about the lower-casing of *white*.

4   While historically women (African American and European American) have been constructed as sex objects, deriving their worth from the number of children they produce, it was only in the slave community that *men* were encouraged to be fruitful and multiply, it being a fairly common practice for masters to designate certain males as breeders, nurturing their promiscuity on the plantation so as to have as many female slaves pregnant as possible. The point is especially significant in light of current discussions about the supposed weakness of the Black family, "fatherless" homes, and the "irresponsibility" of African American men.

5   "Inversion," turning a negative mainstream linguistic or social concept into its opposite – e.g., *bad* = "good" – was first used to describe the language practices of Black English Vernacular speakers by Holt (1972). "Semantic inversion" (Smitherman 1986) is believed to have its origins in West African language use (Turner 1949; Dalby 1969).

6   Although self-administered questionnaires can be problematic – e.g., low return rate among both African and European Americans – there are often particular problems when racial identification of African Americans is requested. In the C1 sample, 84 of the 210 persons who answered the *African American* question refused to give their race, either implicitly (e.g., through omission) or explicitly (e.g., "Why does it matter?" "What difference does it make?" and similar comments written on several questionnaires). Based on the distribution points for these questionnaires, about 60 of the 84 are believed to be African American.

7   See, however, John Baugh's article in the issue of *American Speech* in which this article first appeared. On 29 January 1991, while this article was under editorial review, *The New York Times* (p. A19) published the results of a national poll by the Joint Center for Political and Economic Studies, a research organization specializing in African American political affairs. Based on a survey of 759 African Americans across the country, results indicate that, depending on region, anywhere from 22–28 percent of African Americans outside the South favor *African American* over *Black*; in the South only 15 percent favor the term. Among African American intellectuals, the Joint Center has long been lauded for its work in Black politics. Typically, though, as in the case with Gallup and other political pollsters, samples are based on *registered voters*, thereby excluding many speakers of what John Baugh calls "Black street speech" (1983), as well as many young adults, among whom "voter apathy" is perhaps strongest. I'm raising a question about a type of class bias in public polls involving African Americans. We tried to control for this with a sampling frame designed to include college students in the C1 group, and in the C2 sample, by targeting areas populated by working, unworking, and under-class African Americans. The success of Jackson's "rainbow coalition" politics in mobilizing large numbers of disempowered and young African Americans demonstrates the latent power of the "root culture" (Pasteur and Toldson 1982) to impact on national politics.

8   Note that I do not hyphenate *African American*. The notion of "hyphenated Americans" is an older expression that most "hyphenated Americans" cringe at because it (the term and the hyphen) suggests a hybrid, lacking in authenticity. Note that I also do not hyphenate *European American*. Of course the only (nationally) authentic, i.e. indigenous, group is the Native American/Indian. By a similar line of reasoning, I no longer advocate AfroAmerican (nor its current alternative, AfriAmerican), with or without the hyphen. Both smack of something hybrid, truncated, cut off – "Afro," "Afri," but not "African."

3   WHITE ENGLISH IN BLACKFACE OR, WHO DO I BE?

1   For examples of such programs, see *Non-Standard Dialect*, Board of Education of the City of New York (National Council of Teachers of English, 1968); San-Su C. Lin, *Pattern Practices in the Teaching of Standard English to Students with a Non-Standard Dialect* (USOE Project 1339, 1965); Arno Jewett, Joseph Mersand, Doris Gunderson, *Improving English Skills of Culturally Different Youth in Large Cities* (US Department of Health, Education and Welfare, 1964); *Language Programs for the Disadvantaged* (NCTE, 1965).

2   See, for example, Joan Baratz and Roger Shuy, eds, *Teaching Black Children to Read* (Center for Applied Linguistics, 1969); A. L. Davis, ed., *On the Dialects of Children* (NCTE, 1968); Eldonna L. Evertts, ed., *Dimensions of Dialect* (NCTE, 1967).

3   For the most racist and glaring of these charges, see Fred Hechinger, ed., *Pre-School Education Today* (Doubleday, 1966); for an excellent rebuttal, see William Labov, *Nonstandard English* (NCTE 1970); for a complete overview of the controversy and issues involved as well as historical perspective and rebuttal to the non-verbal claim, see my "Black Idiom and White Institutions," *Negro American Literature Forum*, Fall, 1971.

4   The most thorough and scholarly of these, though a bit technical, is Walter Wolfram, *Detroit Negro Speech* (Center for Applied Linguistics, 1969).

5   Kochman is one linguist who done gone this route; see for instance his "Rapping in the Black Ghetto," *Trans-action*, February 1969. However, he

makes some black folks mad because of what one of my students called his "superfluity," and others shame cause of his exposure of our "bad" street elements. Kochman's data: jam up with muthafuckas and pussy-copping raps collected from Southside Chicago.

6   Johnnetta B. Cole, "Culture: Negro, Black and Nigger," *The Black Scholar*, June, 1970.

7   Amiri Baraka, "Expressive Language," *Home*, pp. 166–72.

8   See her "Toward a New Perspective in Negro English Dialectology," *American Speech* (1965) and "Language and Communicative Styles of Afro-American Children in the United States," *Florida FL Reporter*, VII (Spring/Summer, 1969).

9   See Thomas Kochman, "The Kinetic Element in Black Idiom," paper read at the American Anthropological Association Convention, Seattle, Washington, 1968; also his *Rappin' and Stylin' Out: Communication in Urban Black America*.

10 Frantz Fanon, *Black Skin, White Masks*, pp. 17–40.

4   DISCRIMINATORY DISCOURSE ON AFRICAN AMERICAN SPEECH

1   Scholars pursued this line of linguistic illogic despite scholarly evidence that was being advanced by Hugo Schuchardt of Austria. According to Gilbert's research (1985), Schuchardt, a nineteenth-century language scholar and the first to advance the Creole origins theory of US black English, corresponded with several members of the American Dialect Society, including Harrison. Schuchardt strongly exhorted this newly formed organization to do fieldwork on Gullah, looking particularly at its African linguistic linkage and its Caribbean connection, as well as empirical studies of the black speech communities elsewhere in the Southeastern US. Despite Schuchardt's urgings that such research would be "a real challenge to its skill and ability," neither the American Dialect Society nor other scholars did any research in this vein until forty years later.

2   The "noninvolvement" and "objectivity" of such scholars is akin to the urban policy formulated by Daniel Patrick Moynihan, chief domestic adviser to President Richard Nixon. In a secret memorandum to Nixon, Moynihan advised a policy of what he termed "benign neglect" toward America's racial problem. Specifically, he was recommending nonenforcement of earlier legislation regarding voting laws, laws prohibiting discrimination against blacks and minorities in employment, laws outlawing both *de jure* and *de facto* educational segregation, and in general racial discrimination laws the federal government had clear legal powers to enforce. Black leadership denounced this noninvolvement, nonenforcement "benign neglect" for what it was: criminal negligence.

3   In the US the media shape and control public opinion and thought more than any other institution. In full recognition of this, Labov appeared recently on national network television ("CBS Reports," December 1985) and was extensively interviewed in the *New York Times* (March 1985) and other national press clarifying the significance and implications of his latest research findings that black and white speech in the US are diverging (Labov, 1985). As one of the principal linguists in the research team I organized and coordinated for the *King* case, he also appears in the British Broadcasting Corporation's 1980 film on King and US black English in general. On the role of linguists in social change, Labov states: "The [King] trial was the initiative of black people . . . The whites who have been privileged to play an auxiliary role in this affair know that they are marginal to the success that was achieved. The only permanent advance in

the conditions of life in any field occurs when people take their affairs into their own hands. I believe that this is true of the study of Black English as it is true everywhere" (Labov 1982).

5 "A NEW WAY OF TALKIN' ": LANGUAGE, SOCIAL CHANGE, AND POLITICAL THEORY

1   Presented at the conference, "Race and Class in the Twentieth Century," Oxford University, Oxford, UK, 28–31 January 1988.

6 REVIEW OF NOAM CHOMSKY'S *LANGUAGE AND RESPONSIBILITY*

1   Noam Chomsky, *Language and Responsibility. Based on Conversations with Mitsou Ronat.* Translated from the French by J. Viertel in Collaboration with Noam Chomsky. (New York: Pantheon Books, 1979.)
2   The case of *Martin Luther King Junior Elementary School Children v. Ann Arbor School District Board* was filed in 1977 and tried in Federal court in Detroit, Michigan, in 1979. It represents the first test of the applicability of 1703(f), the language provision of the 1974 Equal Educational Opportunity Act, to Black English speakers. Ruling in favor of the plaintiff children, Judge Charles C. Joiner ordered the Ann Arbor School District to remedy its failure to overcome the language barriers which had prevented the children from exercising their right to equal educational opportunity. In so doing, he relied heavily on the academic scholarship and research on Black English in conjunction with testimony by linguists, educators, and psychologists who had done research in the field. Citing such work in his forty-three-page opinion, Joiner's ruling establishes, within a legal framework, that Black English is a systematic language with roots in Africa and America. For a thorough analysis of the case, see Smitherman (1981a, 1981b) and Labov (1982).
3   Borrowing from Muhammad Ali's famous "rope-a-dope," Gates (1988b) coined the term "trope-a-dope" to refer to rhetorical tropes employed by black signifiers in their verbal devastation of opponents in both the literary and oral traditions.
4   DuBois's use of generic "he" simply reflects the common practice of his time. A supporter of women's causes long before it was fashionable, he is well-known for his tribute to black women, long before this was fashionable too. See DuBois (1887, 1905, [1924] 1970).

7 ENGLISH TEACHER, WHY YOU BE DOING THE THANGS YOU DON'T DO?

1   "Blackman/an unfinished history" by Don L. Lee in *We Walk the Way of the New World*. Copyright © 1970 by Don L. Lee. Reprinted by permission of Broadside Press.
2   James Sledd, "Bi-Dialectalism: The Linguistics of White Supremacy," *English Journal*, 58 (December 1969).
3   Reprinted by permission of Harold Ober Associates Incorporated. Based on *Simple Takes a Wife*, Copyright 1953, by Langston Hughes. *Simply Heavenly*, Copyright © 1956, 1958, 1959 by Langston Hughes and David Martin.

4   Lyrics are from "Deep in Love with You" by Langston Hughes and David
     Martin. © Copyright 1958, Bourne Co., New York City, New York. Used
     by permission.
5   Thomas Kochman, "Rapping in the Black Ghetto," *Trans-Action* (February
     1969) pp. 26–34.
6   William Labov, *The Study of Nonstandard English* (Urbana, Illinois: National
     Council of Teachers of English, 1970).
7   LeRoi, Jones (Amiri Bakara), "Expressive Language," in *Home* (New York:
     Morrow and Company, 1966), pp. 166–72.

8   "WHAT GO ROUND COME ROUND": *KING* IN PERSPECTIVE

1   Since their children's low reading level was among the parents' chief concerns,
     one of Joiner's early attempts at mediation was to suggest that we draft a pro-
     gram targeted at reading. Philosophically, the program stressed inservice train-
     ing, school-wide involvement, community input, youth-training-youth, and
     the integration of multicultural material in all school subjects, at all grade lev-
     els, and for *all* children at King School. Pedagogically, emphasis was on a mul-
     tidisciplinary approach to the teaching of reading, on the use of a language
     experience and black cultural approach, and on oral and written activities aimed
     at developing communicative competence. The defendants objected, contend-
     ing that the program was too broad in scope, that it did not address the spe-
     cific, individual cases of the fifteen plaintiff children, and finally, that they had
     already been using some of the suggested approaches and materials with the
     plaintiff children, but nothing seemed to work.
2   In addition to myself, the biracial team of experts included: Richard Bailey,
     University of Michigan; J. L. Dillard, Northern Louisiana State University;
     Ronald Edmonds, Harvard Graduate School of Education; Daniel N. Fader,
     University of Michigan; Kenneth Haskins, Roxbury Community College;
     Milford Jeremiah, Morgan State University; William Labov, University of
     Pennsylvania; Jerrie Scott, University of Florida; and Gary Simpkins, Watts
     Health Foundation.
3   In 1970, the NAACP, acting on behalf of one white parent and several black
     parents, filed a federal suit against the Detroit School District and the State of
     Michigan (Milliken was governor). The claim was that black children had been
     deliberately segregated and were receiving an inferior education. In his historic
     1971 decision, Judge Stephen Roth ruled that Detroit schools had been inten-
     tionally segregated, and he ordered cross-district busing between Detroit and
     its predominantly white suburbs. At that time, Detroit's schools were 65 per-
     cent black. In his decision, Roth indicated that following the 1967 "civil dis-
     turbance," Detroit had suffered the most rapid exodus of whites of any
     Northern city school system. In 1974 the Supreme Court overturned the Roth
     decision on cross-district busing and thus sounded the death knell for integrat-
     ing Detroit's schools which today are 86 percent black.

9   EBONICS, *KING*, AND OAKLAND: SOME FOLK DON'T BELIEVE FAT MEAT IS GREASY

1   "Some folk don't believe fat meat is greasy" is an Ebonics folk saying, signifyin on fools who insist on adhering to certain beliefs and/or practices in the face of all logical evidence to the contrary.

10 "THE BLACKER THE BERRY, THE SWEETER THE JUICE"

1   Acknowledgements: Special thanks to Joshua Bagakas, Michigan State University statistician, for assistance with statistical design and analysis; to Dr. Jules Goodison, Director of National Assessment for Educational Testing Service and his staff, without whose help this project could not even have been started, much less finished; to family members, Sam and Kathy Brogdon and Bobbi White for those gruelling, twelve-hour days of work at ETS in the summer of 1989; to my Michigan State University research assistants Chanille Bouldes, Tyronda Curry, Angeletta Gourdine, and Ronnie Hopkins for assistance with data entry, coding and most of all, for their patience; to Dr. Schavi Ali, Dr Denise Troutman-Robinson and Ms. Wanda Larrier, for assistance with coding, and for their wisdom and sound advice; and to my secretary, Debbi Sudduth, for persevering. Any mistakes or shortcomings are entirely my own.

11 "HOW I GOT OVUH": AFRICAN WORLD VIEW AND AFRO-AMERICAN ORAL TRADITION

1   *Signification* refers to the act of talking negatively about somebody through stunning and clever verbal put downs. In the black vernacular, it is more commonly referred to as *sigging* or *signifyin*. *The Dozens* is a verbal game based on negative talk about somebody's mother.
2   Also referred to as "announcing" his text, this involves a fairly consistent three-part structure: (1) the act of citing the Scriptural reference from which the message of the sermon is to be taken, followed by (2) the reading of the passage, and concluding with (3) a usually cleverly worded statement articulating the "theme" (message) of the sermon.

12 "IF I'M LYIN, I'M FLYIN": THE GAME OF INSULT IN BLACK LANGUAGE

1   Hurston's classic novel is based on her fieldwork research while she was living in rural Florida, from about 1927–32.
2   In his 1958 *Partisan Review* essay, "Change the Joke and Slip the Yoke," Ellison argued that the "Negro American folk tradition . . . has . . . much to tell us of the faith, humor and adaptability to reality necessary to live in a world which has taken on much of the insecurity and blueslike absurdity known to those who brought it into being."
3   Jess B. Simple (also Semple) is a Harlem folk hero created by Langston Hughes during World War II, who became the subject of hundreds of stories that displayed African American humor and mother wit. The best stories from Hughes's several books about Simple are collected in his 1961 *The Best of Simple*.

4   Of the several references I've noted here, Holloway and Vass (1993) is of particular interest because it seeks to "correct the mistaken assumption that only West Africans had a linguistic influence on African American culture" (p. xiii) by demonstrating the linguistic impact of Central Africa on Ebonics.

5   Speckled Red's famous recording was reissued on an album entitled *The Dirty Dozens*. Although he says he had to "clean it up a bit" for broader distribution, it is so "clean" that it seems like a different song.

6   "Kansas City Papa" can be heard on *Leadbelly: King of the 12-String Guitar*, Sony Music, 1991.

7   Memphis Minnie's "New Dirty Dozen" was re-released on the album, *Blues Classics*, Arhoolie Productions, 1984.

8   In Labov's in-depth analysis of the rhetorical complexity of Black insult rituals, he concludes that there are at least ten different "shapes" of the "yo momma" disses (1972).

9   From the basketball courts of Lansing, Michigan, 1992.

10   From Chicago, 1994.

11   A "lie" is an anecdote, experience, reflection, or story, rendered with clever eloquence and oratorical embellishment. Though it may be exaggerated in the telling, the lie generally has a kernel of truth and is distinguished from an outright, blatant falsehood. As Fishbelly asks, in reference to his friend Zeke's having "cut" (had sex with) Laura: "Zeke, this lie about Laura Green . . . is that a *true* lie or just a *plain* old lie?" (From Richard Wright's 1958 novel, *The Long Dream*.)

13 "MAKIN A WAY OUTA NO WAY": THE PROVERB TRADITION IN THE BLACK EXPERIENCE

1   Authors' note: This article is based on our panel presentation at the Second World Congress on Communication and Development in Africa and the African Diaspora, Bridgetown, Barbados, 24–8 July 1983. We are indebted to the Center for Black Studies, Wayne State University, Detroit, for its continuing support of this collaborative effort over the past several years. Particular thanks are in order to Ms. Nubia Salaam, Black Studies Research Assistant and Ms. Adrienne Gregg, Office Supervisor at the Center. We gratefully acknowledge the support of our families and the Black communities that gave us birth and continue to sustain and believe in us. Most of all, this work pays tribute to all of those souls who have kept the proverb tradition alive.

15 "THE CHAIN REMAIN THE SAME": COMMUNICATIVE PRACTICES IN THE HIP HOP NATION

1   From Naughty By Nature, (1995). Chains remain. *Poverty's Paradise*. Tommy Boy Records.

2   Although "Rapper's Delight" was the first big rap hit, selling over 2 million copies in the United States (Rose, 1994, p. 196), it was not the first rap record. That "first" occurred earlier in 1979: "King Tim III (The Personality Jock)," recorded by the Fatback Band (George, 1992, p. 16).

3   Their name derives from a central tenet of the Five Percent Nation. The people who are all wise and know who the true living God is are only 5 percent of the population. This 5 percent are called the "poor righteous teachers." The

Poor Righteous Teachers rap group comes from a ghetto project in Trenton, New Jersey, dubbed "Divineland" (Ahearn, 1991).

16 AFRICAN AMERICANS AND "ENGLISH ONLY"

1   This article is based on my presentation at the Conference, "Language Pluralism in the US: Linguistic Minorities and 'English Only,'" 13 April 1991. The Conference was convened by Dr. Denise Troutman at Michigan State University. My thanks to Vice President Garrett Heberlein at Wayne State University for the research grant that made the five-city survey possible. I also wish to acknowledge the assistance of Dr. Thomas Kochman, Professor Laverne Summerlin, and Mr. Ronald Stephens, for assistance with data collection; Dr. Alida Quick for assistance with research design, instrumentation and statistical analysis; and Mr. Joshua Bagakas, statistician. Finally, a very special thank-you to Dr. Ana Celia Zentella whose sisterly challenge inspired me. Any short-comings or limitations are entirely my own.

17 THE MIS-EDUCATION OF THE NEGRO – AND YOU TOO

1   Bureau of the Census, 1980, p. 292, Table 2. Since this article was written, however, the number of Polish speakers in Michigan has apparently experienced a sharp decline. The 1990 Census data (which were unavailable when this article was being written in 1989) put the number of speakers at 64,527 persons who speak Polish at home and are five years of age and older (1990 Census of Population and Housing Summary, Tape File 3A). However, the same critique of Census methods applies to this new number that applied to the 1980 Census data, namely that the question did not ask about language spoken in the church or community, but only inquired about language spoken in the home. Local demographers give significantly higher estimates of Polish speakers. For a penetrating critique of Census methods that have undoubtedly produced significant undercounts of foreign language speakers, see Hart-Gonzalez and Feingold, 1990.

2   I note in passing that the call for "Black" to be replaced by "African American" is right on time and what many African American intellectuals have long advocated. It symbolizes our connection with Mother Africa while simultaneously affirming, as Langston Hughes once put it, that "we too sing America." Although "Black" was suitable and even necessary in its day, it remains an anomaly that is asymmetrical with the naming practices of America's other groups. (See "From African to African American," this volume, pp. 41–56, for a detailed historical analysis of racial semantics in African America and also for a correction as to who initially launched the "African American" call. It was not Reverend Jesse Jackson as I had originally indicated.)

3   A more recent survey of English speakers on the global scene (Crystal, 1997) gives some different numbers. Using population estimates for mid-1995, Crystal estimates that 337 million people learned English as a first language, a number that would be higher if there were data available for every country, "especially in such areas as West Africa, where it is not known how many use a variety of English as a first language" (1997, pp. 60–61). For those who learned English as a second language, which is also subject to the same problem, i.e., of countries where estimates are not available, the figure is 235 million persons. Finally

for those who learned English as a foreign language, the estimate ranges from 100 million to 1,000 million. For a grand total, Crystal suggests the figure of 1,200–1,500 million persons who speak English (p. 61).

20 SOUL 'N STYLE

1   Langston Hughes, *Simple Stakes a Claim*. See Smitherman ([1972] 1973) for the full quote.
2   The poem was written by Georgia Walker, a student in my Black Communications class at Wayne State. According to Georgia, the poem reflects her heightened consciousness resulting from systematic study of Black Language and culture to which, as a white middle class student, she had not been previously exposed.

22 "STILL I RISE": EDUCATION AGAINST THE ODDS IN CUBA

1   Excerpted from title poem in And Still I Rise (Random House, 1978), by African American poet, Maya Angelou. Despite over a generation of work in literature, film, and dramatic performance, Angelou seems to be only known for having composed and read a poem at Clinton's Inaugural.

23 CCCC AND THE "STUDENTS RIGHT TO THEIR OWN LANGUAGE"

1   A different version of this essay is slated for publication in 1999 for the special 50th Anniversary issue of the journal, *College Composition and Communication* (*CCC*). I would like to express special thanks to David Sheridan, Ph.D. candidate in English at Michigan State University, for his most capable assistance and archival work. Also a shout-out to David Kirkland, recent secondary school English teacher and my research assistant, for his efforts to make me computer literate. Any shortcomings are entirely my own doing.
2   Kwame Ture, then Stokely Carmichael, first used the "Black Power" slogan in a speech in June 1966 on a protest march in Greenville, Mississippi. The march, designed to go across the state of Mississippi, had been initiated by James Meredith, the first Black to be admitted to the University of Mississippi, who had been ambushed and shot early on during the march. Carmichael and other Civil Rights leaders had come to Mississippi to continue Meredith's march. The concept of empowerment, as well as the accompanying rhetorical strategy, had been carefully worked out by the leadership of the Student Non-Violent Coordinating Committee (SNCC), which was waiting for the opportune moment to introduce the "Black Power" slogan into the discourse of the Civil Rights Movement. A few days before Stokely's speech, SNCC worker, Willie Ricks, had begun using the slogan in local meetings to rally the people. And it was actually Ricks who convinced SNCC leadership – and Carmichael – that this was the historical moment to drop "Black Power." In retrospect, Kwame Ture confessed that Stokely Carmichael "did not expect that 'enthusiastic response' from his audience of sharecroppers, farm workers, and other everyday Black people in Mississippi." [From "The Time Has Come, 1964–6," *Eyes on the Prize II: America at the Racial Crossroads* 1965–85.]

3   Donald J. Lloyd, who taught for years at Detroit's Wayne State University, was
     a major figure in the early years of Composition Studies and Linguistics. His
     Ph.D. in literature from Yale University hardly equipped him to teach literacy
     and language, and he notes that he learned, through trial and error over the
     years with his students, how to teach writing. He is co-author of *American
     English in Its Cultural Setting* (1962) and is credited with coining the phrase, the
     "national mania for correctness." On a personal note, while doing the research
     for this essay, I remembered that Lloyd had taught me introductory linguistics
     at Wayne State. At the time, his ideas about language were profoundly shock-
     ing to most of his students – including me, who at the time was an untutored,
     fresh-from-the-ghetto very young teen-ager. Being the first of my family to go
     beyond the seventh grade – much less college – and on whom the family hopes
     for educational success were riding, I recall being highly attracted to – but at
     the same time fearful of – Lloyd's "heretical" challenge to prevailing language
     norms.

4   The other "Students' Right" Committee members were: Adam Casmier, Ninfa
     Flores, Jenefer Giannasi, Myrna Harrison, Richard Lloyd-Jones, Richard A.
     Long, Elizabeth Martin, the late Elisabeth McPherson, and Ross Winterowd.
     Robert F. Hogan and Nancy S. Prichard served as NCTE *ex-officio* members.

5   The other LPC members were: Elizabeth McTiernan Auleta; Ana Celia
     Zentella; Thomas Kochman, Jeffery Youdelman; Guadalupe Valdes; Elisabeth
     McPherson. Of the original group, Ana Celia Zentella, Elizabeth McTiernan,
     and I are still on the (now reconstituted) Language Policy Committee. Other
     current Committee members are: Richard Lloyd-Jones, Victoria Cliett, Gail
     Okawa, Victor Villanueva, Rashidah Muhammad, Elaine Richardson, Kim
     Lovejoy, and Jan Swearingen.

REFERENCES

Note:

For references to Smitherman, see Publications by the author section on pp. .

Abraham, W. E. (1962), *The Mind of Africa*, Chicago: University of Chicago Press.

Abrahams, R. (1964), *Deep Down in the Jungle*, Chicago: Aldine Publishing Co.

Achebe, C. (1959), *Things Fall Apart*, New York: Fawcett.

Advocates for Language Learning, (1989), "Governors Stress Foreign Language Education, *Newsletter*, 5(1) 1.

Ahearn, C. (1991, February), "The Five Percent Solution," *Spin*, pp. 55–7, 76.

Akrofi, C. A. [n.d.], *Twi Mmebusem*, Accra: Waterville.

Alexander, N. (1989), *Language Policy and National Unity in South Africa/Azania*, Cape Town: Buchu Books.

Allen, E. Jr. (1996), "Making the Strong Survive: The Contours and Contradictions of 'Message Rap,' " in W. E. Perkins (ed.), *Dropping Science: Critical Essays on Rap Music and Hip-Hop Culture*, Philadelphia: Temple University Press, pp. 159–81.

Allen, H. B. (1952), "Preparing the Teacher of Composition and Communication – A Report." *College Composition and Communication*, 3 May (2).

Allen, H. B. (1954), "Linguistic Research Needed in Composition and Communication," *College Composition and Communication*, 5, pp. 55–60.

Allen, V. (1969), "Teaching Standard English as a Second Dialect," *Florida Foreign Language Reporter*, spring–summer, pp. 123–9.

Alleyne, M. (1980), *Comparative Afro-American*, Ann Arbor: Karoma.

Alvarez, L., and Kolker, A. (1987), *American Tongues*, [instructional videotape], New York: Center for New American Media.

Angelou, M. (1971), *Just Give Me a Cool Drink of Water 'Fore I Diiie*, New York: Random House.

Angelou, M. (1981), *The Heart of a Woman*, New York: Random House.

Anonymous. (1989, July), "African-American or Black: What's in a Name? Prominent Black and/or African Americans Express Their Views," *Ebony*, 76–80.

Applebee, A., Langer, J., and Mullis, I. (1985), *Writing Trends Across the Decade, 1974–84*, Princeton, NJ: Educational Testing Service.

Applebee, A., Langer, J., Mullis, I., and Jenkins, L. (1990), *The Writing Report Card 1984–8*, Princeton, NJ: Educational Testing Service.

Arewa, E. O. and Dundes, A. (1964, October), "Proverbs and the Ethnography of Speaking Folklore," *American Anthropologist*, p. 66.

Asante, M. K. [published as Smith, A.] (1972), *Language, Communication and Rhetoric in Black America*, New York: Harper & Row.

Asante, M. K. (1988), *Afrocentricity*, Trenton, NJ: African World Press.

Asante, M. K. (1990), "African Elements in African American English," in J. Holloway (ed.), *Africanisms in American Culture*, Bloomington: Indiana University Press, pp. 19–33.

Bailey, B. L. (1965), "Toward a New Perspective in Negro English Dialectology," *American Speech* 40, pp. 171–7.

Bailey, B. L. (1966), *Jamaican Creole Syntax*, Cambridge: Cambridge University.

Bailey, B. L. (1968), "Some Aspects of the Impact of Linguistics on Language Teaching in Disadvantaged Communities," in A. L. Davis (ed.), *On the Dialects of Children*, Champaign/Urbana, IL: National Council of Teachers.

Bailey, B. L. (1969), "Language and Communicative Styles of Afro-American Children in the United States," *Florida Reporter*, spring/summer.

Bailey, G., Maynor, N., and Cukor-Avila, P. (eds), (1991), *The Emergence of Black English: Text and Commentary*, Philadelphia and Amsterdam: John Benjamins.

Bailey, R. W. (1981), "Press Coverage of the *King* Case," in Smitherman, G. (ed.), *Black English and the Education of Black Children and Youth: Proceeding of the National Invitational Symposium on the* King *Decision*, Detroit: Wayne State University Center for Black Studies, pp. 359–89.

Baldwin, J. (1979, July 29), "If Black English Isn't a Language, Then Tell Me What Is," *New York Times*, p. 19.

Baldwin, J. (1981), "Black English: A Dishonest Argument," in Smitherman, G. (ed.), *Black English and the Education of Black Children and Youth: Proceedings of the National Invitational Symposium on the* King *Decision*, Detroit: Wayne State University Center for Black Studies, pp. 54–60.

Ball, A., and Lardner, T. (1997), "Dispositions Toward Language: Teacher Constructs of Knowledge and the Ann Arbor Black English Case," *College Composition and Communication*, 48, pp. 469–85.

Balliro, L. and Nash, A. (1990), *English Only/English Plus: A Curriculum Sourcebook for ESL and ABE Teachers*, Massachusetts: English Plus Coalition.

Bamgbose, A. (1976), "Introduction: The Changing Role of the Mother Tongue in Education," in A. Bamgbose (ed.), *Mother Tongue Education: The West African Experience*, Paris: Unesco Press.

Banks, J. A. (1968), "A Profile of the Black American: Implications for Teaching," *College Composition and Communication*, 19, pp. 288–96.

Barrett, L. E. (1976), *The Sun and the Drum*, Kingston: Sangster's Book Stores.

Baugh, J. (1979), "Linguistic Style-Shifting in Black English," Ph.D. dissertation, University of Pennsylvania.

Baugh, J. (1983), *Black Street Speech*, Austin: University of Texas Press.

Baugh, J. (1991), "The Politicization of Changing Terms of Self Reference Among American Slave Descendants," *American Speech*, 66(2), pp. 133–46.

Beckwith, Martha Warren ([1925] 1970), *Jamaican Proverbs*, New York: Negro Universities Press.

Bell, D. (1987), "*And We Are Not Saved*," New York: Basic Books.

Bennett, J. (1908), "Gullah: A Negro Patois," *South Atlantic Quarterly*, 7, pp. 332–47.

Bennett, J. (1909), "Gullah: A Negro Patois," *South Atlantic Quarterly*, 8, pp. 39–52.

Bennett, L. (1961), *Before the Mayflower*, Chicago: Johnson.

Bennett, L. (1967, November), "What's in a Name?," *Ebony*, pp. 45–54.

Bereiter, C. (1965), "Language Program for Culturally Deprived Children," in *Language Programs for the Disadvantaged* (Report of the National Council of Teachers of English Task Force on Teaching English to the Disadvantaged), Champaign, IL: National Council of Teachers of English.

Bereiter, C., and Engelmann, S. (1966), *Teaching Disadvantaged Children in Pre-school*, Englewood Cliffs, NJ: Prentice Hall.

Berger, P. and Luckmann, T. (1966), *The Social Construction of Reality: A Treatise in the Sociology of Knowledge*, New York: Doubleday and Co.

Bickerton, D. (1981), *Roots of Language*, Ann Arbor, MI: Karoma.

Blackshire-Belay, C. A. (1996), "The Location of Ebonics within the Framework of the Africological Paradigm," *Journal of Black Studies*, 27, pp. 5–23.

Blackwell, J. E. (1981), *Mainstreaming Outsiders: The Production of Black Professionals*, Bayside, New York: General Hall.

Blassingame, John W. (1972), *The Slave Community*, New York: Dial Press.

Bliss, L., and Allen, D. (1978), *Language Screening and Assessment Test for Pre-school Children of Diverse Backgrounds* (Interim Report to National Institute of Health, Research Project NIH–NINCDS-76-03), Detroit: Wayne State University.

Bloomfield, L. (1933), *Language*, New York: Holt, Rinehart.

Boggs, J. (1982), *Manifesto for an American Revolutionary Party*, Philadelphia: National Organization For an American Revolution.

Bokamba, E. (1981), "Language and National Development: Black English in America," in Smitherman, G. (ed.), *Black English and the Education of Black Children and Youth: Proceedings of the National Invitational Symposium on the* King *Decision*, Detroit: Wayne State University Center for Black Studies.

Bond, H. M. (1966), *The Education of the Negro in the American Social Order*, New York: Random House.

Bosmajian, H. (1984), "Reagan's Evil Empire–Virus–Cancer–Mickey Mouse: Phantasmagoria," *Quarterly Review of Doublespeak*, 11(1) pp. 5–6.

Botan, C. and Smitherman, G. (1983), "*White Faces, Black Tongues: Black English and White Workers*," paper presented at the Speech Communication Association Convention, Washington, DC.

Boyd, H. (1996, December 27–9), "Karenga on Jackson Criticism: 'Jesse is Versed in Ebonics,'" *Daily Challenge, weekend edition*, 25, p. 198.

Bray, R. (1990, December), "Reclaiming our Culture," *Essence*, 84–6, pp. 116, 119.

Brewer, J. M. (1972), *American Negro Folklore*, Chicago: Quadrangle.

Brookover, W. B. and Beady, C. (1978), *School Social Climate and Student Achievement*, New York: Praeger.

Brooks, R. L. (1990), *Rethinking the American Race Problem*, Berkeley: University of California Press.

Brown, G. (1851), *Grammar of English Grammars*, New York: W. Wood.

Brown, H. R. (1969), *Die Nigger, Die!*, New York: Dial Press.

Buck, P. D. (1999), "Prison Labor: Racism and Rhetoric," in Spears, A. (ed.), *Race and Ideology*, Detroit: Wayne State University Press.

Burchfield, R. W. (1985), *The English Language*, Oxford: Oxford University Press.

Bureau of the Census (1979), *Current population reports*, 116, November, Washington, DC: Government Printing Office.

Bureau of the Census (1980), "Nativity and Language for Divisions and States," *General Social and Economic Characteristics: United States Summary, table 236*, Washington, DC: Government Printing Office.

Butler, M. (ed.) (1974), "Students' Right to Their Own Language," (Special Issue), *College Composition and Communication*, 25, Fall, pp. 1–32.

Califa, A. J. (1989), "English-Only Laws Would Mean Loss of Rights," *Civil Liberties*, Winter.

Califa, A. J. (1991), "*The Attack on Minority Language Speakers*," paper available from the American Civil Liberties Union, Washington, DC, unpublished manuscript.

Carmichael, S., and Hamilton, S. (1967), *Black Power*, New York: Random House.

Cassidy, F. (1985, continuing), *Dictionary of American Regional English*, Cambridge: Belknap Press of Harvard University Press.

Chambers, G. and Morgan, J. (1992, September), "Droppin Knowledge," *Essence*, 83–85, pp. 116–20.

Champion, T. and Bloome, D. (1995), (eds) *Linguistics and Education, Special Issue: Africanized English and Education*, 7(1).

Chaplin, M. (1987), "An Analysis of Writing Features Found in the Essays of Students in the National Assessment of Educational Progress and the New Jersey High School Proficiency Test," unpublished manuscript, Rutgers University, Department of English, Camden, NJ.

Chaplin, M. (1990), "A Closer Look at Black and White Students' Assessment Essays," *Iowa English Bulletin*, 38, 15–27.

Chomsky, N. (1957), *Syntactic Structures*, The Hague: Mouton.

Chomsky, N. (1959), (Review of the book *Verbal Behavior*), *Language*, 35, pp. 26–58.

Chomsky, N. (1966), *Cartesian Linguistics*, New York: Harper & Row.

Chomsky, N. (1972), *Language and Mind* (enlarged edn), New York: Harcourt Brace Jovanovich.

Chomsky, N. (1975), Introduction, in Blackstock N. (ed.), *Cointelpro*, New York: Random House.

Chomsky, N. (1979), *Rules and Representations*, New York: Columbia University Press.

Christaller, J. G. (1873), "Two Mmebuseum Mpensa-Ahansia Mmoaano," Basel.

Christensen, J. B. (1973), "The Role of Proverbs in Fante Culture," in Skinner, E. P. (ed.), *Peoples and Cultures of Africa*.

Clark, W. G. (1975), "In Responses to Students' Right to Their Own Language," *College Communication and Composition*, 27, p. 217.

Clemente, F. and Watkins, F. (eds) (1989), *Keep Hope Alive: Jesse Jackson's Presidential Campaign: A Collection of Major Speeches, Issue Papers, Photographs, and Campaign Analysis*, Boston: South End.

Cohen, R. A. (1969), "Conceptual Styles, Cultural Conflicts and Non-Verbal Tests of Intelligence," *American Anthropologist*, 71, pp. 828–56.

Coleman, C. F. (1997), "Our Students Write with Accents – Oral Paradigms for ESD Students, *College Composition and Communication*, 48, pp. 486–500.

Committee on Public Doublespeak (1992, January), *Quarterly Review of Doublespeak*, 18.

Conference on College Composition and Communication (1974), "Students' Right to Their Own Language," (special issue), *College Composition and Communication*, 25.

Conference on College Composition and Communication (1991), "The National Language Policy," (brochure available from NCTE headquarters), Champaign-Urbana, Illinois.

Conyers, J. (congressman), (1988, 15 August), personal communication.

Cooper, G. (1979), "The Relationship Between Errors in Standard Usage in Written Compositions of College Students and the Students' Cognitive Styles," unpublished doctoral dissertation, Howard University, Washington, DC.

Costello, M. and Wallace, D. F. (1990), *Signifying Rappers: Rap and Race in the Urban Present*, New York: Penguin.

Crawford, J. (1989), *Bilingual Education: History, Politics, Theory, and Practice*, Trenton: Crane.

Crawford, J. (ed.) (1992), *Language Loyalties: A Source Book on the Official English Controversy*, Chicago: University of Chicago Press.

Crystal, D. (1997), *English as a Global Language*, Cambridge: Cambridge University Press.

Cullen, C. (1925), "Heritage," in Davis, A. P. and Redding, S. (eds), *Calvacade*, Boston: Houghton, pp. 326–37.

Curry, O. (1971), "Black English," *American Teacher*, 45.

Dalby, D. (1969), "Americanisms that May Once Have Been Africanisms," *New York Times*, (19 July).

Dalby, D. (1970), *Black through White: Patterns of Communication*, Bloomington: Indiana University Press.

Dalby, D. (1972), "The African Element in American English," in Kochman, T. (ed.), *Rappin' and Stylin' Out: Communication in Urban Black America*, Urbana: University of Illinois Press, pp. 170–86.

Dance, D. C. (1978), *Shuckin' and Jivin': Folklore from Contemporary Black Americans*, Bloomington: Indiana University Press.

Dandy, E. (1991), *Black Communication: Breaking Down the Barriers*, Chicago: African American Images.

Daniel, J. L. (1972, winter), "Towards an Ethnography of Afro-American Proverbial Usage," *Black Lines*.

Daniel, J. L. (ed.) (1974), *Black Communication: Dimensions of Research and Instruction*, New York: Speech Communication Association.

Daniel, J. L. (1979), *The Wisdom of Sixth Mount Zion from the Members of Sixth Mount Zion and Those Who Begot Them*, Pittsburgh. [available from the author.]

Daniels, H. A. (ed.) (1990), *Not Only English – Affirming America's Multilingual Heritage*, Urbana: National Council of Teachers of English.

Danquah, J. B. (1968), *The Akan Doctrine of God*, London: Frank Cass.

Davis, A. P., and Redding, S. (eds) (1971), *Calvacade*, Boston: Houghton.

Davis, V. I. (1990), "Paranoia in Language Politics," in Daniels, H. A. (ed.), *Not Only English – Affirming America's Multilingual Heritage*, Urbana: National Council of Teachers of English, pp. 71–7.

Dawsey, K. M. (1994, June), "Caught up in the (Gangsta) Rapture," *The Source*, 58–62.

DeBose, C. and Faraclas, N. (1993), "An Africanist Approach to the Linguistic Study of Black English: Getting to the Roots of the Tense–Aspect–Modality and Copula Systems in Afro-American," in Mufwene, S. S. (ed.), *Africanisms in Afro-American Language Varieties*, Athens, GA: University of Georgia Press, pp. 364–87.

Delano, I. O. (1966), *Yoruba Proverbs: Their Meaning and Use*, Ibadan: Oxford University Press.

Desai, Z. (1994), "Praat or Speak but Don't Theta: On Language Rights in South Africa," *Language and Education*, 8 (1–2.).

Deutsch, M. (1963), "The Disadvantaged Child and the Learning Process," in Passow, A. (ed.), *Education in Depressed Areas*, New York: Columbia University Press.

Dillard, J. L. (1972), *Black English*. New York: Random House.

Dillard, J. L. (1977), *Lexicon of Black English*. New York: Seabury Press.

Dollard, J. (1939), "The Dozens: Dialectic of Insult," *The American Imago*, 1 November, pp. 3–25.

Douglass, F. (1881), *Life and Times*, New York: Collier Books.

Dowd, J. (1926), *The Negro in American Life*, New York: The Century Company.

Drake, S. C. (1966), "Negro Americans and the African Interest," in Davis, J. P. (ed.), *The American Negro Reference Book*, Englewood Cliffs: Prentice, pp. 662–705.

Drake, S. C. (1987), "Black Folk Here and There: An Essay in History and Anthropology," (Center for Afro-American Studies, Monograph Series 17), Los Angeles: Center for Afro-American Studies, University of California.

DuBois, W. E. B. (1887, November), editorial, *Fisk Herald*.

DuBois, W. E. B. (1896), *The Suppression of the African Slave Trade to the United States of America, 1638–1870*, New York: Longmans, Green.

DuBois, W. E. B. ([1903] 1961), *The Souls of Black Folk*, New York: Fawcett.

Dubois, W. E. B. (1905, 26 October), "The Negro Ideals of Life," *The Christian Register*.

DuBois, W. E. B. ([1930] 1973), "Education and Work," in Aptheker, H. (ed.), *The Education of Black People: Ten Critiques, 1906–60*, Amherst: University of Massachusetts Press, pp. 61–82.

DuBois, W. E. B. ([1933] 1973), "The Field and Function of the Negro College," in Aptheker, H. (ed.), *The Education of Black People: Ten Critiques, 1906–60*, Amherst: University of Massachusetts Press, pp. 83–102.

DuBois, W. E. B. (1968), *The Autobiography of W. E. B. DuBois*, New York: International Publishers.

DuBois, W. E. B. (1970), "The Freedom of Womanhood," in *The Gift of Black Folk*, New York: Washington Square Press.

Dundes, A. (1973), *Mother Wit from the Laughing Barrel: Readings in the Interpretation of Afro-American Folklore*, Englewood Cliffs, NJ: Prentice-Hall.

Edmonds, R. (1979), "Some Schools Work and More Can," *Social Policy*, 9(5), pp. 28–32.

Edmonds, R, (1981), Educational Policy and the Urban Poor: Search for Effective Schools," in Smitherman, G. (ed.), *Black English and the Education of Black Children and Youth: Proceedings of the National Invitational Symposium on the King Decision*, Detroit: Wayne State University Center for Black Studies.

Elias, R. (1986), "Nukespeak and Beyond," *Quarterly Review of Doublespeak*, 12(4), pp. 9–10.

Ellison, R. (1958), "Change the Joke and Slip the Yoke," in Ellison, R. *Shadow and Act*. New York: Random House.

Elton, W. (1950), "Playing the Dozens," in "Miscellany," *American Speech*, 25 (1).

Esselman, B. (1977), "An Investigation of Third and Fourth Grade Reading Teachers' Perceptions as Related to Those Who Speak Black Dialect in the School District of the City of Highland Park, Michigan," Dissertation Abstracts International, 39, 03A, (University Microfilms No. DK78-16019)

Fabio, S. W. (1968), "What is Black?," *College Composition and Communication*, 19, pp. 286–7.

Fairclough, N. L. (1985), "Critical and Descriptive Goals in Discourse Analysis," *Journal of Pragmatics*, 9, pp. 739–63.

Fanon, F. (1963), *The Wretched of the Earth*, New York: Fawcett Edition.

Fanon, F. (1967), "The Negro and Language," in Fanon, F. (ed.), *Black Skin, White Masks*, New York: Grove.

Farrakhan, L. (1995), "Day of Atonement," in Madhubuti, H. R. and Karenga, M. (eds), *Million Man March/Day of Absence – A Commemorative Anthology*, Chicago: Third World Press.

Farrell, T. J. (1983), "IQ and Standard English," *College Composition and Communication*, 34, pp. 470–84.

Fasold, R. W. (1964), "Tense and Form 'Be' in Black English," *Language*, 45, pp. 763–76.

Fasold, R. and Shuy, R. (1970), *Teaching Standard English in the Inner City*, Washington, DC: Center for Applied Linguistics.

Fasold, R. W. and Wolfram, W. (1970), "Some Linguistic Features of Negro Dialect," in R. W. Fasold and R. Shuy (eds), *Teaching Standard English in the Inner City*, Washington, DC: Center for Applied Linguistics.

Fernando, S. H. (1994), *The New Beats: Exploring the Music, Culture, and Attitudes of Hip-Hop*, New York: Doubleday.

Finnegan, R. (1976), *Oral Literature in Africa*, Nairobi: Oxford University Press.

Fishman, J., Cooper, R. and Conrad, A. (1977), *The Spread of English*, Rowley: Newbury House.

Fishman, J. A. (1989), *Language and Ethnicity in Minority Sociolinguistic Perspective*, Clevedon and Philadelphia: Multilingual Matters, Ltd.

Fishman, J. A. (1991), *Reversing Language Shift*, Clevedon and Philadelphia: Multilingual Matters, Ltd.

Fishman, W. K. and Wainer, I. (1982), "A History of the Concept of Race," *Science for the People*, vol. 14, pp. 6–33.

Folb, E. (1980), *Runnin Down Some Lines*, Cambridge: Harvard University Press.

Fowler, R. and Kress, G. (1979), "Critical Linguistics," in Fowler, R. *et al.*, (eds), *Language and Control*, London: Routledge & Kegan Paul.

Fowler, R. and Kress, G. (1979), "Rules and Regulations," in Fowler, R. *et al.*, (eds), *Language and Control*, London: Routledge & Kegan Paul.

Francis, W. N. (1958), *The Structure of American English*, New York: Ronald Press.

Franklin, B. (1753), "The German Language in Pennsylvania," in Crawford, J. (ed.),
   Language Loyalties: A Source Book on the Official English Controversy, Chicago:
   University of Chicago Press, pp. 18–19.

Franklin, J. H. (1967), *From Slavery to Freedom: A History of Negro Americans*, New
   York: Alfred A. Knopf, Inc.

Frazier, E. F. (1966), *The Negro Family in the United States*, Chicago: University of
   Chicago Press.

Freeman, L. D. (1975), "The Students' Right to Their Own Language: Its Legal
   Basis," *College Composition and Communication*, vol. 26, 25–9.

Freire, P. (1985), *The Politics of Education: Culture, Power, and Liberation*, Hadley, MA:
   Bergin and Garvey.

Fries, C. C. (1940), *American English Grammar*, New York: Appleton-Century.

Gallup Organization, Inc. (1991), *A Gallup Study of Attitudes Toward English as
   the Official Language of US Government*, Princeton: The Gallup Organization,
   Inc.

Garofalo, R. (ed.). (1992), *Rockin' the Boat: Mass Music and Mass Movements*, Boston:
   South End Press.

Gaspar, D. B. and Hine, D. C. (1996), *More than Chattel: Black Women and Slavery
   in the Americas*, Bloomington: Indiana University Press.

Gates, H. L. (1988a), *Contending Forces*, New York: Oxford University Press.

Gates, H. L. (1988b), *The Signifying Monkey: A Theory of Afro-American Literary
   Criticism*, New York: Oxford University Press.

Gawthrop, B. (1965), "1911–1929," in McDavid, Jr., R. (ed.), *An Examination of
   the Attitudes of the NCTE Toward Language*, Champaign/Urbana, IL: The
   National Council of Teachers of English, pp. 7–15.

George, N. (1992), *Buppies, B-Boys, Baps & Bohos: Notes on Post-Soul Black Culture*,
   New York: HarperCollins.

Gere, A. R. and Smith, E. (1979), *Attitudes, Language, and Change*, Urbana: National
   Council of Teachers of English.

Giddings, P. (1984), *When and Where I Enter: The Impact of Black Women on Race and
   Sex in America*, New York: William Morrow.

Gilbert, G. G. (1985), "Hugo Schuchardt and the Atlantic Creoles: A Newly
   Discovered Manuscript on the Negro of West Africa," *American Speech*, 60, pp,
   31–63.

Giovanni, N. (1971), *Gemini (An Extended Autobiographical Statement on my First
   Twenty-Five Years of Being a Black Poet)*, New York: Penguin Books.

Golden, R. I. (1959), *Improving Patterns of Language Usage*, Detroit: Wayne State
   University Press.

Gonzales, A. (1922), *Black Border*, Columbia, SC: The State Co.

Gordon, M. (1964), *Assimilation in American Life*, New York: Oxford University Press.

Gough, D. (1996), "Black English in South Africa," in de Klerk, V. (ed.), *Focus on
   South Africa*, Amsterdam: Benjamins.

Green, C. G. (1963), "Negro Dialect, the Last Barrier to Integration," *The Journal
   of Negro Education*, 32, pp. 81–3.

Green, R. L. (1975), "Tips on Educational Testing: What Teachers and Parents
   Should Know, *Phi Delta Kappan*, pp. 89–93.

Greenbaum, L. (1968), "Prejudice and Purpose in Compensatory Programs," *College
   Composition and Communication*, 19, pp. 305–11.

Greenberg, K. (1984), "Responses to Thomas J. Farrell, IQ and Standard English,"
   College Composition and Communication, 35, pp. 455–60.

Gwaltney, J. L. (1980), *Drylongso: A Self-Portrait of Black America*, New York:
   Random House.

Hacker, A. (1992), *Two Nations*, New York: Maxwell MacMillan.

Hacker, D. (1989), "Petoskey Doctor Leads English-Only Crusade," *Detroit Free Press*, (14 February) p. 3A.

Hall, R. A. (1950), "The African Substratum in Negro English: Review of Africanisms in the Gullah Dialect," *American Speech*, 25.

Hall, R. A. (1966), *Pidgin and Creole Languages*, Ithaca, NY: Cornell University Press.

Halliday, M. A. K. (1976), "Anti-Languages," *UEA Papers in Linguistics*, pp. 15–45.

Halliday, M. A. K. (1978), *Language as Social Semiotic: The Social Interpretation of Language and Meaning*, London: Arnold.

Harris, M. A. (1974), *The Black Book*, New York: Random House.

Harrison, J. A. (1884), Negro English, *Anglia*, 7, pp. 232–79.

Hart-Gonzalez, L. and Feingold, M. (1990), "Retention of Spanish in the Home," (special issue), *International Journal of Sociolinguistics, Spanish in the United States*, 83.

Hayakawa, S. I. (1949) *Language in Thought and Action*, New York: Harcourt Brace.

Hayakawa, S. I. (1992), "The Case for Official English," in Crawford, J. (ed.), *Language Loyalties: A Source Book on the Official English Controversy*, Chicago: University of Chicago Press.

Hendrickson, J. R. (1972), "Responses to CCCC Executive Committee's Resolution 'The Student's Right to His Own Language,'" *College Composition and Communication*, 23, 300–1.

Herrnstein, R. (1994), *The Bell Curve: Intelligence and Class Structure in American Life*. New York and London: Free Press.

Herskovits, M. (1941), *Myth of the Negro Past*, Boston: Beacon Press.

Herskovits, M. (1949), Commentary in *Funk and Wagnalls Standard Dictionary of Folklore, Mythology, and Legend*, vol. 1, New York: Funk and Wagnalls, p. 322.

Herskovits, M. (1966), *The New World Negro*, New York: Random House.

Heugh, K. Siegruhn, A. and Pluddemann, P. (eds) (1995) *Multilingual Education for South Africa*, Johannesburg (Isando): Heinemann.

Hirshberg, J. (1982), "Towards a Dictionary of Black American English on Historical Principles," *American Speech*, 57, pp. 163–82.

Holloway, J. E. (ed.) (1990), *Africanisms in American Culture*, Bloomington: Indiana University Press.

Holloway, J. E. and Vass, W. K. (1993), *The African Heritage of American English*, Bloomington: Indiana University Press.

Holm, J. (1984), "Variability of the Copula in Black English and its Creole Kin," *American Speech*, 59, pp. 291–309.

Holm, J. (1992), "A Theoretical Model for Semi-Creolization," paper presented at the Ninth Biennial Conference of the Society for Caribbean Linguistics, Barbados: University of the West Indies.

Holt, G. (1972), " 'Inversion' in Black Communication," in Kochman, T. (ed.), *Rappin' and Stylin' Out: Communication in Urban Black America*, Urbana: University of Illinois Press, pp. 152–9.

Holt, G. (1972), "The Ethnolinguistic Approach to Speech–Language Learning," in Smith, A. (ed.), *Language, Communication and Rhetoric in Black America*, New York: Harper.

hooks, b. (1992, February), "A Feminist Challenge: Must we Call all Women Sister?" *Z*, pp. 19–22.

Hoover, M. (1978), "Community Attitudes Towards Black English," *Language in Society*, 7, 65–87.

Hughes, L. (1961), *The Best of Simple*, New York: Hill and Wang.

Humboldt, W. V. (1841), *Uber die Verschiedenheiten des Meschlichen Sprachbaus, Gesammelte werke*, VI [On the Varieties of Human Linguistic Structures, Collected Works], Berlin.

Hurston, Z. N. (1935), *Mules and Men*, New York: Harper.

Hurston, Z. N. (1937), *Their Eyes Were Watching God*, (perennial library edition, H. L. Gates Jr., ed.), New York: Harper & Row.

Hurston, Z. N. (1942), "Story in Harlem Slang," *The American Mercury*, 55(223), pp. 190–215.

Hymes, D. (1956), "The Supposed Spanish Loanword in Hopi for Jaybird," *International Journal of American Linguistics*, 22, 186.

Hymes, D. (1961), "On Typology of Cognitive Styles in Language," *Anthropological Linguistics*, 3, 22–54.

Hymes, D. (1974), *Foundations in Sociolinguistics*, Philadelphia: University of Pennsylvania Press.

Hymes, D. (1979), "The Religious Aspect of Language in Native American Humanities," in Grindal, B. T. and Warren, D. M. (eds), *Essays in Humanistic Anthropology: A Festschrift in Honor of David Bidney*, Washington, DC: University Press of America, pp: 83–114.

Irmscher, W. F. (1968), "*In Memoriam*: Rev. Dr Martin Luther King, Jr. 1929–68," *College Composition and Communication*, vol. 19, p. 105.

Ives, S. (1954, December), "Grammatical Assumptions," *College Composition and Communication*, 5, pp. 149–55.

Iyasere, S. O. (1975), "Oral Tradition in the Criticism of African Literature," *Journal of Modern African Studies*, 13(1).

Ice-T. (with Siegmund, H.),. (1994). *The Ice Opinion*, New York: St. Martin's Press.

Jackson, B. (1974), *"Get your Ass in the Water and Swim Like Me": Narrative Poetry From Black Oral Tradition*, Cambridge, MA: Harvard University Press.

Jaffe, H. (1994), *European Colonial Despotism: A History of Oppression and Resistance in South Africa*, London: Karnak House.

Jahn, J. (1961), *Muntu*, London: Faber & Faber.

Jeanty, E. A. and Brown, C. O. (1976), *Haitian Popular Wisdom*, Port-au-Prince: Editions Learning.

Jensen, A. R. (1968), Social Class and Verbal Learning, in Deutsch, M. (ed.), *Social Class, Race, and Psychological Development*.

Jensen, A. R. (1980), *Bias in Mental Testing*, New York: Free Press.

Johnson, C. (1998), "Holding on to a Language of Our Own: An Interview with John Rickford," Reprinted from the San Francisco Chronicle, February 26, 1997, in Perry, T. and Delpits, L. (eds), *The Real Ebonics Debate: Power, Language and the Education of African American Children*, Boston: Beacon Press.

Joiner, C. W. (1978), 451 F. Supp. 1324 and 463 F. Supp. 1027, In G. Smitherman (ed.), *Black English and the Education of Children and Youth: Proceedings of the National Symposium on the King decision*, Detroit: Center For Black Studies.

Joiner, C. W. (1979), "Memorandum Opinion and Order," (Civil Action No. 7-71861, 473F, Supp, 1371, pp, 336–58), in Smitherman, G. (ed.), (1981), *Black English and the Education of Black Children and Youth: Proceedings of the National Invitational Symposium on the King Decision*, Detroit: Center For Black Studies.

Jones, K. M. (1994), *Say it Loud: The Story of Rap Music*, Brookfield, CT: Millbrook.

Jones, L. (1963), *Blues People*, New York: William Morrow.

Jordan, J. (1973), "White English: The Politics of Language", *Black World* (August).

Kaimowitz, G. (1981), "Commentary on the *King* Case," in Smitherman, G. (ed.), *Black English and the Education of Black Children and Youth: Proceedings of the National Invitational Symposium on the King Decision*, Detroit: Wayne State University Center for Black Studies.

Kamwangamalu, N. M. (1996), *Multilingualism and Education Policy in Post-Apartheid South Africa*, paper presented at the Fifth Conference of the International Society for the Scientific Study of European Ideas, 19–24 August, Utrecht, The Netherlands.

Kelly, D. (1997, April), Native Tongues, *The Source*, pp. 26–7.

Kelly, E. B. (1968, May), "Murder of the American Dream," *College Composition and Communication*, 19, pp. 106–8.

Kidd, D. (1906), *Savage Childhood*, London.

Kloss, H. (1977), *The American Bilingual Tradition*, Rowley: Newbury House.

Knickerbocker, K. L. (1950, December), "The Freshman is King: Or, Who Teaches Who?" *College Composition and Communication*, 1(4), pp. 11–15.

Kochman, T. (ed.) (1972), *Rappin' and Stylin' Out: Communication in Urban Black America*, Urbana: University of Illinois Press.

Kochman, T. (1981), *Black and White Styles in Conflict*, Chicago: University of Chicago Press.

Kozol, J. (1975), The Politics of Syntax, *English Journal*, December, pp. 22–7.

Kramarae, C. (1974), Stereotypes of Women's Speech, *Journal of Popular Culture*, 8, pp. 622–38.

Krapp, G. (1924), The English of the Negro, *The American Mercury*, 2, pp. 190–5.

Krapp, G. (1925), *The English Language in America*, New York: Modern Language Association.

Kress, G. and Hodge, R. (1979), *Language as Ideology*, London: Routledge & Kegan Paul.

Kurath, H. (1928), "The Origin of Dialectal Differences in Spoken American English," *Modern Philology*, 25.

Labov, W. (1970), *The Logic of Non-Standard English*, Urbana: National Council of Teachers.

Labov, W. (1971), "The Notion of Systems," in Hymes, D. (ed.), *Pidginization and Creolization of Languages*, Cambridge: Cambridge University Press.

Labov, W. (1972a), *Sociolinguistic Patterns*, Philadelphia: University of Pennsylvania.

Labov, W. (1972b), *Language in the Inner City*, Philadelphia: University of Pennsylvania.

Labov, W. (1982), Objectivity and Commitment in Linguistic Science: The Case of the Black English Trial in Ann Arbor, *Language in Society*, 11, pp. 165–201.

Labov, W. (1985), *The Increasing Divergence of Black and White Vernaculars*, National Science Foundation Research Project, University of Pennsylvania.

Labov, W., and Harris, W. A. (1986), "*De Facto* Segregation of Black and White Vernaculars," in Sankoff, D. (ed.), *Diversity and Diachrony*, Amsterdam: John Benjamins, pp. 1–24.

Labov, W., Cohen, P., Robbins, C. and Lewis, J. (1968), *A Study of the Non-Standard English of Negro and Puerto-Rican Speakers in New York City*, (final report, US Office of Education), Cooperative Research Project no. 3288.

Lacayo, R. and Monroe, S. (1989), "In Search of a Good Name," *Time*, 6 March, p. 32.

Ladner, J. (ed.) (1973), *The Death of White Sociology*, New York: Random House.

Lakoff, R. (1975), *Language and Woman's Place*, New York: Harper & Row.

Landers, A. (1989), "'African American' Label Draws Fire from all Races," *Detroit Free Press*, 2 April, p. 2L.

Landers, S. (1989), English-Only Debate Asks: Is it Polarizing or Uniting? *Monitor*, January, p. 26.

Language Policy Committee (1987), Conference on College Composition and Communication, 19 October, *Interim Report*, 1.

Larry P. v Riles. (1979, October), No. C–712270 RFP (N. C. Cal.).

Lee, C. (1993), *Signifying as a Scaffold for Literary Interpretation*, Urbana, IL: National Council of Teachers of English.

Leggett, J. C. (1968), *Class, Race and Labor: Working-class Consciousness in Detroit*, Oxford: Oxford University Press.

Leslau, C. and Leslau, W. (1962), *African Proverbs*, Mount Vernon: Peter Pauper.

Leland, J. and Joseph, N. (1997), "Hooked on Ebonics," *Newsweek*, 13 January pp. 78–9.

Lewis, N. (1988), "Chancellor Aims to Purge 'What-Cha's and Aint's," *New York Times*, 28 February p. 5B.

Lewontin, R., Rose, S. and Kamin, L. (1982), "Bourgeois Ideology and the Origins of Biological Determinism," *Race and Class*, 24, pp. 70–92.

Lincoln, C. E. (1990), *The Black Church in the African American Experience*, Durham, NC: Duke University Press.

Linn, M. (1982), "Black and White Adolescents and Pre-Adolescent Attitudes toward Black English," *Research in the Teaching of English*, 16, pp. 53–69.

Lloyd, D. J. (1951, February), "Darkness is King: A Reply to Professor Knickerbocker," *College Composition and Communication*, 2(1).

Lloyd, D. J. (1953, May), "An English Composition Course Built around Linguistics," *College Composition and Communication*, 4(2).

Lloyd, D. J. (1962a), *American English in its Cultural Setting*, New York: Alfred A. Knopf.

Lloyd, D. J. (1962b), "On not Sitting Like a Toad," *College Composition and Communication*, 12(1).

Lloyd-Jones, R. (1992, December), "Who We Were, Who We Should Become," *College Composition and Communication*, 43(4).

Long, R. B. (1958, December), "Grammarians Still Have Funerals," *College Composition and Communication*, 9(4).

Lowth, R. ([1762] 1979), *A Short Introduction to English Grammar*, Delmar, New York: Scholars' Facsimiles and Reprints.

Lutz, W. (1987), "Notes Toward a Description of Doublespeak," *Quarterly Review of Doublespeak*, 13(2), pp. 10–12.

MacKaye, S. (1988), "California Proposition 63 and Public Perceptions of Language", paper given at Stanford University Conference on language rights, April.

Madhubuti, H. (formerly Don L. Lee), (1968, December), "Directions for Black Writers," *Black Scholar*, pp. 53–7.

Magubane, B. and Mandaza, I. (eds). (1988), *Whither South Africa?*, Trenton: Africa World Press.

Major, C. (1970), *Dictionary of Afro-American Slang*, New York: International Publishers.

Major, C. (1994), *From Juba to Jive: A Dictionary of African-American Slang*, New York: Penguin Books.

Mandela, N. (1994), *Long Walk to Freedom*, Randburg, South Africa: MacDonald Purnell.

Mannheim, K. (1936), *Ideology and Utopia*, New York: Harcourt, Brace.

Marable, M. (1982), *How Capitalism Underdeveloped Black America: Problems in Race, Political Economy, and Society*, Boston: South End Press.

Marable, M. (1989), "African-American or Black? The Politics of Cultural Identity," *Black Issues in Higher Education*, 13 April, p. 72.

Marshall, T. (1987), " 'We the People': Not all Americans Were Included," 15 May, *Detroit Free Press*, p. 2.

Martin Luther King Junior Elementary School Children v. Ann Arbor School District Board, (12 July 1979), Civil Action No. 7-71861 (E. D. Mich.).

Marx, K. (1844), *Economic and Philosophical Manuscripts of 1844*.

Mayer, P. (1951), "The Joking of 'Pals' in Gusii Age-Sets," *African Studies*, 10, pp. 27–41.

McDavid, R. I. (1950), Review of *Africanisms in the Gullah Dialect*, by Lorenzo Turner, *Language*, vol. 26, pp. 328–30.

McDavid, R. I. (1967), "Historical, Regional and Social Variation," *Journal of English Linguistics*, 15, pp. 15–40.

McDavid, R. I and McDavid, V. (1951), "The Relationship of the Speech of American Negroes to the Speech of Whites," *American Speech*, 26, 3–17.

McPherson, E. (1968, December), "Hats Off-Or On-To the Junior College," *College Composition and Communication*, 19, pp. 316–22.

McWorter, G. (1969), "Ideology of a Black Social Science," *Black Scholar*, pp. 28–35.

Mencken, H. L. ([1919] 1936), *The American Language: An Inquiry into the Development of English in the United States*, New York: Knopf.

Merrick, G. (1969), *Hausa Proverbs*, New York: Negro University Press.

Messenger, J. C., Jr. (1959), "The Role of Proverbs in a Nigerian Judicial System," *Southwestern Journal of Anthropology*, 15.

Mieder, W. and Dundes, A. (eds) (1981), *The Wisdom of Many*, New York: Garland.

Milimo, J. T. (1972), *Bantu Wisdom*, Lusaka: Zambia Printing Company.

Mitchell, H. (1970), *Black Preaching*, Philadelphia: Lippincott.

Mitchell, H. (1975), *Black Belief*, New York: Harper & Row.

Mitchell-Kernan, C. (1969), *Language Behavior in a Black Urban Community* (Working Paper No. 23). Berkeley, CA: Language Behavior Research Laboratory

Mitchell-Kernan, C. (1972), "Signifying, Loud-Talking, and Marking," in Kochman, T. (ed.), *Rappin' and Stylin' Out: Communication in Urban Black America*, Urbana: University of Illinois Press, pp. 315–35.

Morgan, M. (1989), "From Down South to Up South: The Language Behavior of Three Generations of Black Women Residing in Chicago," unpublished doctoral dissertation, University of Pennsylvania, Philadelphia.

Morgan, M. (1993), "The Africannes of Counter-Language among Afro-Americans," in Mufwene, S. S. (ed.), *Africanisms in Afro-American Language Varieties*, Athens, GA: University of Georgia Press.

Morgan, M. (unpublished manuscript), " 'Hip Hop Hooray': The Linguistic Production of Identity," unpublished manuscript, Department of Anthropology, University of California at Los Angeles.

Morrison, T. (1971), "What the Black Woman Thinks about Women's Lib," *New York Times Magazine*, 22 August, pp. 14–15, 63–4, 66.

Morrison, T. (1981), "The Language Must not Sweat," *The New Republic*, 21 March.

Morrison, T. (1994), *The Nobel Lecture in Literature*, London: Chatto and Windus.

Mufwene, S. S. (1992), "Ideology and facts on African American Vernacular English," *Pragmatics* 2(2), pp. 141–66.

Mufwene, S. S. (1993), (ed.) *Africanisms in Afro-American Language Varieties*, Athens, GA: University of Georgia Press.

Mufwene, S. S. (1997), "Jargons, Pidgins, Creoles, and Koines: What are They?" in Spears, A. K. and Winford, D. (eds) *The Structure and Status of Pidgins and Creoles*, Philadelphia and Amsterdam: John Benjamins.

Murray, L. ([1795] 1819), *English Grammar*, New York: Collins and Company.

Muxlow, K. (1990), telephone interview, 15 May.

Myrdal, G. (1944), *An American Dilemma*, New York: Harper & Row.

National Advisory Commission on Civil Disorders, (1968), report [popularly known as the "Kerner Commission Report" after its chair, Otto Kerner], Washington, DC: Government Printing Office.

National Assessment of Educational Progress, (1980), "Writing Achievement, 1969–79," (Report No. 10-W-01), Denver, CO: Education Commission of the States.

National Organization for an American Revolution, (1982), *Manifesto for an American Revolutionary Party*.

Nelson, H. and Gonzales, M. A. (1991), *Bring the Noise: A Guide to Rap Music and Hip-Hop Culture* (with foreword by Fab 5 Freddy), New York: Harmony.

N'Namdi, G. (1978), "Analysis of Parent–Child Interaction in the Two-Child Black Family," unpublished doctoral dissertation, University of Michigan.

Nunberg, G. (1992), "The Official English Movement: Reimaging America," in Crawford, J. (ed.), *Language Loyalties: A Source Book on the Official English Controversy*, Chicago: University of Chicago Press.

Oakland California School Board. (1996), "Resolution of the Board of Education Adopting the Report and Recommendations of the African-American Task Force," 18 December, Oakland, CA.

Odum, H. W. (1910), *Social and Mental Traits of the Negro*, New York: AMS Press.

Okezie, J. A. (1978, August), "Function and use of Igbo proverbs in conflict," presented at the Annual Seminar on Igbo Language and Culture, University of Nigeria, Nsukka.

Olson, D. R. (1977), "From Utterance to Text: The Bias of Language in Speech and Writing," *Harvard Educational Reviews*, 47, pp. 257–281.

Olson, G. A. (1997, May), "Critical Pedagogy and Composition Scholarship," [Review of books by J. A. Berlin, J. Coleman and J. Sledd.], *College Composition and Communication*, 48, (2).

Opoku, K. A. (1975), *Speak to the Winds*, New York: Lothrop, Lee & Shephard.

Page, C. (1989), "African American or Black? It's Debatable," *Detroit Free Press*, 1 January, pp. A1, A12.

Pasteur, A. B. and Toldson, I. L. (1982), *Roots of Soul: The Psychology of Black Expressiveness*, New York: Doubleday.

Patterson, O. (1991), "Race, Gender and Liberal Fallacies," *New York Times*, sec 4, p. 15.

Percelay, J., Dweck, S. and Ivey, M. (1995), *Double Snaps*, New York: William Morrow.

Peñalosa, F. (1972), "Chicano Multilingualism and Multiglossia," *Aztlan*, vol. 3, pp. 15–22.

Peñalosa, F. (1980), *Chicano Sociolinguistics*, Rowley, MA: Newbury House.

Phaswana, N. E. (1994), "African Language Planning Policies at the University of Venda and the Medium of Instruction Question," unpublished Master's thesis, University of Cape Town.

Phillips, D. B., Greenberg, R. and Gibson, S. (1993, December), "College Composition and Communication: Chronicling a Discipline's Genesis," *College Composition and Communication*, 44.

Phillipson, R. (1992), *Linguistic Imperialism*, Oxford: Oxford University Press.

Phillipson, R. and Skutnabb-Kangas, T. (1986, August), "English: The Language of Wider Colonisation," paper presented at the 11th World Congress of Sociology, New Delhi, India.

Pooley, R. (1969), "The Oral Usage of English Teachers," in McDavid V. (ed.), *Language and Teaching: Essays in Honor of W. Wilber Hatfield*, Chicago: Chicago State College.

Pooley, R. (1974), "The Teaching of English Usage," Urbana, IL: National Council of Teachers of English.

Postman, N. and Weingartner, C. (1969), *Teaching as a Subversive Activity*, New York: Delacourte.

Pouissant, A. (1967), "A Negro Psychiatrist Explains the Negro Psyche," *The New York Times Magazine*, p. 52.

Progressive Composition Caucus, (1987, April) Newsletter.

Quirk, R. (1995), Keynote Address, English in Africa Conference, 11–14 September Grahamstown, South Africa.

Read, A. W. (1939), "The Speech of Negroes in Colonial America," *Journal of Negro History*, 24, pp. 247–58.

Richardson, E. (1998), "The Anti-Ebonics Movement: 'Standard' English Only," *Journal of English Linguistics*, 26, 2.

Rickford, J. R. (1979), "Variation in a Creole Continuum: Quantitative and Implicational Approaches," Ph.D. dissertation, University of Pennsylvania.

Rickford, J. R. (1992), "Rappin on the Copula Coffin: Theoretical and Methodological Issues in the Analysis of Copula Variation in African American Vernacular English," *Language Variation and Change*, 3, pp. 103–32.

Rickford, J. R. and Rickford, A. E. (1976), "Cut-Eye and Suck-Teeth: Masked Africanisms in New World Guise," *Journal of American Folklore*, 89, 353, 294–309.

Rickford, J. R. (1998), "The Creole Origins of African American Vernacular English: Evidence from Copula Absence," in Mufwene, S. S. et. al., *African American English: Structure, History and Use*, London and New York: Routledge.

Rogers, J. A. (1917), *From Superman to Man*, Chicago: M. A. Donohue.

Rogers, J. A. (1934), *100 Amazing Facts about the Negro, with Complete Proof; A Short Cut to the World History of the Negro*, New York: J. A. Rogers Publication.

Rose, T. (1994), *Black Noise: Rap Music and Black Culture in Contemporary America*, Hanover, NH: Wesleyan University Press.

Rowan, C. T. (1979), "Black English would Doom Blacks to Fail," *Detroit News*, 11 July, p. 19A.

Rowan, C. T. (1990, 15 October), interview, *USA Today*, p. 6A.

Roy, A. M. (1991), "The English-Only Movement: A Review Essay," *College Composition and Communication* 42(4), pp. 520–3.

Russell, J. (1980), "Many Kinds of English," *New York Times Book Review*, 6 January.

Safire, W. (1981), "Getting Down," *The New York Times Magazine*, 18 January.

Safire, W. (1985), "The Case of the President's Case," *New York Times Magazine*, p. 18.

Salaam, N. (1976), "Proverbial Data Collection Critique," unpublished research report, Detroit: Wayne State University, Center for Black Studies.

Sapir, E. (1929), *Language: An Introduction to the Study of Speech*, New York: Harcourt, Brace.

Samuels, M. L. (1995), Headmistress, Battswood Educare Center, interview by G. Smitherman and Ezra Hyland, 22 August, Cape Town, South Africa.

Schechter, W. (1970), *The History of Negro Humor in America*, New York: Fleet Press.

Schneider, E. W. (1993), "Africanisms in the Grammar of Afro-American English: Weighing the Evidence," in Mufwene, S. S. (ed.), *Africanisms in Afro-American Language Varieties*, Athens, GA: University of Georgia Press, pp. 209–21.

Schwartz, J. (1988), (Michigan State Senator), personal communication, 24 May.

Scott, J. C. (1981), "Mixed Dialects in the Composition Classroom," in Montgomery, M. (ed.), *Language Variety in the South: Perspectives in Black and White*, Montgomery: University of Alabama Press.

Scruton, Roger, (1980), "English and Where it's at," *London Times Literary Supplement*, 22 February.

Seymour, D. (1971), "Black Children, Black Speech," *Commonweal*, 95, pp. 175–8.

Sheridan, D. (1998), personal communication, 17 May.

Shuy, R. and Fasold, R. W. (1973), *Language Attitudes: Current Trends and Prospects*, Washington, DC: Georgetown University Press.

Silverman-Weinreech, G. (1981), "Towards a Structural Analysis of Yiddish Proverbs," in Miedner, W. and Dundes, A. (eds), *The Wisdom of Many*, New York: Garland.

Simmons, D. C. (1963), "Possible West African Sources for the American Negro 'Dozens'," *Journal of American Folklore*, 76, pp. 339–40.

Simmons, G. (1972) (ed.), *Black Culture: Reading and Writing Black*, Holt, Rinehart.

Simmons, J. D. (1997), "Ebonics Plagues Policymakers," *Daily Challenge, Weekend Edition*, 3–5 January.

Simpkins, G. (1976), "Cross-Cultural Approach to Reading," (doctoral dissertation, University of Massachusetts-Amherst), Dissertation Abstracts International, University Microfilms. No. DCJ77-06404.

Simpkins, G., Holt, G., and Simpkins, C. (1975), *Bridge: A Cross-Culture Reading Program Field Test Report*. Boston: Houghton Mifflin.

Sledd, J. (1956), "Coordination (Faulty) and Subordination (Upside-Down)," *College Composition and Communication*.

Sledd, J. (1969), "Bidialectalism: The Linguistics of White Supremacy," *English Journal*, 1307–29.

Sledd, J. (1996), "Grammar for Social Awareness in Time of Class Warfare," *English Journal*, November.

Smith, A. (Molefi K. Asante) (1969), *Rhetoric of Black Revolution*, Boston: Allyn and Bacon.

Smith, A. (1972) (ed.) *Language, Communication, and Rhetoric in Black America*, New York: Harper & Row.

Smith, A. N. (1976, May), "No one has a Right to his Own Language," *College Composition and Communication*, 27, pp. 155–9.

Smith, E. (1978), "The Retention of the Phonological, Phonemic and Morpho-phonemic Features of Africa in Afro-American Ebonics," seminar paper No. 43, Fullerton, CA: California State University.

Smith, E. (1998), "What is Black English? What is Ebonics?" in Delpit, L. and Perry, T. (eds), *The Real Ebonics Debate: Power, Language and the Education of African American Children*, Boston: Beacon Press.

Smith, M. G. (1965), *The Plural Society in the British West Indies*, Berkeley: University of California Press.

Smitherman, G.: *For references to Smitherman, see Publications by the author, pp. 430–3*.

Spears, A. K. (1982), The Black English semi-auxiliary "come." *Language*, 58(4), 850-72.

Spears, A. K. and Winford, D. (1997), *Structure and Status of Pidgins and Creoles*. Philadelphia and Amsterdam: John Benjamins.

Spears, A. K. (1998), African-American Language Use: Ideology and So-Called Obscenity," in Mufwene, S. S. (ed.), *African-American English*, London and New York: Routledge, pp. 226–50.

Specter, M. (1990), Men and Women of their Word: But Should that be Black or African American? *The Washington Post National Weekly Edition*, 28 October, p. 10.

Spillers, H. (1983), "A Hateful Passion, A Lost Love: Three Women's Fiction," *Feminist Studies*, vol. 9.

Stalin, J. (1951), *Marxism and Linguistics*, New York: International Publishers.

Staples, R. (1971), Towards a Sociology of the Black Family: A Theoretical and Methodological Assessment, *Journal of Marriage and Family*, 33, 119–39.

State of Michigan 83rd Legislature (1985), *Amendment to Act No. 451 of the Public Acts of 1976, Section 1157a*.

State of Michigan House of Representatives (1987), *Journal of the House*, 21 October, pp. 2754–5.

State of New Mexico 39th Legislature (1989), *House Joint Memorial*, 16.

Steinman, M. Jr. (1951), Darkness is Still King: A Reply to Professor Lloyd, *College Composition and Communication*.

Stewart, B. (1973) " 'Sesame Street': A Linguistic Detour for Black-Language Speakers," *Black World* (August).

Stewart, W. A. (1967, spring), "Sociolinguistic Factors in the History of American Negro Dialects," *Florida Foreign Language Reporter*, pp. 2–4.

Stewart, W. A. (1967, 1968, in 1972), "Toward a History of American Negro Dialect," in Williams, F. (ed.), *Language and Poverty: Perspectives on a Theme*, Chicago: Markham (pp. 351–79).

Stone, C. (1975), "A Black Paper: Standardized Tests: True or False?" *The Black Collegian*, pp. 44–56.

Sykes, M. (1988), "From Rights to Needs: Official Discourse and the Welfarization of Race," in Smitherman, G. and van Dijk, T. A. (eds), *Discourse and Discrimination*, Detroit: Wayne State University Press.

"Task Force on Language Policy and National Development," (1981), in Smitherman, G. (ed.), *Black English and the Education of Black Children and Youth: Proceedings of the National Invitational Symposium on the King Decision*, Detroit: Wayne State University Center for Black Studies.

"Task Force on Media and Information Dissemination," (1981), in Smitherman, G. (ed.), *Black English and the Education of Black Children and Youth: Proceedings of the National Invitational Symposium on the King Decision*, Detroit: Wayne State University Center for Black Studies.

Taylor, O. (1971), "Recent Developments in Sociolinguistics: Some Implications for AHSA," *American Speech and Hearing Association Journal*, 13, pp. 341–8.

Taylor, O. (1992, June), Presentation at African American English in Schools and Society Conference, Stanford University, Stanford, CA.

Taylor, H. U. (1989), *Standard English, Black English and Bidialectalism*, New York: Peter Lang.

Thomas, G. (1926), "South Texas Negro Work-Songs," in *Publications of the Texas Folklore Society*, No. 5, reprinted in Dobie, F. (ed.), *Rainbow in the Morning*, Hatboro, PA: Folklore Associates, Inc.

Thompson, R. F. (1983), *Flash of the Spirit: African and Afro-American Art and Philosophy*, New York: Random House.

Tillinghast, J. A. (1902), *The Negro in Africa and the Americas*, New York: MacMillan.

Tollefson, J. A. (1991), *Planning Language, Planning Inequality*, London: Longman Group Limited.

Turner, L. D. (1949), *Africanisms in the Gullah Dialect*, Chicago: University of Chicago Press.

Upski. (1993, May), "We Use Words Like 'Mackadocious'," *The Source*, pp. 48–56.

Valdman, A. (1977), *Creole and Pidgin Linguistics*, Bloomington: University of Indiana Press.

Van Dijk, T. A. (1988), "How 'They' Hit the Headlines: Ethnic Minorities in the Press," in Smitherman, G. and van Dijk, T. A. (eds), *Discourse and Discrimination*, Detroit: Wayne State University Press.

Van Sertima, I. (1976), "My Gullah Brother and I: Exploration into a Community's Language and Myth through its Oral Tradition," in Harrison, D. S. and Trabasso, T. (eds), *Black English: A Seminar*, Hillsdale, NJ: Erlbaum Associates.

Vass, W. K. (1979), *The Bantu-Speaking Heritage of the United States*, Los Angeles: University of California Center for Afro-American Studies.

Vaughn-Cooke, F. (1980), "Evaluating Language Assessment Procedures: An

Examination of Linguistic Guidelines and Public Law 94–142 guidelines," in Atlatis, J. E.and Tucker, R. (eds) *Language and Public Life*, Washington, DC: Georgetown University Press.

Vaughn-Cooke, F. (1987), "Are Black and White Vernaculars Diverging?" *American Speech*, vol. 62, pp. 62–72.

Vibe (1995), "Who's Zoomin' Whom?" August, p. 67.

Veltman, C. (1988), *The Future of the Spanish Language in the United States*, New York and Washington, DC: Hispanic Policy Development Project.

Vološinov, V. N. ([1929] 1973), *Marxism and the Philosophy of Language*, translated by L. Matjka and I. R. Tutnik, Cambridge: MIT.

Von Humboldt, W. ([1810] 1963), "Man's Intrinsic Humanity: His Language," in Cowan, M. (ed.), *Humanist Without Portfolio*, Detroit: Wayne State University Press.

Vygotsky, L. S. (1962), *Thought and Language*, Cambridge: MIT.

Walker, A. (1982), *The Color Purple*, New York: Harcourt Brace Jovanovich.

Walker, A. (1983), *In Search of our Mother's Garden*, New York: Harcourt, Brace, Jovanovich.

Walker, D. ([1829] 1965), *Appeal, in Four Articles: Together with a Preamble to the Coloured Citizens of the World, but in Particular, and very Expressly, to those in the United States of America*, (C. M. Wiltse, ed.), New York: Hill and Wang.

Walker, S. (1971), "Black English: Expression of the Afro-American Experiences," *Black World* (August 1973).

Walters, R. W. (1993), *Pan Africanism in the African Diaspora: The African American Linkage*, Detroit: Wayne State University Press.

wa Thiong'o, N. (1984), "The Politics of Language in African Literature," in Turner, L. and Alan, J. (eds), *Frantz Fanon, Soweto and American Black thought*.

Watkins, F. (1991), telephone interview, 8 April.

Watkins, M. (1978), "Books: Black Language Gets New Dimension," *New York Times*, (29 March).

Watkins, M. (1994), *On the real side: Laughing, Lying, and Signifying: The Underground Tradition of African-American Humor*, New York: Simon & Schuster.

Weber, G. (1971), *Inner City Children can be Taught to Read: Four Successful Schools*, Washington, DC: Council for Basic Education.

Webster, N. ([1784] 1980), *A Grammatical Institute of the English Language*, Part II, Delmar, New York: Scholars Facsimiles and Reprints.

Weinrich, M. T. (1931) "Mutershpracht un tsveyte shpraks," *Yivo-Bleter*, 1, pp. 301–16.

Weinrich, U. (1963), *Languages in Contact*, The Hague: Mouton.

Whiteman, M. (1976), "Dialect Influence and the Writing of Black and White Working-Class Americans," unpublished doctoral dissertation, Georgetown University, Washington, DC.

Whorf, B. (1956), *Language, Thought and Reality: Selected Writings of Benjamin Lee Whorf*, Carroll, J. B. (ed.), Cambridge: MIT Press.

Wilkerson, I. (1989), "Many Who are Black Favor New Term for Who They Are," *New York Times*, 31 January, pp. 1, 8.

Wilkins, R. (1971), "Black Nonsense," *Crisis*, 78.

Wilks, M. (1981), "Black English and Media," in Smitherman, G. (ed.), *Black English and the Education of Black Children and Youth: Proceedings of the National Symposium on the King Decision*, Detroit: Wayne State University Center for Black Studies.

Williams, F., Whitehead, J., and Miller, L. (1971), *Attitudinal Correlates of Children's Speech Characteristics*, Austin: University of Texas, Center for Communication Research.

Williams, R. L. (1972), *The Bitch 100: A Culture-Specific Test*, St. Louis: Washington University.

Williams, R. L. (1973), "Developing Culture Specific Assessment Devices: An Empirical Rationale," in Williams, R. L. (ed.), *Ebonics: The True Language of Black Folks*, St. Louis: Institute of Black Studies, pp. 110–32.

Williams, R. L. (1974), "The Silent Mugging of the Black Community," *Psychology Today*, pp. 32–41, 101.

Williams, R. L. (ed.) (1975), *Ebonics: The True Language of Black Folks*, St. Louis: Institute of Black Studies.

Williams, R. L., Rivers, W., and Brantley, M. (1975), "The Effects of Language on the Test Performance of Black Children," in *Ebonics: The True Language of Black Folks*, (ed.) Williams, R. L., St. Louis, MO: Institute of Black Studies.

William, S. W. (1982, March), "Language Consciousness and Cultural Liberation in Black America," paper presented at the Sixth Annual Conference of the National Council for Black Studies, Chicago.

Williams, S. W. (1993), "Substantive Africanisms at the End of the African Linguistic Diaspora," in Mufwene, S. S. (ed.), *Africanisms in Afro American Language Varieties*, Athens, GA: University of Georgia Press.

Wilson, R. (1971), "A Comparison of Learning Styles in African Tribal Groups with African American Learning Situations and the Channels of Cultural Connection: An Analysis of Documentary Material," unpublished doctoral dissertation, Wayne State University.

Wilson, T. L. (1972), "Notes Toward a Process of Afro-American Education," *Harvard Educational Review*, 42, pp. 374–89.

Winford, D. (1997), "On the Origins of African American Vernacular English – A Creolist Perspective," *Diachronica*, XIV, pp. 305–44.

Wodak, R. (1995), "Critical Linguistics and Critical Discourse," in Verschueren, J. Ostman, J. and Blommaert, J. (eds), *Handbook of Pragmatics*, (pp. 204–10), Philadelphia and Amsterdam: John Benjamins,

Wolfram, W. (1970), *Detroit Negro Speech*, Washington, DC: Center for Applied Linguistics.

Wolfram, W. (1990), "Re-examining Vernacular Black Speech," *Language*, vol. 66, pp. 121–35.

Wolfram, W. (1997), "The Myth of the Verbally Deprived Black Child," in Bauer L. and Trudgill, P. (eds), *Language Myths*.

Wolfram, W. (1998, June), Language Ideology and Dialect: Understanding the Oakland Ebonics Controversy, *Journal of English Linguistics*, 26(2).

Wonder, S. (1995, Jul 9), "Quote Bag," *Detroit Free Press*, p. 4.

Woodson, C. G. (1915), *The Education of the Negro Prior to 1861*, Washington, DC: Associated Publishers.

Woodson, C. G. (1921), *The History of the Negro Church*, Washington, DC: Associated Publishers.

Woodson, C. G. (ed.) (1925), *Negro Orators and their Orations*, Washington, DC: Associated Publishers.

Woodson, C. G. ([1933] 1969), *The Mis-Education of the Negro*, Washington, DC: Associated Publishers.

Woodson, C. G. ([1936] 1969), *The African Background Outlined*, or *Handbook for the Study of the Negro*, New York: New American Library.

Wright, G. (1983, March), "US English," *San Francisco Chronicle*, 20, p. B9.

Wright, R. (1958), *The Long Dream*, New York: Ace Publishing Corporation.

Wright, R. (1963), *Lawd Today*, New York: Walker and Company.

Wright, S. (1984) "A Description between the Oral and Written Language Patterns of a Group of Black Community College Students," unpublished Ph.D. dissertation, Wayne State University, Detroit.

Yasim, J. (1995), "In Yo Face: Rapping Beats Coming at You," unpublished doctoral dissertation, Columbia University, Teachers College, New York.

Young, J., Jr. (1990), telephone interview, 15 May.

Zentella, A. C. (1988a), "Language Politics in the USA: The English-Only Movement," in Craige, B. (ed.), *Literature, Language and Politics*, Athens: University of Georgia Press, pp. 39–53.

Zentella, A. C. (1988b), personal communication.

Zentella, A. C. (1997), *Growing Up Bilingual*, Malden, MA: Blackwell Publishers.

Zinn, H. (1970), *The Politics of History*, Boston: Beacon Press.

PUBLISHED BY THE AUTHOR

(1971) "The Black Idiom and White Institutions," *Negro American Literature Forum*, autumn, pp. 88–91, 115–17.

(1972a), "Black Power is Black Language," in *Black Culture: Reading and Writing Black*, (ed.) Simmons, G., New York: Holt, Rinehart and Winston, pp. 78–89.

(1972b), "English Teacher, Why You Be Doing The Thangs You Don't Do?" *English Journal*, January, pp. 59–65.

(1972c), "The Legitimacy of the Black Idiom," National Council of Teachers of English cassette recording series, March.

([1972] 1973), "After Bi-Dialectism – What?" National Council of Teachers of English cassette recording series, November. Revised version published as "Grammar and Goodness," in *English Journal*, May, pp. 774–7.

([1973] 1980), "White English in Blackface, or Who Do I Be?" *Black Scholar*, May–June, 1973, pp. 3–15. Reprinted in *The State of the Language*, (eds) Michaels, L. and Ricks, C., Berkeley: University of California, pp. 158–68. Excerpts reprinted in (ed.) Goshgarian, G. *Exploring Language*, Little, 1983 and *Black English, Standard English and Bi-Dialectalism*, Hanni Taylor, Peter Lang, 1989.

(1973a), "The Black Idiom: What the English Curriculum Bees Needin," *Arizona English Bulletin*, April, pp. 76–8.

(1973b), "The Power of the Rap: The Black Idiom and the New Black Poetry," *Twentieth Century Literature*, October, pp. 259–74.

(1974), "Everybody Wants to Know Why I Sing the Blues: Ed Bullings/Stage One," *Black World*, April, pp. 3–17.

(1975a), "Linguistic Diversity in the Classroom," in *The Cultural Revolution in Foreign Language Teaching*, (ed.) Lafayette, R., Skokie: National Textbook Company, pp. 32–48.

(1975b), *Black Language and Culture: Sounds of Soul*, New York: Harper & Row.

([1976] 1988), "'How I Got Over': Communication Dynamics in the Black Community," with Daniel, J. L. in *Quarterly Journal of Speech*, February, pp. 26–39. Reprinted in D. Carbaugh, *Cultural Communication and Intercultural Contact*, Excerpt of article reprinted in "The Prospect for Cultural Communication," by G. Philipsen in *Communication Theory From Eastern and Western Perspectives*, Academic Press.

(1976), "We Are The Music: Ron Milner, People's Playwright," *Black World*, April, pp. 10–20.

([1977] 1986), *Talkin and Testifyin: The Language of Black America*, Boston: Houghton Mifflin; reissued, with revisions, Detroit: Wayne State University Press.

(1977), "Black Language and Black Liberation: Implications for Public Policy," with McGinnis, J. in *Black Books Bulletin*, June, pp. 8–14, 69.

(1978), "Sociolinguistic Conflict in the Schools," with McGinnis, J. in *Journal of Non-White Concerns*, January, pp. 9–19.

(1979a), "Black English and Black Identity: Message to the Talented Tenth," with Daniel, J. L. in *Journal of Educational and Social Analysis*, April, pp. 20–30.

(1979b), "Soul 'N Style," monthly columns from *English Journal*, reprinted as a chapter in *Alternatives in Teaching English: Essays on the Future of the Profession*, (ed.) Judy, S., New York: Hayden Book Company, pp. 2–14.

(1979c), "Toward Educational Linguistics for the First World," *College English*, November, pp. 202–11.

(1981a), *Black English and the Education of Black Children and Youth: Proceedings of the National Invitational Symposium on the King Decision*, 213 February, edited, with an introduction, Detroit: Center for Black Studies, Wayne State University.

(1981b), "Black English: So Good It's Bad," *Essence* Magazine.

(1981c), "Talkin and Testifyin on Ann Arbor's Green Road," *John Dewey Society Occasional Papers Series*, pp. 26–51.

([1981d] 1985), "'What Go Round Come Round': *King* in Perspective," *Harvard Educational Review*, February, pp. 40–56. Reprinted in *Tapping Potential*, (ed.) Brooks, C.

(1983a), "American English in its Death Throes: Is We Sick?," *North Carolina English Teacher*, winter, pp. 4–7.

(1983b), "Language and Liberation," *Journal of Negro Education*, 52(1), winter, pp. 15–23.

(1983c), review of *Language and Responsibility*, by Chomsky, N. in *Language in Society*, 12(3), autumn pp. 349–56.

(1984a), "Deadly Force and Its Effects on PoliceCommunity Relations," with Littlejohn, E., and Quick, A. in *Howard Law Review*, September, pp. 1131–84.

(1984b), "Language Attitudes and Self-Fulfilling Prophecies in the Elementary School," with Scott, J. In *The English Language Today*, (ed.) Greenbaum, S., Oxford: Pergamon Press, pp. 302–14.

(1984c), "The Contemporary Merger of Linguistics and the Law: Black Language as Power," in *Language and Power*, (eds), Kramarae, C., and Schulz, M., Beverly Hills: Sage, pp. 101–15.

(1986a) "Talkin and Testifyin: Black English and the Black Experience," in *Les Temps Modernes*, (ed.) Santamaria, U., December, pp. 112–29. [Article translated into French, in special journal issue on Black Americans.]

(1986b), "Upside the Wall: The Afro-American Mural Movement," with Donaldson, J. R., in *The People's Art: Black Murals, 1967–78*, (ed.) Burnham, I., Philadelphia: Afro-American Historical and Cultural Museum.

(1987a), "'Makin A Way Outa No Way': the Proverb Tradition in the Black Experience," with Daniel, J. L., and Jeremiah, M. in *Journal of Black Studies*, 17(4), June, pp. 482–508.

(1987b), "The Nurturing Role of Black Church Women," with Daniel, Daniel, and Poag, in *The Griot*, autumn, pp. 33–43.

(1987c), "Toward a National Public Policy on Language," *College English*, 49(1), January, pp. 29–36.

(1988a), "Discriminatory Discourse on Afro-American Speech," in *Discourse and Discrimination* (eds), Smitherman, G., and van Dijk, T. A., Detroit: Wayne State University Press, pp. 144–75.

(1988b), *Discourse and Discrimination*, co-edited with van Dijk, T. A., Detroit: Wayne State University Press.

(1989), "A 'New Way of Talkin': Language, Social Change, and Political Theory," *Sage Race Relations Abstracts*, 14(1), February, pp. 5–23. [Based on updated survey of Black and White automobile assembly line workers in Detroit.]

(1989, July), *"And Ain't I A Woman?": African American Women and Affirmative Action*, special issue of *Sex Roles*, co-edited with Taylor, D.

(1990a), "The 'Miseducation of the Negro' – and You Too," in *Not Only English: Affirming America's Multilingual Heritage*, (ed.) Daniels, H., Urbana: National Council of Teachers of English, pp. 10920.

(1990b), *Improving Self-Concept for At-Risk Black Students, With Emphasis on Saving the Black Male*, edited conference proceedings, Detroit: Detroit Public Schools.

([1991] 1993) " 'What is Africa to Me?': Language, Ideology and *African American*," *American Speech*, 66(2), summer, pp. 115–32. Reprinted in *Word: A Black Culture Journal*, 1993, and as a chapter in Ward, 1993.

(1991a), "Black English in the Integrated Workplace," with Botan, C. In *Journal of Black Studies*, December. [Based on language survey of Black and White speakers, working and middle class, in Detroit.]

(1992a), "African Americans and 'English Only'," *Language Problems and Language Planning*, autumn.

(1992b), *Strategies for Educating African American Males: the Detroit Model*, with Watson, C. And Gourdine, A., Detroit: Detroit Public Schools.

(1992c), "Language, Dialects and the Fourth of July" in *Why Don't You Talk Right?*, (ed.) Elliott, A., Kendall Hunt.

(1992d), "Black English, Diverging or Converging?: the View from the National Assessment of Educational Progress," *Language and Education*, 6(1).

([1992e] 1995), "African Americans and English Only," *E Pluribus Unum*, (ed.) Troutman-Robinson, D., MSU College of Arts and Letters.

(1993), " 'Still I Rise': Education Against the Odds in Cuba," *East Lansing Voice*, winter.

(1994a), " 'The Blacker the Berry, the Sweeter the Juice': African American Student Writers and the NAEP," in *The Need for Story: Cultural Diversity in Classroom and Community*, (eds) Dyson, A. H., and Genishi, C., Urbana: National Council of Teachers of English, 1994.

(1994b), *Black Talk: Words and Phrases from the Hood to the Amen Corner*, Boston: Houghton Mifflin.

(1994c), "Juvenile Justice: Multicultural Issues," with Corley, C. in *Multicultural Perspectives in Criminal Justice and Criminology*, (eds) Hendricks, J. E., and Byers, B., Springfield: Charles C. Thomas Publishers.

(1995a), " 'If I'm Lyin, I'm Flyin': An Introduction to the Art of the Snap," in *Double Snaps* by Percelay, J., Dweck, S., and Ivey, M., New York: Morrow and Company, 1995.

(1995b), "African American English: Language Attitudes and Public Policy," *Twelve Pages*, 4(3), City University of New York, autumn.

(1995c), "Non-Standard English," in *The Oxford Companion To Women's Writing in the United States*, (eds) Davidson, C. N., and Wagner-Martin, L., New York: Oxford University.

(1995d), "Testifyin, Sermonizin, and Signifyin: Anita Hill, Clarence Thomas, and the African American Verbal Tradition," in *African American Women Speak Out on Anita HillClarence Thomas*, (ed.), Detroit: Wayne State University Press.

(1995e), *African American Women Speak Out on Anita HillClarence Thomas*, edited with an introduction and article, Detroit: Wayne State University Press.

(1995f), " 'Students' Right to Their Own Language': A Retrospective," *English Journal*, 84(1), January.

(1996a), "The Hit and the Miss: The African American Art of the Pickup Line," with Randle, G. in *You're So Fine, I'd Drink a Tub of Your Bathwater*, by Dweck, S. And Ivey, M., New York: Hyperion.

(1996b), "A Womanist Looks at the Million Man March," in *Million Man March: A Commemorative Anthology*, (eds) Madhubuti, H., and Karenga, M., Chicago: Third World Press.

(1996c), *Educating African American Males: Detroit's Malcolm X Academy Solution*, with Watson, C., Chicago: Third World Press.

(1997a), " 'The Chain Remain the Same': Communicative Practices in the Hip-Hop Nation," *Journal of Black Studies*, September.

(1997b), "African American Language," in *Dictionary of Multicultural Education*, Phoenix: Oryx Press.

(1997c), "Black Language and the Education of Black Children – One Mo Once," *The Black Scholar*, 27(1), spring.

(1997d), "Discourse, Ethnicity, Culture and Racism," with van Dijk, T. A., Ting-Toomey, S. and Troutman, D. in *Discourse as Social Interaction*, (ed.) van Dijk, T. A., Thousand Oaks, California: Sage.

(1997e), "Forms of Address," with Randle, G. in *Oxford Companion to African American Literature*, (eds), Andrews, W. L., Foster, F. S. and Harris, T., New York: Oxford University Press.

(1997f), "Moving Beyond Resistance: Ebonics and African American Youth," with Cunningham, S., *Journal of Black Psychology*, 23(3), August.

(1998a), " 'What Go Round Come Round': *King* in Perspective," revised version of 1981 article, reprinted in *The Real Ebonics Debate: Power, Language, and the Education of African American Children*, (eds) Perry, T. and Delpit, L., Boston: Beacon Press.

(1998b), "Black English/Ebonics: What it Be Like?" in *The Real Ebonics Debate: Power, Language, and the Education of African American Children*, (eds) Perry, T. and Delpit, L., Boston: Beacon Press.

(1998c), "Black Women's Language", with Troutman-Robinson, D., in *The Reader's Companion to US Women's History*, (eds) Mankiller, W., Mink, G., Navarro, M., Smith, B., Steinem, G., Boston and New York: Houghton Mifflin Company.

(1998d), "Ebonics and Tesol," in "Teaching Issues," *Tesol Quarterly*, spring.

(1998e), "Ebonics, *King*, and Oakland: Some Folk Don't Believe Fat Meat is Greasy," in *Journal of English Linguistics*, special issue on Ebonics, June.

(1998f), "From 'Hujambo' to 'Molo': Study of and Interest in African Languages Among African Americans," in *Between Distinction and Extinction: The Harmonization and Standardization of African Languages*, ed., Kwesi Kwaa Prah, Johannesburg: University of Witwatersrand.

(1998g), "Word from the Hood: The Lexicon of African American Vernacular English," in *The Structure of African American Vernacular English*, (eds) Salikoko, S., Mufwene, S. S., Rickford, J. R., Bailey, G., and Baugh, J., New York: Routledge.

(1998h), review of *Multilingual Education for South Africa*, (eds) Heugh, K., Siegruhn, A., and Pluddemann, P. In *Multilingua*, with Thiba, T., 17(2/3), special issue, "Aspects of Multilingualism in Post-Apartheid South Africa," (ed.), Kamwangamalu, N. M.

(1999), "CCCC's Role in the Struggle for Language Rights," *College Composition and Communication*, 50th anniversary issue, February.

(2000), *Black Talk: Words and Phrases from the Hood to the Amen Corner*, revised, updated edition, Boston and New York: Houghton Mifflin.

"English Plus" policy 315, 329
enslavement 19, 30, 33, 44, 225, 270,
  351; African population 42;
  historical 98; rebellion against 46
EPIC (English Plus Information
  Clearinghouse) 292, 312
Equal Education Opportunity Act
  (1974) 132, 144
equal educational opportunity 134,
  135, 139
equality: ambivalence on the question
  of 71; claim to 310; dream of 37;
  moral and Constitutional questions of
  387; struggle for 294; women's 267
Equiana, Olaudah (Gustavus Vassa) 44
equity: political and economic demand
  for 50; racial 47; struggle for 293
eradicationism 346–7, 357
Essence (Black women's magazine) 41,
  340
ethnic groups 51, 56; African,
  linguistically diverse 100
ethnicity 159, 181, 321
ethnocentrism: Anglo-American 364;
  bias 74; linguistic 295
ethnography 83, 85, 86, 101
ethnolinguistics 83, 160, 182; Black
  Tradition 262
ETS (Educational Testing Service) 167,
  172
Eurocentrism: cultural dominance 271;
  discourse 257
European Americans 53, 254, 296;
  Abolitionists 46; linguistic and
  cultural domination 157–8; students
  178, 179; see also EAL
existential "it" 24
expletives 24, 62
exploitation 355; capitalist 316;
  economic 316; foreign laborers 309;
  labor 101; material 317; racial 98;
  rhetorical 263; sexual 93; white
  working class 71, 102; women 98
eye-rolling 350, 351

Fabio, Sarah Webster 382
FAIR (Federation for American
  Immigration Reform) 309

"fakelore" 232
Fanon, Frantz 66, 157–8, 203, 317,
  354
Farrakhan, Louis 260, 265, 316
Farrell, Thomas J. 88–9, 392
Faulkner, W. 343–4
Fauset, Arthur Huff 267
FBI 257, 261
Federal law 37
feminists 311, 360; white 98
Fernando, S. H. 268
field dependency 178–9, 180, 182,
  183, 186, 257–8
Finnegan, Ruth 233, 234–5
Fishman, J. 308
"fives" see "giving five"
"flippin the script" 279–80
Florida 157, 292
Fodor, Jerry 110
Folb, E. 84, 86, 147
folklore 85, 86, 208, 232; sayings 204;
  song 225; tales 212
Forde, Darryll 200
Foucault, Michel 112
Fowler, R. 94, 95, 99
France 100
Franck, Harry 237
Franklin, Aretha 216, 218
Franklin, Benjamin 323
Frazier, E. Franklin 30, 77
Free African Society 44
freedmen 71
freedom 35, 44, 48, 49, 70, 88, 101,
  369
Freeman, L. D. 89–90
Freire, P. 154, 159, 161
French 97, 110, 307
Fresno Bee 42
Fries, Charles C. 378

Gallup Poll 299–302
games 27; verbal 21
"gangsta" rap 271
Gates, Henry Louis 112, 278
Gawthrop, B. 151–2
Gazette (North Carolina) 70
gender 26, 252, 254, 266, 294, 388
genetic inferiority 72, 74, 179

sacred and secular commandments 242,
  248
sacred style 63, 64, 212; singers 216
"saddity" 264
Safire, W. 89
St Louis 28
Salem witch trial (1692) 31
Salt N Pepa (rappers) 277–8
Sapir, E. 179
Saunders, R. 267
SCA (Speech Communication
  Association) 376
"Schleppers" 307
scholarship 33, 70–1, 77, 82, 86, 87,
  113, 135; elitist 67; European, on
  Africa 200; institutionalized 74;
  linguistic 87; literacy 88; racist 68,
  89; traditions 80
School Talk 21
schools: bourgeois sociolinguistic
  character of 91; seen as guardians of
  the national tongue 141; white
  middle-class 126
science: ideological warfare waged by
  71; paradigms of 80; philosophical
  bases of 68; philosophy of 112
Scott, J. C. 178
Scottish 72
SE (Standard English) 20, 37, 38, 79,
  91, 148, 150, 153, 155, 161, 350;
  attempting to teach students how to
  speak 142; BE diverging from 165;
  competence in 143, 145; departures
  from 274; divergence from 166;
  educating youth to acquire literacy
  in 322; everyday 385; features of 88;
  grammar 89; middle-class speakers
  159; need to master 382; second
  language 357; underdeveloped
  version of 78; written, interference
  in production of 177
Sea Islands 75, 136–8
secular style 64, 65, 212, 216
segregation 47, 68, 143, 316; de facto
  101
Seiler, Friedrich 231
semantic inversion 21, 26, 48, 101,
  137, 279–80, 365

semantics 41, 55, 56, 104, 139, 350;
  BE 102, 104; Black Language 26;
  "deep" essence 82; EAL structure
  279; focal, unifying 45; generative
  113; Hayakawa's work on 87; race
  relations 362; racial 34, 41, 43,
  48; strategies 272; tonal 217,
  222, 258–60, 269, 358; verbal
  symbols 98
"semi-creole" 33
sentences 21; "new" 236; patterns 62,
  130; spoken 141; "translated" 354
sermons 204, 219
sexism 97, 277; in language 388; WE
  reflects and reproduces 99
sexual issues 228, 229, 266;
  exploitation 251; harassment 251,
  263, 266; interaction, male–female
  85; objectification of women 277;
  social subordination based on 97;
  speech data 84
Seymour, D. 84
Shakur, Tupac 279
Sharpton, Revd Al 321
shucking 83, 84
signification/signifyin 26, 66, 83, 84,
  101, 110, 204, 207, 220, 224, 228,
  229, 255–7, 269, 277; clever 138;
  structural 278
Silverman-Weinreech, Beatrice 232
Simmons, J. D. 322
Simone, Nina 216, 349
Simpkins, G. & C. 161
singular: plural distinction 90, 141;
  third possessive 273
skin color see color
Skinner, B. F. 110
Skutnabb-Kangas, T. 288
"slang" 19, 59, 151, 255, 279, 351;
  Afro-American 63
Slave Trade Act (1808) 45
slavery 19, 32, 60, 65, 69, 100, 201,
  213, 283; abolition of 46, 70, 71,
  387; aftermath of 30; introduction of
  34, 315; "philosophy" and
  ideological attacks on 71; shuffling
  speech of 84; struggle to preserve
  71; temporary 45